BVR Legal & Court Case Yearbook 2016

BVR
What It's Worth
1000 SW Broadway, Suite 1200, Portland, OR 97205
(503) 291-7963 • www.bvresources.com

BVR

What It's Worth

Editor: Sylvia Golden

Publisher: Sarah Andersen

Managing Editor: Monique Nijhout-Rowe

Senior Copy Editor: David Solomon

Chair and CEO: David Foster

President: Lucretia Lyons

Vice President of Sales: Lexie Gross

Customer Service Manager: Retta Dodge

ISBN: 978-1-62150-061-2

Library of Congress Control Number: 2016930114

Table of Contents

INTRODUCTION 5

COURT CASE SUMMARY TABLE 7

COURT CASE DIGESTS[1] 11

Advanced Drainage Systems v. Quality Culvert, Inc. 11
American Aerial Services v. Terex United States 15
American Eagle Waste Industries, LLC v. St. Louis County 19
In re Ancestry 22
Anchor Savings Bank v. United States 26
Apple, Inc. v. Samsung Electronics Co. 29
AstraZeneca AB v. Apotex Corp. 31
Bank of America, N.A. v. Veluchamy (In re Veluchamy) 35
Berg v. Young 40
Bohme v. Bohme 42
Cartwright v. Jackson Capital Partners, Limited Partnership 46
Chambers v. Fike 50
Charron v. Sallyport Global Holdings, Inc. 53
Chico's Fas, Inc. v. Clair 57
City of Baton Rouge v. Jay's Donuts, Inc. 61
Clear-View Technologies, Inc. v. Rasnick (I), (II) 65
Cohen & Company v. Breen 69
Cortes v. 3A N. Park Ave Rest Corp. 72
Crile v. Commissioner 76
Cullifer v. Commissioner 80
In re Dole Food Co. (Dole I) 84
In re Dole Food Co., Inc. Stockholder Litigation (Dole II) 87
In re Dole Food Co. (Dole III) 89
In re El Paso Pipeline Partners, L.P. Derivative Litigation 94
Finjan, Inc. v. Blue Coat Systems, Inc. 100
Fox v. CDx Holdings 104
Freihage v. Freihage 109
Gallo v. Gallo 112
Estate of Giustina v. Commissioner 115
Glickenhaus & Co. v. Household International, Inc. 117
In re Groupon Securities Litigation 120
Guardian Energy, LLC v. County of Waseca 125
In re Marriage of Hartung 130
Hewlett-Packard Co. v. Benton Cnty. Assessor 131
In re Honer 136
Immersion Corp. v. HTC Corp. 140
J&M Distributing, Inc. v. Hearth & Home Technologies, Inc. 144
Kardash v. Commissioner (Kardash I) 147
Kardash v. Comm'r (Kardash II) 150
K.T. v. M.T. 152
Lane v. Lampkin 156
LongPath Capital, LLC v. Ramtron International Corp. 159
Lunn v. Lunn 164

1 For the full court opinion of each case, subscribe to *BVLaw*. Visit www.bvresources.com for more information.

In re Mauer 166
McCarter v. McCarter 168
Merlin Partners LP v. AutoInfo, Inc. 171
Moore v. Getahun 176
Moore v. Moore 179
Nordock, Inc. v. Systems, Inc. 184
Owen v. Cannon 187
Perez v. Bruister 193
Rabe v. Rabe 199
Reedy-Huffman v. Huffman 201
Ross v. Rothstein 203
Rowe v. DPI Specialty Foods 204
Russell v. Allianze Life Insurance Co. of North America 207
Schickner v. Schickner 210
SEC v. Wyly (I), (II) 213
Settele v. Settele 218
Shaffer v. Visaggio's, Inc. 222
Sieber v. Sieber 227
Tilstra v. Boumatic LLC 231
Tri Cnty. Wholesale Distribs. v. Labatt USA Operating Co. LLC 234
TWC I, L.L.C. v. Damos 240
Utah Resources International, Inc. v. Mark Technologies Corp. 243
Warsaw Orthopedic, Inc. v. NuVasive, Inc. 249
Washington v. Kellwood Co. 251
Wright v. Irish (Hudson Valley Clean Energy, Inc.) 257
Zelouf International Corp. v. Zelouf 260

Introduction

Dear Reader,

Valuation now plays a role in most civil litigation. Appraisers testify in divorce cases, contract disputes, bankruptcy proceedings, statutory appraisal actions, patent litigation, and a host of other suits. All of this activity produces a wealth of case law, which the *BVR Legal & Court Case Yearbook 2016* perfectly captures.

Although no practitioner can be an expert in everything, there are great benefits to reviewing cases from subject areas other than one's own to see how different courts and different experts deal with common valuation problems. This publication is a compendium of legal cases and analysis that puts the year's most meaningful valuation-related cases within easy reach.

Few areas of law are as dynamic as divorce cases, at least when it comes to valuation issues. At the center of many of the disputes discussed in this publication are the evergreen issues of goodwill (personal versus enterprise) and double dipping. A case of first impression from the South Carolina Supreme Court on enterprise goodwill was one of the year's highlights. *Moore v. Moore* centered on the valuation of a light fixtures retail store that the wife had built and, later, with some help from the husband, had transformed into a successful Internet business. Illustrious experts for both sides argued over the value of personal goodwill attributable to the wife, and the parties subsequently argued over whether the remaining enterprise goodwill was a marital asset subject to division. In answering the question with a hesitant "yes," the state Supreme Court provides a thorough review of goodwill jurisprudence across the country and also discusses issues such as the discount for lack of marketability and the appropriate valuation date.

In terms of double dipping, the court to follow has been the Ohio Court of Appeals. It made news in 2008 with its *Heller* decision, prohibiting double counting. Early in 2015, however, the court issued in quick succession two decisions that announced its retreat from *Heller* and the double dip framework. The cases, *Bohme v. Bohme* and *Gallo v. Gallo*, offer complementary analyses that any practitioner in family law cases should know. But the Ohio appeals court has not been able to put the double dip issue to rest, as several subsequent cases, which are all available in the compendium, make clear.

One of the most industrious courts is the Delaware Court of Chancery. Its judges distinguish themselves with their understanding of valuation. During the summer, when one might expect activity to slow down, the court issued a number of long and deep decisions in dissenting shareholder lawsuits, which are discussed in this book. In line with the court's 2014 *Huff Fund* decision, the court in several instances decided the merger price was a more reliable indicator of value than standard valuation techniques, including the generally favored discounted cash flow analysis. But leave it to the court's new chief, Chancellor Andre Bouchard, to upend the trend. In *Owen v. Cannon*, he performed his own DCF analysis, based on expert testimony, and in so doing also explored the issue of tax affecting and the continuing significance of the *Kessler* model.

Daubert cases are a dime a dozen, but occasionally one stands out. In 2015, it was *Washington v. Kellwood*, in which an aspiring entrepreneur sued a marketing and branding company for breach of a licensing agreement that he hoped would lead to success in the sports apparel market along the lines of the leading "Under Armour" brand. Facing a dearth of financial evidence on which to base damages, the plaintiff's expert performed a yardstick analysis using sales figures from Under Armour. The expert's conclusions may be "improbable," the court said, but the analysis is good enough to warrant admission under *Daubert*. However, as the compendium also shows, other courts are not so liberal in their interpretation of *Daubert*.

Patent litigation slowed in 2014 but gathered speed in 2015. In terms of damages, questions as to how to interpret the entire market value rule (EMVR) and how to apportion continue to dominate the conversation. The cases featured in this book—many of which ended up at the Court of Appeals for the Federal Circuit—illustrate how plaintiff's experts wrestle with damages calculations involving high-tech devices that contain a multitude of components beside the patented feature. The question is no longer simply "is the patent-related feature the basis for customer demand," but "what value the protected feature is able to add to what component of the accused device."

But do concepts such as EMVR and apportionment have a role to play in big pharmaceutical patent infringement cases? That was the question at the heart of *AstraZeneca v. Apotex*, which revolved around AstraZeneca's drug "Prilosec." The Federal Circuit's opinion explains why EMVR is inapplicable in the case but does not endorse the proposition that EMVR is per se inapplicable in the pharmaceutical context. Stay tuned.

This introduction only provides a snapshot of the valuation cases that have shaped the past year. Financial experts wanting a more complete picture of the litigation landscape need only dive into the *BVR Legal & Court Case Yearbook 2016*.

Sincerely,

Sylvia Golden, Esq.
Executive Legal Editor

Court Case Summary Table

Presented in order of case type, then by jurisdiction.

Case Name	Date	State/ Jurisdiction	Court	Summary	Page
Bankruptcy					
Bank of America, N.A. v. Veluchamy (In re Veluchamy)	12/18/14	Federal/ Illinois	United States Bankruptcy Court	Bankruptcy Court Accepts Rationale for Tax Affecting	35
Condemnation					
City of Baton Rouge v. Jay's Donuts, Inc.	12/17/14	Louisiana	Court of Appeal	Valuators in Taking Case Disagree Over Measure of Damages	61
Contract					
Tilstra v. Boumatic LLC	6/30/15	Federal	United States Court of Appeals for the 7th Circuit	'Blunderbuss of Objections' Aims to Kill Loss of Goodwill Calculation	231
Advanced Drainage Systems v. Quality Culvert, Inc.	3/23/15	Federal/ Illinois	United States District Court	Court Endorses Before and After Method for Lost Profits	11
Ross v. Rothstein	3/12/15	Federal/ Kansas	United States District Court	FRE 702 Ruling Puts Expert in 'Uncommon Position'	203
J&M Distributing, Inc. v. Hearth & Home Technologies, Inc.	1/9/15	Federal/ Minnesota	United States District Court	What Role for RR 59-60 Factors in Valuing Closely Held Business?	144
Russell v. Allianze Life Insurance Co. of North America	1/8/15	Federal/ Mississippi	United States District Court	Expert's Failure to Adhere to Objective Standard Spoils Analysis	207
Charron v. Sallyport Global Holdings, Inc.	12/10/14	Federal/ New York	United States District Court	High Company-Specific Risk Adjustment Distorts Valuation	53
Cohen & Company v. Breen	9/11/14	Ohio	Court of Appeals	Expert Fee Dispute Devolves Into Malpractice Claim	69
Damages					
Clear-View Technologies, Inc. v. Rasnick (I), (II)	6/3/15 6/2/15	Federal/ California	United States District Court	Expert Rebuttal Fails to Engage With Initial Valuation	65
Chambers v. Fike	1/29/15	Federal/ Kansas	United States District Court	Court Draws Line Between Data Quality and Data Quantity	50
American Aerial Services v. Terex United States	4/29/15	Federal/ Maine	United States District Court	Failure to Test Causation Narrative Clouds Analysis of Lost Profits	15
Washington v. Kellwood Co.	4/21/15	Federal/ New York	United States District Court	*Daubert* Allows for Generous View on Yardstick Analysis	251
Tri Cnty. Wholesale Distribs. v. Labatt USA Operating Co. LLC	6/24/15	Federal/ Ohio	United States District Court	'Hybrid' Approach to Quantify Loss of Beer Franchise Contracts	234
Rowe v. DPI Specialty Foods	8/19/15	Federal/ Utah	United States District Court	Damages Opinion Reveals 'Serious Misconception' of Role of Expert	204
Lane v. Lampkin	9/16/14	Mississippi	Court of Appeals	What Rationale for Net Book Value in Damages Analysis?	156
American Eagle Waste Industries, LLC v. St. Louis County	2/24/15	Missouri	Court of Appeals	Admissibility Does Not Depend on Personal Knowledge of Facts	19
In re El Paso Pipeline Partners, L.P. Derivative Litigation	4/20/15	Delaware	Court of Chancery of Delaware	Financial Advisor's 'Real Client Was the Deal,' Says Chancery	94
Cartwright v. Jackson Capital Partners, Limited Partnership	5/21/15	Tennessee	Court of Appeals	No Place for Asset Appraisal in Trust Dispute, Court Says	46

Case Name	Date	State/ Jurisdiction	Court	Summary	Page
Dissenting Shareholder					
In re Ancestry	1/30/15	Delaware	Court of Chancery of Delaware	Chancery Assigns Secondary Role to Post-Merger DCF	22
In re Dole Food Co. (Dole I)	12/9/14	Delaware	Court of Chancery of Delaware	Delaware Chancery Orders Disclosure of Nonexpert Internal Valuations	84
In re Dole Food Co., Inc. Stockholder Litigation (Dole II)	2/27/15	Delaware	Court of Chancery of Delaware	Can a Valuation Firm Serve as Expert Witness?	87
In re Dole Food Co. (Dole III)	8/27/15	Delaware	Court of Chancery of Delaware	Chancery Lauds Advisor's 'Heroic' Efforts at Credible DCF	89
Merlin Partners LP v. AutoInfo, Inc.	4/30/15	Delaware	Court of Chancery of Delaware	Chancery Adopts Merger Price *Sans* Cost Savings Reduction	171
LongPath Capital, LLC v. Ramtron International Corp.	6/30/15	Delaware	Court of Chancery of Delaware	Adjusted Merger Price Superior to Other Valuation Methods	159
Owen v. Cannon	6/17/15	Delaware	Court of Chancery of Delaware	Chancery Validates Tax Affecting in Fair Value Case	187
TWC I, L.L.C. v. Damos	5/20/15	Iowa	Court of Appeals	Discovery Evidence Casts Doubt on Valuator's Independence	240
Shaffer v. Visaggio's, Inc.	7/29/15	Pennsylvania	Superior Court of Pennsylvania (Court of Appeals)	Appraiser Lacks Necessary Valuation Expertise, Dissent Says	222
Utah Resources International, Inc. v. Mark Technologies Corp.	12/23/14	Utah	Supreme Court	Use of Asset-Level Deductions Hinges on Business Strategy	243
ESOP					
Perez v. Bruister	10/16/14	Federal/ Mississippi	United States District Court	Averaging Multiple Appraisals Yields Most Reliable FMV	193
Evidence					
Moore v. Getahun	1/29/15	Ontario-Canada	Court of Appeal	Canadian Ruling on Use of Expert Draft Reports Crumbles on Appeal	176
Federal Taxation					
Crile v. Commissioner	10/2/14	Federal	United States Tax Court	Court Rejects Art Market Expert's Profitability Analysis	76
Cullifer v. Commissioner	10/7/14	Federal	United States Tax Court	Valuations Bolster IRS's Transferee Liability Claim	80
Estate of Giustina v. Commissioner	12/5/14	Federal	United States Court of Appeals for 9th Circuit	9th Circuit Calls Tax Court Out Over 'Imaginary Scenarios'	115
Kardash v. Commissioner (Kardash I)	3/18/15	Federal	United States Tax Court	Tax Court Tacitly Approves of IRS Solvency Assessment	147
Kardash v. Commissioner (Kardash II)	10/6/15	Federal	United States Tax Court	Tax Court Explains Valuation Method Behind Solvency Ruling	150
Intellectual Property					
Apple, Inc. v. Samsung Electronics Co.	5/18/15	Federal	United States Court of Appeals for the Federal Circuit	Federal Circuit Resists Samsung's 'Quest for Apportionment'	29
AstraZeneca AB v. Apotex Corp.	4/7/15	Federal	United States Court of Appeals for the Federal Circuit	Federal Circuit Weighs Use of EMVR in Pharmaceutical Case	31
Nordock, Inc. v. Systems, Inc.	9/29/15	Federal	United States Court of Appeals for the Federal Circuit	Trial Court Misinterprets Damages Rules for Design Patent Violation	184

Case Name	Date	State/ Jurisdiction	Court	Summary	Page
Warsaw Orthopedic, Inc. v. NuVasive, Inc.	3/2/15	Federal	United States Court of Appeals for the Federal Circuit	Federal Circuit Sweeps Aside Lost Profits Theories and Award	249
Finjan, Inc. v. Blue Coat Systems, Inc.	7/14/15	Federal/ California	United States District Court	Complex Facts Test Patent Experts' Apportionment Skills	100
Immersion Corp. v. HTC Corp.	2/24/15	Federal/ Delaware	United States District Court	Court Declares Lost Profits Analysis 'Goes Too Far'	140
Chico's Fas, Inc. v. Clair	6/3/15	Federal/ Florida	United States District Court	Uncritical Use of Royalty Rate Data Spoils Damages Opinion	57
Judicial Dissolution					
Cortes v. 3A N. Park Ave Rest Corp.	10/28/14 (Slip Op)	New York	Supreme Court of New York (Trial Court)	Lack of Marketability a Factor in Valuing Minority Interest	72
Wright v. Irish (Hudson Valley Clean Energy, Inc.)	11/7/14	New York	New York Supreme Court (Trial Court)	Expert's Solid DCF and Industry Research Sway Court	257
Zelouf International Corp. v. Zelouf	12/22/14	New York	Supreme Court of New York (Trial Court)	*Zelouf* Court Reasserts Its Objection to DLOM	260
Marital Dissolution					
Lunn v. Lunn	6/29/15	Tennessee	Court of Appeals	Tennessee Appeals Court Straddles Goodwill Issue in Divorce	164
Schickner v. Schickner	4/16/15	Arizona	Court of Appeals	No Automatic Bar to Minority Discount in Divorce Cases	210
In re Honer	4/9/15	California	Court of Appeal	Court Affirms Rightness of Expert's 'Marital Value' Calculation	136
Freihage v. Freihage	1/7/15	Illinois	Appellate Court of Illinois	Treatment of Debt Skews Valuation of Franchise Business	109
In re Mauer	2/25/15	Iowa	Court of Appeals	Asset Approach Avoids Double Counting of Future Earnings	166
Bohme v. Bohme	1/30/15	Ohio	Court of Appeals	Court Backs Away From Support for Double Dip Theory	42
Gallo v. Gallo	3/17/15	Ohio	Court of Appeals	Court Rejects Flat Prohibition Against Double Dipping	112
Moore v. Moore	10/7/15	South Carolina	Supreme Court	S.C. Supreme Court Makes New Law on Business Goodwill	179
Reedy-Huffman v. Huffman	5/20/15	Alaska	Supreme Court of Alaska	Court Validates Zero Goodwill for Naturopathic Practice	201
Berg v. Young	9/2/15	Florida	Court of Appeals	Different Ways to Find No Claim to Enhanced Value of Nonmarital Asset	40
In re Marriage of Hartung	8/5/15	Iowa	Court of Appeals	Expert's Application of Asset Approach 'Defies Common Sense'	130
Rabe v. Rabe	5/29/15	Kentucky	Court of Appeals	Court Infers Nature of Goodwill From Nature of Business	199
Settele v. Settele	9/15/15	Ohio	Court of Appeals	Court Nixes Double Dip Claim Based on Accounts Receivable Treatment	218
Sieber v. Sieber	6/15/15	Ohio	Court of Appeals	Husband's Roles in Company Negate Need for DLOC	227
McCarter v. McCarter	12/1/14	Tennessee	Court of Appeals	Goodwill Determination Turns on Classification of Auction Business	168
K.T. v. M.T.	8/13/15	Texas	Court of Appeals	Court Declines to Attribute Commercial Goodwill to Solo Practice	152

Case Name	Date	State/ Jurisdiction	Court	Summary	Page
Securities					
Fox v. CDx Holdings	7/28/15	Delaware	Court of Chancery of Delaware	Chancery Decries Accounting Firm's Compromised Valuation	104
Glickenhaus & Co. v. Household International, Inc.	5/21/15	Federal	United States Court of Appeals for the 7th Circuit	7th Circuit Proposes Solution for Loss Causation Conundrum	117
In re Groupon Securities Litigation	3/5/15	Federal/ Illinois	United States District Court	Fraud Litigation Highlights Dispute Over 'Market Efficiency'	120
SEC v. Wyly	12/19/14 9/25/14	Federal/ New York	United States District Court	Court Sanctions SEC's Novel, Alternative Disgorgement Measure	213
State Taxation					
Guardian Energy, LLC v. County of Waseca	8/12/15	Minnesota	Supreme Court	Obsolescence Analysis Kills Tax Court's Property Valuation	125
Hewlett-Packard Co. v. Benton Cnty. Assessor	8/6/15	Oregon	Supreme Court of Oregon	Shaky Industrial Plant Valuation Survives High Court Review	131
Winstar					
Anchor Savings Bank v. United States	8/31/15	Federal	United States Court of Federal Claims	Court Approves *Winstar* Plaintiff's Tax Gross Up Calculation	26

Court Case Digests

Presented in alphabetical order.

Advanced Drainage Systems v. Quality Culvert, Inc.

Citation: 2015 U.S. Dist. LEXIS 36037
Date of decision: March 23, 2015
Experts: Rebekah Smith (plaintiff); unknown (defendants)
Judge: Economus
State/Jurisdiction: Federal/Illinois
Court: United States District Court
Type of case: Contract
SIC code: 3084 Plastics Pipe
NAICS code: 326122 Plastics Pipe and Pipe Fitting Manufacturing

Court Endorses Before and After Method for Lost Profits

A recent *Daubert* ruling on lost profits offers a detailed description of the challenged expert's methodology and the myriad objections from the opposing party. The court carefully combed through the testimony and explained why some parts met the legal requirements for admission and others did not.

Two types of damages. Both the plaintiff and the defendants were manufacturers of high-density polyethylene (HDPE) pipe products. They agreed that the plaintiff would buy the defendants' plastic pipe business. The parties' asset purchase agreement (APA) prohibited the defendants from competing for five years following closing and required them to work with the plaintiff on continuing business relations with customers and contractors. At the same time, the contract permitted the defendants to conduct an inventory liquidation sale for 90 days following the closing of the deal.

The plaintiff sued for breach of contract, alleging the defendants continued doing business for nearly a year after the end of the liquidation period. The plaintiff retained an expert to calculate two types of damages: (1) lost profits based on the defendants' unauthorized sales outside the liquidation period (violation sales); and (2) lost profits and diminution of value stemming from temporary or permanent damage to customer relationships. (The court redacted all damages figures.)

1. *Violation sales.* For this category of damages, the plaintiff's expert assumed that all of the alleged sales that took place after the inventory liquidation period were violation sales. Moreover, she assumed that, if the defendants had not made the sales, the plaintiff would have made a sale for a comparable product. To determine what a comparable product was, the expert reviewed product descriptions in the defendants' sales reports and cross-referenced those to a product the plaintiff offered. She used the plaintiff's accounting system to determine the product price and, based on price and incremental gross margin, calculated lost revenue and profits.

2. *Lost profits and diminution of value.* The expert used the before and after method to determine losses stemming from damaged customer relations. The method rests on the theory that, but for the defendant's alleged misconduct, the plaintiff would have reached the same level of revenues and profits after the defendant's action as before. In her report, the expert expressly said that a damages calculation had to "consider other factors that could have affected the plaintiff's level of revenues and demonstrate how those factors have been taken into consideration."

She said she analyzed the plaintiff's customers and the HDPE market as they were before and after the transaction date to pinpoint differences both with respect to the industry and customers. The method required an analysis of the market, she said. Her study led her to conclude that, "at a minimum, the before and after periods should be the same." There was nothing in the overall market that explained the decrease in the plaintiff's sales to the defendants' companies, the expert said.

Further, she analyzed individual customers to determine customer-specific differences in the before and after periods. Her analysis included customers with revenues over $50,000 in 2011 (the year before the APA) to whom the defendants: (1) made inventory liquidates sales; (2) made violation sales; and (3) to whom the plaintiff made sales in 2012. She found this type of customer accounted for over 95% of the defendants' revenues.

At the same time, the plaintiff's expert excluded five categories of customers with respect to whom sales decreased for reasons other than the defendants' alleged misconduct. She said sales occurring during the liquidation period might have affected a customer's need to buy a product from the plaintiff later and added sales made during that period to the plaintiff's actual sales during the after period. Her calculation excluded customers with regard to whom sales did not decrease in the after period. She explained that she adjusted her analysis based on feedback from the company—adding back two customers because the plaintiff claimed these customers were purchasing from competitors but excluding others as directed by the company.

The expert then categorized customer relations as temporarily or permanently damaged.

For temporarily damaged relationships, the expert used the plaintiff's retention rate to determine what percentage they were in relation to the 2011 sales and what sales should have been in the after period. She analyzed pre- and post-transaction revenues by customer for three other acquisitions the plaintiff recently had made to determine the revenue the plaintiff generally retained.

After calculating lost sales, she calculated lost profits by applying the gross profit margin the plaintiff provided to her and relying on the company's statement that there would not be any additional fixed costs related to additional sales.

In terms of calculating losses related to permanently damaged customer relations, she said she used the valuation formula "implicit" in the asset purchase transaction, including anticipated earnings figures. She explained that determining a diminution in value based on damaged customer relations required adjusting the revenue and related EBITDA stream and applying the appropriate multiple. Her report included a table that showed the revenue figure reduced by total cost to arrive at EBITDA. That number was multiplied by "EBITDA Multiple With Synergies" taken from the plaintiff's pretransaction analysis.

Expert's affidavit no cure for analytical flaws. The defendants filed a pretrial motion claiming the testimony failed to meet the requirements of Rule 702 of the Federal Rules of Evidence and *Daubert*. Broadly speaking, the claims were that the plaintiff's expert lacked the necessary qualifications, her lost profit calculation regarding violations sales was unreliable, and her analysis regarding temporarily and permanently damaged customer relations lacked foundation.

In response to the defendants' motion, the expert submitted an affidavit as to the violation sales to the court. It stated that a number of factors "make it reasonable to assume a Violation Sale caused a lost [plaintiff] sales on a one to one basis." As examples, it noted the provision in the APA that provided only a limited window for the defendants to sell the remaining inventory and the requirement that the defendants assist the plaintiff in transitioning former customers to the plaintiff. The affidavit also said, "The Violation Sales appear to be clear breaches of both of these provisions. An expert is allowed to make assumptions as long as they are reasonable."

Some of the defendants' arguments had traction with the court, but some did not.

1. *Qualification.* The defendants claimed the expert lacked expertise specific to the market for HDPE products. The court dismissed that argument, promptly noting that an expert need not have industry-specific training to perform a damages analysis.

2. *Violation sales.* The defendants contended the expert failed to perform an analysis of factors that could have affected sales but simply adopted the plaintiff's positions. Further, her calculations were basic math and as such did not require expert analysis and were not admissible as expert testimony.

The plaintiff countered that the expert undertook an independent analysis of the company's lost profits and, in instances where she relied on company information or assumptions, she tested that information. Also, the math computations were only a last step in the expert's analytical process.

The court sided with the defendants. It said the expert's belated affidavit was devoid of any analysis but merely stated facts related to the parties' asset purchasing agreement and included a legal conclusion as to breach of contract that the expert was not qualified to make. The expert report also provided no analysis but adopted the company's position that it would have made all of the violation sales. The only independent analysis the expert undertook, aside from performing simple math, was comparing product descriptions to determine comparable company products, the court said. But, since she lacked industry-specific expertise, this analysis was not helpful outside the context of an independent damages analysis—which was missing. Therefore, the testimony as to violation sales was inadmissible.

3. *Damaged customer relations.* In the most general terms, the defendants claimed the testimony unreasonably relied on company information. More specifically, the expert simply adopted certain information the plaintiff provided, including its identification of temporarily or permanently damaged customer relations, its revenue forecast for temporarily damaged customer relations, its claim that there were no additional incremental costs related to the additional sales it would have made, and its anticipated earnings figures.

The court disagreed. It noted that the expert properly applied the before and after methodology, and it called the defendants' claim a "conclusory argument" that ignored the expert's independent analysis as to damaged customers based on sales information, market factors, and other information. The expert did not simply adopt the plaintiff's revenue forecast but analyzed other plaintiff acquisitions to calculate the revenue the company generally retained. To the extent she used the financial information from the plaintiff as a basis for her own independent damages analysis, her reliance would be subject to cross-examination as questions on this point went toward weight, not admissibility, the court added.

Finally, the defendants maintained the expert failed to take into account other explanations or factors as to why the plaintiff lost sales. With regard to missed sales for one customer in particular, she failed to consider price, relationship issues, and the customer's decision to leave the plastic pipe business. The defendants also suggested that the expert should have contacted customers to ask why they temporarily or permanently stopped buying from the plaintiff.

The court found these claims baseless. The expert considered many alternative reasons for the reduced or lost sales, including market forces and customer-specific issues. The argument that she could have considered additional factors is not a legal basis for excluding her opinion. It may be a valid attack on the accuracy of the expert's conclusion but not on the soundness of her methodology. For admissibility's sake, "an expert's testimony need not eliminate all other possible causes of the injury."

Also, the defendants failed to recognize that the plaintiff had business reasons to prevent its expert witness from "quizzing" their customers or potential future customers.

For all of these reasons, the court admitted the expert's testimony on lost profits and diminution of value. Moreover, the court denied the defendants' summary judgment motion, which allowed the plaintiffs to go forward with their case.

American Aerial Services v. Terex United States

Citation: 2015 U.S. Dist. LEXIS 55997
Date of decision: April 29, 2015
Experts: Reginald Perry (plaintiff); unknown (defendants)
Judge: Levy
State/Jurisdiction: Federal/Maine
Court: United States District Court
Type of case: Damages
SIC code: 3531 Construction Machinery and Equipment
NAICS code: 333120 Construction Machinery Manufacturing

Failure to Test Causation Narrative Clouds Analysis of Lost Profits

Causation is a critical element of damages. It also often derails experts because they assume the plaintiff will create the necessary link between the plaintiff's losses and the defendant's conduct. At the same time, the plaintiff in turn may hope the expert's financial analysis will establish the cause-and-effect connection the law requires. A recent *Daubert* case exemplifies the risk of an expert's assuming too much and scrutinizing the client's narrative too little before proceeding to court.

Backstory. In December 2011, the plaintiff bought a Terex T780 truck crane from a major crane dealer. After taking delivery, it experienced significant problems with the equipment's engine and other components. Neither the dealer nor the crane manufacturer provided a satisfactory remedy. When the crane failed inspections and became unusable, the plaintiff sued both entities on a number of theories in state court. The case was transferred to federal court (D. Me). A breach of contract/breach of warranty claim survived the defendants' motions to dismiss. The company had four other cranes.

The plaintiff asked for lost profits and offered testimony from a damages expert, which the defendants tried to preclude under Federal Rule of Evidence 702 and *Daubert*.

The plaintiff's expert submitted two written reports that explained his lost profits calculation. The expert, a veteran CPA, had a deep knowledge of the construction industry from working with clients who owned and operated heavy equipment. He determined that there were essentially two parts to the damages. One component was the loss of crane rental net revenue in the amount of nearly $617,000. Moreover, the plaintiff suffered consequential damages in the amount of over $138,000 because a segment of its business was steel erection and it lost customer confidence once the crane was taken out of service (the "luster effect," see below).

Four findings were central to the expert's lost profits analysis.

1. *Overall lost revenue.* According to the expert, the plaintiff had lost gross revenue as a result of the defective crane. He said January 2012 was the "date when the T780 was fully equipped with additional components" and when the plaintiff began to generate extra revenue from the crane. He based this observation on a comparison of the plaintiff's total revenue generated in the six-month period preceding the delivery of the crane (July 2011 through December 2011) with the revenue

generated in the subsequent six months (January 2012 through June 2012). He determined there was an increase of over $325,000. The expert noted that the company's overall revenue continued to increase through February 2013, but it "dropped precipitously for the period of March 2013 through July 2013." He noted that the owner of the plaintiff company directly tied the steep revenue drop in 2013 to the market's awareness that the plaintiff had abandoned the crane rental business and a perception among customers that the plaintiff was in a precarious financial position. Having the crane gave the company luster and increased revenue; both the luster and the extra revenue went away when the crane became unusable.

The expert admitted that he did not independently verify the executive's narrative. Nor did he explore other reasons for the increase and decrease in revenue. The expert also conceded that the only actual data he based his statement on were financial data he had obtained from the company.

In arguing this part of the testimony was inadmissible, the defendants zeroed in on the expert's failure to perform a "quantitative analysis" to bolster his assumption that there was a cause-and-effect connection between the crane and the plaintiff's ability to generate revenue. The defendants also attacked the expert for relying on the plaintiff's financial data without conducting his own analysis of the financial records.

The court pointed out that *Daubert* does not require an expert to independently verify the financial data the client supplies and on which the expert bases his or her analysis. However, it added that a damages determination based on "pure speculation" did not meet the Rule 702 reliability requirement.

The court agreed with the defendants that it was inappropriate for the expert to assume a causal connection between the availability of the crane and the company's financial fortune based on nothing more than the company owner's luster effect theory. It noted that the expert could have gathered anecdotal evidence supporting this assertion. The expert also failed to break out data as to the revenue the plaintiff was able to generate when the crane was in service and the expenses related to the crane's use. He failed to research the market for the T780 to determine what the rate of demand for a crane with that capacity actually was. And it observed that the plaintiff had other cranes that were in service but that the expert failed to establish how much revenue renting them out generated for the company.

The court also found the expert wrongly assumed that the company abandoned the rental business because of the inability to use the T780. Yet an exhibit attached to the expert's report indicated that, even though the plaintiff stopped using the T780 in August 2012, it still continued to generate crane rental income in the ensuing 12 months.

The court concluded: "Pinning the company's overall financial performance on the Crane, untethered from any data or methodology" that illuminates the plaintiff's real experience when it comes to renting cranes made that aspect of the expert testimony speculative and inadmissible.

2. *Lost crane rental net revenue.* The expert explained that lost rental revenue was a function of a "reasonable utilization rate" and a "reasonable hourly rate net of related expenses." For the first part

of the damages period, January 2012 through August 2012, he used a two-day-per-week utilization rate. For the remainder, September 2012 into July 2014, he increased the rate to three days per week. He assumed that on the utilization days the crane would be in use for 10 hours a day because that kind of day was standard for the plaintiff. He said the three-day utilization rate was based on his conversations with the plaintiff's owner about past rental experience as well as with the CFO of another company that rented cranes similar to the T780. The two-day rate for the initial period was to account for the fact that the plaintiff "was effectively re-entering the crane rental market." The expert also said in deciding on the utilization rates he relied on his professional experience as an accountant serving the construction industry.

He explained that he assumed a gross hourly rate of $225 that ultimately reduced to $181 considering various expenses related to the pay and benefits for crane operators ($30), the pro rata cost of diesel fuel ($6), insurance ($5), and various repairs ($3). He said he derived the individual estimates from industry research and information from crane rental companies, i.e., the plaintiff's owner, as well as the expert's own experience with the construction industry.

He concluded that lost net rental revenue was nearly $617,000.

The defendants claimed there was insufficient information to determine the two-day-per-week utilization rate. Also, the increase in the rate to three days per week was based on the expert's unsupported belief that there was an uptick in the construction business. Moreover, he failed to verify expense-related information he received from the plaintiff's owner.

The court acknowledged that aspects of the expert's determination of the crane's utilization rate as well as the reasonable crane rental rate might "have a weak factual basis," but it found the analysis overall satisfied the admissibility requirement. The law favored vigorous cross-examination as to the foundation for the expert's opinion over exclusion, the court added.

'Luster effect' theory. The expert's claim for consequential damages also was based on the "luster effect" theory the company's owner had developed. As the expert explained it, "confidence engendered by having a large piece of industrial equipment opened up business opportunities otherwise not available." But once the T780 was out of service at the end of August 2012, "the 'confidence engendered' effect was lost and revenues began to fall after February 2013." He explained there was a lag between the drop in business and the drop in revenue.

3. *Lost profits related to steel erection segment of business.* The expert explained that he calculated damages for lost business opportunities by assuming the 20% annual rate of increase in revenue, which the company experienced in 2012, would have continued. Since total revenues in 2012 were almost $2.43 million, he assumed that 20% of that amount would have been generated as additional revenue for the period from March 2013 through February 2014 and he decided that 10% of that amount represented net income loss—$48,570.

Moreover, he claimed the company incurred almost $90,000 in additional costs for "substitute crane rentals" to enable the steel erection business to meet its obligations on projects. This figure was based on a business record the plaintiff provided. Therefore, the total amount of loss related to the plaintiff's steel erection business was almost $138,400.

The court agreed with the defendants that the luster effect theory was lacking in substance and precluded the expert from testifying regarding the alleged $48,570 in lost net income.

However, the court declined to exclude the testimony as to the cost to the plaintiff of renting cranes from other companies to perform on its contracts. For the purpose of admissibility, the expert did not have to independently verify the accuracy of the figure, the court said. But it allowed that at trial the substitute crane rental cost was "grist for cross-examination."

4. *Explanation for delay in realizing decrease in revenues.* The expert explained the gap between the crane's removal from service in August 2012 and the delayed signs of a decrease in revenues in February 2013 by noting there was a "lag between the booking [of] revenues and its recognition in the accounting records."

The defendants claimed the expert "did not even conduct a rudimentary analysis" of the plaintiff's financial records to support his explanation for the continued increase in revenues even after the crane was out of service.

The court allowed the expert's "lag" statement in. It was based on the expert's conversations with the company's owner, the expert's general knowledge of the construction industry, his extensive experience as an accountant, and his review of the plaintiff's financial statements, the court said.

In conclusion, the court precluded the expert from testifying that there was a link between the plaintiff's overall increase in revenues and the crane's luster effect on the company's public profile, nor was he able to propose the company incurred additional consequential damages based on the loss of luster related to the crane's nonusability.

American Eagle Waste Industries, LLC v. St. Louis County

Citation: 2015 Mo. App. LEXIS 168
Date of decision: Feb. 24, 2015
Experts: C. Eric Ficken (haulers/plaintiffs); none (county/defendant)
Judge: Clayton III
State/Jurisdiction: Missouri
Court: Court of Appeals
Type of case: Damages
SIC code: 4212 Local Trucking without Storage
NAICS code: 562111 Solid Waste Collection

Admissibility Does Not Depend on Personal Knowledge of Facts

The latest dispute in the long-running litigation between several garbage disposal companies and a Missouri county focused on the trial court's damages findings. The county argued damages were based on inadmissible and unreliable lost profits testimony from the haulers' expert. In addressing the county's objections, the appeals court chided the county for failing to challenge the factual underpinnings of the testimony at trial through cross-examination and a counterexpert opinion.

Two-year waiting period. The suit involved three waste disposal services (haulers) and St. Louis County (county). When the county implemented a new trash collection program in 2007, it stopped using the three haulers and awarded the contracts to other companies. However, a statutory provision required the county to give the existing haulers two years of notice before the county could enter the business of trash collection.

Initially, the county contested the applicability of the statute to the situation at hand. But it lost that argument in the state Court of Appeals. Subsequently, the trial court found the county was liable for violating the statute and held a trial on damages during which the haulers presented testimony from a damages expert who was a CPA, a certified valuation analyst, and a financial forensics analyst. The court awarded the companies $1.2 million.

The county and the haulers appealed the trial court's judgment to the state Supreme Court, which affirmed as to liability, finding the haulers had a right to continue providing trash collection services during the two-year waiting period. It also said the haulers were entitled to "their projected receipts from their contract price [for their services], minus any business and operational costs Haulers would have incurred while providing [trash] collection services, considering all the circumstances." The state high court remanded, ordering the trial court to allow the parties to conduct discovery, present additional evidence, and cross-examine witnesses as to the amount of damages.

In a second trial, the haulers relied on the same expert testimony they had offered in the first trial. The county did not present any witnesses or additional evidence. Instead, it repeated its earlier objections to the damages testimony, claiming it lacked foundation and was based on inadmissible hearsay.

Expansive view of damages. The haulers' expert first calculated lost revenue based on the number of customers each hauler lost during the two-year waiting period and then subtracted variable costs incurred in the production of the revenue. He explained that he relied on information the haulers provided, specifically their databases and their unaudited profit and loss statements covering a two-year period. The databases provided customer information, including a customer's name, address, the type of trash collection available, the applicable monthly rate, and the start and end dates of service. The expert said he received the information from the haulers via a "data dump." He called the actual database "a live system" that reflected the most current information. He then tested the information using a mapping program to confirm the address of each listed customer. Once he knew the location of a property, he was able to identify the revenue associated with the lost services for each property based on each lost customer's monthly rate. Finally, he multiplied that amount by 24 months to cover the two-year waiting period.

He had "[no] reason to doubt the accuracy of the information," he said on the stand. He repeatedly noted that his calculations relied on information reasonably relied on by experts in his field.

He said determining variable costs was "a matter of obtaining profit and loss statements and reviewing the individual line item expenses to understand the nature of the expense, how it's affected by daily operations, its ties to revenue, and just overall professional judgment and experience." He explained that subtracting variable costs from revenue was a method that "experts in [his] field would normally use to calculate lost business profits."

Moreover, he decided to include damages related to growth, rate increases, disposal fees, uncollectible accounts receivable, and layoff costs in his lost profits calculation. The county objected to the expansion of damages based on these categories. When cross-examined on these components, the expert conceded weaknesses. For example, he said that "damages for growth" stood for revenue that the haulers lost from customers "they never had." He admitted that in determining damages for one hauler he used rate increases even though the company president refused to furnish the backup information the expert had sought. The expert allowed that the disposal fees included in another hauler's damages did not go back to the county's violation of the waiting period. He agreed that in terms of uncollectible accounts receivable, nothing stopped the hauler from recovering the amounts by filing suit against the customer or taking other actions. As for layoff costs, he conceded that he was not aware of any contract that required a hauler to pay severance to its laid-off employees.

The expert concluded that damages for all three haulers amounted to over $10.1 million.

The trial court found that the expert was well qualified, used a methodology and information that experts in his field rely on, and also based his calculations on sources that were reasonably reliable. However, the court found the damages related to growth, rate increases, disposal fees, uncollectible accounts receivable, and layoff costs were too speculative. Therefore, it excluded the respective amounts. Accordingly, it arrived at a total amount of damages of approximately $5.9 million.

Dearth of contradictory evidence. The trial court's findings on damages prompted a second appeal from both sides.

1. *County.* The county's main argument was that the expert relied on information of which he had no firsthand knowledge, i.e., the haulers' databases and unaudited profit and loss statements.

That argument had no force of persuasion. The appeals court noted that, under applicable state law, an expert was allowed to base his opinions on information "derived from sources outside of court and other than by his own perspective." In fact, said the court, most of the time, expert testimony is based on facts that the expert did not observe firsthand and of which he had no personal knowledge. The key is whether the facts and data are reasonably relied on by experts in the field and are otherwise reasonably reliable.

Here, the county "put on no evidence to contradict" the expert's assertions that his methodology and the information he used for his calculations satisfied those criteria even though the county had the opportunity to do so. The trial court did not err in deferring to the expert's testimony. Further, "any weaknesses in the factual underpinnings" of the expert's testimony did not go toward admissibility but credibility of the witness, the appeals court said. The county could have conducted discovery and cross-examined the experts on the facts and data he relied on and impeached him. It could have introduced its own expert testimony to convince the trial court that the haulers' expert was wrong. It failed to do so. As a result, the trial court for the most part relied on the sole expert's damages calculation and "implicitly" found the expert to be credible. But the trial court did not simply adopt the testimony but rejected damages that it considered too speculative. Therefore, the appeals court deferred to the trial court's findings.

The county also attacked the expert's methodology, claiming: (1) the lost profits calculation included revenues the haulers would have received from customers who decided to halt trash collection services before the county's new program started; and (2) the expert improperly used the haulers' unaudited profit and loss statements instead of their income tax returns.

The appeals court noted that the county contested these particular factual issues earlier, but the trial court discounted the objections. The trial court, as the finder of fact, "was free to believe or disbelieve any, all, or none of [the expert's] testimony." It is not the appeals court's role to "re-evaluate [the] testimony through its own perspective."

2. *Haulers.* The haulers cross-appealed as to one point. They said the trial court erred when it subtracted from the award amounts related to growth, rate increases, disposal fees, uncollectible accounts receivable, and layoff costs.

According to the appeals court, this objection, too, related to determinations of witness credibility, which were the province of the finder of fact—here the trial court.

Because the haulers established damages with reasonable certainty, the trial court's lost profits award was based on substantial evidence, the state Court of Appeals said and affirmed the award.

In re Ancestry

Citation: 2015 Del. Ch. LEXIS 21
Date of decision: Jan. 30, 2015
Experts: William S. Wisialowski (petitioners); Gregg A. Jarrell (company/respondent)
Judge: Glasscock
State/Jurisdiction: Delaware
Court: Delaware Court of Chancery
Type of case: Dissenting Shareholder
SIC code: 8732 Commercial Economic, Sociological, and Educational Research
NAICS code: 541720 Research and Development in the Social Sciences and Humanities

Chancery Assigns Secondary Role to Post-Merger DCF

As he did in *Huff Fund*, Vice Chancellor Glasscock of the Delaware Court of Chancery recently lamented "the difficulties, if not outright incongruities of a law-trained judge determining fair value of a company in light of an auction sale." Various factors complicated the court's task in the new case, including the wildly differing values the parties' experts proposed using the same—discounted cash flow—method. Again, the court proved up to the challenge. In a careful critique of expert testimony, it explained why the merger price ultimately proved to be the most reliable indicator of value.

Backstory. Ancestry described itself as "a pioneer and the leader in the online family research market." In late 2009, the company went public and its shares traded at $13.50 apiece. In spring 2010, it became the financial and research sponsor of a popular NBC show—"Who Do You Think You Are?"—featuring celebrities who wanted to explore their family history. Soon, the company experienced exponential growth, such that by early 2011 its stock was trading at over $40 per share. But within a year the company's fortune changed. The NBC show's ratings started to decline, and in May 2012 the show was cancelled. Also, the company began to feel the weight of various competitors encroaching on its territory.

By early 2012, Ancestry's stock had dropped to about $20 per share. Its board then retained a financial advisor to explore strategic options. Once news of the potential sale of the company reached the public, a number of possible bidders and strategic buyers as well as financial sponsors lined up. Preliminary indications of interests fell in the range of $30-$31 to $35-$38. The three highest bidders performed due diligence by doing extensive analyses of key metrics—gross subscriber additions (GSA), cancellation of subscriptions in a given period (chum), and subscriber acquisition cost (SAC)—and also cohort analyses that tested the engagement among different segments. The latter in particular indicated a declining trend among every cohort of monthly subscribers. None of the bidders submitted a final bid by the company's early August deadline.

The company then also hired Goldman Sachs to explore "what the company could do as an ongoing stand-alone public company." Eventually, one of the three bidders, the buyer, offered $31 per share but raised its offer to $32 after further negotiations and pressure from the company's board members. The sales price represented a 41% premium on the unaffected trading price of company stock. In October 2012, the company entered into a merger agreement with the buyer. Between the announcement of the merger and the closing, in December 2012, no topping bid emerged. Ninety-nine percent of the voting shares approved of the transaction.

Among the dissenters petitioning the Delaware Court of Chancery for a fair value determination under Delaware's Appraisal Rights Statute, Section 262, was Merion Capital, L.P., which in the past had challenged similar transactions. See *Merion Capital, L.P. v. 3M Cogent, Inc.*, 2013 Del. Ch. LEXIS 172 (July 8, 2013) (available at *BVLaw*).

Sale-oriented management projections. Company management did not generate long-term projections in the regular course of business. But it developed some forecasts in May 2012 in connection with the impending sales process. The initial May projections met with an exhortation from the board to make the projections more aggressive. This feedback resulted in the May sales projections for which management "turned the dials—GSA, SAC, chum—as much as [they] could while maintaining … credibility." These projections were available to interested buyers during the sales process.

But subsequently the potential bidders argued the assumptions underlying the May projections were too optimistic and aggressive. In response to bidder feedback and tighter numbers emerging from the actual budget process that had begun in August 2012, management developed the October projections, which were more conservative. These projections included a Scenario A and a Scenario B that served as outer "goalposts." Management said these were best estimates of the company's future performance. At the time management created the scenarios, it also contemplated equity rollovers into a new company. The $32-per-share merger price included a rollover of $82 million in equity.

Compromised expert DCFs. For the appraisal proceedings, both sides retained experts who agreed that the best, and only, way to determine the company's fair value was by using a discounted cash flow (DCF) analysis. Because the company was so unique in the services it provided, there were no comparable companies or transactions on which to base a comparative analysis.

But the experts disagreed on key inputs of the DCF as well as the factors that made up the components and, as a consequence, reached vastly different results. As the Chancery put it, the petitioners' expert "proved something of a moving target," in that he proposed at different points in the litigation a figure as high as $47 per share and a minimum value of $42.81. The company's expert concluded the stock was only worth $30.63 per share. As the court pointed out, that price was actually below the value the buyer, a nonstrategic investor, was willing to pay.

In terms of expert testimony, the Chancery observed that, although both experts were respected and well qualified, their approaches were "less than fully persuasive." Their valuations appeared to be "result-oriented riffs on the market price." By his own account, the petitioners' expert "tortured the numbers until they confess[ed]." For example, he worked the more realistic October management projections into an "unbelievable" best-case scenario to come up with a "defensible" number—higher than the merger price but not ridiculously so. The company's expert "candidly suggested" that, if his valuation had been as far from the merger price as that of the petitioners' expert, he "would have tried to find out a way to reconcile those two numbers."

The court said these statements showed the limited use of a post hoc DCF analysis. "If an analysis, relied upon to assess whether a sales price presents the fair value in turn uses that very sales price as a check on its own plausibility, and if it must be revised if it fails that check, then the process itself approaches tautology."

The court went on to say that "the problem with relying on torture is the possibility of false confession." Instead of relying on either expert's analysis completely, the court decided to conduct its own analysis. In describing how it went about doing so, it explored some of the major areas of disagreements between the experts.

a. Cash flow projections. Management projections were the input that most drove the valuation gap between the experts' DCF, the court noted. Although the petitioners' expert "tout[ed]" the initial May forecast as the most reliable, he ultimately decided to blend that forecast with the best-case October scenario he created. Presumably he did so realizing that relying solely on the aggressively optimist May forecast would produce a valuation "so high as to be likely rejected out-of-hand," the court said.

The company's expert relied on the October projections, "despite evidence suggesting they were produced in light of the need to justify the sales price," the court noted. Ultimately, however, the Chancery found the two October forecasts represented management's best view of the company, and it decided to use them, weighting Scenarios A and B equally.

b. Terminal value. A significant dispute between the experts centered on the normalization of EBIT margins. The company's expert contended normalizing was important, but the petitioners' expert did not. The petitioners claimed that, since the October projections, which the company's expert used, already represented a pessimistic view, normalizing was not necessary.

The court disagreed. The October projections reflected a best view of the company going forward, it said. Therefore, the court adopted the company expert's approach: averaging the 2013 through 2016 EBIT margin projections and using that figure as the future projection.

c. Discount rate. One of the issues was the calculation of beta. The petitioners' expert used Nasdaq as the market proxy, reasoning it contained a number of companies similar to Ancestry. He next applied this beta to an S&P 500-based equity risk premium, although his report stated that it was appropriate to multiply a Nasdaq-based beta by a Nasdaq equity risk premium.

The company's expert used the S&P 500 as his market proxy.

Also, the petitioners' expert used a weekly observation point, whereas the company's expert used monthly data—a choice the petitioners' expert criticized because it only yielded 30 data points, when the valuation literature recommended using at least 36 and some sources even preferred using at least 60 data points.

The court declined to adopt either expert's discount rate in full. The S&P 500 was the better market proxy because it provided a broader sampling of the market, it stated. But the company's expert should have used weekly rather than monthly data to obtain a larger sample size, the court said.

By the court's calculation, beta was 1.137.

The experts also clashed over the equity risk premium (ERP). Both experts agreed it was appropriate to use the supply-side ERP from the Ibbotson yearbook, but disagreed over which edition to use. The petitioners' expert used the 2013 edition to come up with an ERP of 6.11%; the company's expert used the 2012 edition of the yearbook to arrive at an ERP of 6.14%. This disagreement carried over into the equity size premium.

The court agreed with the petitioners' expert that it was appropriate to use the 2013 edition since the merger date (Dec. 28, 2012) was very close to the end of 2012 and "the 2013 edition would not have contained any information not available as of the Merger Date, aside from one day of trading information."

Both experts relied on the weighted average cost of capital (WACC) method to calculate the discount rate, and both used the capital asset pricing model (CAPM) to calculate the cost of equity. The court did, too, and arrived at a WACC of 10.71%.

d. Stock-based compensation. Since startups such as Ancestry customarily compensate employees heavily with stock, "[t]he effect of that practice is significant in a valuation of such a company," the court observed. "[O]nce it reaches a material level, SBC must in some manner be accounted for in order to reach a reasonable calculation of fair value," it went on to say. The problem was how to do so: whether to consider the dilutive effect of SBC or to consider it in expenses.

The company's expert chose the latter approach, deducting the noncash stock expense from EBIT, treating it as tax deductible to approximate the anticipated deductions when options were exercised, and not adding the expense back. The petitioners argued that nowhere had the Chancery approved of this treatment. In fact, they said, in *Merion Capital v. 3M Cogent*, the court rejected the proposition that SBC should be treated as a cash expense because there was no showing that SBC would "have any effect on the actual cash flows of the Company." At the same time, the court in *3M Cogent* said it made sense "to adjust earnings to take into account the dilutive effect of SBC."

In his initial analysis, the petitioners' expert did not account for SBC. But, for his rebuttal report, he created a model "to measure the cash flow required to eliminate any dilution from future option rants and their exercise." Nevertheless, in the end, he decided "not to include any impact for SBC in my DCF analysis," explaining that adding the future stock-trading price would add "yet another level of assumptions which are difficult to prove."

The court adopted the approach the company's expert proposed, saying the petitioners did not present a reliable alternative.

Check on merger price. Using its own inputs, the court concluded that under Scenario A the shares were worth $30.33 per unit and under Scenario B they were worth $33.24 per unit. Since it decided to weight the values equally, it arrived at a DCF-derived value of $31.79 per share of Ancestry stock.

But this calculation did not end the court's analysis. The bigger issue was whether to rely on the DCF valuation, using the market-derived valuation as a check, or using the DCF-derived value as a check on the plausibility of the merger price. Considering all the projections underlying any DCF analysis were problematic in this case, the court decided to use the DCF as a check only.

The sales process here was "reasonable, wide-ranging and produced a motivated buyer," the Chancery said. The sales price first came under scrutiny earlier in the proceedings when the petitioners asked the court to enjoin the merger. The court then declined to do so, finding the process "had a lot of vibrancy and integrity." There was no showing that the director defendants acted under a conflict of interest that would give rise to a breach of the duty of loyalty. While it was unlikely that the auction "left significant stockholder value unaccounted for," there also was no indication that synergies pushed the merger price above fair value, the court subsequently determined. The company's expert conceded as much, the court pointed out.

In concluding, the vice chancellor said that the court's DCF valuation "gives me comfort that no undetected factor skewed the sales process." But the DCF value was still below the actual sales price. According to the court, it would be "hubristic" to elevate that estimate of value over the value an entity "for which investment represents a real—not merely an academic—risk" placed on the company. Therefore, the Chancery found the $32 merger price represented the fair value of company stock.

Anchor Savings Bank v. United States

Citation: 2015 U.S. Claims LEXIS 1110
Date of decision: Aug. 31, 2015
Experts: Unknown (plaintiff); unknown (defendant)
Judge: Block
State/Jurisdiction: Federal
Court: United States Court of Federal Claims
Type of case: Winstar
SIC code: 6211 Security Brokers, Dealers, and Flotation Companies
NAICS code: 523120

Court Approves *Winstar* Plaintiff's Tax Gross Up Calculation

Another *Winstar* case inched closer to conclusion when the Federal Claims court recently approved the plaintiff's projection of tax liability for damages stemming from the bank's successful breach of contract suit against the government. A sticking point in the tax gross up calculation was the value of the *Anchor* litigation at the time JPMorgan acquired the assets of Anchor Savings Bank, the plaintiff.

FIRREA litigation. The litigation was a consequence of the savings and loan crisis that occurred in the late 1970s and early 1980s. Anchor had committed to buying several failing savings and loan associations in exchange for the government's allowing Anchor to count more than $550 million in supervisory goodwill toward its capital requirements, amortized over decades. But in the late 1980s Congress passed the Financial Institutions Reform, Recovery and Enforcement Act (FIRREA)—legislation that effectively terminated the favorable accounting treatment the government had promised to Anchor. The change in law caused Anchor to become severely undercapitalized. To avoid regulatory closure, Anchor had to sell valuable assets at a loss. In 1995, Anchor sued the government for breach of contract.

In 2008, the U.S. Court of Federal Claims found the government liable and awarded Anchor over $356.4 million in damages, including net lost profits, damages for reduced stock proceeds, mitigation costs, damages from branch sales, and "wounded bank" damages. On appeal from the government, in 2010, the U.S. Court of Appeals for the Federal Circuit essentially affirmed the judgment but remanded for clarification of the lower court's calculation of mitigation costs. (A detailed discussion of the damages testimony and the Federal Circuit's ruling in *Anchor Savings Bank v. United States,* 2010 WL 786578 (C.A. Fed.) (March 10, 2010) is available at *BVLaw.*)

Five years later, the Federal Claims court awarded the bank an additional $63.2 million in mitigation costs and determined the pregross judgment owed to Anchor was over $419.6 million. It also found that approximately $228.1 million of the award was subject to a "tax gross up." (In an earlier 2015 ruling, the same court said the amount that was subject to a tax gross up was $227.1 million.)

A tax gross up is an additional award that seeks to "zero out" the tax liability that attaches to the plaintiff's damages award. It ensures that the plaintiff is fully compensated for the harm the defendant's conduct caused.

Here, calculating the final tax gross up rate was the last step in the determination of damages and quite likely the end of the litigation.

Bank's ownership change. The court noted that the resolution of the case was delayed owing to the repeated change in ownership of Anchor. First, the bank merged into the Dime Savings Bank of New York (Dime). Subsequently, Dime merged with Washington Mutual Bank (WMB). In 2008, the government seized WMB and placed it in receivership with the Federal Deposit Insurance Corporation (FDIC). The FDIC sold substantially all of WMB's assets, including the *Anchor* litigation, to JPMorgan Chase Bank (JPMC) for $1.8 billion.

Key in terms of determining the gross up rate was that, when Dime took over Anchor, it issued litigation tracking warrants (LTWs) to its shareholders. When Washington Mutual acquired Dime, it ratified the LTW agreement. The LTWs were trading on the Nasdaq.

Gross up calculation. For purposes of calculating the gross up, the plaintiff acknowledged that it was only entitled to gross up the portion of the $228.1 million that represented taxable gain. Taxable gain is the difference between the present value of the asset and the price the asset commanded at the time of acquisition, including adjustments for depreciation and other factors.

Here, the plaintiff maintained, the present value of the *Anchor* litigation was the court's award of $419.6 million. To determine the price JMPC paid for the litigation, the plaintiff looked to the price the LTWs were trading on the day JMPC acquired Anchor's assets. Although JPMC did not acquire the *Anchor* litigation at a specific price but as part of the package the FDIC sold, it argued an examination of the LTWs established that the fair market value or tax basis of the *Anchor* litigation was nearly $55.4 million.

The plaintiff also explained that it was appropriate to deduct only a fraction—54.3%—of the basis from the pregross judgment since only a portion of the award—$228.1 million of $419.6 million—was subject to a gross up. It said that 54.3% of the $55.4 million basis meant only $30.1 million was to be deducted from the $228.1 million the court had designated for the gross up.

Accordingly, the plaintiff arrived at a taxable gain of nearly $198 million. It claimed that the appropriate combined federal and state marginal rate was 37.535%. Thirty-five percent represented the federal tax rate; in terms of the applicable state tax rate, it noted that JPMC was subject to multiple state jurisdictions. The rate for all unitary jurisdictions was 3.9%. "But, since state and local taxes are deductions for Federal Tax purposes, the 3.9% becomes 2.535% (3.9% × 65%)." The plaintiff concluded that taxing the projected $198 million taxable gain at a 37.535% rate resulted in a gross up of nearly $119 million. Assuming this was the additional amount the court would award it, the plaintiff stipulated that JPMC intended to report the $119 million as taxable income.

The government did not object to the plaintiff's calculation but asked the court to defer the gross up award given a possibility that the Internal Revenue Service might determine the LTWs understated the fair market value of the *Anchor* litigation and might use a different method to value Anchor's tax basis.

The court declined to delay the gross up award based on what it called "this purported uncertainty." Projecting a plaintiff's tax liability "inevitably entails a certain degree of uncertainty," the court said. It observed that the plaintiff showed that the ownership interests in the *Anchor* litigation were actively traded on the day JPMC bought them and that courts "in other contexts" agreed that the value of a stock reflected information about the value of a company or its asset.

Adding the $119 million gross up award to the pre-gross-up judgment, the court found the plaintiff was entitled to over $538.6 million in damages resulting from the FIRREA litigation.

Apple, Inc. v. Samsung Electronics Co.

Citation: 2015 U.S. App. LEXIS 8096
Date of decision: May 18, 2015
Experts: Terry Musika, Julie L. Davis (plaintiff); Michael Wagner (defendants)
Judge: Probst
State/Jurisdiction: Federal
Court: United States Court of Appeals for the Federal Circuit
Type of case: Intellectual Property
SIC code: 4813 Telephone Communications

Federal Circuit Resists Samsung's 'Quest for Apportionment'

In the most recent twist of the infringement saga featuring the tech giants Apple and Samsung, the Federal Circuit rejected Samsung's various calls for apportionment in calculating damages for design patent infringement. The court also affirmed damages related to utility patent infringement but not those based on trade dress claims. The appellate ruling suggests that Apple's $1 billion award remains largely intact.

Backstory. In April 2011, Apple sued Samsung. In August 2012, a jury found Samsung infringed critical features of the iPhone and iPad and awarded Apple just over $1 billion in damages. The infringement claims involved patents related to design elements in the iPhone and utility patents related to the phone's user interface. Samsung first challenged the outcome in post-trial motions. The district court upheld the jury's liability findings but struck down about 40% of the damages, finding Apple's expert had used an improper notice date in calculating part of the damages. In the partial retrial on damages, the jury awarded Apple over $290 million. Samsung again attacked the trial proceedings in post-trial motions. After the district court rejected Samsung's claims, the defendant appealed the final judgment at the Federal Circuit.

Design patent infringement. In terms of damages stemming from design patent infringement, Samsung primarily contended that the district court committed legal error when it allowed the jury to award damages based on Samsung's entire profits from its infringing smartphones. Damages should be a function of "basic causation principles," Samsung said. And "Apple failed to establish that infringement of its limited design patents … caused *any* Samsung sales or profits." (emphasis in original) Hence, Apple suffered no loss. Samsung also said consumers bought its phones for a variety of other factors.

According to the Federal Circuit, Samsung was on a "quest for apportionment." Samsung's causation arguments militated in favor of an apportionment requirement that Congress, in the Patent Act, 35 USC § 289, specifically rejected. The court explained that under the apportionment theory a patent holder would have to show what portion of the infringer's profit, or of its own lost profit, was due to the design and what was due to the article itself.

In contrast, Section 289 provides:

> Whoever during the term of a patent for a design, without license of the owner, (1) applies the patented design, or any colorable imitation thereof, to any article of manufacture for the purpose of sale, or (2) sells or exposes for sale any article of manufacture to which such design or colorable imitation has been applied shall be liable to the owner to the extent of his total profit, but not less than $250, recoverable in any United States district court having jurisdiction of the parties.

Therefore, section 289 explicitly entitles the patent holder to "the total profit from the article of manufacture bearing the patented design." The Federal Circuit noted in passing that in their "friend of the court" brief, law professors, supporting Samsung's position on this issue, argued that allowing entire profits for design patent infringement "makes no sense in the modern world." The court called this a "policy argument" that should be made to Congress. Good or bad policy, the court was under an obligation to uphold the existing statutory requirement, the Federal Circuit said.

Alternatively, Samsung proposed limiting the profits awarded to "the portion of the product as sold that incorporates or embodies the subject matter of the patent." In other words, the court should construe the term "article of manufacture" narrowly based on a 2nd Circuit case from 1915. The Federal Circuit found the facts underlying both cases were too dissimilar. There was no authority requiring the district court in this case to limit damages for design patent infringement, the Federal Circuit said.

Utility patent infringement. Samsung also contested aspects of damages for the infringement of Apple's utility patents.

1. *Lost profits.* The jury found that for certain Samsung phones there was no reasonable noninfringing alternative available. Consequently, the appropriate measure of damages was lost profits. Under Federal Circuit precedent, "market sales of an acceptable noninfringing substitute often suffice alone to defeat a case for lost profits." *Grain Processing Corp. v. American Maize Products,* 185 F.3d 1541 (Fed. Cir. 1999).

On appeal, Samsung claimed there were two Samsung phones that the jury should have considered as noninfringing substitutes and whose existence negated an award for lost profits.

The Federal Circuit disagreed, noting that Samsung was unable to support its claim that the two noninfringing phones included a feature that was comparable to the patented feature. The jury had every reason not to consider the Samsung phones as acceptable substitutes: One phone's features were significantly different from those of the patented product; the other phone was never sold by a U.S. carrier.

2. *Reasonable royalty.* For a certain set of phones, Apple was only entitled to a reasonable royalty. Samsung claimed on appeal that one of Apple's experts failed to explain in detail how she arrived at the royalty rates based on the *Georgia-Pacific* factors, particularly with regard to showing demand.

The Federal Circuit dismissed that objection. The expert expressly considered what it would cost Samsung to be out of the market long enough to design around the patents, the profits related to

Samsung's use of the patented functions, and the commercial relationship between the parties. The expert testimony was sufficient to support the reasonable royalty award.

Trade dress claims. The only portion of the damages the Federal Circuit struck down was related to Apple's trade dress dilution claim. Specifically, the appeals court found that the trade dresses were functional and as such not protected under trademark law.

Accordingly, the Federal Circuit remanded for "immediate entry of final judgment on all damages awards not predicated on Apple's trade dress claims."

Editor's note: Tom F. Cotter, one of the law professors signing the amicus brief, regrets the Federal Circuit's refusal to consider apportionment in instances of design patent infringement. A rule requiring an award of "total profit" is "indefensible," he says, because it "means that a court may award the defendant's entire profit from the sale of design patent-infringing goods, even if the design patent in suit accounts for only a small portion of that profit." He wonders whether Samsung might consider asking the U.S. Supreme Court for review of the current Section 289 interpretation. See comparativepatentremedies.blogspot.com/2015/05/federal-circuit-affirms-damages-awards.html.

AstraZeneca AB v. Apotex Corp.

Citation: 2015 U.S. App. LEXIS 5543
Date of decision: April 7, 2015
Experts: unknown (plaintiff); unknown (defendant)
Judge: Bryson
State/Jurisdiction: Federal
Court: U.S. Court of Appeals for the Federal Circuit
Type of case: Intellectual Property
SIC code: 2834 Pharmaceutical Preparations
NAICS code: 325412 Pharmaceutical Preparation Manufacturing

Federal Circuit Weighs Use of EMVR in Pharmaceutical Case

A patent suit involving two major drug companies explored the issue of using the entire market value rule in the pharmaceutical context. Typically, the rule comes into play when the subject is a multicomponent product such as a machine. In this case, however, the subject was a pill that contained a novel drug at its core and two coatings to enable delivery of the active ingredient to the patient. The defendant wanted apportionment because the patentee's patent for the active ingredient had expired. The patentee claimed its formulation patents covered the entire product, not just a single component of the product.

Backstory. The litigation centered on omeprazole, a proton pump inhibitor effective in treating acid-related gastrointestinal disorders. Omeprazole, however, is susceptible to degradation in acidic and neutral media. The plaintiff, AstraZeneca (Astra), held two patents that enabled delivery to the patient by designing a pill that protected the active ingredient, omeprazole, with a water-soluble subcoating and an enteric coating. Astra's patents covered both the active ingredient and the formulations for delivering it. The company's active ingredient patent expired in 2001, but the two patents in suit related to the formulation did not expire until April 2007. Astra sold its highly successful prescription drug under the name Prilosec.

The defendant, Apotex, started selling generic omeprazole until the district court (S.D.N.Y.) ruled Apotex's formulation infringed Astra's patents. Subsequently, the court held a trial on damages for infringement from 2003 until 2007.

***Georgia-Pacific* factors favor plaintiff.** The parties agreed that damages should take the form of a reasonable royalty. Consequently, the district court used the *Georgia-Pacific* framework to determine what royalty the parties would have agreed upon had they negotiated a license before Apotex began to infringe.

In essence, the district court found that:

1. At the time of infringement, Apotex expected a gross margin on sales of its generic omeprazole that was more than twice as large as the average gross margin on other generic products the company sold in the U.S. According to the district court, if Apotex had a license to Astra's patents, its profit estimates would be even higher since there would be no litigation and it would have more leeway to price its generic product than an "at risk" entrant into the generic market generally has.

2. At the time of the hypothetical negotiation, Apotex had a poor chance of finding a noninfringing omeprazole formulation. A number of generic drug companies had developed versions and sought approval from the Food and Drug Administration to manufacture and sell them. Apotex was a late entrant into the market and faced a high risk of being shut out of it altogether. Because most pharmacies keep only one generic version of a drug on hand, producers of generic drugs are in a race to enter the market.

3. There was only a slim chance that in 2003 Astra would have granted a license to Apotex because the appearance on the scene of another generic manufacturer would have interfered with Astra's long-term strategy concerning proton pump inhibitors. There was a risk that third-party payers (TPPs) would impose a "maximum allowable cost" for prescription omeprazole based on the generic price of the drug or would otherwise limit the use of branded drugs such as Prilosec.

4. Other licenses and settlements Astra had made in connection with omeprazole, although not a "perfect benchmark," supported the court's royalty rate determination, the court decided. It noted that pursuant to one settlement Astra was entitled to 54% of the manufacturer's net profits on its comparable sales and, under a settlement offer with another manufacturer, Astra would obtain 50% to 70% of the manufacturer's profits on certain dosages of omeprazole.

The district court concluded that Astra had a right to 50% of Apotex's gross margin (gross sales minus cost of goods) on the infringing sales, which translated into over $76 million plus prejudgment interest.

'Intermingling' lost profits and reasonable royalty. Apotex appealed the district court's findings with the Federal Circuit on numerous grounds. The theme of its objections was that the district court "lost sight of the essential purpose of the exercise to compensate Astra for harm actually suffered."

Apotex contended that, since it was the fourth generic manufacturer entering the omeprazole market, its participation would have inflicted little marginal harm to Astra. Further, in actuality, it did not cut prices aggressively.

The Federal Circuit found the district court properly concluded that Apotex's actual pricing history provided few clues as to how it would have priced omeprazole had it obtained a license from Astra.

The appeals court also noted Apotex's "intermingling" of lost profits and reasonable royalty damages measures. Apotex's concern with compensation based on the harm Astra actually suffered illustrated the problem, the Federal Circuit said. Actual harm was a relevant consideration in a lost profits case but not a reasonable royalty determination, the court explained. A lost profits determination seeks to compensate the patent holder for lost sales owing to infringement; a reasonable royalty analysis tries to compensate the patent holder for the lost opportunity to obtain a reasonable royalty that the infringer would have been willing to pay if it had been barred from infringing.

Since the measure of damages here was a reasonable royalty, the district court was required to calculate the rate Astra would have asked for in exchange for licensing its patents to Apotex at the beginning of Apotex's infringement in late 2003. Here, the district court extensively detailed the immense benefits to Apotex and the considerable costs to Astra of a license for the formulation patents. Even with a 50% royalty payment to Astra, Apotex would be able to count on a 36% profit margin, which was in the range of the 31%-to-48% margins the company at the time typically earned on products.

As part of its "overcompensation" argument, Astrotex also seemed to claim that the costs to the infringer of producing a noninfringing product were irrelevant to a reasonable royalty calculation. The Federal Circuit disagreed, pointing out that, where an infringer can easily design around a patent and develop a noninfringing product, the hypothetical royalty rate typically is low. Conversely, if it is difficult to avoid a patent, an infringer is willing to pay a higher royalty for a license. Here, the district court found that Apotex would have confronted considerable obstacles in marketing a noninfringing generic omeprazole formulation. This fact could not but influence the royalty rate a company in Apotex's position would be willing to pay for a license from Astra.

Apotex also attacked the district court's consideration of some of the licenses and settlements Astra had made, arguing that the transactions occurred in the context of litigation and were irrelevant to determining a reasonable royalty rate in this case.

"That contention goes too far," the Federal Circuit said, noting "there is no per se rule barring reference to settlements simply because they arise from litigation." In the two instances, the third parties' decisions to settle with or take a license from Astra occurred after the district court had held that Astra's patents were valid and that both of the third-party defendants had infringed. "The setting in which those events took place was therefore similar to the setting of a hypothetical negotiation in which infringement and patent validity are assumed," the Federal Circuit observed.

Defendant advocates for apportionment. Finally, Apotex claimed that the district court overcompensated Astra because it based its damages calculation on the value of the entire omeprazole product—the active ingredient at the core and the two coatings. But since the patent for the active ingredient, omeprazole, had expired at the time of the infringement, the district court should have apportioned the value of the "inventive element" of the drug, that is, the subcoating.

Apotex argued that apportionment was necessary under the entire market value rule (EMVR), which requires that in a multicomponent product a patent holder may only claim damages based on the value of the entire product where the patented feature "creates the basis for customer demand or substantially creates the value of the component parts."

The district court had rejected the use of EMVR in the generic pharmaceutical context, finding it typically applied to multicomponent products such as machines. The Federal Circuit did not go as far. It declined to hold that EMVR was per se inapplicable in the pharmaceutical context but said EMVR was inapplicable in this case.

The Federal Circuit clarified that in a multicomponent product EMVR aimed to tease out the value of the patented feature to the whole. "This case does not fit the pattern in which the entire market value rule applies," the court said. Astra's formulation patents covered three key elements—the drug core, the enteric coating, and the subcoating—which in combination represented the omeprazole product that was the subject of the claims. "Thus, Astra's patents cover the infringing product as a whole, not a single component of a multi-component product. There is no unpatented or non-infringing feature in the product."

But the Federal Circuit also pointed out that, even if EMVR did not apply, the district court's damages analysis had "to account for the relative value of the patentee's invention in comparison to the value of the conventional elements recited in the claim, standing alone." See *Ericsson, Inc. v. D-Link Systems, Inc.*, 773 F.3d 1201 (Fed. Cir. 2014) (available at *BVLaw*). The district court did so by way of a *Georgia-Pacific* analysis, several of whose factors directly addressed this issue, the Federal Circuit found.

Moreover, "it is improper to assume that a conventional element cannot be rendered more valuable by its use in combination with an invention," the court said. According to the Federal Circuit, "the question is how much new value is created by the novel combination, beyond the value conferred by the conventional elements alone."

Here, the history of omeprazole showed that the patented formulation "substantially create[d] the value" of the entire omeprazole product. Although omeprazole was effective in reducing stomach acid, the issue was how to deliver the active ingredient to the part of the human body where it could be effective. Astra's scientists resolved the problem by developing a water-soluble subcoating, which in turn allowed them to formulate a commercially viable product. Accordingly, "the subcoating was substantially responsible for the value of the product." Astra's formulation resulted in a novel product, the Federal Circuit said.

For all of these reasons, the district court was correct in not excluding the value of the active ingredient from its damages calculation, the Federal Circuit decided. The only modification it required the district court to make was shortening the damages period.

Bank of America, N.A. v. Veluchamy (In re Veluchamy)

Citation: 2014 Bankr. LEXIS 5106
Date of decision: Dec. 18, 2014
Experts: G. William Kennedy (estate); Daniel Van Vleet (defendants)
Judge: Wedoff
State/Jurisdiction: Federal/Illinois
Court: United States Bankruptcy Court
Type of case: Bankruptcy
SIC code: 7331 Direct Mail Advertising Services
NAICS code: 511140 Directory and Mailing List Publishers

Bankruptcy Court Accepts Rationale for Tax Affecting

A noteworthy discussion involving reputed valuation experts over how to value stock in one of the defendants' S corporations lies buried in a bankruptcy case that features over 20 claims of fraudulent transfers. The court ruled on bread-and-butter valuation issues, such as cash flow, capitalization rate, discount for lack of marketability, and tax affecting.

Background. The defendants established a number of direct-mailing and marketing operations. When those businesses proved a success, the defendants invested in banking institutions but foundered when the government began to investigate the institutions' loan practices and financial conditions. To keep the banks afloat, the defendants borrowed tens of millions of dollars from a predecessor of Bank of America (BoA), the plaintiff.

In 2007, before the defendants defaulted on their loans, they reported a net worth of nearly $500 million. But, in subsequent years, while BoA took measures to collect the outstanding loans, the defendants disposed of almost all of their major assets by transferring many millions of dollars to their two children and other family members, the co-defendants. They sold stock and real estate in the U.S. and India at discounted prices to the co-defendants and gave them the remaining cash and other assets, such as jewelry. When BoA was poised to go to trial to collect on judgments totaling over $47 million, the defendants filed for Chapter 7 bankruptcy and caused their businesses to file for Chapter 11 bankruptcy. The Chapter 11 bankruptcy case is pending.

The Chapter 7 bankruptcy is the subject of this controversy. Because BoA's interests aligned with those of the trustee and other creditors, it came to represent the estate in suing the defendants on 23 claims for fraudulent transfers. The theory was that the defendants and co-defendants carried out a scheme to move the high-value assets out of reach of creditors. To make the transfers look legitimate, they destroyed genuine documents and created false ones.

The Bankruptcy Court found the estate "amply" proved liability and fashioned a remedy for each of the counts based on expert testimony. The estate and the defendants retained respected financial professionals to support their positions. Two counts in particular raise important issues for valuators.

1. Valuation dispute. One value dispute centered on the defendants' sales of stock in a holding company that owned seven profitable direct marketing companies. The company operated as an S corporation.

Before the defendants defaulted on their BoA loans, they owned a 70% interest in the company and a right to most of its income. Both children owned the remainder of the stock, 15% each. Once BoA filed suit against the defendants, the latter orchestrated two transfers to sell a controlling interest in the company to their two children for less than fair value by having the company issue new shares. The result was a dilution of the defendants' interest from 70% to 19.8% in voting stock and from 70% to 52.0% in nonvoting stock. Transferring control of the company to the children meant that any creditor who seized the defendants' stock would be unable to control the company and its subsidiaries. There was some evidence that the stock in the first transfer was worth $2.75 per share and the stock in the second transfer was worth $1.99. In the first transfer, the children paid only $0.63 per share for voting stock; in the second transaction, they paid $0.61 per share for voting stock and $0.60 for nonvoting stock. When the children were asked how the parties determined the price of the stock, they invoked their right not to incriminate themselves. The stock valuation was the subject of conflicting expert testimony at trial.

Income approach preferable. Since the estate wanted to obtain a cash award rather than the children's interest in the proceeds of the company's bankruptcy sale, it had the burden of establishing the value of the shares at the time of the transfers. The estate's expert used both a market and an income approach.

a. *Market approach.* To compute the subject company's value, he selected a number of publicly traded companies that he said were similar to the subject company and applied average sales and earnings multiples from the chosen group to the subject's sales and earnings. (The opinion does not provide specifics.)

The defendants' expert argued that the selection included some companies that were much larger than the subject and others that were "penny stock" companies whose precarious financial situation put them at risk of being delisted from the exchanges on which their stock traded. He also questioned the way in which the estate's expert had derived multiples from the selected set's financial data.

The court said that, while these criticisms did not invalidate the market approach, they were strong enough to make the income approach the more persuasive valuation method.

b. Income approach. Under the income approach, the estate's expert performed a capitalization of net cash flow analysis. The defendants' expert objected to components of the normalized cash flow analysis and the determination of the capitalization rate. The court concluded that with modifications the estate's expert's analysis provided "a reasonable value" of the company's stock.

Three cash flow issues. Because the estate's expert lacked access to the company's cash flow statements, he estimated future capital expenditures that would lower normalized cash flow. In so doing, he added a smaller amount of depreciation in calculating the normalized cash flow for the relevant year than the company had deducted from income in the past.

1. The defendants' expert claimed the rivaling expert's calculation of the expenditures was incorrect. Capital expenditures must equal depreciation costs, he claimed; otherwise, "the assets of [the] company would disappear within five years because of lack of replenishment and replacement."

The court found this claim was without basis. "Fully depreciated property may continue to be used or it may be discarded either with no need for replacement or with the replacement incurring a lower cost," the court said. The estate's expert used an amount that was smaller than the historical deduction, "presumably because the deduction available to [the company] would be declining," the court observed. The amount of capital expenditures was independent of the depreciation costs.

2. Moreover, the estate's expert eliminated the defendants' compensation from the annual cash flow, explaining that they did not provide remunerative services but simply took equity distribution in the form of compensation.

The defendants' expert said that adding the compensation to the cash flow was error since only a controlling shareholder would be able to prevent the defendants from withdrawing excessive personal payments from the company.

The court disagreed. The stock transfers conveyed control to the children, who together had control of the business. Under applicable law, there was an assumption that siblings likely would work together to control a business. Also, the company had management that was separate from the defendants. A third party acquiring the children's interests would be able to stop the defendants from withdrawing "inappropriate" compensation, the court said. It was proper to increase the amount of income for the company by the amount of the compensation the defendants had withdrawn.

3. A final disagreement centered on the estate expert's decision not to tax affect the company's income. He explained that whether and how to account for the taxation applicable to S corporations was a matter of debate in the valuation community. Moreover, he said, multiple decisions from the U.S. Tax Court have held that it is inappropriate to reduce the value of an S corp to capture the tax effects on S corp owners.

The defendants' expert argued that not to tax affect was error. A proper valuation had to consider the taxation of the shareholders on the income of an S corp. The best way was to charge the corporation's income with taxes at the rate reduced by the owners' tax savings. He adjusted the company's income by reducing "income before taxes" by 38%. The rate was based on 35% and 3% federal and state ordinary income tax rates, respectively.

The court found the defendant expert's argument was persuasive, but he did not execute the approach he proposed. Therefore, the court did not adopt his calculation. Although the owner of stock in an S corporation avoids the double taxation imposed on an owner of an ordinary C corporation, there is taxation on the shareholder level, the court noted. "Purchasers of S corporations would in fact experience a reduction in the value of the corporations' earnings because of the need to pay personal income taxes on those earnings, and recognizing that tax effect in valuing S corporations is appropriate," the Bankruptcy Court said. But the defendant expert's calculation simply reduced the company's income by the marginal tax rate of individual owners, which was higher than the rate corporations would pay. And he failed to reflect the savings flowing from the elimination of the double taxation.

Ultimately, the court decided that, instead of correcting the defendant expert's calculation to align with the approach—correct—to which he testified, it would use the midpoint between the defendant expert's tax-affected net cash flow ($7.3 million) and the estate expert's non-tax-affected cash flow ($8.5 million). According to the Bankruptcy Court, $7.9 million was the amount to be used in the estate expert's income-based valuation.

Corrections to capitalization rate. The defendants' expert raised two valid concerns about the estate expert's calculation of the discount rate, the court said.

The first related to the estate expert's use of a company-specific risk premium. The defendants' expert explained the valuation profession disfavored its use and proposed the use of an approximately 2.9% industry risk adjustment (the text provides conflicting rates) based on Ibbotson. The court agreed.

There also was a discussion about the appropriateness of an additional small-firm risk premium. The defendants' expert suggested a 5.9% discount, whereas the estate's expert declined to use one, noting that studies showed that purchasers did not currently apply small-firm risk premiums. The court rejected an all-or-nothing approach and chose to apply a 2.95% rate.

The estate's expert provided a high and a low rate for the equity risk premium: 4.36% and 5.00% based on "two reliable sources." The defendants' expert had no objections, but the court found choosing the midpoint rate—4.68%—"is the best reflection of the evidence."

Based on the adjustments, the applicable capitalization rate was 11.66%, the court concluded. Applying that rate to the $7.9 million annualized cash flow resulted in a company value of nearly $68 million at the relevant time.

DLOM applies. Both experts agreed that the valuation should include a discount for lack of marketability to recognize the difficulty a seller would experience in finding willing buyers. They disagreed over the applicable rate. The defendants' expert proposed a 35% rate. He claimed this was the appropriate rate to account for the increased difficulty of selling an interest in a business controlled by others. The estate's expert used a 15% rate.

The court credited the estate's expert, noting that the children received a controlling interest by way of the two stock sales.

The court next considered the percentage of outstanding stock the children received in the two transfers to calculate their individual liability. It found that they each were liable to the estate for $1.37 million for the initial stock transfer and $7.9 million for the second transfer. In total, under this count for fraudulent transfer alone, each child was liable for nearly $9.3 million.

2. Admissibility issues. One count dealing with the fraudulent transfer of real estate raised questions as to the admissibility of testimony from the estate's expert. The expert's calculation relied on a report Colliers International had prepared for him.

The defendants claimed the expert's testimony was inadmissible for various reasons. For one, he was a business valuator, not a real estate appraiser, and, therefore, lacked the qualifications to testify as to the value of this asset. But even if he were qualified, he failed to perform a proper valuation but simply "parrot[ed]" the Colliers opinions. Also, the Colliers appraisal was inadmissible hearsay.

The court found none of the objections valid. As to the expert's qualifications, the court noted that he qualified as an expert on valuation on the basis of his extensive experience in business valuation. Even though he did not have a specialization in real estate valuation, he had been appraising businesses for over 18 years, including entities that owned real estate. Accordingly, his testimony on property values was likely to assist in the determination of the business values at issue. His approach—comparing sales of similar buildings and tracking cash flows—was accepted in the industry and lent itself to testing.

In addition, Rule 703 of the federal rules of evidence permits experts to base their opinions on information other experts in the field would reasonably rely on, "when the opinion falls within the testifying expert's expertise." This was the case here. The estate's expert was capable of assessing "the appropriateness" of the work done by the Colliers experts, and he did so. He did not just convey the Colliers opinion. And even if the Colliers report was inadmissible by itself, it could come into evidence, as it formed the basis of the valuation expert's opinion on the contested real estate. The defendants were liable for the property values the estate's expert had determined, the court concluded.

Berg v. Young

Citation: 2015 Fla. App., LEXIS 13077
Date of decision: Sept. 2, 2015
Experts: Unknown (wife); unknown (husband)
Judge: Levine
State/Jurisdiction: Florida
Court: Court of Appeals
Type of case: Marital Dissolution
SIC code: 5511 Motor Vehicle Dealers (New and Used)
NAICS code: 441120 Used Car Dealers

Different Ways to Find No Claim to Enhanced Value of Nonmarital Asset

In a Florida divorce case, the trial court heard copious expert testimony on the value of the husband's interest in a car dealership. The dispute turned on the validity and interpretation of the parties' prenuptial agreement; a secondary issue was how to treat any appreciation in value, assuming there was an increase in value in the first place and assuming the nonowner spouse had a claim to it. Although part of the trial court's analysis was flawed, it ultimately arrived at the correct outcome.

Valuations all over the place. The husband's father owned a 40% interest in a car dealership in Delray Beach, Fla. The father created a trust for the benefit of the husband that held a 30% interest in the business. During the marriage, the husband bought half of his father's 40% interest in the dealership, "the Delray 20%."

Before marrying, the husband and wife made a prenuptial agreement. Among other things, the contract provided that "any and all real, personal, intangible, mixed, or other property owned by either party prior to the marriage shall be and remain hereafter the separate property of such party, including other property purchased with the proceeds thereon and increases in value during the marriage or changes in form." The contract also included a "title presumption" stating that "any and all real, personal, intangible, mixed, or other property acquired during the marriage in the name of one party alone shall be and remain the separate property of the party in whose name title is taken" and that "[e]ach party waives any claim of a special equity, equitable distribution, or any other claim against any such asset."

The husband bought the Delray 20% with a loan for $1.65 million in 2002 based on a contemporaneous business valuation of the dealership. He paid the loan with funds from his separate accounts. In 2004, the business, Delray Motors, paid off a loan to buy the land on which it was located. The funds to pay off that loan came from the business's earnings that were not distributed to the husband and/or other shareholders.

The husband's income included salary, commissions, and trust stock distributions from the business. The income varied based on the business's success. During most of the marriage, the wife also worked for the business on a salary basis. In line with the prenuptial agreement, both spouses deposited their earnings in separate accounts.

At trial, the parties presented a raft of experts who testified to the value of the business. A personal property appraiser for the wife found the tangible assets of the business were worth $2 million. A real estate appraiser concluded the buildings and improvements on the land yielded a $17 million value. The wife's CPA determined that, based on his valuation in 2010, the valuation year, the husband's 20% interest in the business had increased by $1.85 million. The expert acknowledged that he used a different approach than the firm that did the 2002 appraisal had used.

A financial advisor for the husband said the dealership owned too much land. No reasonable buyer would pay about $19 million—the total amount resulting from the different values the wife's experts assigned to the business—for the dealership. There was not enough gross profit to warrant that kind of investment. This expert determined that, in 2010, the dealership was worth $2.75 million. Accordingly, the husband's interest in the Delray 20% had decreased. An independent analysis by the husband's CPA also concluded that the husband's contested interest in the business had dropped in value from the year of purchase to the valuation year.

In reviewing the prenuptial agreement, the trial court found it was valid. At the same time, it said, "The Wife did not waive her right to equitable distribution of the increase in the value or enhancement in value of all separate assets which have appreciated due to the active marital effort of the Husband." Here, the husband bought the Delray 20% interest with his separate funds, the trial court determined.

The critical follow-up questions in terms of the community's right to any value in the Delray 20% were whether there was an appreciation in the asset. And, if so, was the appreciation in value passive in nature or was it the result of the "active marital efforts of the Husband"? The trial court said that, to the extent the Delray 20% interest increased in value, it "is the result of the passive increase in the value of the underlying land and buildings" of the business, not the husband's efforts during the marriage. The court did not make a conclusive finding that there was an appreciation and how much it was. It declined to award the wife any funds stemming from the Delray 20%.

In appealing the trial court's ruling with the Florida Court of Appeals, the wife claimed it was error not to find any active appreciation in the Delray 20% and not to award the community a share of the appreciation.

'Tipsy coachman' doctrine applies. The appeals court first reviewed the language of the prenuptial agreement to determine whether the trial court's findings were correct. Under controlling case law, "[w]here a prenuptial agreement does not address the right to enhanced value of a non-marital asset, that value is subject to equitable distribution," the appeal court said (citing *Weymouth v. Weymouth*, 87 So. 3d 30 (Fla. 4th DCA 2012)).

The key was the title presumption provision in the agreement, the appeals court noted. This paragraph combined with the agreement's other provisions, including those that addressed property acquired during the marriage, was enough to suggest a waiver of the future enhancement of nonmarital property even if the enhancement resulted from the marital earnings or labor. Consequently, the trial court's interpretation of the prenuptial agreement was wrong. Under the agreement alone, the wife had no claim to any interest in the Delray 20%.

But, the appeals court continued, the trial court ultimately reached the correct conclusion—first, by finding that the Delray 20% represented the husband's separate property; and second, by finding that, if there was a change in the value of the contested interest, it was due to an increase in the value of the land the dealership owned. This kind of increase was the result of market forces, not the husband's efforts. The appeals court pointed out there also was evidence that the part of the business that was under the husband's management, new car sales, had dropped in value from the time the husband bought the Delray 20%.

This was an instance where the "tipsy coachman" doctrine applied, the Court of Appeals said, in affirming the trial court's final determination. The trial court "reach[ed] the right result, but for the wrong reasons."

Bohme v. Bohme

Citation: 2015 Ohio App. LEXIS 325
Date of decision: Jan. 30, 2015
Experts: Milton Zimmerman, J.R. Hochwalt (husband); Alan Duvall (wife)
Judge: Hall
State/Jurisdiction: Ohio
Court: Court of Appeals
Type of case: Marital Dissolution
SIC code: 8021 Offices and Clinics of Dentists
NAICS code: 621210 Offices of Dentists

Court Backs Away From Support for Double Dip Theory

A hot-button issue, "double dip," recently dominated an Ohio divorce case involving a dental practice. The case afforded the Court of Appeals an opportunity to revisit its foundational decision in *Heller v. Heller.* The new opinion shows a court retreating from its earlier support for the double dip framework, saying the latter was of limited use. The court found that considering income "as a tool" to value a professional business and then using the income "as actual income for a spousal support calculation" does not per se amount to impermissible double dipping.

High vs. no DLOM. The husband was a dentist and the sole owner of his practice. On the stipulated valuation date, Dec. 31, 2009, he was 44 years old. In the divorce proceedings, the value of the business and the income the husband derived from it became flashpoints. The main fight centered on the determination of spousal support.

For trial, the husband offered testimony from two experts on the business's fair market value (FMV). The wife retained one expert.

The husband's most recent expert was neither a CPA nor a certified business valuator. However, the witness said he had been involved in the sale of numerous dental practices. He used an average of a market-based approach and an earnings approach to determine a FMV of $240,000.

The husband's original expert was an experienced CPA and a credentialed business valuator who determined the practice was worth $689,000 as of the valuation date using an income—capitalization of earnings—approach. He found the business's invested-capital value was about $1.4 million, from which he subtracted debt of $432,000 to arrive at a marketable interest of $985,000. He applied a 30% discount for lack of marketability (DLOM) because of the time it would take to sell the practice and the "recent" loss to the practice of two major corporate clients.

At trial, the expert said that, if the business had declined by 14% since the valuation date and he were to do a present-time valuation, he would reduce the FMV to $500,000.

The wife's expert also was an experienced CPA and business valuator who used a capitalization of earnings approach "and also incorporated a cash-flow method" to compute a FMV of $1.1 million. He explained that performing an appraisal in this case was "very difficult" because of the problematic underlying documents. He declined to apply a DLOM. For one, he said, the husband was the sole owner of the practice, which meant he had absolute control. This characteristic by itself reduced any marketability discount. Moreover, he said that he factored lack of marketability into his determination of the capitalization rate. Therefore, a DLOM was inappropriate here. He also pointed out that the husband had taken "excessive" distributions from the business, which affected the results the competing experts had proposed.

Another piece of valuation evidence was that, in 2008, prior to the valuation date, the husband had listed the practice for sale for $1.1 million.

The trial court credited the valuation of the husband's original expert, including the expert's decision to apply a 30% DLOM, and adopted his value of $689,000. The trial court divided this asset equally, awarding the wife nearly $345,000.

Different views on additional income. The wife asked for $11,000 per month in spousal support, pointing to the parties' "extravagant lifestyle" during the course of their marriage. The three valuation experts also testified regarding the husband's actual income.

The husband's non-CPA expert proposed spousal support should be based on an annual income figure of $215,000. This amount, he said, was based on the husband's being an employee, not on his being the owner of the practice. He added that any additional income was due to the husband's "entrepreneurial spirit" and was considered in the valuation of the business. Accordingly, it should not count toward calculating spousal support.

The husband's original expert noted that the annual income in 2009, the valuation year, was about $516,500. For 2008, it was less, nearly $464,000. The expert said he did not believe the husband was taking home the corporate net income. Therefore, he proposed to use only $261,000 for the spousal support calculation, reasoning that using the entire $500,000 figure would be double dipping: using the very income that was the basis for valuing the business, of which the wife received her share, again, as the basis for determining spousal support.

The wife's expert maintained the husband's income "available to him through his dental practice" was $520,000. Business records for 2011 showed he had personal cash flow of $521,000, the expert noted.

The trial court found the husband's annual income was approximately $500,000, which translated into monthly spousal support of $9,000 for seven years.

Facts resemble *Heller*. The husband appealed the divorce decree to the state Court of Appeals (2nd Appellate Division). The major argument was that the trial court erred when it disregarded the original expert's opinion on double dipping. The spousal support award included payment to the wife as part of the distribution of property, that is, the dental practice. She "benefitted from the same stream of income twice," the husband contended.

To support the double dip argument, the husband relied on a storied case decided by the Court of Appeals (10th Appellate Division). *See Heller v. Heller*, 2008 Ohio App. LEXIS 2788 (*Heller I*) (June 30, 2008) (available at *BVLaw*).

Specifically, in *Heller*, the husband owned a 39.5% interest in a brokerage firm, organized as a subchapter S corporation. He also worked for the company and drew a base salary of $300,000 per year, and he received an annual bonus in the form of shareholder distribution. The parties' experts both used a capitalization of earnings approach to value the business. The trial court awarded the interest in the firm to the husband and awarded the wife other assets that equaled one-half of the present value of the husband's share in the business. It also ordered spousal support of $8,000 per month based on the husband's normalized annual income of $300,000. Moreover, it required the husband to pay 20% of each payment of additional gross (pretax) income that he received every year from the business. According to the trial court, "the sole purpose of the additional 20% award … was to account for the unpredictable nature of the husband's income from the company in excess of his salary."

In his first appeal (there were three in all), the husband claimed the trial court "double dipped" by distributing his interest in the future profits of his business two times: once, when it awarded the wife an amount equal to one-half the present value of the husband's share in the business and, a second time, when it ordered the husband to pay a percentage of his future shareholder distributions.

Since there was no Ohio case on point, the appeals court looked to the marital dissolution statutes, in particular the provisions governing: (1) the division of property; and (2) the determination of spousal support. The first provision expressly required that trial courts equitably divide marital property "prior to making any award of spousal support … and without regard to any spousal support so awarded," the court said. Under the second provision, "spousal support does not include any payment made to a spouse ... that is made as a division or distribution." Taking both provisions together:

> We discern a statutory mandate to keep marital property division and spousal support separate, and to consider the potential "double dip" when ruling upon these issues in cases where one spouse's ownership in a going concern is discounted to present value and divided, and where excess earnings arising from that ownership interest will constitute part of the spouse's stream of income into the future.

The appeals court in *Heller* found the trial court had discretion to credit the opinion of the husband's expert who had advocated in favor of an income approach because 99% of the business's value was made up of "blue sky intangible assets." The expert further explained that the husband's income from the business consisted of dividends, or the return on his investment that arose directly from his ownership interest. Commissions, which were similar to salary, came from the husband's book of business.

The appeals court in *Heller* said the trial court abused its discretion "in drawing twice from the same well." Accordingly, it remanded the case for an award that did not treat the husband's share of his firm's future profits "as both an asset and as income for spousal support purposes."

Court computes value from excess earnings. In the instant case, the Court of Appeals was not receptive to the double dip argument, its earlier ruling in *Heller* notwithstanding. At the start of its analysis it said:

> The double-counting analytical framework works well for fixed assets that produce an income stream, such as a pension or annuity. But it is not as easily applied for suggesting that income from a closely-held business, particularly a wholly-owned professional practice, is counted twice when that income is considered as a tool to value the business and then as actual income for a spousal support calculation.

The appeals court then went on to perform a computation of the present value to the husband of the additional income stream. It found that, under the scenario most favorable to the husband, if his additional income was $300,000 per year and he were to retire at age 54, there would be $3 million in additional income. Using a 5% discount rate, the present value would be $2.4 million. If one were to assume the $300,000 per year was pretax income and reduced it by one-third to reflect post-tax income, the present value would be over $1.6 million. "Therefore, even construing income and retirement most favorably to the practitioner, the present value of the future stream of income is almost *one million dollars* more than the determined value of the business," the Court of Appeals stated with emphasis. Consequently, valuing the business using an income methodology does not "double count" income to the husband's detriment, the court said.

Along this line of thinking, it added that if the business were valued using another methodology, "no one reasonably would assert" the income was counted twice.

Next, the court distinguished the facts in *Heller* from the facts in the case in front of it. In *Heller*, the appeals court said, the husband only had a minority interest in the practice, with no indication that he had complete control. In contrast, the husband in the instant case owned and controlled the business. In *Heller,* the company had no fixed assets; its value consisted of "blue sky intangibles." Here, the appeals court said, the husband's dental practice had fixed assets and over $50,000 in receivables, "although we recognize it also had more than $400,000 in debt."

The appeals court concluded: "In any event, to the extent that the present case may resemble *Heller,* we decline to follow it because of the difficulty in the double-dipping analysis when dealing with solely owned, closely-held business valuation as opposed to defined income-stream distribution."

It upheld the trial court's business valuation and related spousal support determination.

Cartwright v. Jackson Capital Partners, Limited Partnership

Citation: 2015 Tenn. App. LEXIS 361
Date of decision: May 21, 2015
Experts: Z. Christopher Mercer (plaintiff); N. Gordon Thompson; (defendants)
Judge: Gibson
State/Jurisdiction: Tennessee
Court: Court of Appeals
Type of case: Damages
SIC code: N/A
NAICS code: N/A

No Place for Asset Appraisal in Trust Dispute, Court Says

Did the appraiser use the wrong method for the case? This question took center stage in a lawsuit featuring the beneficiary of a grantor trust who claimed the trustee had deprived him of all the distributions to which he was entitled The beneficiary hired a renowned business valuator to prove damages, but the trial court excluded the testimony, stating the case did not require the type of financial valuation the expert performed. An appeal to the ruling followed.

Protracted litigation. The plaintiff-appellant was the beneficiary of several trusts that his parents established. His sister, one of the defendants-appellees, was the other beneficiary and also served as trustee for some of the trusts. The father, an attorney, entrepreneur, and investor, set up a grantor trust, as well as a series of other trusts, to protect the plaintiff against what the father knew to be the plaintiff's spendthrift ways. The trust agreement provided the plaintiff with a lifetime income but limited his access to funds that were not under the trust's protection. After the father's death in 1994, the plaintiff's mother became the trustee, and, when she died in 2005, the sister became the sole trustee of the grantor trust. As part of their estate planning, the parents also established a family limited partnership (FLP).

The multilayered litigation, which unfolded in state and federal courts, began in 2004, when the mother sued both children and others, challenging the family tax-planning structure. Before the mother died and the defendants settled her estate claims, the plaintiff filed a cross-claim in state court, alleging, among other things, the defendants had deprived him of assets and asking the court to remove the sister as trustee and grant him access to the trust corpus as the court saw fit.

Trial court finds no financial injury. The focus in the damages case was the grantor trust and two amendments to the trust instrument. The original agreement provided that the plaintiff would receive 75% of the net income of the trust. The agreement could only be amended with the written agreement of the trustee and the plaintiff.

Amendment 1 poured the distributions to the plaintiff from 15 other trusts into the corpus of the grantor trust and made them subject to the grantor trust agreement. Further, it increased the plaintiff's distribution from 75% to 100% of the income of the trust but imposed an annual "cap." It provided he would receive the lesser of: (1) $84,000 per year; or (2) 100% of the net annual income of the trust, plus any amount the trustee considered necessary to pay the beneficiary's state and federal income taxes. The plaintiff agreed to it.

When the plaintiff's mother, who was then the trustee, learned he had purchased several cars and collected high-interest car notes and speeding tickets, she and the plaintiff executed Amendment 2, which lowered the yearly distribution amount from $84,000 to $60,000 (reducing the monthly payments to the plaintiff from $7,000 to $5,000). When the sister replaced the mother as trustee, she increased the distributions again to $84,000 but did not memorialize the change in another amendment.

In asking the court to dismiss the claims against her, the sister said she had acted in accordance with the trust agreement and even more generously. She claimed she based the distributions to the plaintiff on the specific dollar amounts appearing in the amendments and even made them at that level during the downturn in the market or when there was little or no income for distribution. Consequently, the direct distribution per month to the plaintiff was never less than $5,000 or $7,000 per month; moreover, the trust paid for the plaintiff's major expenses. Per the sister's calculation, the plaintiff had received over $592,000 in the past five years and over $696,000 in expenses.

In response, the plaintiff claimed he had signed the amendments under duress and accused the sister and others of exercising undue influence over him. The trial court dismissed the claim, but the state Court of Appeals, in Round 1, determined there was a genuine issue as to the undue influence issue and remanded. It pointed out that there was no evidence as to the trust income generated in any given year. Even though the sister testified that the plaintiff had received the "lump sum" figure reflected in the amendments, how much money he might have received if the cap resulting from Amendment 1 had not been imposed on his annual distributions was not clear. Also, at the pretrial stage, it was reasonable to infer that the cap might have resulted in increasing the amount of money in the trust corpus. If the son died without spouse or children, his sister would have been the beneficiary of the remaining money.

How to measure damages? On remand, both sides retained experts to argue the financial effect, if any, resulting from the plaintiff's executing the amendments. The defendants challenged the testimony of the plaintiff's expert under the state's Rule of Evidence 702.

The defendants claimed the narrow issue on remand was whether the amendments were the result of undue influence and resulted in a benefit to the sister. Damages, to the extent the plaintiff suffered any, should be calculated by computing the amount of net income distributable to the plaintiff absent the amendments and comparing that amount with the amount of the actual distributions to the plaintiff.

The defendants' financial expert was a CPA as well as a certified financial planner and valuation analyst. He determined that the pour-over provision and the cap that were at the heart of Amendment 1 did not result in more money remaining in the corpus of the grantor trust for potential future distribution to the sister. He emphasized that, between 1995 (the date of the first amendment) and 2011, the plaintiff received over $1.3 million *more* in distributions than he would have without the amendments. Instead of receiving 75% of the net income of grantor trust and a specified share of the net income from the other trusts, the plaintiff received an amount equal to all of the cumulative net income, in addition to principal distributions in the amount of over $1 million, the defendant's financial expert concluded.

According to the defendants' expert, the plaintiff's expert used a methodology for determining damages that conflicted with state law, accounting principles, and prior trial court and appeals court rulings as to how to determine damages on remand. Since the opposing expert's testimony was based on an improper methodology, it would not "substantially assist the trier of fact to understand the evidence or determine a fact in issue."

Specifically, the defendants' expert described the rival expert report as an "asset valuation report" and said it had "nothing to do with the narrow issue on remand." The plaintiff's expert should have traced the distributable net income stemming from the grantor trust and the pour-over trusts, but instead he compared the "net appreciation of a hypothetical portfolio" against what he estimated to be the actual "net appreciation" of the FLP since 1995 and then computed the plaintiff's loss as a percentage of the theoretical "net appreciation." Based on this treatment, the plaintiff's expert determined the plaintiff was entitled to $12.8 million in trust income. In a supplemental report, he lowered the damages amount to $3.6 million. (The opinion provides little detail on either expert report.)

The trial court agreed with the defendant expert's analysis and struck the plaintiff expert's report. It also precluded the expert from testifying at trial. The court acknowledged he was "a nationally recognized expert in the area of business/asset appraisal and valuation," but it said "asset appraisal and valuation" were "not an issue in the case on remand." The court also found the expert's supplemental report included opinions on trust administration for which the expert lacked "foundational expertise" and said he used a definition of "net income" that did not accord with the governing trust documents.

Ultimately, the trial court granted the defendants summary judgment on the undue influence issue. It found the defendants' expert conclusively showed that the plaintiff "received over a million dollars more than he would have received absent the signing of the amendments." In other words, the plaintiff failed to show financial harm.

'Detailed financial accounting.' The plaintiff appealed the trial court's ruling a second time. He objected to "evidentiary rulings" the trial court had made in the context of the summary judgment but failed to specify which rulings he attacked. His brief, the appeals court noted, included "a few scattered references to evidentiary matters" but was devoid of a cogent argument that would have supported a reversal of the trial court's exclusion of the plaintiff expert's testimony.

Moreover, the appeals court found there was ample support for the trial court's ruling in favor of summary judgment for the defendants. The defendants' expert "provided a detailed financial accounting of the impact" of the amendments to the grantor trust and negated any claim of harm.

In affirming the trial court's ruling, the state Court of Appeals dismissed the plaintiff's argument that, for the 17-year period the defendants' expert reviewed, the amendments did reduce the plaintiff's annual income during three particular years. According to the appeals court, the plaintiff failed to show how this fact "demonstrates an entitlement to damages, considering he benefitted from the Amendments during the other fourteen years" and over the entire period received a total of over $1.3 million more in distributions as a result of executing the amendments.

The plaintiff next contended the defendants' expert improperly treated the trust's payment of about $1.7 million toward his personal income tax liability as a benefit specific to the amendments. The expert wrongly assumed that the plaintiff would not have received this benefit under the terms of the pretrust agreement when there was language in the original agreement allowing the trustee to invade the trust corpus if he or she thought the distributions were insufficient to ensure the beneficiary's well-being. The court agreed with the defendants that it was "idle speculation" to say what would have occurred without the amendments.

Further, the plaintiff claimed there was ambiguity surrounding the term "net annual income." The defendants' expert subtracted capital gains from the total income reported on the tax returns to determine distributable income. The plaintiff claimed he also had a right to a share of the capital gains. He believed "net income" meant all of the income of the trust. He referred to *Black's Law Dictionary*, which he said defined net income as total income from all sources minus deductions, exemptions, and other tax deductions.

The defendants countered that the expert's treatment concurred with the applicable state law under which a trust was required to allocate proceeds from a sale of productive trust property, including capital gain, to the trust principal. The appeals court agreed, observing that another justification for the treatment was that the grantor trust specifically gave the trustee discretion in terms of allocating receipts and disbursements between income and principal of the trust.

In affirming the trial court's findings, the appeals court also dismissed the plaintiff's contention that the existence of damages was never in question. The defendants' expert had disproved the claim of financial harm resulting from the execution of the amendments, the state Court of Appeals concluded.

Chambers v. Fike

Citation: 2015 U.S. LEXIS 10228
Date of decision: Jan. 29, 2015
Experts: Chet Buchman (plaintiff); unknown (defendants)
Judge: Rogers
State/Jurisdiction: Federal/Kansas
Court: United States District Court
Type of case: Damages
SIC code: 5261 Retail Nurseries, Lawn and Garden Supply Stores
NAICS code: 444220 Nursery, Garden Center, and Farm Supply Stores

Court Draws Line Between Data Quality and Data Quantity

A recent *Daubert* decision in a personal injury case involving the single owner of a limited liability business is noteworthy for the court's deference to the 7th Circuit's *Manpower* decision circumscribing the role of the trial court. As such, the court took care to distinguish objections to the proffered lost income calculation that attacked the expert's methodology from those that aimed at the underlying data.

Lost income vs. lost profits. The plaintiff was the sole owner of a nursery that operated as a limited liability company. It sold and planted trees and performed landscaping. The plaintiff sustained injuries in a collision with the defendant company's truck and sued the driver and company alleging negligence. Based on expert calculations, he claimed over $980,000 in lost income and earning capacity. The expert, in turn, relied on information from the plaintiff.

In related pretrial motions, the defendants sought to exclude the expert testimony and by extension defeat the plaintiff's case.

One of the defendants' arguments was that the loss of income the plaintiff claimed was actually the income of the company. The plaintiff had no legal right to claim that income, the defendants contended. The court (D. Kan.) found that, even though the plaintiff owner could not recover his LLC's lost profits, he was able to sue for lost income. Also, the court said it did not rule out the possibility that evidence as to the business's lost profits would be admissible as proof of the plaintiff's economic loss.

Moreover, the court pointed out that state law does not require expert testimony to prove lost income. Therefore, it was possible that the plaintiff could support his claim for damages even if the court were to exclude the complete expert testimony under Federal Rule of Evidence 702 and *Daubert*—which the court did not.

Limited role for court. The defendant attacked several aspects of the lost income analysis. The court considered the arguments in turn.

1. *Mileage analysis.* One of the ways in which the expert tried to measure the plaintiff's loss of income was determining the mileage of a vehicle on which the plaintiff relied for his work and linking the

mileage to revenue. The vehicle was a tree spade that the plaintiff used to dig up and transplant trees. When he bought it in 2004, it had 250 miles on it. In 2013, the date of the expert analysis, it had over 83,000 miles on it. The plaintiff's accident took place in late 2011.

The defendants averred that the analysis was unreliable for a number of reasons. For one, it was impossible to verify the plaintiff's mileage information. Also, the expert's calculation failed to account for the many other factors that might affect the revenue-per-mile average from year to year. And the expert's revenue-per-mile averages, based on post-injury numbers, did not correlate with the averages for the years prior to the accident. (The opinion does not provide further details on this last point.)

The court observed that the defendants' objections essentially went to the data inputs, as opposed to the logic of the expert's mileage analysis. Since the plaintiff's business generated revenue from using the tree spade, determining annual revenue and dividing the result by the mileage the vehicle traveled in a given year showed revenue average per mile. That average was helpful to estimating income loss by multiplying the average revenue per mile by the estimated reduction in miles driven as a consequence of the plaintiff's injuries. According to the court, even though the plaintiff's expert may not have used the best methodology to calculate the plaintiff's loss, there was a point to this analysis and his testimony was not inadmissible. For purposes of admissibility under *Daubert,* the plaintiff only had to show the expert used a reliable methodology. The method did not have to be "indisputably correct."

The court observed that there was no evidence that the expert lacked the expertise to apply the methodology. And although the expert failed to show that the type of analysis he performed was generally accepted or had undergone peer review, "these factors are not always determinative," the court said—particularly where the objection is to data inputs rather than the methodology itself.

The court said it based its finding on the 7th Circuit's *Manpower* decision, which the Court of Appeals in its own circuit had cited with approval. In *Manpower,* the trial court found the plaintiff's expert had relied too heavily on assurances of the plaintiff's business managers when choosing an estimated growth rate to project total revenues and excluded the testimony under *Daubert.* The 7th Circuit overruled the trial court, noting the lower court had usurped the role of the jury by impermissibly scrutinizing "the quality of the expert's data and conclusions, rather than the reliability of the methodology the expert employed." (*Manpower, Inc. v. Insurance Company of Pennsylvania,* 732 F.3d 796 (7th Cir. 2013), is available at *BVLaw).*

The situation in *Manpower* resembled the instant case, the court here decided.

2. *Missed customer jobs analysis.* Another approach the plaintiff's expert used to measure lost income was calculating the number of "missed jobs" to the plaintiff because of the injuries. Specifically, the expert reviewed phone logs of calls the nursery received that were not returned while the plaintiff attended to his injuries. Based on the plaintiff's information, the expert assumed that 80% of the missed calls would have resulted in revenue-generating business had the plaintiff been able to respond to them.

The defendants attacked the analysis, saying the 80% conversion rate lacked support in hard data. The expert failed to account for the possibility that not every caller was likely to accept the plaintiff's quote for a job or that the plaintiff might have been unable to do the work even without the injuries. The expert failed to check whether a call was the result of a caller's simply returning the plaintiff's call. The expert also did not calculate the costs to the business if the plaintiff had performed the job.

The plaintiff countered that the information he provided to the expert was based on his experience of doing business in a small community. He said he reviewed his records to come up with a conversion rate. He maintained that the costs to the business, including labor costs, were irrelevant to the expert's analysis because he, the plaintiff, did not charge the business for his labor.

The court again sided with the plaintiff. For one, an expert may assume facts provided the expert assumes facts rather than confirms facts being assumed. Also, Rule 702 was concerned with the quantity of data rather than quality of data. If the opposing side attacks an assumption for being based on personal experience or limited record keeping, the attack raises primarily a question of data quality. This, rather than a lack of data, seemed to drive the defendants' objection to the missed jobs analysis, the court noted. It added that this type of objection was best "fleshed out" at trial, through testimony and cross-examination.

3. *Future earnings analysis.* To calculate the plaintiff's loss of future earnings, the expert relied on a doctor's opinion that said the plaintiff had suffered a 25% functional disability as a result of the injuries. The expert first assumed that two employees could perform the job functions the plaintiff used to perform at an annual cost of $103,000 and then took 25% of the cost to determine lost future income.

The defendants claimed the analysis was inadmissible because there was no vocational analysis of the plaintiff's employment that linked to the functional disability rating and no showing that the functional disability correlated to the plaintiff's earnings capacity. In fact, since the accident, the plaintiff had been able to operate the tree spade and perform other aspects of the job, the defendants pointed out.

The court agreed with the defendants. The issue in this instance was one of methodology: whether the functional disability rating was a proper measure of the plaintiff's future earnings capacity, the court explained. Given the shortage of data correlating the two components, "multiplying that measure against the replacement cost of plaintiff's labor appears unreliable." Case law in the area of workers' compensation suggested there was a "significant distinction" between functional disability ratings and work disability ratings, the court observed. Therefore, it decided to exclude the testimony "at this time" but said it was open to further proof from the plaintiff.

4. *Tree loss analysis.* Finally, the expert included in his loss analysis an estimate of the lost sales value of tree crops that, but for the plaintiff's injuries, "were planted or would have been planted." He said he considered the tree crop in the year before the accident, the year of the accident, and the two years following the accident. He assumed there were 300 trees in each year's crop, of which

about 8% would have died. The surviving trees would have sold either as ball and burlap trees for $550 per tree or as spaded trees for $1,200 per tree.

The defendants were able to show that many of the assumptions were problematic. For one year, the expert assumed the plaintiff did not plant a tree crop, when in fact he did. For the two most recent years, the plaintiff in effect did not plant tree crops, but the failure to do so had nothing to do with his injuries. The plaintiff's inventory of trees purchased and planted as well as trees that died was spotty. The plaintiff was unable to provide a cause of death for some of the planted trees. The expert did not account for replacement cost for dead trees, which would have mitigated the loss of income for a tree dying before reaching the age assumed for sale.

The court found the defendants' arguments convincing. Regarding this analysis, it noted the shortage of reliable data and the questionable assumptions the expert made. In fact, the analysis was so defective that it was not only not helpful to a jury, but also might confuse the jury, the court said. Therefore, it decided to exclude the testimony but again left the record open for further proof.

Charron v. Sallyport Global Holdings, Inc.

Citation: 2014 U.S. Dist. LEXIS 170964
Date of decision: Dec. 10, 2014
Experts: Jeffrey Risius (plaintiff); none (defendants)
Judge: Pauley III
State/Jurisdiction: Federal/New York
Court: United States District Court
Type of case: Contract
SIC code: 8748 Business Consulting Services N.E.C.

High Company-Specific Risk Adjustment Distorts Valuation

A breach of contract dispute turned on the valuation of a rollover equity interest the defendant received after reselling the company he had obtained by buying out the plaintiff. The defendant undervalued the interest to avoid triggering a windfall protection provision that would give the plaintiff a percentage of the proceeds from the resale, the plaintiff alleged. Accounting for risks specific to the company became a contested element of the valuation.

Windfall provision. In 2004, two West Point graduates and former servicemen decided to collaborate. Over the next few years they built a spectacularly successful military contracting business that benefited from the U.S. government's involvement in Iraq and Afghanistan. Both men owned half of the company, SGH, which spawned a number of subsidiaries.

By 2009, the partners decided to sell the company, in part because of concern over the dwindling opportunities in the Middle East and in part because of their increasingly hostile relationship. No offers materialized at that time. In late December 2010, in a rushed transaction, the plaintiff sold his interest to the defendant for $40.7 million. The sale came with a windfall protection, which in essence said that, if the defendant sold 20% of the company, as measured by "voting power" or "economic value," within one year of the buyout in one or a series of related transactions "for a price that reflects an enterprise value of the Company equal to or greater than $65,000,000 (a 'Windfall Sale')," the defendant had to pay the plaintiff 20% of the proceeds from the sale.

Some six months after the buyout, the defendant, who was now the sole shareholder, sold the company and its affiliated companies to a private equity firm, DC Capital. Under the parties' agreement, the equity firm paid $60.7 million in cash and gave the defendant a 38% equity interest in the acquiring company. Importantly, the agreement assigned a $3.8 million value to the 38% rollover equity interest. Therefore, the total sales price was $64.5 million—just short of the $65 million that triggered the windfall provision.

Also under the agreement, the acquiring company would merge with another company DC Capital owned to form a new entity, KSI. As part of the merger, the defendant's 38% equity interest converted to a 19.38% interest in KSI.

The defendant failed to inform the plaintiff of the sale of SGH. Instead, the plaintiff found out about it when his lawyer contacted the defendant's lawyer and received "an opaque two-sentence letter" describing the event. The plaintiff subsequently sued in federal court (S.D.N.Y.), alleging the defendant breached their contract. The true value of the equity interest was much higher than the $3.8 million the defendant and DC Capital assigned to it, the plaintiff claimed. Accordingly, the enterprise value was greater than $65 million. Further, the plaintiff contended the defendant had removed assets from the company prior to the sale and kept them for himself so that their value did not appear as payment from the new buyer. The enterprise value had to reflect the value of these "stripped out" assets, the plaintiff argued.

Disparate EBITDA projections. Whether there was a breach of contract came down to the value of the rollover equity interest, the court found. Notwithstanding the defendant's claim that the company sold for $64.5 million, what complicated the deal was that payment was partly in cash and partly in stock in the acquiring company. Even if the transaction on the whole were an arm's-length transaction, "it does not follow that the rollover equity is actually worth the $3.8 million attributed to it," the court said.

It found that a number of inconsistencies made it necessary to "probe behind the $64.5 million figure." For example, in unrelated court proceedings, SGH's lawyers stated that the defendant gave up only 64.09% of his ownership interest in the company and its affiliates. If that was the case, the court said, then "the transaction reflected a total enterprise value of well over $65 million." Also, within the sales transaction, the parties assigned different values to identical shares of SGH. At one point, they valued them at $6,449 each, at another, at $4,000. At trial, they failed to explain the reason for the discrepancy.

All indications suggested that $64.5 million was an "unrealistically low enterprise value" considering the company's earnings projections, the court observed. At the time of the transaction, various parties, including the buyer, DC Capital, and third parties, prepared nine sets of six-year EBITDA projections for SGH. The lowest projected annual EBITDA was $20.5 million, and the highest was over $55 million.

In a presentation to the company with which SGH eventually merged, DC Capital stated EBITDA for SGH for 2011 was $39.4 million; for 2012, it was $35.3 million; for 2013, it was $27.4 million; and, for 2014, it was $24.9 million. Yet, at trial, witnesses for DC Capital claimed that future EBITDA was only about $10 million given the various risks the company confronted, including an unstable Middle East and the pullout of U.S. troops. They also tried to disavow the other projections by saying these were "overly optimistic and everyone knew it."

The plaintiff offered expert testimony from an experienced, credentialed business valuator who explained that, at a projected EBITDA of $35 million, a sale of the company for $64.5 million equated to a value of 1.8 times EBITDA. But valuators typically assigned a range of five times to 10 times EBITDA to government contractors. SGH actually was "hard-wired" into the defense department's military operations, and many of its contracts were "no-bid."

The court discredited the $10 million EBITDA figure. Contemporaneous documents showed EBITDA was at least twice as much, it said. Assuming a valuation of at least five times EBITDA, based on the plaintiff expert's testimony, the court concluded that $64.5 million was "too good a price to be true."

Problematic purchase price allocation. In connection with the transaction, DC Capital retained an investment bank to conduct a purchase price allocation. Specifically, the bank was to calculate the fair value of the 19.38% interest the defendant received once SGH merged to form KSI. The bank valued an incorrect percentage and also subtracted an amount of $2 million from the KSI valuation when that value was already considered in the projections underpinning the valuation. Adjusting for these two errors alone brought the total consideration in the transaction to over $65 million, the court noted.

There also was a notable discrepancy between the projections DC Capital gave to the investment bank for the purchase price allocation and the projections it gave to a second investment bank it retained to sell KSI. For 2014, the projected EBITDA available to the latter financial advisor was twice that given to the first one. A DC Capital representative explained that he had removed a number of contracts, including the largest contract, from the projections used for the purchase price allocation. He also took out earnings that the company had in fact earned. His explanation for doing so was not credible, the court concluded, and the $3.8 million value the investment bank assigned to the defendant's stake in KSI was a "malleable figure that could be titrated" to the defendant's and DC Capital's needs.

DCF achieves best indicator of value. The plaintiff's expert offered the most credible valuation of the rollover interest in KSI, the court concluded. To value KSI, he first performed a discounted cash flow (DCF) analysis using the most conservative projections out of the nine EBITDA forecasts. These projections excluded revenue from a number of contracts, including revenue that was earned at the time DC Capital removed them. Up to that point, the expert's valuation tracked the investment bank's purchase price allocation analysis.

But the plaintiff's expert objected to the investment bank's treatment of company-specific risk. He pointed out that the bank doing the price allocation used a 22.25% discount rate that included a company-specific risk adjustment of 10%. But downward adjustments to cash flow projections already accounted for the very same risks. The bank double counted the negative factor, he maintained.

Accordingly, his company-specific risk adjustment was zero. Together with other modifications, his value calculation for the defendant's rollover interest was approximately $18.3 million.

He also conducted a guideline public company analysis, which led him to conclude that KSI was worth between $200 million and $400 million. After comparing the DCF and guideline public company results, he decided KSI's value was $210 million. Therefore, the defendant's rollover interest was worth approximately $20.1 million, he said.

The defendant stood by his position that the rollover equity interest was worth $3.8 million, as reflected in the transaction documents. He did not offer an independent expert valuation but attacked the analysis of the plaintiff's expert, alleging the latter relied on unreliable figures and used companies that were not truly similar.

The court dismissed the defendant's objections but agreed that the guideline public company analysis the plaintiff's expert performed was flawed. According to the court, "the dissimilarities with the supposed guideline companies are glaring." On the other hand, the court completely agreed with the expert's DCF reasoning.

The projections the expert and the investment bank used were "ultraconservative," the court said. The DC Capital representative removed seven contracts that carried a 100% win chance—"what should have been sure things." Moreover, he took out three contracts that had a 90% win probability. The effect was that the projections for 2011 excluded $111.1 million in revenues; for 2012, $97.1 million; and, for 2013, $96.6 million. The only explanation DC Capital gave for eliminating hundreds of millions of dollars from the projected cash flows and applying a high company-specific risk rate was that KSI faced uncertainty having to do with its size, its geographic concentration, and the negative effects from troop withdrawals, the court noted. This was double counting, it said. There also was contemporaneous evidence that the risks were overstated, the court observed. A third-party report analyzing the risks to the company from the potential troop drawdown said that "nation-building" work would replace defense-related work, resulting in a "positive outlook for the future" of the company.

The plaintiff's expert reasonably applied a company-specific adjustment of zero, the court found. His DCF analysis also corrected other errors the investment bank had made in the purchase price allocation valuation, and he achieved a reasonable value for the defendant's equity interest. The court adopted his $18.3 million figure.

It further found that two loans worth $2.75 million were operating assets of the company and their worth needed to be included in the enterprise value. In all, the proceeds from the transaction yielded an enterprise value of nearly $79.9 million, the court concluded. And it agreed with the plaintiff that the windfall provision in the contract expressly entitled the plaintiff to 20% of *all* proceeds, not, as the defendant strained to show, 20% of the proceeds above the $65 million mark. Therefore, the court awarded the plaintiff nearly $15.8 million in damages.

Chico's Fas, Inc. v. Clair

Citation: 2015 U.S. Dist. LEXIS 71716
Date of decision: June 3, 2015
Experts: Adam Falconer (defendants); unknown (plaintiff)
Judge: Chappell
State/Jurisdiction: Federal/Florida
Court: United States District Court
Type of case: Intellectual Property
SIC code: 2341 Women's, Misses', Children's and Infants' Underwear and Nightwear
NAICS code: 315240 Women's, Girls', and Infants' Cut and Sew Apparel Manufacturing

Uncritical Use of Royalty Rate Data Spoils Damages Opinion

A patent infringement case explores the use of royalty rate data available to experts working in the area of intellectual property. The opposing party's *Daubert* attack for the most part succeeded in excluding damages testimony because the expert failed to perform a rigorous analysis of data gleaned from various intellectual property databases and publications.

Unsubstantial credentials. Both parties in this patent dispute sold camisole bras. The defendants/counterclaimants contended the plaintiff's "Oh My Gorgeous" garments infringed their design and utility patents. The plaintiff sued in federal court (M.D. Fla.) to obtain a declaration from the court that there was no infringement and that the patents were invalid and unenforceable.

The defendant patent holders hired a damages expert who prepared a report that was filed under seal. In a pretrial motion, the plaintiff claimed the testimony failed all three *Daubert* requirements: qualification, relevance, and reliability. The court agreed in large part.

The expert was an intellectual property consultant, who held a J.D. and had an undergraduate degree in management information systems. He had been a guest lecturer on intellectual property commercialization, damages, and valuation in several universities. He said he also had worked for a time at Ernst & Young, but he did not explain what his job duties were.

The plaintiff's attack on his qualifications related to his proposed testimony on financial issues such as revenue, profits, margins, and costs of a publicly traded company. The expert's "total profits" calculation in connection with the patent holders' one design patent was problematic, in particular his failing to account for fixed and indirect costs, the plaintiff claimed. In deposition, the expert was unable to answer basic questions as to what direct and indirect costs were, the plaintiff pointed out. Also, the expert was not a CPA or certified valuation analyst and had no accounting, finance, or economics degree. Except for his employment with companies that performed financial analysis, he was unable to point to any expertise in accounting matters that would make him fit to give guidance to the jury.

The court said it "shares" the plaintiff's concerns. It observed that it was unclear what exactly the expert did at Ernst & Young and how that experience made him an expert on damages. But rather than disqualify him at this stage, the court decided to allow the plaintiff to conduct voir dire before permitting the expert to testify at trial. It warned that evasive answers might lead to disqualification.

Shaky basis for royalty analysis. The major target of the plaintiff's attack was the expert's reasonable royalty determination. First, there was a problem with the royalty rate the expert proposed, the plaintiff found. The expert said it could range from 3.24% to 8.9%. Based on a case that was litigated last year in the same court and centered on a similar undergarment, he said he settled on a rate of 3.35%. The plaintiff noted that the expert's royalty base inexplicably was six times the base applicable in the case that served as a reference point.

Moreover, the rate determination was based on questionable data from the following sources:

1. *RoyaltySource database.* By its own account, the RoyaltySource database tracks licenses and IP-related transactions in diverse fields. A preliminary search provides a summarized list of records from which a subscriber may choose those that seem of interest. The company then sends additional information on royalty payments, rates, other compensation, and the source of information.

The expert said he used this database to obtain information related to bras, combination bras, tank tops, camisoles, and camisole bras.

The plaintiff noted that the expert's search resulted in a summary of nine licenses, none of which involved the garments at issue. Instead, the licenses related to furniture products, enzymes for processing hemp, and spider silk textiles.

Also, five of the agreements were between related parties and as such less relevant. One was not a proper license but an option to license.

The court agreed that the licenses the expert considered were not comparable to the patents in suit and could have no bearing on estimating a royalty for camisole bras. Testimony based on RoyaltySource database information was inadmissible.

2. Licensing Economic Review (LER) *data. LER* is a monthly newsletter indicating royalty rates for 15 industries. This service uses the same database as RoyaltySource.

According to the expert, he used "the most relevant *LER* industries for his research." He conceded that the data were "less relevant" than the RoyalSource data.

The plaintiff pointed out that if the RoyaltySource search failed to produce a single license summary related to bras, the *LER* data were even more unreliable and also were duplicative. According to the plaintiff, the expert performed a broad search of all "consumer goods, retail and leisure" and obtained data that provided nothing more than "generalities" of royalty rates for a wide range of goods. It was impossible to determine from *LER* what licenses formed the basis of the quoted royalty rates and what the terms of the specific licenses were. Without this particularized information, the patent holder was unable to prove that the *LER* data were meaningful to the hypothetical licenses at issue in this case, the plaintiff stated.

The court observed the *LER* data were much too broad and, therefore, were not useful for comparison with the patents in suit. Therefore, testimony based on *LER* data was unreliable.

3. Licensing Letter Royalty Trends Report. According to the publication, its 2014 edition provides royalty rates and 10-year trend lines in a variety of fields, including art, entertainment/character, fashion, sports, and trademark/brand, enabling users to "benchmark your deals against industry norms."

The expert said he used royalty rates in the category of fashion, the subcategory of apparel, and the next subcategory of hosiery.

The plaintiff objected that this data source provided generic industry data without offering an analysis for a particular product line. The expert failed to review any of the licenses cited in the report or identify any of the parties to any of the licenses. There was no way to know how the available data related to the case, and the expert failed to establish the requisite link.

The court agreed that, since this report covered generic industry data rather than data for specific product lines, such as bras, it was not reliable evidence and any opinion based on it was inadmissible.

4. *2012 KPMG article.* The expert also used a 2012 article from KPMG titled "Profitability and Royalty Rates Across Industries: Some Preliminary Evidence." He acknowledged that the article relied on RoyaltySource data and said his takeaway from the article was the suggestion that a 15% benchmark royalty rate could be used in almost every case. He applied that rate to the plaintiff's gross margin.

The plaintiff noted that the suggested 15% baseline royalty rate was akin to the 25% rule of thumb whose use the Federal Circuit had rejected soundly in its 2011 *Uniloc* decision. See *Uniloc USA, Inc. v. Microsoft Corp.*, 632 F.3d 1292 (Fed. Cir. 2011) (available at *BVLaw*).

The court said it was impossible to determine whether the licenses that formed the basis of the article's conclusions related to bras or similar products. Moreover, under controlling precedent, it was improper to use a 15% baseline royalty rate in a hypothetical negotiation without linking this general rate to the facts of the case. Consequently, testimony based on the KPMG article was inadmissible.

5. *Patent holder's expectation.* The patent holders admitted that they had no formal licensing policy at the time a hypothetical negotiation between the parties would have taken place. But they said they currently expected or wanted to license the patents at issue at a rate of between 7% and 10%. The expert said he considered this potential rate in crafting his opinion.

The plaintiff said "regurgitating a client's naked and baseless demands" was not the same as providing an expert opinion. One "does not need any specialized knowledge to make a royalty demand," the plaintiff argued.

The court dismissed this objection, noting that excluding such evidence—even if weak—was not appropriate. The expert was permitted to rely on the patent holders' representations "and even hindsight assertions." The court added that the plaintiff served its case best by exploring weaknesses in the testimony in cross-examination. Testimony considering the patent holders' royalty rate expectation was admissible.

6. *Survey data.* The expert explained that he concluded the patents in suit produced four major benefits in products: convenience, usability, comfort, and innovative product. He said he explored the plaintiff's website and used approximately 550 customer reviews to determine whether the plaintiff's contested products shared those four benefits.

The plaintiff decried this approach. It said the reviews were unsolicited and represented a minuscule part of the company's sales of camisole bras. Also, the expert did not undertake an analysis to determine whether his findings were statistically significant. He did not show that his methodology had undergone peer review. And he was "not qualified … to interpret benefits of a product through these reviews."

This objection also had no traction with the court. In terms of admissibility, there was nothing problematic about the expert's review of customer surveys appearing on the plaintiff's website, the court said. Any argument against the use of that information was best made in the context of cross-examination and left for the fact finder to decide. Accordingly, the court admitted statements based on the survey data.

Apportionment error. In a final blow to the testimony, the plaintiff claimed the rate determination was unreliable because the expert applied his 3.35% royalty rate to the entire camisole bra rather than the swatch of fabric that covers cleavage and allegedly represents the invention in this garment. He should have calculated only the value added by the novel feature and excluded any value attributable to the nonpatented elements of the bra. Moreover, he failed to consider noninfringing alternative bras and their effect on the damages analysis.

The court agreed with the plaintiff that Federal Circuit case law requires apportionment. Specifically, where a product has patented and unpatented features, royalties are not based on the entire product but on the "smallest salable patent-pricing unit." See *Laser Dynamics, Inc. v. Quanta Computer, Inc.*, 694 F.3d 51 (Fed. Cir. 2012) (available at *BVLaw*). The court explained that the entire market value rule was a narrow exception to the rule, but its use required a showing that demand for the entire product was attributable to the patented features, which the expert in this case failed to do. The court also noted the expert's failure to take into account noninfringing alternative bras.

But rather than exclude the calculation, the court allowed the expert for trial to revise his calculation, narrowing compensation to infringement only.

City of Baton Rouge v. Jay's Donuts, Inc.

Citation: 2014 La. App. Unpub. LEXIS 722
Date of decision: Dec. 17, 2014
Experts: Dr. Daryl Burckel (City/appellee); Michael Daigle (company/appellant)
Judge: Theriot
State/Jurisdiction: Louisiana
Court: Court of Appeal
Type of case: Condemnation
SIC code: 5461 Retail Bakeries
NAICS code: 722213 Snack and Nonalcoholic Beverage Bars

Valuators in Taking Case Disagree Over Measure of Damages

An expropriation case centering on taking a successful donut shop for public use raised fundamental valuation issues, such as the proper methodology for capturing the full extent of the owner's loss. The city's business valuator relied on fair market value, whereas the company's expert contended that only a valuation based on the discretionary cash flows to the owner ensured full compensation. The trial court's decision prompted an appeal; the appeals court decision, in turn, triggered a spirited dissent.

'Full extent of his loss.' In 2010, the City of Baton Rouge went to court to expropriate property belonging to Jay's Donuts, a successful business that was organized as a C corporation and owned by a sole stockholder. The city proposed to pay $599,000 in just compensation.

The state's constitution stipulated that in an expropriation "the owner shall be compensated to the full extent of his loss." Under case law, compensation was not restricted to the market value of the property taken. Any compensation had to put the owner whose property was taken in an "equivalent financial position to that which he enjoyed before the taking."

Jay's Donuts sued, arguing the compensation the city offered did not cover the full extent of the loss. During the initial trial, the city offered testimony from three experts on the value of the business. The first witness was a real estate appraiser who said just compensation was about $883,000. This amount represented $190,000 for the market value of the land, nearly $150,000 for the market value of the improvements, $46,300 for the value of anticipated revenue from a billboard lease, and $496,500 for the market value of the business. The business value relied on the determination of the city's business valuation expert.

The city's second witness was an expert in appraising real estate and billboard leasing who said just compensation was over $844,000, including $190,000 for the land taken, $155,000 for the improvements taken, $44,100 for anticipated revenue from the billboard lease, and $455,000 for the business value.

Valuation based on rule of thumb book. The city's third witness was the business valuation expert. He affirmed the value of Jay's Donuts, exclusive of real estate, was $496,500. Initially, he used three methods for the calculation: an asset approach, an income approach by way of a capitalization of net cash flow, and a market approach by way of a multiple of discretionary earnings. He relied on financial data, including income tax returns, from the three years preceding the taking, that is, 2007, 2008, and 2009. He disregarded the value resulting from the asset approach because it was the lowest figure. He noted that the capitalization of earnings analysis yielded a value of over $485,100 using a 15.86% rate and the seller's discretionary earnings analysis using a 3.47% rate yielded a $540,300 value. But he based the final value—$496,500—on the company's annual sales in 2009. He explained that he arrived at it by using a "rule of thumb" book—a guide to what businesses sell for—and found a donut shop generally was worth 45% to 50% of annual sales. However, for a very successful business, the value could be up to 100% of sales, he noted.

Jay's Donuts, he said, was successful and profitable. It was "innovative" and had an excellent reputation and loyal customer base. It also had no debt. Accordingly, he valued it at 100% of sales for 2009. He further explained that he used "[f]air market value without any sort of discount for marketability or minority interest which translates into fair value." He allowed that the fair market value standard of value was based on the assumption of a voluntary sale. He also noted that it was standard practice to normalize expenses, such as salary and benefits, to determine a company's earnings because "many small businesses operate their business activities to minimize taxes." In this instance, he explained, if the owner/operator of Jay's Donuts received $100,000 in salary and estimated wages based on market data were $78,000, "we would actually reduce the labor that he showed on the return. And that would go to the bottom line."

The owner of Jay's Donuts also testified, noting that he was involved in the day-to-day operations of the company and that he worked 10-and-a-half-hour days. He envisioned working even more in the future. On behalf of the company, he tried to offer expert testimony from a CPA, who was certified in financial forensics. But the trial court disqualified the expert, ostensibly because of a misunderstanding about the expert's methodology.

The trial court ordered just compensation of nearly $888,000. Both parties appealed. The state's Court of Appeals found the trial court erred in precluding the expert for Jay's Donuts from testifying and remanded the case to the trial court for a new determination of what constituted the full extent of the loss to Jay's Donuts.

Valuation based on discretionary cash flows. On remand, the company's expert described the "full extent of the owner's loss" as "the value of the owner's pecuniary position in the business enterprise on the date of taking plus any additional compensation necessary to the full extent of his or her losses."

The first step in his calculation was defining the value of the owner's pecuniary position as of the taking date, he said. Since Jay's Donuts was an owner-operated business, the owner's pecuniary position was that he was the sole beneficiary of all discretionary cash flows stemming from the business. Accordingly, the expert had to compute the cash flows and then capitalize them by using an appropriate risk rate.

He explained that for this valuation it was inappropriate to consider fair market value. Fair market value applied when there was an open-market transaction between a willing buyer and a willing seller and when neither party was under compulsion to act. Also, in using a fair market value standard of value, an expert might be making normalization adjustments to "mimic an average typical business," which did not reflect the actual cash flow the business would have generated.

He said his calculation relied on tax returns for the three years preceding 2010 because the tax documents were certified and signed by the owner and as such represented the most credible starting point for determining the discretionary cash flow to the owner. He then adjusted the figures in the tax forms because calculations for tax purposes were not intended to calculate discretionary cash flow to the owner.

Specifically, he added back to taxable income owner's compensation, bonuses, personal expenses, and other items. He then projected the short-term discretionary cash flows the business would generate in 2010, 2011, and 2012 and concluded the owner of Jay's Donuts would receive $230,925 per year in discretionary cash flows.

Next he used the build-up method to determine a 15.41% capitalization rate. Dividing the discretionary cash flow by the cap rate yielded $1.5 million as the value of the full extent of Jay's Donuts' loss, he concluded.

On cross-examination, Jay's Donuts' expert explained that added-back owner's compensation included the amounts paid to the owner and his wife. Whether and how much they paid themselves was "totally discretionary because the corporation's owners decide how they want to distribute earnings, whether as bonuses, dividends, salaries, or personal expense items." Here, the owners chose to distribute the cash as earnings for tax purposes. He added that small businesses sought to create a "zeroed taxable event for the C corporation."

The expert admitted that the owner was considered a separate entity from the business for purposes of receiving retirement and tax benefits and to limit personal liability. But he said that the characterization on income tax return forms did not affect the determination of the owner's pecuniary position in this situation.

The city attacked the expert's credibility by asking him about his valuations in other expropriation cases in which he had used the term "fair market value" and which revealed discrepancies in the capitalization rates. The expert explained that these were typos in two draft reports (out of 14), not in the final copies. He maintained the errors "do not undermine the fundamental opinions offered in these reports." What's more, the errors had no effect on the work he did in the matter of Jay's Donuts. He also said he used a 15.1% capitalization rate, which aligned with the rate the city's own business valuator used.

The trial court wanted to know why the expert added back the owner's and his wife's earnings to the discretionary cash flow but not the earnings of the rest of the employees. Jay's Donuts' expert explained that the income subject to the valuation was the discretionary cash flow to the owner generated by the business. The owner had complete discretion as to whether, when, and how to pay that income but had no discretion as to whether to pay regular employees.

The trial court did not find this explanation persuasive. In discrediting the testimony, it also noted the errors in the draft reports.

Second appeal on measure of damages. Jay's Donuts appealed a second time to the state Court of Appeal, arguing its expert's valuation of loss was the correct measure of damages. The trial court erred when it based just compensation on the market value of its land and business rather than the value of discretionary cash flow to the owner generated by the business.

The city contended the company's expert erred when he added back the salaries to the owner and his wife since they were not the owners of the business. Rather, "the corporation owns itself." The owners wanted it both ways, the city said: separate themselves from Jay's Donuts for tax and liability purposes, but claim ownership for the purpose of valuing the business in an expropriation proceeding.

A majority of the appeals court agreed with the city. Although there was support in case law for the proposition that the award in an expropriation should be based on the business's income, the law did not prescribe a method with which to compensate the owner. The city presented credible evidence by which to determine the compensation amount. Therefore, the trial court's decision was not "manifestly erroneous."

Dissent credits company expert's valuation. One judge issued a vigorous dissent. It was inappropriate in this case for the city's business valuator to rely on fair market value, the dissent said. The company's valuator was the "only expert qualified to determine Jay's Donuts' loss of its pecuniary position in its assets based on the cash flows those assets produced." The expert adequately explained what the discretionary cash flow to the owner was, why it should be used as the basis of value, and why its characterization on an income tax return did not change the fact that it was owned by the business and through the business by the business's sole shareholder (and his wife). "The legal separateness of a corporation from its owners is irrelevant to whether the portion of its cash flow that it chooses to pay its owners is in fact cash flow that the business lost due to the taking," the dissent said.

It observed that the city's own valuator added back owner compensation and benefits to determine income but not as much as the company's owner because the city's valuator mistakenly looked to fair market value. The trial court also erred in discrediting the testimony of the company's expert based on draft reports concerning other expropriation cases. According to the dissent, those were "irrelevant" to the instant case. The trial court erred when it declined to credit the valuation of Jay's Donut's expert and failed to increase the award to the business to $1.5 million, the dissent concluded.

Clear-View Technologies, Inc. v. Rasnick (I), (II)

Citation: 2015 U.S. Dist. LEXIS 71990
Date of decision: June 2, 2015
Experts: Dr. Jonathan Neuberger (plaintiff); James A. Turner (defendants/valuation), Earl McCune (defendants/technology)
Judge: Freeman
State/Jurisdiction: Federal/California
Court: United States District Court
Type of case: Damages
SIC code: 7373 Computer Integrated Systems Design
NAICS code: 541512 Computer Systems Design Services

Citation: 2015 U.S. Dist.. LEXIS 72601
Date of Decision: June 3, 2015
Experts: Dr. Jonathan Neuberger (plaintiff); James A. Turner (defendants/valuation), Earl McCune (defendants/technology)
Judge: Freeman
State/Jurisdiction: Federal/California
Court: United States District Court
Type of case: Damages
SIC code: 7373 Computer Integrated Systems Design
NAICS code: 541512 Computer Systems Design Services

Expert Rebuttal Fails to Engage With Initial Valuation

In an intellectual property case, the court determined what qualifies as admissible rebuttal testimony under Rule 26 of the Federal Rules of Civil Procedure. The defendants failed to designate a technical expert to support their affirmative defense and counterclaims as an initial expert but tried to salvage the crucial testimony by appending it to their valuation expert's rebuttal report. The court called this tactic impermissible "gamesmanship." Its exclusion of the technical testimony came at a cost to the rebuttal valuation testimony.

Backstory. The dispute centered on the parties' agreement to develop and sell a product called "The BarMaster," a beverage inventory control system. The plaintiff argued in 2011 that the defendants conspired with a group of plaintiff employees to wring control from the plaintiff company's management, and it sued for tortious interference with contract, unfair competition, civil conspiracy, and breach of contract.

The key issue in the case was whether The BarMaster was a viable product such that the plaintiff could produce a functioning machine and sell it at a profit. The defendants claimed that, at the relevant time, the plaintiff did not have a version that worked. They used this argument both to defend against the suit and to go on the attack, alleging the plaintiff breached their agreement by failing to develop a working, marketable product. The plaintiff countered that, prior to litigation, it successfully installed The BarMaster at one establishment and that it had other orders waiting.

The plaintiff presented expert valuation testimony, which the defendants sought to exclude under Federal Rule of Evidence 702 and *Daubert*.

Plaintiff's expert assumes product works and sells. The plaintiff's expert specialized in financial economics, valuation, and damages analysis across a variety of areas, including in intellectual property. To value the company, he examined its business plan; financial statements and projections based on a third-party valuation that was done prior to and without an eye to litigation.

In his report, the expert explained that sales projections for The BarMaster represented the backbone of his valuation and that he made several assumptions to create them. In essence, he assumed that, in 2011, the year the dispute unfolded, the plaintiff would "book no revenue." The following year, sales would be limited to preliminary orders the plaintiff received at a March 2011 trade show in Las Vegas. Also, in line with "the enormous size of the potential market identified by [the plaintiff's] market research," the expert projected sales for The BarMaster to increase over the first five years to make up 5% of the plaintiff's target market and assumed a 1% annual revenue growth in the following years. He concluded that, in June 2011, at the time of the defendants' alleged misconduct, the plaintiff was worth about $88.7 million.

Moreover, the expert assumed that the company presently had value. Specifically, by his analysis, the 60 million shares of the company would be "potentially valuable if the company is able to restart its operation." He assigned each stock a nominal value of $0.01 to arrive at a present value of $600,000.

The defendants claimed the assumptions the expert made rendered the valuation unreliable. They first took aim at the assumption that the Las Vegas preorders would develop into actual sales.

The court noted that other courts have distinguished between expert testimony that is "unpersuasive" but capable of being submitted to the jury and testimony that is wholly "unreliable" and, therefore, inadmissible under *Daubert*. The thinking behind this distinction was that courts should abstain from judging the factual underpinnings of an expert's analysis or the correctness of the expert's conclusions.

Here, basing future sales projections on the assumption that orders placed at the 2011 trade show would convert into sales did not make the expert's calculation so unreliable as to make it inadmissible, the court said. The reason was that the expert did not simply make up sales numbers to use as a baseline or rely on "mere expression of corporate hope" but relied on "clear indicia of demand for the product." The defendants would get an opportunity to attack this assumption in cross-examination, the court said.

The defendants also took issue with the expert's assumptions that the plaintiff: (1) would be able to complete The BarMaster; (2) would be able to take the product to market according to its business plan; and (3) would subsequently develop a "more efficient" version of the product. According to the defendants, on the valuation date, the plaintiff did not yet have a working version of The BarMaster.

The court pointed out that the issue of whether or not there was a working machine was contested. Under the Advisory Committee Notes to Federal Rule of Evidence 702, it was improper for a court to exclude one expert's testimony based on "the ground that the court believes one version of the facts and not the other." The bar to excluding expert testimony based on faulty assumptions was high, the court added, and none of the defendants' objections met them.

The defendants said the expert's assumption that there was a huge market for the product and a potential for international sales also lacked a foundation.

The court disagreed again. The expert analyzed the plaintiff's competitors and undertook studies of the domestic and international market for the product to support this assumption, the court observed.

Finally, the defendants attacked the expert's assumption that the company currently was valuable. They objected that, under the expert's scenario, "an individual can start a company, arbitrarily choose the number of 100 million shares of stock, and [the expert's] methodology would value that entity at $1 million."

The court found the defendants had provided no evidence that showed the number of outstanding shares the expert used was arbitrary.

Accordingly, it admitted the plaintiff expert testimony in its entirety.

Contortions to qualify testimony as rebuttal. The defendants did not offer initial (affirmative) valuation testimony, but, at the last minute, submitted a rebuttal report from a CPA and credentialed business valuator. This rebuttal report drew on a technical report from a specialist in wireless communications and radio frequency technology that concluded that The BarMaster technology was "fatally flawed." The defendants' valuation expert attached the technical expert report as an exhibit to his report.

The plaintiff asked the court to strike both the technical report and those portions of the rebuttal valuation report that were based on it. Its primary claim was that the technical expert report violated Fed. Rule. Civ. P. 26(a)(1)(D) that governs the parties' disclosure obligations. Specifically, the technical report was an initial report since it spoke to the heart of the matter; it supported the defendants' affirmative defense that The BarMaster did not work and their breach of contract counterallegation. At the same time, the technical report did not qualify as an initial report since the defendants failed to disclose their technical expert in time.

The defendants strained to argue the technical report was rebuttal testimony. They said it spoke to the "same subject matter" as the plaintiff expert's valuation report and it disputed the plaintiff valuator's conclusion that The BarMaster was a viable product.

The court dismissed the defendants' line of argument. It emphasized that the defendants had the burden to support their affirmative defense with *initial* expert testimony as to the technical feasibility of The BarMaster and were responsible to offer the testimony during the relevant time frame. By failing to do so, they deprived the plaintiff of the opportunity to offer rivaling technical expert testimony.

Here, the court said, statements from the defendants' technical expert made it clear that he was not rebutting the plaintiff expert's valuation report. He admitted that he had not seen and was not familiar with the plaintiff's valuation report prior to drafting his own report.

As the court put it, "an expert cannot be said to 'rebut' testimony he or she has never seen or reviewed." Moreover, the two reports did not engage with each other, as became obvious when one read the technical report alongside the plaintiff expert's valuation report. The valuation report did not include a technical analysis of The BarMaster but presented a sales projection to value the company at the time of the tortious interference. Although the valuation report assumed the machine was viable and that the company in time would develop a more efficient version that would improve sales, the valuation report was not focused on whether the technology worked and whether it could be sold to and installed in businesses. Whether the technology worked or could ever work was the issue at the heart of the dispute, the court noted. "If the purpose of expert testimony is to contradict an expected or anticipated portion of the other party's case-in-chief, then the witness is not a rebuttal witness or anything analogous to one," the court continued to say.

As the court saw it, when, as here, a party's case—particularly in terms of damages—pivots on the workability of a product, one might expect the defendants to introduce testimony on this question by way of an initial expert. Here, the defendants failed to do so, but then they tried to "backdoor" the testimony by calling it "rebuttal" testimony and appending it to the rebuttal testimony their valuation expert prepared. The court called this tactic an attempt "to sandbag" the plaintiff, which ran afoul of Rule 26.

Valuator as mouthpiece. The court also rebuffed the defendants' argument that the testimony should come in because its author was the type of expert on which the defendants' valuation expert could reasonably be expected to rely. In support of their point, the defendants cited a case in which a federal court found that it was reasonable for an expert real estate appraiser to rely on calculations from an architect because appraisal experts normally rely on such data to form opinions on the diminution of the market value of property resulting from deferred maintenance.

The circumstances in the two cases were not comparable, the court in the instant case said. The defendants failed to show how an expert in radio frequency systems was the kind of expert on which a CPA and valuator would normally rely on for his or her business valuation. Moreover, the defendants' valuation expert did not state that he independently verified the work of the technical expert or state that he would be qualified to do so. Here, the valuation expert merely served as the mouthpiece of a scientific technical expert who operated in a wholly different field.

Excluding the technical report meant that the defendants' valuation expert was not allowed to testify about The BarMaster's technical flaws since he lacked the expertise to comment on this point. But the court allowed him to say he had seen no evidence that supported an assumption that The BarMaster was a viable product—thus, rebutting the opposing valuation expert's assumption.

Finally, the court struck parts of the rebuttal expert's valuation on the ground that they went beyond the scope of expert testimony. Several statements were legal conclusions, including a section that stated the plaintiff had failed to mitigate damages and parts that claimed the plaintiff expert's valuation report lacked evidentiary value. The statement that the plaintiff "had the elements of a [P]onzi scheme," was inadmissible since the term "Ponzi scheme" was a "loaded term" that required evidentiary support before it came in front of the jury. Here, the defendants' valuation expert did not point to indications that the plaintiff's leadership raised money to pay amounts due to earlier investors. Also, the rebuttal valuation expert maintained the plaintiff had "no patentable IP," but he lacked the expertise to make such a sweeping statement, the court noted. It limited his opinion on patents to statements that the plaintiff "held no issued patents."

The court's numerous prohibitions severely restricted the defendants designated rebuttal testimony.

Cohen & Company v. Breen

Citation: 2014 Ohio App. LEXIS 3847
Date of decision: Sept. 11, 2014
Experts: Andrew Finger, Cohen & Company (appellee); none (appellant)
Judge: McCormack
State/Jurisdiction: Ohio
Court: Court of Appeals
Type of case: Contract
SIC code: 6512 Operators of Nonresidential Buildings
NAICS code: 531120 Lessors of Nonresidential Buildings

Expert Fee Dispute Devolves Into Malpractice Claim

When an accounting firm that provided valuation services in a divorce case sued its former client over unpaid fees, the client responded by accusing the appraiser of having breached its promise to perform work in compliance with the applicable Statement on Standards for Valuation Services #1 (SSVS #1). Although the firm ultimately prevailed, it found itself repeatedly in the position of having to defend its work against the second-guessing client. The case serves as a reminder that an expert needs to guard as much against the client as against the opposing side.

Three valuations for divorce. The client-appraiser dispute had its origin in the client's divorce case. The client owned five businesses that held significant real estate in the form of office buildings. At divorce, the value of the real estate became a point of contention between the spouses. The client-husband tried to show that the value of the properties declined during the marriage, leaving no appreciation in value that would be subject to division.

To do so, the client-husband hired the accounting firm. The firm's engagement letter specified that the partner hourly rates ranged from $295 to $395, the professional staff rates ranged from $135 to $295, and support staff rates ranged from $115 to $155. The contract further said the firm would provide services related to a valuation engagement, as defined by the SSVS #1 issued by the American Institute of Certified Public Accountants, "in order to determine or to evaluate and reply to an opposing expert's opinion" of the fair market value of the client's ownership interests.

The partner who handled the matter was a certified appraiser and was certified in financial forensics. In subsequent testimony, he said that for the divorce case his staff reviewed more than 25 boxes of documents containing information on the client's personal and business finances covering over 12 years. At the request of the client's attorney, the appraiser wrote three reports related to property division and spousal and child support.

In essence, the first report determined the fair market value of the client's interest in the five businesses that owned and operated the contested real estate. It showed that during the 12-year marriage all the entities had dropped in value and four of the five entities had zero value at the time of the divorce. The report also noted that the firm performed a valuation as the term was defined by SSVS#1 and that the valuation "was conducted in accordance with the 'SSVS#1.'"

The second report was an income and cash flow analysis, and the third report was a labor-intensive "tracing" analysis to show the client's premarital portion in the assets. For a 12-year period, it followed the flow of money in each of the five businesses. The work required sorting out the loan transactions that occurred among the five entities. According to the appraiser, while working on the case, he began to realize that most of the properties were "under water" and discussed with counsel whether it was necessary to perform the costly valuation and tracing analyses. The client's attorney assured him the work was critical to making a case for the client's retention of ownership in all of his assets.

In the divorce trial, the wife's attorney challenged the appraiser's valuation, specifically the methodology of valuing the real estate. The expert explained what he did at length. He used the capitalization of earnings method to determine the fair market value of the property owned by the businesses. It required him to forecast the annual earnings from the property and determine the appropriate capitalization rate. He said that for purposes of calculating the applicable rate he considered the appraisal report the wife's expert had prepared. He admitted that the opposing report included a "restrictive use" provision. He also made it very clear that he independently calculated the net operating income of the properties.

After the appraiser's testimony, the wife's attorney asked the court to exclude the opinion. But prior to the court's decision on the attorney's motion, the parties settled. The husband was able to hold on to all five businesses.

Fee dispute. Fees for all appraisal reports and court testimony added up to $163,300. The client paid the initial retainer of $10,000 and subsequently paid $12,000. The appraiser's work went from April 2011 to May 2012. According to the appraiser, the client did not dispute the amount of the fees and the firm kept working up the three reports as the months went by. But the client failed to keep up with the payments. When the outstanding balance reached $86,000, the firm set up a payment plan. The client acknowledged the fees owed and agreed to pay $2,000 per month. After a few payments, he stopped. By the time the appraiser sued for breach of contract, the unpaid fee amount was over $166,000.

The client filed a counterclaim alleging accounting malpractice and professional negligence. At the heart of the client's accusations was the claim that the appraiser erred when he adopted the appraisal report the wife's expert had submitted. Ultimately, however, the client gave up on the claim because he could not find an expert to help him prove the allegations.

In the fee dispute trial, the court permitted the client to cross-examine the appraiser about the services the firm had provided and their compliance with the engagement letter. But the court prohibited the client from pursuing questions related to the applicable accounting standards. Under case law, knowledge related to the standard of care in various professions requires expert testimony.

When asked about his use of the opposing expert's report, the appraiser explained that he had considered a range of items to compute the capitalization rate, including another appraisal, the county tax valuation, capital-rate-related statistics from PricewaterhouseCoopers, and rates from CB Richard Ellis. He admitted that the wife's attorney challenged his use of the wife's expert's report but said the challenge had nothing to do with the "restrictive use" provision on the report. Also, he said, when one side prepared a valuation report for litigation, it was customary to let the other side use it. Moreover, the issue of whether his reports were admissible in the divorce trial had nothing to do with his professional responsibilities related to the reports.

The client also maintained the appraiser had failed to rebut the rival expert report and as such had failed to honor the promise in the engagement letter. The client believed the opposing expert had valued the property based on an "extraordinary" assumption that a tenant in one of the buildings who had been six months late in rent would become current. The client's appraiser should have challenged the valuation and underlying assumption, the client complained. The appraiser responded that he did not use "rent roll" information from the opposing expert's report but independently calculated the net operating income of the property to arrive at the property's value.

The client further tried to claim that there were inconsistencies between the appraiser's testimony in the divorce trial and the valuation method in the appraiser's report. The court in the contract dispute cut that line of argumentation short because it required expert testimony.

The jury awarded the accounting firm over $200,000, including accrued interest. The trial court denied the client's request for a new trial but reduced the award to $166,000. The client appealed to the state's Court of Appeals.

No second-guessing trial court. The issue on appeal was whether the trial court erred when it barred the client in the contracts dispute from showing the appraiser had failed to perform in accordance with the standards underlying the engagement letter.

The appeals court engaged in a thorough discussion of the appraiser's divorce-related work, his testimony, and the fee arrangement and dispute. Ultimately, it found the issue in front of it came down to malpractice. After the client voluntarily withdrew his counterclaim for malpractice, he tried to revamp the allegation as a breach of contract claim—arguing by way of his own testimony that the accounting firm had breached its promise in the engagement letter to him when it failed to adhere to the applicable accounting standards. Malpractice or breach of contract claim, the client required expert testimony to prove his allegations, the appellate court said. The trial court did not abuse its discretion in excluding the client's testimony related to accounting standards and technical valuation issues.

Cortes v. 3A N. Park Ave Rest Corp.

Citation: 2014 N.Y. Misc. LEXIS 4693
Date of decision: Oct. 28, 2014 (Slip Op)
Experts: Michael J. Garibaldi (plaintiff); Howard Cannon (defendants)
Judge: Demarest
State/Jurisdiction: New York
Court: Supreme Court of New York (Trial Court)
Type of case: Judicial Dissolution
SIC code: 5812 Eating Places
NAICS code: 722511 Full-Service Restaurants

Lack of Marketability a Factor in Valuing Minority Interest

How do you establish a business's actual profits when you have almost no reliable data? In yet another fascinating New York fair value case, the minority shareholder in a restaurant turned for help to a noted forensic accountant to prove the defendants had diverted considerable amounts of cash to deprive him of his share of the profits. The court's decision provides an in-depth assessment of the expert's profitability analysis and resulting business valuation and an explanation of the court's conditional dissolution remedy.

Minority interest in restaurant. In 2003, the individual defendants offered the plaintiff a "partnership" in a Mexican restaurant if he paid $50,000 for a 16.67% ownership interest in the defendant corporation that owned the business. A written agreement specified that the plaintiff was to be the restaurant's managing partner and would receive a salary and his proportionate share of the profit in the enterprise. The contract also gave the corporation the right to buy back the plaintiff's shares if he decided to resign from his position, but it did not specify a share price or a formula for calculating it.

In 2010, because he was "miserable" working long hours and enduring a long commute, the plaintiff "quit." When he sought to sell his shares to the defendants, they offered him $50,000, insisting that, under the agreement, the plaintiff was only entitled to the return of his investment. When he asked for his 16.67% share of the profits, the defendants replied they were going to recoup their investment first. Corporate financials and tax returns showed the business had made minimal or no profit.

In June 2011, the plaintiff sued, claiming the defendants breached their fiduciary duty to the corporation and to him by, among other things, siphoning off profits from the corporation, failing to purchase his shares at fair value, and failing to declare a dividend to enable him to obtain his fair share of the profits proportionate to his ownership interest. In a series of pretrial rulings, the court dismissed certain claims, but the plaintiff's diversion claim and his individual request for dissolution of the business under common law survived.

The defendants countered that the plaintiff frequently drank on the job and failed to carry out his managerial responsibilities in a responsible way. The company only became profitable in 2013, after the plaintiff had left. According to the defendants, business then "exploded" in part because they were active in managing the place and in part because they expanded the restaurant. They admitted that a New York State sales tax audit earlier had found they had underreported sales and owed about $90,000 in tax, which they paid without contest.

The case resulted in a bench trial, and valuators took center stage.

'Critical' server reports. The principal challenge for the plaintiff was how to prove his allegation that customers paid substantial amounts of cash that never appeared on the corporate books or in tax filings. Because the defendants consistently thwarted the plaintiff's discovery efforts, ultimately the only documents he was able to obtain were server reports from July 2011 to July 2012. These, the court noted, "proved critical to the plaintiff's case."

Once servers take an order, they enter data into a computerized system that summarizes the amount and form of payment—cash or credit card—as well as tax and tip and the amount of alcohol and food and drink items customers consumed. The resulting server report is unalterable and typically is stored and retrievable for a year.

The plaintiff retained an experienced forensic accountant and business valuator to determine the ratio of the restaurant's known and verifiable credit card revenues to the cash received as reflected in the limited set of server reports. The expert based his projection of business activity over an 11-year period on a sample of dates from a single year. The sample was the work of an expert statistician, who selected a number of random dates during the period in which server reports were available to create a statistically significant sample size from which to discern the percentage of the restaurant's revenue in cash. The valuation expert explained that relying on the sample for his projections was "entirely appropriate and a generally accepted procedure in the forensic accounting community, which frequently uses sampling in both forensic accounting and auditing."

He determined that, between July 2011 and July 2012, 45.6% of the revenue was paid by credit card and 54.4% was paid in cash. After adjusting for sales tax and tip, he applied the ratio to the automatic credit card bank deposits to estimate the cash revenue received during this period. Moreover, he applied that ratio to all credit card deposits from 2003 through 2013. He explained he only used the sample dates to calculate the ratio of credit card to cash payments but not to determine total sales revenue. As such, increased sales on a given date were irrelevant for his calculation. He concluded that only a small fraction of the cash received made it into the corporation's bank account and that the corporation's estimated profits were significantly underreported. Using the credit card-to-cash ratio and deducting costs and expenses, as they appeared in tax returns, he determined the restaurant had a projected profit of over $7.3 million from when it opened at the end of 2003 through the end of 2013. Accordingly, the plaintiff's 16.67% share of the profits was over $1.2 million. He suggested that to determine the present value of the business "a multiple of between 3 and 5 of net income is appropriate to estimate the value of the business." Based on an estimated adjusted net income of nearly $1.1 million for 2012, he found the value of the company was between $3.3 million and $5.5 million and the plaintiff's interest would be worth between $547,000 and $911,000.

Defendant expert's report full of caveats. The defendants offered an expert in "restaurant operations and business restaurant evaluation," who had an MBA and extensive practical experience in the industry, but who was not a CPA and had no background in business valuation. He "did not belong to any professional organizations," the court noted. The defendants' expert said he reviewed 88 pages of documents, but these did not include the restaurant's bank statements or server reports. Based on client instructions, he relied on statements from the company's accountant and on tax returns and financial statements the accountant had prepared; the expert also considered verbal communication with the defendants' attorney and an affidavit from one of the defendants. He admitted he did not consider liabilities of the corporation.

Given the limited information available to him, the expert used the "verifiable gross sales method to determine an initial value for this subject establishment." He noted that, under industry norms, "a restaurant valuation can most easily be gleaned by assessing a value that is equal to 30% to 35% of the verifiable gross sales of the business." Assuming the restaurant had $5 million in gross sales volume from November 2010 through October 2013, he divided the figure by three to determine the average of annual gross sales. He then multiplied the result by 30% and 35% to arrive at an "initial data-point for the Fair Market Value" of between $501,000 and $586,000. He mentioned the "potential impact of yet-to-be determined minor influences of plus or minus fifteen-percent" but did not expand on what those influences might be. The defendants' expert projected the plaintiff's share would be worth somewhere in the neighborhood of $70,800 and $112,300. He also suggested that, since the plaintiff had no decision-making authority in the business, his shares were not "desirable," reducing their value by an additional 30% to 50% to arrive at a range of $35,400 to $78,600.

The expert's report included multiple caveats. For example, he emphasized that "a valuation is only as good as the verifiable data and verifiable information" available to the valuator. Also, he said the gross sales method requires gross sales numbers "verifiable by a Certified Public Accountant (CPA) that is licensed in the state where the establishment is operating." He went on to say: "It should be noted that I am not a Certified Public Accountant nor was I asked to review any of the numbers pertaining to this matter" to arrive at a valuation. Further, because of time and cost constraints, the defendants objected to his performing an in-depth review of the opposing expert's report as well as the underlying financial data informing the latter's analysis.

The defendants' accountant also testified, critiquing the plaintiff's expert's report. Although he did not argue with the report's mathematical computations, he said it was "impossible" that credit card sales were only 45.6%. He offered a projection based on a rent-based formula that he said showed the cash-to-credit revenue was about 35% to 65%. In general, he said, the credit card percentage in the restaurant business was never below 60%. He admitted he had no basis for knowing whether the cash-to-credit ratio would vary depending on certain days. He also said he disagreed with the plaintiff's expert's valuation and claimed the value of a restaurant was between 40% and 60% of gross sales. He admitted that the restaurant had been the subject of a state tax audit and that the assessed liability was accurate. He explained he had prepared financial documents, including tax returns, based on the company's bank statements and on the defendants' verbal statements regarding sales in cash. He also conceded that he did not know about the plaintiff's ownership interest until the litigation.

Court accepts credit/cash ratio analysis. The court quickly dismissed the accountant's testimony. Basing his determination of the company's cash revenue on the defendants' verbal reports, without asking for documentary support, "seriously undermines [his] professional competence as an accountant and renders him incredible as a witness regarding corporate earnings," the court said. Records he prepared were not reliable indicators of the company's value. The court added that the accountant lacked the expertise to comment on the value of the restaurant.

The court also discredited the valuation of the defendants' expert. For one, he relied on the accountant's "completely unreliable" revenue report while expressly stating that the accuracy of his valuation depended on the accuracy of the data regarding the restaurant's gross sales. He did not review any "primary records or such independent sources as the bank records to verify the accuracy of the information he was given," the court observed. Moreover, by his own account, the expert only prepared "phase one" of a valuation and never followed up with a more in-depth analysis.

According to the court, there was clear evidence that the defendants diverted substantial receipts in cash. The defendants did not present any evidence that negated the projections of unreported cash that the plaintiff's expert produced, nor did they offer an alternative business valuation. Instead, throughout litigation, they "deliberately frustrated" the plaintiff's requests for records concerning the restaurant's profits. "It is the defendants' deliberate concealment of the sales records, particularly the server reports, that they knew would reveal their defalcations, that warrants acceptance of the projections of the expert based upon the limited records produced," the court said.

The court's finding came with its own caveat. With regard to the diversion, the plaintiff had only shown the defendants owed a fiduciary duty to the corporation, not to him individually. Therefore, the court said, the judgment belonged to the entity. It added that the appropriate measure of damages in this case was the difference between the actual revenue that was deposited in the company's bank account and the total sales the plaintiff's expert projected based on his credit-to-cash ratio analysis. The court concluded that the amount diverted was $3.7 million and that interest was appropriate, yielding a judgment of over $4.9 million to the corporation.

DLOM evidence is missing. The court next turned to the plaintiff's request for dissolution. It pointed out that, even though it was clear that "the parties do not wish to continue their association in this highly profitable business," liquidation was "not warranted unless defendants fail to buy [the plaintiff] out at fair value." The court found the net income approach the plaintiff's expert used was generally accurate, but it noted he had failed to address whether a discount for lack of marketability (DLOM) should apply in this case. Further, the defendants' expert essentially applied a minority discount, which the state courts expressly prohibit. According to the court, "the lack of marketability of shares in a closely-held corporation is recognized to be a factor to be considered in valuing such shares." At the same time, in this case, the parties did not present DLOM evidence. Accordingly, the court chose to apply only a 10% DLOM.

The court also found that neither expert used the proper valuation date for his calculation. It, therefore, adjusted the profit calculations the plaintiff's expert presented for the year prior to the suit to arrive at a net income of about $1.1 million. In accordance with the plaintiff expert's statement that the value of a business was equal to three to five times the net income of the proceeding year, it arrived at a base valuation of $3.2 million, It then added that amount to the $4.9 million judgment it granted to the corporation to arrive at a fair value of the company of about $8.1 million. Factoring in the 10% DLOM and a few other minor adjustments, the court determined the fair value of the plaintiff's share in the restaurant was $1.2 million. In other words, the court gave the defendants the option either to buy out the plaintiff for $1.2 million or face dissolution of the business.

Crile v. Commissioner

Citation: 2014 Tax Ct. Memo LEXIS 198
Date of decision: Oct. 2, 2014
Experts: Elizabeth von Habsburg (art appraiser, respondent); none (petitioner)
Judge: Lauber
State/Jurisdiction: Federal
Court: United States Tax Court
Type of case: Federal Taxation
SIC code: 8999 Services N.E.C.
NAICS code: 711510 Independent Artists

Court Rejects Art Market Expert's Profitability Analysis

Can an artist have a profit motive when she incurred losses related to making her art for most of her career? A recent Section 183 tax court case involving an acclaimed creative artist delved into the taxpayer's claim that she pursued art as a business rather than a hobby and, therefore, was justified in claiming major art-related expenses as business deductions. In contesting the claim, the Internal Revenue Service retained an art appraiser to assess the commercial viability of the artist's work, but the Tax Court took issue with the appraiser's valuation methodology and conclusions.

Critical, but not financial, success. The taxpayer was a distinguished painter and printmaker who practiced her art for over four decades, created more than 2,000 pieces of art, and along the way achieved critical, if not financial, success. In the early 1980s, she also began teaching part time at Hunter College in New York City and in 1994 received tenure as a full professor. During the academic year, she spent about 30 hours a week on her art, but, during the summer, she worked full time on her art business.

The permanent collections of at least 25 museums, including New York's Metropolitan Museum of Art and the Guggenheim, included her works. The artist also sold works to major corporations and received funding from the National Endowment for the Arts and other arts institutions. During her career, she was represented by at least five New York galleries. In 2004, she switched to a gallery she believed would increase access to collectors interested in her politically charged work and thus profitability. However, that gallery went out of business in 2009. From 2004 to 2009, the relevant period, the artist also started a project of printing on silk after colleagues had suggested this as a way to expand the market for her works.

Much of the artist's work required considerable research and even international travel. To complement the marketing efforts of the galleries, the artist maintained a mailing list of 3,000 collectors to whom she sent exhibition announcements and promos. She carefully documented her inventory and maintained decent, but not complete, sales records. Because galleries often failed to provide her with precise sales data, some of the records were not entirely accurate. She also hired a bookkeeper to assist her with record keeping, and she used an accountant to prepare her tax returns.

From 1971 until 2013, she sold a total of 356 works of art yielding approximately $1.2 million in gross proceeds. Subtracting a standard 50% gallery commission, this amount represented about $668,000 in earned income for her. In 1995, her best year to date, she reported a Schedule C profit of $34,204, but it was offset by a net operating loss carry forward. Likewise, the year 2013 seemed to be a profitable year because she earned at least $75,000 from sales of her art. All the other years, however, amounted to losses. For the relevant five years, from 2004 through 2009, she claimed significant business-related deductions ranging from $37,100 to $63,300.

The IRS accused the artist of underpaying her taxes by more than $81,000 from 2004 to 2009, and the artist petitioned the Tax Court for review.

Limited commercial market? The agency relied on two legal theories. For one, it said the artist's art-related activities represented "an activity not engaged in for profit" within the meaning of 26 U.S.C. Section 183, which is also known as the "hobby loss rule." Her profession was that of a teacher, and she pursued her art to retain her teaching position. Consequently, the expenses resulting from doing her art were not business expenses but unreimbursed employee expenses. She could not use the losses from that activity to offset other income. In the alternative, if the court found her art-related work represented a business activity, it should disallow many of the deductions she claimed because they were personal, family, or living expenses and failed to fit the definition of "ordinary and necessary expenses" in Section 162(a).

The artist argued she was involved in two distinct activities, artist and teacher, and while her art-making rarely was profitable she pursued the work with an intent to earn a profit. Therefore, the claimed deductions were business expenses.

The crux of the case was whether she could show an expectation of overall profit when, in her long career as an artist, she rarely had made a profit. To support their positions, both sides presented expert testimony.

The artist offered testimony from three experts on industry practice. One was the dean of the Yale School of Art, who discussed the factors influencing the price of an artist's work, including exhibition history, noteworthy reviews, awards, and other forms of acclaim. He said that generally speaking the greater the exposure to an artist's work, the greater the potential for an increase in price. Significant events such as an acquisition of the work by a museum and solo exhibitions drove prices higher. These factors were present in the artist's case. In general, few artists expected to make a consistent annual income and many took another job to counteract the uncertainty. The second expert, an owner of an art gallery, said that representation by a gallery was important as it increased visibility. Galleries were businesses that strove to represent artists who had or could develop successful professional careers. Artists often experienced fluctuating income and confronted uncertainty as to when success would occur, he said.

The artist's third expert was an art appraiser and art consultant with 30 years of experience in the field, who visited the artist's studios to inspect her artwork and assess her inventory and storage practices. She found the artist kept a log of all her stored works and stored her paintings in accordance with industry practice. The expert concluded the artist was "a professional in the business of selling and/or attempting to sell her art."

The IRS retained an expert in the art market and art appraisal. She pointed to several factors that indicated an artist's commercial viability, including strong sales of the artist's works, detailed and accurate recordkeeping, income trending upward, and increasing price levels for the artist's works. She noted that, since 2009, the artist had not had gallery representation and sold few of her works at auctions. According to the expert, the artist's recordkeeping was wanting.

The expert calculated that, during the relevant five years, the artist received aggregate net proceeds of about $15,700 from the sale of her art. Although she sold an additional 13 pieces during that period and should have received $17,250, she was not paid. From 2000 to 2013, her annual net proceeds were only about $10,000. During her 42-year career, the artist's average annual net proceeds were about $17,000 related to the sale of her art, the appraiser found.

To determine whether there was a consistent increase in price paid for the artist's works, the expert reviewed the prices paid for the artist's oil paintings. She found the average net price ranged from zero for years in which no oil painting was sold to a high of nearly $30,000 in 1995. She disregarded the years in which no oils were sold and the year1995, which she considered to be an outlier year, and concluded that the average net price per oil painting did not "trend upward" but stayed within a range of $1,825 to $9,000 from 1971 through 2013. The expert said that she had not personally looked at any of these works. She concluded that based on the works' sales history and other factors there seemed to be a limited commercial market for the artist's works.

The Tax Court first sided with the artist when it came to defining the scope of her activities. Her art business and her salaried position at the college were two distinct activities, the court found. She had practiced her art years before she took up teaching. Also, she spent hundreds of hours a year on "tedious or unpleasant" tasks related to her art business. The IRS failed to explain why she would do so if her only aim were to make art to retain her tenured position.

The court also found that the artist pursued her art with the requisite profit motive, notwithstanding the small profitability rate. She kept records that were detailed and "relatively" accurate, and, while she did not use them to contain costs, she used them for marketing purposes. She had a large inventory, and expert testimony proved that she tracked and stored her works effectively, in the way a successful practitioner of her craft would do. There were two instances—moving to a different gallery and undertaking printing on silk—that proved she changed operating methods to increase the chances of making a profit. And even though she did not have a written business plan, she had a plan and followed it consistently.

The court disagreed with the IRS's contention that the artist failed to show her work would ever appreciate in value to the point where it would exceed the accumulated claimed losses. This proposition, the court said, misstated the law, which required merely a showing that the petitioner "could reasonably entertain an expectation that the value of her inventory would eventually appreciate significantly."

The court called the IRS expert's method for gauging the potential for asset appreciation "unreliable as applied here." The expert based her conclusion on the average sales price of oil paintings over the years, but she did not consider sales of the same painting at two distinct times and then determine the price change for the work. "Where an expert relies on comparable sales, it is necessary to determine whether the items compared, if not identical, are at least similar," the court said. Here the expert focused only on the prices paid for the paintings but failed to consider other crucial factors, such as size, quality, subject matter, or the conditions in the art market at the time an artwork sold. "Other things equal, it seems obvious that a very large painting will sell for a higher price than a very small painting," the court noted. The expert also did not view the works. For all these reasons, the court gave the expert's appreciation analysis little weight.

The court found the artist had a long history of sales and was able to earn income of almost $112,000 from the sale of art in 1995. She could "plausibly expect that such good years would recur," the court said. This expectation explained her "willingness to sustain operating losses."

The court also found that the magnitude of the losses the artist had reported for income tax purposes might be less because her Schedule C deductions seemed to include many personal expenses. The line between business and personal expenses may appear blurred to creative artists, the court said. "Petitioner is not alone in resolving doubts in favor of deductibility." The court promised to resolve the question of the character of the expenses "in due course."

Cullifer v. Commissioner

Citation: 2014 Tax Ct. Memo LEXIS 204
Date of decision: Oct. 7, 2014
Experts: S. Todd Burchett (petitioner); Francis Burns, Steven Hastings (respondent/IRS)
Judge: Laro
State/Jurisdiction: Federal
Court: United States Tax Court
Type of case: Federal Taxation
SIC code: 4226 Special Warehousing and Storage N.E.C.
NAICS code: 493110 General Warehousing and Storage

Valuations Bolster IRS's Transferee Liability Claim

In a multilayered tax shelter case, the IRS used the theory of transferee liability to pursue a $9 million claim against the petitioner in connection with the sale of company assets and company stock. Since the applicable transfer liability statute merely provided a remedy, but did not impose liability, the IRS used state law to establish an independent basis of liability. In particular, it relied on Texas fraud statutes to argue the company, through the petitioner, made unlawful asset transfers. Solvency analyses from experts played a key role in the court's determination of whether there was fraud and whether the transactions left the company insolvent.

Minimizing tax liability. In the early 1990s, the petitioner rehabilitated an old plant to make it suitable for storing ammonia and, eventually, other chemicals. He was the sole officer and director and in 1996 became a 50% shareholder. A Canadian corporation owned the remaining 50% interest. The storage company was incorporated in Texas and did business there. Starting in 2000, the petitioner, who by then worked mostly remotely from Florida, where he owned other businesses dealing in commercial real estate, was looking to sell the facility. He made contact with MidCoast Investments, which was in the business of pursuing corporations "suitable for conversion into the asset recovery business." It promised to "help buyers and sellers achieve the best of both worlds" by buying a company shortly before or after its sale of assets and using high-basis, low-market-value assets—e.g., charged-off receivables—to offset the taxable gain from the asset sale. It also would pay sellers a premium calculated on the size of the taxable gain.

In June 2004, the petitioner sold all the company's operational assets, as well as intangible assets, to a third party. The company retained its preclosing liabilities, including environmental liabilities. At the same time, the petitioner signed a noncompete agreement with the acquirer that prevented the company from working in the ammonia storage and handling business for 10 years. In exchange, he received $1.5 million. As a result of the sale, the company had no operating assets and no ability to function as an ammonia facility. The buyer also hired half of the company's employees.

While the asset sale was in the works, the petitioner prepared the way for a stock enhancement transaction. He caused the company to transfer many of its remaining assets to entities that were under his control or the control of the other shareholder. He agreed with MidCoast that the latter would buy 100% of the company stock at a $3.76 million premium—about 50% of the assumed capital gains tax liability stemming from the asset sale. He performed minimal due diligence related to the stock sale. He also became the 100% shareholder of the company, which he then caused to declare a special dividend to him in the amount of $3.73 million.

Subsequently—but prior to the stock sale—the company's accounting firm calculated the federal and state tax liabilities without checking the books for accuracy. By its estimation, the company's assets were worth $6.23 million, and its liabilities amounted to $6.5 million. Federal income tax was almost $6 million, and Texas franchise tax was almost $750,000. The accountants did not reduce the taxable income by the Texas tax amount because it was not deductible until paid.

The stock sale took place in late August 2004. MidCoast had set up a holding company as the buyer. An attorney cautioned the petitioner about the risk of not making MidCoast itself a party to the agreement. MidCoast paid the petitioner about $3.5 million and paid $275,000 to the petitioner's advisor for his investment banking fees. Pursuant to an agreement, the holding company was to be responsible for the state and federal income tax liability accompanying the stock sale. The petitioner did not report income from the sale on his personal federal income tax return.

Post-stock sale, MidCoast and the holding company performed a number of other transactions to remove about $5.7 million from the company and offset taxable gain before selling it to the ultimate buyer, who sought to wring more value out of it. The last buyer reported that the company had a capital gain of $15.2 million from the asset sale and $5.3 million from rental income. He offset the gain by way of a 90.39% interest in a loan that was part of a portfolio of distressed debts his company had bought at auction for $300,000 in 2003. The purported bad debt amount was nearly $17.8 million. As a result, the company claimed an $825,000 loss for the period ending September 2004.

Transferee liability. Upon an audit by the IRS, the government disallowed the bad debt loss and several other deductions and issued a notice of deficiency to the company. It determined that the company was liable for almost $9 million, including penalties. But its efforts to collect on the outstanding tax were futile. An investigation showed the company had no tangible assets. Consequently, the IRS issued a notice of transferee liability to the petitioner pursuant to I.R.C. Section 6901. Because this provision of the law represents a remedy only, the IRS looked to Texas fraud statutes to establish liability. In essence, the IRS argued that, following the asset sale, the company, through the petitioner, made several asset transfers to the petitioner or entities he controlled between the date of the asset sale and the stock enhancement sale that were fraudulent. Moreover, he became a transferee of the holding company and was liable for the fraudulent transfer the holding company made to him in connection with the stock sale.

The overriding issue in front of the Tax Court was whether the petitioner was liable for the company's $9 million deficiency. A trial took place in September 2013. Subsequently, the presiding judge resigned and the case came to Judge Laro. As he points out in the opinion, the reassignment left him without an opportunity to assess the credibility of the witnesses, including the experts. The decision, therefore, is based solely on the written record.

To prove fraud, the IRS had to show that the debtor did not receive reasonably equivalent value for the transfer and was insolvent at the time of the transfer. Both sides presented expert testimony on this and a range of other issues.

Expert relies on state tax assumption. The petitioner's expert was certified in financial forensics and accredited in business valuation by the American Institute of Certified Public Accountants (AICPA). He claimed that, under a solvency analysis, there was an assumption that the Texas franchise tax had been paid and, therefore, would be treated as a deductible expense. Consequently, the company's federal income tax liability would decrease by about $284,000, leaving the company with equity of nearly $22,100 on the relevant dates: when it declared a special dividend to the petitioner and when the parties executed the stock sale agreement. Accordingly, the company was not insolvent.

The IRS presented the opinions of two experts. The first expert was a highly credentialed appraiser with graduate degrees in finance and economics and with over 25 years of valuation experience. The second expert was a CPA who had AICPA certification in financial forensics and over 20 years of financial and valuation experience.

Expert finds no going-concern value. The first expert submitted two reports: One valued the company's intangible assets as of the stock sale date, and the other valued the 90.39% interest in the bad loan that the ultimate buyer used to offset the company's capital gains. The expert found the intangible assets included rights to intellectual property, including patents and trademarks; licenses and permits used in operation; accounts, instruments, and intangibles; and goodwill. He determined that following the sale of the company's assets it no longer had any "going concern value," having given up its income-generating assets. Regarding the personal goodwill attributable to the petitioner, the expert said that, if the personal goodwill related to the petitioner's special skills or reputation, it was not transferable or marketable. Moreover, the petitioner had resigned from the company and also had signed a 10-year noncompete agreement in connection with the asset sale. There was no value to the company. The expert concluded that the only identifiable intangible asset of value was the company's incorporation status as well as the previously incurred incorporation costs, which the expert estimated to be less than $10,000.

As for the value attributable to the company's 90.39% interest in the bad loan, the expert determined it was part of a nonperforming loan portfolio that in its entirety commanded only $300,000 and which had a total outstanding balance of over $139.2 million. The loan at issue had an outstanding balance of over $19.7 million and represented 28.1% of the loans not designated "not collectable" or 55.2% of loans designated "collectible." Accordingly, the expert valued the loan at a midpoint value of $124,900 and found a 90.39% interest of the loan was worth $112,900.

'Very limited' profit potential. The IRS's second expert also submitted two expert reports. One concerned industry due diligence standards for a stock sale, and the other concerned the ultimate profit potential to the company from the 90.39% interest in the loan portfolio. In terms of the stock sale, the expert claimed the petitioner failed to meet industry standards for financial, legal, commercial, and integration planning due diligence. The reason was the petitioner had: (1) failed to investigate MidCoast's financial status and funding sources; (2) failed to research MidCoast's legal standing and litigation record; (3) failed to research the business mechanics of the asset recovery business; and (4) failed to investigate the operations of previously acquired entities that had undergone conversion into the asset recovery business.

In terms of the loan contribution, the expert concluded that the potential for profit was "very limited." An asset recovery firm generally expected to collect $3 for every $1 spent on a debt portfolio, he explained. One of those dollars would pay for collection costs, another for the investment itself, and the third would be profit. The loan portfolio consisted of 202 individual loans all originating before the end of 1999. The age of the loans suggested a low probability of collection related to difficulties in locating the debtors and the likely existence of previous collection attempts, he explained. Historical collection rates on the loans were low. He also said that the contribution of only a portion of an individual loan was highly unusual in the asset recovery business because nonsyndicated loans of that size were considered illiquid investments and as such not viable candidates for partitioning. Moreover, asset recovery firms typically did not service only portions of a particular loan.

Fraud and insolvency. The court's opinion does not include a detailed assessment of the expert testimony. But the court expressly discredited the petitioner expert's solvency opinion. Since his conclusion was contingent on the payment of the company's Texas franchise tax liability and that liability was never paid, the company was not solvent on the date the company declared a special dividend to the petitioner or on the date of the stock purchase sale, the court said.

Moreover, the court found the IRS proved that it was a creditor of the company and that the petitioner was a transferee under the applicable statute. He was liable for the company's fraudulent transactions. Following the asset sale, he caused it to declare a special dividend of nearly $3.73 million for which the company received no value in return and which left it insolvent. In terms of the stock sale, the IRS's claim against the holding company arose after the latter transferred the stock sale proceeds to the petitioner. The holding company's sole purpose was to profit by avoiding federal tax liability, the court said. Because the petitioner received a fraudulent transfer from the holding company in the amount of $3.77 million, he also was liable as a transferee of a transferee of the company.

In re Dole Food Co. (Dole I)

Citation: 2014 Del. Ch. LEXIS 258
Date of decision: Dec. 9, 2014
Judge: Laster
State/Jurisdiction: Delaware
Court: Delaware Court of Chancery
Type of case: Dissenting Shareholder
SIC code: 2033 Canned, Frozen, and Preserved Fruits, Vegetables, and Food Specialties

Delaware Chancery Orders Disclosure of Nonexpert Internal Valuations

In a discovery dispute in a statutory appraisal action, the Delaware Court of Chancery delved deep into case law and academic literature on valuation to determine whether a party's prelitigation, valuation-related information was discoverable by the opposing side. Finance professionals of all stripes will want to read the court's take on what valuation is and what role experts play in relation to it. The court's assessment of expert testimony in litigation is instructive.

Prelitigation appraisals. The chairman and controlling shareholder of Dole Food Co. (the defendant) proposed a take-private merger in which he would buy all of Dole's common stock that he did not already own for $12 per share in cash. Two months later, he and the company agreed on a $13.50-per-share price. The record date for the merger was Sept. 27, 2013. At the end of October 2013, the company's stockholders approved the merger in a special meeting. The transaction closed on Nov. 1, 2013.

The two petitioners in this case were investment firms that appeared to pursue an "appraisal arbitrage" strategy. One investor, Hudson Bay, bought 4.6 million shares of Dole stock after the company announced the take-private proposal and before the merger closed. Hudson Bay received the merger consideration. Around the time the take-private proposal became public, Hudson Bay also sold over 156,000 shares of Dole stock for amounts ranging from $12.69 per share to $12.90 per share. Similarly, the second investor, Ripe Holdings, bought 2.8 million shares in Dole after the announcement of the take-private proposal and before the merger closed.

Subsequently, the petitioners filed a dissenting shareholder suit in the Delaware Court of Chancery contesting the adequacy of the merger price and asking the court for a fair value appraisal. In discovery, Dole tried to obtain from each of the petitioners valuation-related information, such as written documents and Excel files. This information included: (1) any internal valuations the petitioners had performed of Dole or Dole stock prior to the litigation; and (2) any valuations the petitioners had reviewed or considered in connection with buying and selling Dole stock and with the appraisal action. The petitioners refused to disclose the information. Initially, they claimed this information was irrelevant; moreover, they said, disclosure on valuation was premature before the expert discovery phase.

In addition, Dole wanted to depose financial professionals in the companies. Each of the petitioners designated a witness, but, during the actual depositions, the witnesses, on instruction of counsel, refused to answer most of the questions Dole's counsel posed.

Specifically, Hudson Bay designated a portfolio manager who worked on the Dole stock transactions. His education was in finance and information systems, and he had worked as an investment banker for various firms, including Goldman Sachs. He said he regularly made decisions on buying and selling stocks, sometimes based on market events and sometimes based on extensive research and analysis. He based the Dole transactions on a valuation that used three methods: discounted cash flow (DCF), comparable companies analysis, and sum of the parts. He spoke in general terms about the methods, displaying a familiarity with valuation concepts.

Ripe's designated witness was a managing director with the firm. He also had a law degree and originally worked for the firm's legal department. As managing director, he sourced investments and frequently prepared valuations using the DCF and other financial analyses. He had the lead responsibility for the Dole investment, including the buying of Dole shares. Before the merger, he prepared a seven-to-10-page memo for the firm's investment management committee detailing his recommendation about the investment strategy related to Dole stock. It included a DCF analysis for Dole and a downside analysis that valued Dole at less than the merger consideration.

Following the stunted depositions, Dole filed a motion to compel disclosure of prelitigation information addressing the value of its stock. The petitioners objected.

Valuation not an 'esoteric specialty.' At the outset of its analysis, the court noted that under the state's rule of discovery (Rule 26(b)(1)) generally anything not privileged was discoverable as long as the material was relevant. Importantly, the relevant material need not be admissible but need only appear "reasonably calculated to lead to the discovery of admissible evidence." The court called this aspect "potential admissibility."

1. *Relevance.* In this case, there was no question that the valuations Dole wanted to discover were relevant, the court said. It noted that the petitioners seemed to admit as much because, even though early in the dispute they argued the contested material was not relevant, they had dropped "that implausible objection" by the time they responded to Dole's motion to compel.

2. *Potential admissibility.* The petitioners subsequently hitched their refusal to disclose the information on a claim that the contested material would not lead to the discovery of admissible evidence. The prelitigation valuations were opinions, not facts, they said, and valuation in an appraisal action is "purely a matter for the experts." Since the witnesses were not experts under Rule 702, they could only give lay opinions under Rule 701. However, their value opinions did not meet the requirements for the admission of lay opinions. In sum, there was no basis on which any information about their opinions could be admissible at trial.

The court rejected those claims. It found that under precedent the valuation-related material Dole wanted "easily satisfies the potential admissibility requirement." It disagreed with the premise underlying the petitioners' claim: that valuation was exclusively the province of experts. Although valuation was a topic where expert testimony was "appropriate" and "helpful," the court said, valuation was not an "esoteric specialty" nor was it "a rare discipline like nuclear physics, brain surgery, or accident reconstruction." According to the Chancery, "valuation resembles more closely the common skill of driving a car" in that there are professional drivers and your average commuter. While the former have greater abilities and knowledge, the latter still are knowledgeable enough to comment on how a fellow driver handles himself on the road.

There was an irony to the petitioners' position, the court noted, in that "the appraisal statute mandates that a lay individual express the final conclusion of the fair value of the petitioners' shares." That "lay individual" was a "law-trained judge." In making its determination, the court may consider a range of factual evidence, the court pointed out. This evidence includes, but is not limited to, the market price, the merger price, other offers for the company or its assets, prices at which knowledgeable insiders sold their shares, internal corporate documents from the respondent, and valuation work prepared for nonlitigation purposes. And even if the parties offer expert testimony and the court relies on it to determine fair value, the court may and does consider factual evidence to cross-check the experts' "litigation-driven figures."

The court also observed that in this case the designated witnesses were only "technically lay witnesses" and "were hardly unqualified." If the petitioners believed them to be otherwise, "then perhaps they should begin disclosing to their investors that the financial professionals who manage their funds are not qualified to do their jobs."

Given the witnesses' training and experience, both "likely" could qualify as experts, the court said. But, even if they were deemed lay witnesses, their opinions would be admissible under Rule 701 because their assessments would be helpful to "the determination of a fact in issue."

'Battle of the experts' trope. To support their argument that valuation was a matter for experts only, the petitioners relied on the description of an appraisal proceeding as a "battle of experts," which has appeared in many court decisions. The Chancery noted that courts "have not employed this phrase approvingly to suggest limitations on the scope of admissible evidence." Instead, it serves them as shorthand for the "contrary, and often antagonistic" opinions experts proffer in a litigation setting. Experts tend to generate widely divergent valuations "as they strive to bracket the outer limits of plausibility," the court said.

The petitioners presented an "idealized depiction of valuation as a scientific process" when the "martial metaphor suggests the need to consider other evidence as a check on the warring experts' model," the court stated. One piece of evidence was the contemporaneous view of financial professionals "who make investment decisions with real money." Here, the petitioners' internal contemporaneous valuations represented "real-world" assessments by "astute" investors. How they value the company and its stock may "be as or even more credible than the litigation-crafted opinions of valuation experts."

For all these reasons, the Chancery found that almost all of the valuation-related information Dole requested from the petitioners was discoverable. The attorney-client privilege or work product doctrine potentially protected only the memo that Ripe's witness prepared for the investment committee on Dole and Dole stock. The question was whether the author—Ripe's designated witness, the managing director—was acting as a lawyer or whether he prepared the document as a business analyst. In his deposition, he said the memo contained an analysis of an appraisal statute and that he had prepared it after consultation with outside counsel. The court wanted to inspect the document *in camera* (behind closed doors) to decide whether it contained legal advice or litigation-related information that needed to be redacted before making it available to the opposing side.

Finally, the court found the petitioners had no basis on which to refuse discovery of the information and awarded Dole the reasonable costs it incurred to obtain access to the prelitigation valuation material.

In re Dole Food Co., Inc. Stockholder Litigation (Dole II)

Citation: 2015 Del. Ch. LEXIS 47
Date of decision: Feb. 27, 2015
Experts: Seth Ferguson/Stifel, Nicolaus & Company, Inc. (defendants); unknown (plaintiffs)
Judge: Laster
State/Jurisdiction: Delaware
Court: Delaware Court of Chancery
Type of case: Dissenting Shareholder
SIC code: 2033 Canned Fruits, Vegetables, Preserves, Jams, and Jellies
NAICS code: 311421 Fruit and Vegetable Canning

Can a Valuation Firm Serve as Expert Witness?

Not long ago, in this shareholder litigation in front of the Delaware Court of Chancery, the court was asked to decide whether the plaintiffs' prelitigation, valuation-related information was discoverable by the defendants, where the proceedings had not yet reached the expert discovery phase. Recently, the court addressed another aspect of the case that affects financial experts: whether a financial advisory firm—an entity—could serve as the defendants' expert, as opposed to the human being(s) in the firm who prepared the expert report.

Backstory. In late 2013, the defendant, Dole Food Co. (Dole), effected a take-private merger. Subsequently, the plaintiffs, two investment firms that appeared to pursue an "appraisal arbitrage" strategy, challenged the transaction in the Delaware Chancery, where they asserted a breach of fiduciary duty claim and also petitioned for statutory appraisal.

Dole named an investment banking firm, Stifel, Nicolaus & Co. Inc. (Stifel), as its expert witness on the subject of the company's value at the time of the transaction. The opening expert report named the entity as its author, as did a rebuttal expert report. Two biological persons signed the reports as authorized representatives of the firm. One was a managing director of the firm, the other a firm employee. Neither individual signed in his personal capacity.

For purposes of deposition, Stifel produced the managing director as the person who was most knowledgeable about the reports. The plaintiffs tried to explore whether Dole was distinguishing between the firm and the managing director. When the managing director claimed authorship of the expert reports, Dole's counsel objected that "he is not the expert," claiming that the firm was the expert.

The plaintiffs contended that an expert witness must be a biological person. The distinction was important, they said, because a corporate expert witness might argue that it relied on the collective knowledge and experience of all of its employees and agents, whereas a biological person was only able to rely on the—limited—knowledge and experience that "a living mind might accumulate."

What makes a witness? At the start of its analysis, the court noted that, under Delaware Rule of Evidence 702 on expert testimony, "an expert witness first must be capable of serving as a witness." The Chancery noted that, although the Delaware Code included provisions that "appropriately personif[y]" corporations, companies, and firms in certain commercial and economic contexts, "the Rules of Evidence make clear that a witness must be a biological person." A corporation was an artificial being that only existed "in the contemplation of the law." It had no mind with which to think and no voice with which to speak. Lacking a body, "it cannot even meet Delaware's statutory requirement that a person taking an oath do so, 'with the uplifted hand,'" the court pointed out.

Besides failing the requirements applicable to witnesses generally, a corporation was incapable of meeting the requirements specific to Rule 702. These include that an expert be "qualified" by demonstrating the requisite "knowledge, skill, experience, training or education," the court said. Only a biological person can acquire those, the court continued, "and only a biological person can learn to apply principles and methods." Whatever attributes or abilities a corporation is said to have exist because biological people have them and use them on behalf of the corporation. "The expertise belongs to the individuals, not the corporation," the court observed.

A corporation cannot simply circumvent the requirements by testifying through an agent, as Dole's investment firm attempted to do with the managing director—just as a biological person cannot ask another person to testify on his or her behalf, said the court. At the same time, the corporation's inability to testify did not mean that the testimony of the biological persons who are its agents and decision-makers don't bind the entity, said the court.

In light of the requirements of the evidentiary rules, Vice Chancellor Laster concluded he did "not believe that a corporation can serve as an expert witness." This meant that Stifel could not testify at trial. However, to avoid leaving Dole without an expert, the court allowed the managing director to substitute in and testify to the contents of the expert reports, as long as he confirmed that he had adopted Stifel's expert reports.

In re Dole Food Co. (Dole III)

Citation: 2015 Del. Ch. LEXIS 223
Date of decision: Aug. 27, 2015
Experts: Al Garner, Lazard Frères & Co. LLC (financial advisor to committee); Kevin F. Dages (plaintiffs); unknown (defendants)
Judge: Laster
State/Jurisdiction: Delaware
Court: Delaware Court of Chancery
Type of case: Dissenting shareholder
SIC code: 2033 Canned Fruits, Vegetables, Preserves, Jams, and Jellies
NAICS code: 311421 Fruit and Vegetable Canning

Chancery Lauds Advisor's 'Heroic' Efforts at Credible DCF

After issuing a gaggle of decisions reprimanding financial advisors for producing manipulated valuations in merger transactions, the Delaware Court of Chancery recently had high praise for the financial advisor working on the contested Dole Food take-private merger. Still, the advisor's "heroic" efforts could not overcome the defendants' fraud, the court decided. The defendants both failed to provide material financial information and furnished false information, making a reliable valuation of the company impossible.

Cash-flow problems. The individual defendants in this litigation were David H. Murdock and C. Michael Carter. The plaintiffs, pursuing an appraisal arbitrage strategy, were shareholders challenging the 2013 transaction in which Murdock, who owned approximately 40% of Dole's common stock, bought the remainder shares. Dole Foods is one of the world's largest producers and marketers of fresh fruits and vegetables.

At the time of the merger, Murdock served as chairman, CEO, and de facto controller. Carter was president, COO, and general counsel; he was responsible for the company's day-to-day management. His primary role, the Chancery said, was "to carry out Murdock's plans, and he did so effectively, even ruthlessly."

The merger was in the works for about 18 months. It was the second of a two-step plan to achieve Murdock's goal to take Dole private again. In the wake of the 2008 financial crisis, Dole had experienced financial problems that forced Murdock to sell a part of the company's equity to the public. But he loathed the public-company model and soon began exploring ways to reacquire complete control of the company.

The first step was a 2012 spinoff in which Dole sold its Asia division to a Japanese company, Itochu, for about $1.7 billion in cash. Besides raising funds to pay off its debt, the company expected to benefit from substantial cost savings related to the transaction. At the time, Dole told analysts that it expected to implement $20 million in cost cuts in 2012 and $30 million in 2013. By the end of 2013, it would have arrived at the full run-rate of $50 million per year. A presentation to the board, in December 2012, projected similar savings but with a one-year delay: $35 million would be achieved in 2014, and the entire $50 million would be achieved in 2015. An internal plan identified $62 million in specific cost-cutting initiatives.

Also, before the Itochu transaction, the company began to pursue a long-term strategy of buying farms in Latin America in an effort to produce additional income by capturing the growers' share of profits. But, given its cash-flow problems, it had to delay implementation. The Itochu sale solved the money problem. The expectation was that farm purchases would be about $100 million and produce a $15 million initial return.

Driving down share price. Following the Itochu transaction, Dole's share price climbed to over $14.00 per share. But a rising share price did not align with Murdock's plan to effect a freeze-out at a price most favorable to him. Carter, therefore, took steps to redirect the market. For example, in early 2013, he issued several press releases that downward adjusted EBITDA for the year and predicted cost savings only in the $20 million range. He did not explain to analysts what happened to the other $30 million—an amount, which the court found, represented about 20% of the company's forecasted EBITDA. The announcements came just when the internal discussions about the freeze-out were heating up and caused Dole's stock price to fall 13%.

A few months later, Carter, without informing the board's five outside directors, announced the company indefinitely suspended a planned share repurchase program. This news generated "horrible" press coverage and caused the share price to drop another 10%, the court found.

In June 2013, Murdock made an official proposal to buy the remaining stock for $12 per share. He made it clear he was "a buyer, not a seller." Consequently, the board would be unable to sell the entire company for a higher price to a third party. In response, the board formed a committee made up of its five outside directors to evaluate the proposal from an objective vantage point. Although several of the committee members had strong, longtime ties to Murdock and his businesses, the court found the committee "was in fact independent." One of its first steps was to seek legal and financial advice from a law firm and an investment bank that had not done business with Murdock or Dole in the past.

After Murdock's proposal became public, the committee and its advisors received signs of interest from outside buyers. One of the potential buyers suggested $14 per share, but the committee's financial advisor decided this was not a serious offer. The most promising bidder was Chiquita, which expressed interest in buying all of Dole. But Murdock refused. Ultimately, Murdock and the committee settled on a $13.50-per-share price. Unbeknownst to the committee and its financial advisor, during negotiations over the terms of the merger agreement, Carter and members of Dole's senior management advised Murdock on deal-related issues.

The board approved the transaction. Under the terms of the final deal, the committee had 30 days to shop the company. Even though the financial advisor contacted over 60 parties and two made confidentiality agreements, no one made a bid. In a special meeting of stockholders, 50.9% of the disinterested shares voted for Murdock's offer. The transaction closed on Nov. 1, 2013.

Following the merger, Dole bought between $80 million and $100 million worth of farms. Dole's financial advisor reported that the farms could increase EBITDA by "around $23 million once the acquisitions are fully integrated." Also, the company achieved $30 million in cost savings in 2014 and about $51 million in 2015. "Logically, Dole should have achieved these savings as a result of the ITOCHU Transaction, not the Merger," the court observed.

Doing a number on the projections. No matter the financial advisor's independence, its ability to give reliable advice to the committee depended on having access to sound financial projections, the court said. It found that Carter used his control over Dole's management to provide false information.

Dole typically prepared three-year budgets and financial projections using a bottom-up process. The various operating divisions would create models and forecasts for management's review. Following discussions, senior management would generate the final numbers. But, after Murdock's proposal, in July 2013, Carter ordered senior management and division heads to prepare projections from the top down. He and his team would create only high-case and low-case adjusted EBITDA forecasts. He told division heads to "reverse engineer the supporting budgets after the meeting." The committee had no opportunity to meet with the division heads. The July five-year projections were considerably lower than the prior, December 2012, projections. They reduced EBITDA in Year 3 of the December projections from $211.9 million to $169.2 million, which represented a reduction of more than 20%. Also, they included only $20 million out of the anticipated $50 million in cost savings. And they did not forecast any additional income from the purchase of farms.

At trial, a representative of the financial advisor said the firm at the time did not believe the figures would even support Murdock's $12.00 offer. It seemed, he said, "management had taken a meat cleaver to the projections in a way that it would be difficult, if not inappropriate, for a committee to weight these projections as the basis for determining the adequacy of a price." The committee's chair said he did not find them to be "an accurate representation of the value of the Company."

Moreover, around the same time, Carter organized a lender meeting with Dole management and Murdock's bankers to discuss the take-private proposal. At that meeting, he said that the company would "beat or meet" the July forecasts and discussed the projected $50 million in cost savings. He also stated that Dole would be able to substantially increase its income by buying more farms. Contemporaneous notes suggested that the farm purchases "[e]asily could be $100 [million] ($15 [million] initial return or 20% EBITDA margin)."

Until the litigation, the committee and its financial advisor remained unaware of the scope of the lender meeting. They did not know about Carter's representations about the cost savings and farms. "This information would have been helpful and important to us. We should have known this," the committee chair said. The lender meeting was an "obvious violation of the procedures that the Committee had established," the court said.

Creating fresh projections. The committee and its financial advisor understood that the July projections were unreliable and created their own by using the December projections as a basis to which they made adjustments. The financial advisor considered the result an "aggressive but reasonable and achievable forecast." However, it did not adjust for the additional $30 million in anticipated cost savings or for possible savings attributable to division-level restructuring or for income from farm purchases—all items management did not disclose when providing the committee with information.

The financial advisor's DCF analysis pointed to a per-share price between $11.40 and $14.08. Murdock's final offer, $13.50, was closer to the top price than the midpoint; it also was higher than the value ranges resulting from the financial advisor's public-company and precedent transaction analyses. In sum, the merger price seemed to be a good outcome.

Modified DCF points to unfair price. The plaintiff shareholders' post-merger suit was a combined appraisal and entire fairness action. They alleged the defendants breached their duty of loyalty and were personally liable for damages, and they asked the court to determine the fair value of their shares. The court decided the fairness claims first "because a finding of liability and the resultant remedy could moot the appraisal proceeding."

Here, the court said, Carter's fraud rendered a detailed analysis as to fair dealing unnecessary. His actions made the "highly commendable efforts" to achieve a fair transaction that was in the best interests of Dole's stockholders "useless and ineffective." He changed the company's historic practice by providing earnings guidance, "and the guidance he provided changed Dole's estimate of its ability to achieve cost savings."

As a corporate officer, Carter had a duty to provide accurate and up-to-date financial information to the committee, "even if his principal loyalty is to a controller who is his boss and a source of post-transaction employment," the court said. "The projections Carter provided were knowingly false." They were the most egregious of Carter's actions, but there were other efforts to thwart the bargaining power of the committee, the court observed.

To determine whether the price was fair, the court looked to expert testimony at trial, the financial advisor's opinion at the time of the merger, and market indicators. As tended to be the case in valuation litigation, the court said, the experts' views on company value differed widely. The court found the plaintiffs' expert "relatively speaking" more helpful in that he showed how different assumptions and inputs influenced value. The defendants' expert essentially provided a second fairness opinion "using pro-defendant assumptions." The financial advisor's work was "far more credible," the court stated. However, Carter's actions "tainted both the negotiation process and [the financial advisor's] work product." The court found that in the areas where the financial advisor received complete information from management, its DCF provided the best indication of value at the time of the merger. But, considering the material omissions, the $13.50-per-share price was below the range of fairness.

In terms of cost savings, the financial advisor calculated that the $30 million in incremental savings achieved after the freeze-out would justify an increase in price of $3.80 per share. But, given a degree of uncertainty at the time of the merger as to how much the company could in fact achieve in cost savings, the court found a more reasonable estimate was $1.87 per share. To assume the cash generated from this source was just as certain as the cash generated from the company's core operations would lead to overvaluation, the court decided.

In terms of farm purchases, the plaintiffs' expert determined that buying an incremental $28.6 million in farms would increase the company's value by $1.22 per share, using 3.2% both as perpetual growth rate and for projecting cash flows in Years 4 and 5. In contrast, the financial advisor used 1.5% for these inputs, which reduced the increase in value to $0.87 per share. Using this input and scaling the benefit to the projected $100 million in farm purchases would yield incremental value of $3.04 per share. The court, again accounting for uncertainty, found a more reasonable estimate of the value stemming from the farm purchases was $0.87 per share.

The court rejected the defendants' argument that it was inappropriate to include value from cost savings and farm purchases since these events happened after the merger. "Elements of future value, including the nature of the enterprise, which are known or susceptible of proof as of the date of the merger and not the product of speculation, may be considered," the court noted, citing *Del. Open MRI Radiology Assocs., P.A. v. Kessler*, 898 A.2d 290 (2006) (available at *BVLaw*). Here, the court said, the plans to cut costs and buy farms to increase profits were part of the company's "operative reality" at the time of the merger.

A modified DCF analysis that takes into account all material information suggested that the merger price was not fair, the court concluded. The court dismissed claims by the defendants that the merger price aligned with the way the market valued the company. First, there was no ongoing, consistent market check. The only time Murdock considered selling the company was in the wake of the 2008 financial crisis. He overcame the company's weakness by taking Dole public. During the merger, the period that counted, he was particularly unwilling to sell, the court pointed out.

Also, analyses based on metrics implied by various transactions involving Dole and its peers, Chiquita and Del Monte, led to the same conclusion as the financial advisor's analysis for the committee: If one did not take into account Dole's operative reality of cost savings and farm purchases, the $13.50 merger price was within the range of fairness. But, with the information, the merger price was at best at the low range of fairness and may have dropped below, the court said.

Right to 'fairer price.' In terms of damages stemming from the defendants' breach of fiduciary duty, the court found the stockholders were not limited to "an arguably fair price. They are entitled to a fairer price."

Here, the committee's projections and the financial advisor's analysis, once adjusted for value related to cost savings and farm purchases, could support an award as high as $6.84 per share, the court said. In the final analysis, it found this level of damages "unrealistic and harsh, except as a form of rescissory damages." Carter's fraud, the court observed, might warrant damages on that order, but it declined to go that far.

Instead, it added $2.74 per share to the merger price to arrive at a fair value of $16.24 per share. Considering the maximum of $20.34 per share, the $2.74-per-share figure indicated that the defendants managed to reduce the ultimate deal price by 16.9%. This percentage aligned with academic findings about the average price decrease caused by earnings manipulation before management-led buyouts, the court noted. In sum, the defendants were liable to the plaintiffs for nearly $148.2 million.

In re El Paso Pipeline Partners, L.P. Derivative Litigation

Citation: 2015 Del. Ch. LEXIS 11
Date of decision: April 20, 2015
Experts: Dr. Zachary Nye (plaintiffs); Tudor, Pickering, Holt & Co. (fairness opinions/parent)
Judge: Laster
State/Jurisdiction: Delaware
Court: Court of Chancery of Delaware
Type of case: Damages
SIC code: 4922 Natural Gas Transmission
NAICS code: 486210 Pipeline Transportation of Natural Gas

Financial Advisor's 'Real Client Was the Deal,' Says Chancery

A series of transactions in which the parent company off-loaded risky assets to a limited partnership that it controlled produced a spate of suits from the LP's common unit holders. Many of the claims ended prematurely, but one proceeded to trial. The work product of the financial advisor that valued each of the assets prior to the deals provoked stinging criticism from the Delaware Court of Chancery. The appraiser's performance was fee-driven, the court said. There were instances of manipulating valuations to align the calculations with the parent's asking price. At the same time, the court commended the plaintiffs' expert for producing a valuation on which to base damages.

Dropping assets. In 2010, the parent company sold two of its subsidiaries to a master limited partnership (MLP). The parent controlled the MLP through ownership of a company that served as the sole general partner (GP) of the MLP. One contested transaction took place in March 2010 and involved the parent's selling a 51% interest to the MLP in a subsidiary called Elba. The second transaction involved the sale of the remaining 49% of Elba as well as the sale of a 15% interest in another subsidiary called Southern. The subsidiaries owned a liquefied natural gas (LNG) import terminal and a natural gas pipeline. Both transactions were acquisitions in which ownership interests "dropped down" from the parent company to the MLP.

The parent formed the MLP, a pass-through entity, to maximize the market value of its midstream assets and the amount of capital it could raise based on that valuation. Through dropdowns, the parent was able to reap the tax benefit and obtain capital at the lowest possible cost. The MLP only acquired assets from the parent. The parent initiated each dropdown and proposed the asset for sale. The consideration typically was cash plus the assumption of a share of the acquired entity's debt. In 2010 alone, there were three dropdowns: in spring, summer, and fall.

By 2010, the market for imported LNG was on the decline because of higher levels of domestic production and lower gas prices. Less demand for LNG imports had the parent company concerned about the stability of service contracts Elba had with Shell and British Gas (BG) by way of special purpose entities that had no assets of their own. The risk was that, if the agreements became sufficiently unprofitable, Shell and BG would walk away from them and leave the Elba subsidiary with substantially less than the anticipated revenue.

The plaintiffs challenged the spring and fall dropdowns in the Delaware Court of Chancery. They claimed the transactions served the parent to sell risky assets to the MLP at an inflated price. The issue was whether a special committee, which was comprised of qualified members of the board of directors of the GP and which had to approve the transactions, breached a contractual provision in the partnership agreement governing the MLP. The requirement was that committee members believe in good faith that the dropdown is in the best interests of the MLP.

The Chancery ruled in favor of the defendants' pretrial motion as to the spring transaction but decided there were sufficient triable issues of fact as to the fall dropdown. At the start of its ruling on the latter, the court said it expected that at trial the committee members and their financial advisor would provide a credible account of how they evaluated the fall dropdown but instead found the two "had no explanation for what they did." According to the Chancery, the committee members "went against their better judgment and did what Parent wanted, assisted by a financial advisor that presented each dropdown in the best possible light, regardless of whether the depictions conflicted with the advisor's work on similar transactions or made sense as a matter of valuation theory."

The financial advisor did none of the "real work" an advisor to a committee does, the court said. Instead, the financial advisor's "real client was the deal, and the firm did what it could to justify the Fall Dropdown, get to closing, and collect its contingent fee."

Valuations enabling spring dropdown. Even though the plaintiffs did not prevail as to the spring dropdown, the court found this transaction deserved scrutiny because it exemplified the proneness of the financial advisor to shape its valuations according to the directions of the parent and because the financial advisor treated the fall dropdown as "little more than an update of its work on the Spring Dropdown."

The parent internally decided it wanted to sell a 51% of Elba to the MLP for $900 million in cash and the assumption of debt for a total consideration of $1.05 million. Board members of the parent said that using the MLP to raise equity was the parent's "cheapest source of funds." Also, aiming for a higher price than even the parent's business plan contemplated was a way to maximize cash proceeds to the parent.

Prior to meeting with the special committee, the financial advisor received background material from the parent that stressed Elba's long-term, fixed-fee contracts with Shell and BG. Less prominently, the materials clarified that the direct counterparties to the agreement actually were entities without assets of their own. In effect, the revenue guaranteed according to the service agreements was less than 20% of the total revenue expected under the service agreements. The committee members remained ignorant of this fact until this litigation.

The financial advisor performed three valuations.

1. *DCF.* For the discounted cash flow (DCF) analysis of Elba, it used a five-year projection period; exit multiples of 8x, 10x, and 12x; and discount rates of 8% to 13.9%. The analysis produced a range

of values from $812 million to $1.2 billion. The parent's proposed price was just above the midpoint of the range.

2. *Precedent transactions.* The financial advisor divided the selected transactions into two groups: one comprised acquisitions of a minority interest, which the advisor characterized as less than 50%; a second comprised acquisitions of a controlling interest, which was 50% and above. The minority set generated a range of 8.1x to 8.8x 2010 EBITDA, which amounted to $700 million to $757 million. The controlling interest set produced a range of 6.8x to 13x 2010 EBITDA, or $589 million to $1.13 billion. For this group, the median was 9.3x and the mean was 9.2x, but the financial advisor decided to use the 13x multiple, an outlier.

The Chancery called this breakdown into two sets "curious," noting it did not align with how the parent treated the transaction. The parent originally planned to sell a 51% interest in Elba but after a call with committee members briefly agreed to sell only a 49% interest. However, the parent did not change its pricing. After a call with the financial advisor in which the latter promised the parent it would support a sale of 51%, the parent settled on that percentage. The financial advisor did not tell the committee that changing the percentage had an effect on pricing. According to the Chancery, the financial advisor "split up the precedent transactions because it made Parent's asking price look better."

3. *Comparable companies analysis.* The peer companies supported a range of multiples from 11x to 14.6x 2010 EBITDA and 11.2x to 14.2x 2011 EBITDA. The asking price fell within both ranges.

The Chancery observed that initially there was some pushback from committee members to the parent's asking price. One of the members specifically noted that the flowback of cash to the parent justified a much lower multiple—somewhere in the range of "8 ½ and 9 times EBITDA with no discount on the sponsor's units is in the ball park of fair value to all concerned parties." This suggestion implied a price range of $725 million to $780 million.

In a subsequent presentation to the committee, the financial advisor examined the flowback of cash by calculating the transaction multiple from the point of view of the parent. The financial advisor calculated that the MLP would pay an effective multiple of 16.2x 2010 EBITDA and 14.3x 2011 EBITDA. For the precedent transaction analysis, the financial advisor still divided the transactions into two subsets, but it decided not to show the range of minority acquisitions, which was far below the parent's asking price.

Another committee member reviewed some analyst reports that anticipated a dropdown at a multiple of 9x 2010 EBITDA, which equated to a value of Elba of $780 million.

After some back and forth between the parent and the committee, the parties agreed to a price of $963 million, which implied a multiple of 11.2x 2010 EBITDA. The financial advisor said the transaction "was fair, from a financial point of view, to the holders of common units other than the General Partner and its affiliates."

The market reacted negatively to the transaction. The MLP's common stock traded down 3.6% in response to the news, while the peer index showed a drop of only 0.7% and the S&P 500 a drop of just 0.2%. This prompted a committee member to suggest to other committee members that the market's expectations "exceeded the realities. The next time we will have to negotiate harder."

When the Chancery ruled on the plaintiffs' challenge to the spring dropdown, it found that the bad outcome for MLP reflected ineffective negotiation skills on the committee's part but did not by itself mean the committee members "subjectively believed they were acting against [the partnership's] best interest." In other words, there was not enough there to show the committee members' bad faith. Therefore, the court granted the defendants' pretrial summary judgment motion.

Fall dropdown becomes 'encore' production. In early fall, anticipating another dropdown, several committee members expressed a preference not to acquire more LNG assets. The parent had other plans; it proposed to sell the remaining 49% interest in Elba, asking for $806 million in cash and the assumption of debt for a total consideration of $948 million. In addition, the parent proposed to sell a minority interest in its other subsidiary, Southern. It laid out several options for the MLP, which, the Chancery said, "showed that Parent's principal interest was obtaining low-cost capital."

The financial advisor's internal communication made it clear it viewed the fall dropdown as nothing more than an update on the work of the spring dropdown. The project's code name was "Encore." One partner remarked that this designation was "more tactful than 'Again?'" The committee asked the financial advisor to assess the proposal in light of the weakening LNG market. In response, the financial advisor asked the parent for feedback. The latter replied there had been no changes, and the assets were solid.

At trial, a representative of the financial advisor maintained it would have been "atypical" to ask the opposite side, that is, the parent, for information. The court found this claim unpersuasive. For the dropdown, the financial advisor "*always* asked the Parent for information," the court stressed. It noted that every such transaction began with a due diligence session between the parent and the financial advisor. As the deal shaped up, the latter asked more questions of the parent and the parent provided "anything that [the financial advisor] would ask for."

Prior to proceeding with the deal, a committee member also asked the financial advisor to reassess the service agreements and the strength of the guarantees. The court found the financial advisor did not do so. Instead, the financial advisor used the same slide presentation it had prepared for the spring dropdown but "*reduced the amount of information so that the guarantees looked better*," the court said with emphasis.

Besides these instances of "nonfeasance," the court noted examples of "malfeasance" on the financial advisor's part. They included manipulating the valuation methodologies. For example, in terms of the precedent transactions, for the spring dropdown involving the acquisition of a control interest, the advisor showed only the range for control transactions. To be consistent, for the fall dropdown, it only should have presented the range for noncontrol transactions. Instead, it gave a single range of precedent transactions, the Chancery observed.

The court found this tinkering enabled the financial advisor to achieve multiple ranges of 6.5x to 13.5x for the 2010 EBITDA and 6.8x to 13.0x for the 2011 EBITDA and ensure that the parent's proposed price fell within these ranges.

As for the DCF treatment, for the spring dropdown, the financial advisor prepared one valuation, but for the fall dropdown it prepared three different valuations: one with a five-year projection period, another with a 10-year projection period, and a third one with a 15-year projection period. It calculated terminal value using four exit multiples, instead of the three it had used for the spring dropdown. The lower bound now was a 6x multiple as opposed to the 8x multiple in the spring dropdown analysis. "Most significantly," said the court, the financial advisor "cut off the upper bound of its discount rate at 12%. These changes widened the DCF range, increased the upper bound, and moved Parent's price towards the center."

One other significant aspect of the advisor analysis was its valuing the assets at play (Elba and Southern) in the fall dropdown as a package, even though the parent had valued each interest separately, as had the financial advisor in its internal work. This meant the committee ultimately approved a transaction without knowing what the breakdown in price was between the 49% Elba interest and the 15% interest in Southern. Until litigation, several committee members remained in the dark as to how much the MLP paid for the remainder interest in Elba.

Actually, even though the committee came to see the spring price as too high and thought it had successfully negotiated a lower price for Elba in terms of the fall dropdown, the parent changed the deal in a way that raised the price to the spring dropdown level. By providing only an aggregated price for the deal, the financial advisor helped to conceal that price increase from the committee members.

According to the court, most of the valuation-related changes remained unexplained to the committee members. It noted that, while a financial advisor need not treat every transaction in the same way, "one would expect a financial advisor to have reasoned explanations for its changes, and it would be surprising if every one of the changes moved the analysis in the same direction." Here, all the changes made the parent's asking price more palatable, the court concluded.

Ignoring lessons from spring dropdown. In terms of the fall dropdown, the committee members had breached their contractual duty to conclude the transaction was "in the best interests of the Partnership," the court said. The committee members' preoccupation with accretion rendered them myopic to the point where "Committee members viewed every one of the Parent's opening proposals as fair, simply because distributions could have increased."

The fall dropdown was not just a study in negotiating poorly, the court said. Rather, the committee members had the benefit of a "costly education about Elba" but ignored this expensive lesson. "Rather than returning to their independent assessments of value, they allowed the price from the Spring Dropdown to anchor their counter." They ignored their own desires for a separate analysis of the two components of the fall dropdown, and "even abandoned the price improvement they negotiated in the Fall Dropdown." The committee members' conduct showed "conscious indifference" to their responsibilities to the MLP and resulted in a breach of contract, the court found.

Court adopts plaintiff expert's damage calculation. The court said that the measure of damages was the difference between the price the MLP paid for the 49% interest in Elba and the value of that interest. It found credible the calculation of the plaintiffs' expert. For one, in determining cash flows, he accounted for the risks to Elba's cash flows, estimating the present value of the guaranteed cash flows and the nonguaranteed cash flows. He discounted the guaranteed cash flows at the average yield to maturity of Shell's senior corporate bonds maturing in 2038 and 2040, or 5.581%.

For the nonguaranteed cash flows, he was able to find a comparable LNG import terminal connected to major U.S. natural gas markets and determine that the weighted average cost of capital (WACC) of its owner/operator would have been 11.876% at the time of the spring dropdown. But the expert decided this rate understated the risk associated with Elba because the owner/operator of the comparable terminal had greater creditworthiness. Therefore, he turned to option theory to calculate the nonguaranteed risk implied by that WACC and ultimately concluded that the cost of capital for nonguaranteed investment in a U.S. LNG import terminal was 14.868%. He used this figure to discount Elba's nonguaranteed cash flows.

For the terminal value, he used a multiple of 9.1x EBITDA based on the parent's internal valuations of Elba and the sale of another LNG in which the parent had a 50% interest, which used a 20-year terminal value of 9x EBITDA. The plaintiffs' expert discounted the terminal value using the 14.868% rate.

He calculated that Elba's enterprise value at the time of the fall dropdown was $1.5 billion. This equated to a value of $760 million for a 49% interest. Considering the MLP paid at least $931 million for that interest in the fall dropdown, the MLP sustained damages of $171 million from that transaction alone. The expert also found that analyzing comparable transactions as a cross-check yielded data points that validated his DCF analysis. Further, an event study based on the stock market's reaction to the fall dropdown suggested an even higher loss of value.

The Chancery said that the loss made the $171 million damages figure look conservative and adopted the latter for damages purposes.

Finjan, Inc. v. Blue Coat Systems, Inc.

Citation: 2015 U.S. LEXIS 91528
Date of decision: July 14, 2015
Experts: Dr. Anne Layne-Farrar (plaintiff); Julie Davis (defendant)
Judge: Freeman
State/Jurisdiction: Federal/California
Court: United States District Court
Type of case: Intellectual Property
SIC code: 7372 Prepackaged Software
NAICS code: 511210 Software Publishers

Complex Facts Test Patent Experts' Apportionment Skills

What apportionment techniques can a damages expert use to ensure the capture of the *proceeds* from the infringing features but not the noninfringing components? This question dominated a recent *Daubert* case in which both parties claimed the rival expert's apportionment rendered her reasonable royalty calculation unreliable. The court was partly receptive to the arguments.

Tough assignment. The plaintiff owned a portfolio of patents related to Internet security. It sued the defendant, claiming the latter's suite of Web security appliances and software infringed six patents that focused on protecting network computers from hostile files downloaded from the Internet.

The accused products all had multiple different or overlapping features, and only some of the features were accused of violating one or several of the patents in suit. In other words, some or all of the product or a combination of products might infringe one or several of the plaintiff's patents.

The parties agreed that the proper measure of damages in this case was a reasonable royalty. The plaintiff sought a lump-sum payment not calculated on a per-unit basis. Both parties' experts calculated a reasonable royalty based on the *Georgia-Pacific* framework. Through hypothetical negotiation, they first determined a royalty rate, which they then multiplied by an apportioned royalty base—representing only the portion of a product's revenue attributable to the infringing features. The result was the royalty rate the parties would have agreed upon prior to infringement.

Both sides filed *Daubert* motions to exclude the other side's damages testimony.

At the start of its analysis, the court explained that Federal Circuit law required apportionment where the infringing products included both protected and nonprotected features to ensure the patent holder received no more than the value the patented features added to the infringer's products. Given the many patents in suit and the complexity of the infringing products in this case, apportionment was not child's play.

Scrutinizing defendant expert's apportionment. The plaintiff argued the defendant expert's apportionment analysis was fatally defective in several regards.

1. *Using source code.* One way the defendant's expert apportioned the royalty base was to consider the percentage of infringing source code in each accused product.

The plaintiff claimed this method as such was unreliable because it depended on the competency of the programmer. Specifically, "an accused infringer who has inefficient programmers would pay less because the overall code base would be larger."

The court dismissed this argument promptly. An incompetent programmer would be equally incompetent in programming all of the accused product's code, just as an effective programmer would efficiently program the code of the entire products, the court observed. In other words, the percentage of code for the product would not change, the court said.

It found that this apportionment method was neither inherently unreliable nor prohibited under Federal Circuit law. While it was true that the Federal Circuit has said that apportionment "cannot be reduced to a mere counting of lines of code," it also has recognized that "the glaring imbalance between infringing and non-infringing features must impact the analysis of how much profit can properly be attributed to the use of the [accused feature] compared to non-patented elements."

In addition, the plaintiff contended the defendant expert's focus on the infringing source code meant she did not fully account for the claimed infringement of the plaintiff's patents.

The issue of whether and to what extent the defendant's products actually infringed the patents in suit was at the heart of the litigation, the court observed. It was for the fact finder to decide, not a judge in a *Daubert* proceeding. Since the defendant disputed the value of the plaintiff's protected technology, it was understandable that its expert would work with the facts "as her client sees them." But, said the court, "it is not the role of the trial court to evaluate the correctness of facts underlying one expert's testimony." The source-code-based apportionment analysis was admissible.

2. *Using Web page categorization.* The defendant's expert also apportioned revenues for one of the defendant's accused Web page rating services based on the percentage of "suspicious or malicious" categories of Web pages returned. A product development director told the damages expert that there were numerous categories its ratings service could use to classify a Web page and the patents in suit only implicated a small number of them.

The plaintiff argued this apportionment analysis did not account for all the patents or claim elements the defendant's technology infringed and the approach failed to take into account that the few categorizations considered might be of more importance to the defendant's customers.

According to the court, the expert's analysis was appropriate in light of the Federal Circuit's ruling that "frequency of expected use and predicted value are related" in considering *Georgia-Pacific* Factor 11, which concerns "[t]he extent to which the infringer has made use of the invention; and any evidence probative of the value of that use." Cross-examination was the best way to test whether apportionment relative to this product was able to adequately capture the relative significance of the few categorizations, the court said.

3. *Using plaintiff's patent portfolio.* Relying on plaintiff testimony that all the patents in litigation were "core" and of equal value, the defendant's expert considered all the patents over which the plaintiff had sued thus far—20—as opposed to just the six that were the subject of the case at bar in her apportionment of the proposed reasonable royalty rate.

The plaintiff claimed the expert improperly folded 14 other patents into the plaintiff's portfolio even though those patents were the focus of separate litigation against third parties that occurred after the dates of the hypothetical negotiations.

The court agreed with the plaintiff that the analysis improperly used post-infringement evidence and found this analysis inadmissible. According to the court, "future litigation activity is therefore not probative of the value of the patents-in-suit at the time of the hypothetical negotiation."

4. *Using past-valued dollars.* The plaintiff claimed the defendant's expert improperly stated damages in past-valued as opposed to today's dollars. Specifically, both experts applied the same net present value discount to the hypothesized lump sum but differed on how far back to discount. The plaintiff's expert discounted only to the filing of the complaint, whereas the defendant's expert discounted to the dates of the hypothetical negotiation for each patent.

The court agreed with the plaintiff that discounting to the beginning of the litigation was best. This was the period for which the plaintiff sought damages. Doing so, the court said, compensated the plaintiff for the value of what was taken from it as a result of the defendant's alleged infringement. The defendant expert's opinion on this point was inadmissible.

Parsing plaintiff expert's apportionment. The defendant responded with a series of attacks on the plaintiff expert's apportionment analysis.

1. *Using citation by future patents.* One way to apportion the royalty base, the plaintiff's expert decided, was to consider the number of times a patent was cited as prior art by future patents. The expert said this "forward citation" method was a valuation technique the academic community approved of and some courts have accepted.

As part of this analysis, the expert also assumed a six-patent portfolio consisting of the six patents in suit.

The defendant objected that this treatment did nothing to analyze the value of the infringing features within the accused products. It merely showed the value of each patent in suit relative to the others. Also, it gave no indication of how the market valued the subject patents against other patents that covered the infringing and noninfringing components of the accused products.

The court rebuffed this method. Most problematic, it said, was the expert's failure to tie her analysis to the facts of the case. She failed to explain why this particular technique was an appropriate measure of the value of the subject patents. It was as meaningless as the "25% rule of thumb" and Nash bargaining solution analyses—both approaches the Federal Circuit soundly rejected. "Surely a patent's objective quality cannot be based on the number of times an inventor cites himself in prosecuting related patents," the court stated. It added that pursuant to this method the oldest patent not surprisingly would be the one with the highest number of forward citations. The apportionment at most indicted the relative value of the patents in the abstract, "untethered to any of the facts in this case."

2. *Using totality of features.* The plaintiff's expert also apportioned based on one of the defendant's internal slides that identified 24 functions that ostensibly covered all the features of a suite of security products. The patents in suit "drove" the functionality of about nine of the 24 functions. The expert decided it was appropriate to apportion revenue for each accused product based on the number of functions each patent in suit drove, 24 being the total number of functions. This method, she said, was "highly conservative because not every accused product has 24 features, and yet I apply only 1/24th for each feature to each accused product."

The court likened this approach to the opposing expert's use of lines of infringing code. Neither method was perfect. However, the analysis "reasonably" tied the value the defendant placed on product components to the accused products in the case.

At the same time, the court cautioned that the analysis was still vulnerable in that the plaintiff's expert failed to explain why each of the 24 functions identified in the defendant's presentation should be valued equally. Unless the plaintiff could provide a foundation for her assumption, the court said it would allow the defendant to renew its attack.

3. *Using proposed software license.* The plaintiff's expert also apportioned revenue for one of the defendant's products based on a proposal to license it to original equipment manufacturers.

The defendant pointed out that the product contained noninfringing features. The opposing expert's methodology was unreliable unless there was evidence that the suggested value of the license covered only the infringing features at issue in this case or that the expert apportioned the license fee to cover only the accused features.

The court agreed with the defendant that there was a lack of evidence as to both points, and it excluded this testimony.

Neither expert's reasonable royalty calculation was able to satisfy the apportionment requirements completely and each expert saw parts of her analysis struck down under *Daubert*.

Fox v. CDx Holdings

Citation: 2015 Del. Ch. LEXIS 194
Date of decision: July 28, 2015
Experts: Unknown (Plaintiffs); Grant Thornton, PwC (Defendants)
Judge: Laster
State/Jurisdiction: Delaware
Court: Court of Chancery of Delaware
Type of case: Securities
SIC code: 3829 Measuring and Controlling Devices N.E.C.
NAICS code: 339112 Surgical and Medical Instrument Manufacturing

Chancery Decries Accounting Firm's Compromised Valuation

In several high-profile cases, the Delaware Court of Chancery reprimanded major financial institutions for undertaking "motivated" valuations in connection with merger transactions. But a recent case prompted the court's Vice Chancellor Laster to say the work a major accounting firm had done on a spin/merge transaction "reached a new low." Beholden to the client, the firm's employees were "just copying" another accounting firm's valuation report and calling it their own. When they did their own work, they made inexplicable "fatal errors."

Legal issue. Everything in this complicated case revolved around valuation. Employees who owned stock options in the subject company sued, claiming that members of management, rather than the company's board, determined how much the option holders would receive in connection with a spin/merge transaction and that they intentionally, and to the detriment of the option holders, undervalued certain assets to minimize the controlling stockholders' exposure to corporate tax.

The key defendants were David Halbert, the founder and chairman of the subject company, and Gerald Martino, the company's executive vice president, chief financial officer, and chief operating officer. Martino, the court found, was most deeply involved in crafting the valuations underlying the transaction.

In 2005, Halbert, a successful entrepreneur in the healthcare and information services industries, founded Caris, a company that developed advanced diagnostic and prognostic tools for special illnesses, including cancer. Caris then acquired three other companies:

1. A company known as the "AP business," which focused on anatomic pathology, the diagnosis of human disease through the examination of cells, fluids, and tissues. It was consistently profitable.

2. TargetNow, which profiled genetic and molecular changes specific to a cancer patient's tumor and identified tailored treatments. This business was promising and generated revenue, but no profits.

3. Carisome, which worked on developing blood tests for cancer detection. At the time of the transaction, it was in the developmental stage. Whether it could produce a functioning product was still uncertain, but Halbert and others were optimistic. If Carisome succeeded, it would generate a lot of money; the target market would be in the hundreds of billions.

Halbert owned 70.4% of Caris's fully diluted equity. A private equity fund owned another 26.7% interest, and Caris employees owned most of the remaining 2.9% in the form of stock options.

Working toward zero corporate tax. In the spring of 2011, Caris's board hired an investment bank to explore the sale of the AP business. The aim was to raise money to keep operations at TargetNow and Carisome afloat. The bank recommended using a spin/merge structure to achieve a favorable tax result. The plan was spinning off TargetNow and Carisome (SpinCo.) and subsequently merging what was left of Caris (RetainCo.) with the acquiring entity. (The merged entity was called CDx, which is the name of the defendant entity appearing in litigation documents.) Stockholders could receive the full value for the AP business and only be taxed at the stockholder level. They could use a portion of the proceeds to finance SpinCo.

The success of this strategy hinged on the valuations of TargetNow and Carisome, the Chancery explained. If those entities' fair market value proved to be greater than their tax basis, RetainCo. would be taxed on the difference. Since the buyer of the AP business would also own RetainCo., it would be liable for taxes—an unattractive prospect. On the other hand, if Caris were to show that the value of SpinCo. was lower than the basis, there would be no corporate-level tax due. Martino "made sure to get there," the court said.

In connection with the sales process, the investment bank valued both the AP business and TargetNow but not Carisome. The bank estimated that the AP business was worth between $767 million and $1.18 billion. Also, in the first phases of the sales process, several bidders, including the future buyer, expressed an interest in acquiring both the AP business and TargetNow. At that time, the future buyer proposed to pay $650 million to $700 million for the AP business alone and from $825 million to $900 million for both businesses. The court found that the buyer's bid implied a value of $100 million to $175 million for TargetNow.

Around the same time, Caris employed a big accounting firm (Firm 1) to explore tax issues and get a sense of the value of TargetNow as a going concern. For its estimate, Firm 1 asked Martino what he thought the company was worth. He said between $150 million and $300 million based on projected annual revenue of $70 million and projected EBITDA of $13 million.

Also, the presentation materials Caris gave to interested bidders included projections for TargetNow, which Martino had developed and which the company's board approved. Assuming a linear growth, the forecasts suggested TargetNow's market share could increase from 4.1% in 2011 to 19.4% in 2016. Under an upside scenario, market share could reach as high as 34.5%.

The court noted that, when the plaintiff's expert tried to rely on those optimistic projections when valuing TargetNow for damages purposes, both Martino and Halbert discredited their own forecasts, claiming they provided falsely high numbers to bidders. The court called this a "double-liar problem"; it showed the defendants' willingness to say what might be advantageous in the litigation.

The buyer offered $725 million for RetainCo., making it clear it did not want to assume any tax liability related to SpinCo. As a result, Martino sent an email to Firm 1 instructing the accountants to come up with a transfer tax valuation that ensured zero tax liability. He specified an aggregate value of SpinCo. of about $40 million. He also sent along projections based on falsely low numbers.

Firm 1, the court found, produced a zero corporate-tax valuation that put the worth of TargetNow at $47 million and of Carisome at $15 million. Subsequently, the firm revised this valuation to come closer to the $40 million figure Martino had suggested earlier. Martino was satisfied with the $62 million valuation since it achieved the goal of zero tax liability. Firm 1 informed Caris and the buyer that the valuation was not a fair market valuation of SpinCo., as defined under Revenue Ruling 59-60, but was a Section 482 transfer pricing valuation of the intellectual property of TargetNow and Carisome. As such, it excluded the value of goodwill. Martino and Halbert knew this, the court observed. Use of this valuation to determine the consideration option holders received was one reason why the price was arbitrary and subjective, the court found.

The buyer's tax advisor objected to aspects of the accounting firm's work. For example, it questioned the projections that informed the $62 million valuation and asked why there was no analysis using a transaction involving Clarient, which seemed to be a comparable company, as a data point. In presentations to its board, Caris in fact had identified Clarient as a competitor and it also had made overtures to the company that bought Clarient to market TargetNow. Yet, the court found that Martino told Firm 1 that Clarient was not a comparable company; the firm, in turn, said to the buyer's tax advisor that there were no comparable companies.

Uncomfortable about Firm 1's valuation, the future buyer suggested obtaining a ruling from the IRS on the valuation issues before completing the spinoff. Ultimately, the parties reached a compromise: Caris would provide a second valuation for the separated businesses, TargetNow and Caris, from a different accounting firm (Firm 2).

The board approved the merger, which resulted in the cancellation of all company options. In an announcement to employees, Caris said that, at the time of closing, an option holder would receive a cash amount equal to the per-share value of the company minus the per-share exercise price of the option. The per-share price of the company was between $5.04 and $5.14, a value derived from the sale of the AP business and the value of TargetNow and Carisome. The company claimed that the valuation of TargetNow and Carisome "was based upon a detailed examination of these businesses by two independent and nationally-recognized business valuation firms."

The Chancery found this was not an accurate statement because at the time of the announcement Firm 2 had not yet started work on the second, "independent" valuation. Rather, the range of values for the options was based on an estimate from Martino that was approved by Halbert. Later, after Firm 2 completed its valuation, Martino set the final option payout at $5.07 per share. According to the Chancery, "[t]he fact that Martino could forecast the range of value so precisely shows how deeply he had his hands in the valuation dough."

Not so independent valuation. The court spent extra attention on the valuation work Firm 2 did to back up Firm 1's value determinations. Firm 2 was capable of producing credible valuations for TargetNow and Carisome as going concerns, the court noted. For example, in 2011, it prepared three formal and one draft stock option-related valuations. To do so, it consistently used management projections, the discounted cash flow method, and comparable company analyses. Despite different valuation dates, the inputs were generally consistent and so were the results, the court found.

The valuation determinations also were consistent in another respect, the court observed. They showed that TargetNow and Carisome consistently contributed at least a third of the company's total value.

Moreover, in 2011, Firm 2 performed a formal valuation for Caris for purposes of Accounting Standard Codification 350. It used the same approach for this valuation as it had used for the stock option valuations. It found that TargetNow was worth about $104 million.

But all changed when Martino hired Firm 2 to provide a second, "independent," valuation of TargetNow and Carisome for the spinoff. After meeting with Martino and Firm 1, Firm 2 abandoned its prior methodologies and produced a valuation "so much lower as to be itself suggestive of bad faith," the court found. The evidence showed that the firm's employees believed they were hired to do no more than copy Firm 1's report and claim it as theirs. "And that is predominantly what they did," said the Chancery.

One example of the "copy job" was the valuation of Carisome, the court explained. To make it look as if they did their own valuation, Firm 2 employees asked for costs spent on the company's first failed product. Caris said to exclude $7.587 million in 2010 and $4.036 million in 2011. Using these figures, Firm 2 produced a table that matched a table Firm 1 had included in its earlier valuation report. Only, the inputs Firm 1 had used were markedly different from the ones provided to Firm 2. Caris had told Firm 1 to exclude $13.893 million, not $7.587 million, in 2010 and $12.4 million, not $4.036 million, in 2011. The only possible explanation for the creation of an identical table was that [Firm 2] *"did not prepare its table independently,"* said the court with emphasis. Firm 2 simply copied Firm 1's table.

And, even though Firm 2 had used both the discounted cash flow method and comparable company methods for all of its former valuations, it suddenly relied exclusively on the cost method, claiming it was not possible to accurately forecast the cash flows for Carisome.

The court observed that, when Firm 2 performed its own work on the spinoff valuation, it made grave mistakes. To determine the 2011 revenue figure, employees used the materially lower figure for nine-month trailing revenue rather than 12-month projected revenue. The difference between the wrong and correct figures was over $15.3 million, which meant *"an increase of 39%,"* the court said with emphasis.

The result was a valuation for SpinCo. that was inconsistent with the firm's prior valuation work. It stated the value of TargetNow as $37.1 million and the value of Carisome at $17.6 million. In relation to the deal price, the values represented only 7% of the combined enterprise value for Caris, the court pointed out. It noted that at trial the defendants tried to distance themselves from the valuation, considering it "somewhat flawed."

Firm 1 subsequently submitted a final valuation that assigned a value of $47.23 million to TargetNow's intellectual property and a value of $17.79 million to Carisome's. This was the valuation the company's executives adopted for "book and tax purposes."

Ruling in a nutshell. The court's analysis included the following key points.

1. Probably neither of the defendants intended to harm Caris's employees. The purpose of the valuation exercise was to arrive at a number that would result in zero corporate-level tax for the controlling shareholders, the court said. Once the executives committed themselves to that end, they could not undervalue SpinCo. for tax purposes while valuing it fairly for the option holders. "The option holders were collateral damage," the court said.

2. The stock option plan required the board to determine the fair market value of a share of Caris common stock and adjust options to account for the spinoff. The board failed to do so, leaving the determination to Martino. Halbert signed off on Martino's determination.

3. The valuation determination was not made in good faith and was arbitrary and capricious. Neither Martino nor Halbert believed that TargetNow was worth only $47 million and that Carisome was worth only $17.79 million.

4. Martino manipulated the valuation process. First he pointed Firm 1 to the figure he wanted to achieve to ensure a zero corporate-level tax ($40 million). Then he provided the accountants with reduced forecasts to reach the goal. Finally, rather than leaving Firm 2 to prepare an independent valuation for SpinCo., he directed Firm 1 to instruct Firm 2 as to how to achieve the tax-efficient outcome.

5. Firm 2's report perfectly reflected the flawed process. It was "so egregiously unreasonable as to be essentially inexplicable on any ground other than subjective bad faith," the court said.

6. The question in terms of damages was what the board would have determined to be the fair market value of a share in connection with the merger and taking into account the spinoff. It likely would have retained Firm 2 to prepare a valuation using the methodologies the firm used in prior work, the court said.

7. By the court's calculation, damages to the class of option holders amounted to over $16.26 million.

Freihage v. Freihage

Citation: 2015 Ill. App. Unpub. LEXIS 14
Date of decision: Jan. 7, 2015
Experts: Martin Magida (husband); Ronald Cressman (wife)
Judge: Wright
State/Jurisdiction: Illinois
Court: Appellate Court of Illinois
Type of case: Marital Dissolution
SIC code: 5812 Eating Places
NAICS code: 722513 Limited Service Restaurants

Treatment of Debt Skews Valuation of Franchise Business

A recent divorce case raises interesting issues as to how to value a company owning McDonald's franchises. The dispute featured two experts who were seasoned in franchise valuation, and both performed a discounted cash flow analysis but reached results that were approximately $10 million apart. The trial court's calculation generated its own set of questions with the parties as well as the appeals court.

Divergent views on DCF factors. Over the course of the marriage, the husband bought seven McDonald's restaurants. In the process, he accumulated debt to a bank in the amount of $3.7 million and to a family trust in the amount of $5.8 million. In 2000, the husband created a single-member limited liability company (LLC) that owned the McDonald's franchises. He also was the president and sole shareholder of a management company that operated the franchises.

At divorce, the LLC was the most significant asset and as such fueled the most contention between the spouses. Both parties presented testimony from experts who had deep knowledge of the McDonald's franchise system and who used the discounted cash flow (DCF) analysis to value the company. But the experts disagreed over components, such as the applicable discount rate and sales growth rate. And, although they both allowed that the restaurants required improvements, they disagreed as to whether and how certain rebuilds and reinvestments in the restaurants would take place.

The husband's expert stated that he spent 75% to 80% of his time working with McDonald's operators and franchises and thus far had performed between 50 and 100 valuations of McDonald's restaurants. Moreover, his firm was a member of the National Franchise Consultants and Accountants (NFCA), an organization that had an extensive database on which members could share monthly financial information and compare one firm's clients with stores in the U.S. that showed a similar sales volume. The database included information on 3,400 McDonald's restaurants.

According to the expert, there were two key components to a valuation of the LLC: sales volume and rent. For his calculation, he visited all seven restaurants and reviewed year-end financial statements, an NFCA report, McDonald's "P&L Opportunity Report" for the top 50 stores in the same television market as the LLC's restaurants, and information about possible rebuilds and reinvestments in the LLC's restaurants. He explained that he used the NFCA database, rather than McDonald's opportunity report, to compare the LLC's restaurants with some 200 to 400 McDonald's franchises that had a comparable sales volume. The opportunity report, he said, provided a much smaller pool of comparable restaurants—about 300.

For his DCF analysis, he projected cash flow for 10 years based on a cash flow statement. He said the "standard" discount rate was 20%, but he opted to use a 30% discount rate for one restaurant to account for an "increased risk based on its expected lease expiration in 2016." In projecting future sales, he used a 2% growth rate.

He explained that capital expenditures were an important consideration in valuing the company. He included an average of $20,000 per year to account for routine repairs and equipment replacement in all the restaurants. Based on information he gleaned from a letter from McDonald's, he also included $769,000 in future expenses that would go toward remodeling some of the restaurants over the next five years.

As to financing a rebuild or reinvestment, he explained that McDonald's franchise owners had three choices: (1) they could pay 100% of the cost and receive lower rent costs; (2) they could divide the cost equally; and (3) they could pay one-third of the cost and let McDonald's pay the remaining two-thirds. The husband, the expert said, had a history of paying 100% of the rebuilding costs and indicated to him he would continue to do so. The plan was to rebuild one restaurant in 2014 at a cost of $2.85 million and another in 2016 at a cost of $2.8 million. There was an expectation that the rebuilds would increase sales, the expert said.

Based on all of the data, the husband's expert determined the total value of the restaurants was almost $10 million. Subtracting the cost of reinvestments and "excess liabilities," including the bank debt and the money owed to the family trust, which by the parties' stipulation totaled $9.5 million, the expert arrived at a net value of the LLC of almost $310,000 as of the valuation date.

The wife's expert was equally competent. An experienced CPA and certified valuation analyst, he said that 85% of his business was related to McDonald's. His accounting firm, too, belonged to the NFCA.

For his valuation, he reviewed the LLC's financial statements, franchise and lease agreements, and five-year sales history, and he also visited the restaurants. He said there was information that McDonald's treated the $5.8 million debt to the family trust as equity, not debt, for purposes of determining total business equity. Therefore, he opted to do the same.

For his DCF analysis, he used a 20% discount rate for some, but not all, of the restaurants. He said he had seen discount rates of 19% or 20% for McDonald's restaurants. He decided to apply a 19% discount rate to one restaurant and an 18% discount rate to another because the latter "had a less-than-average sales volume." He explained that a lower sales volume meant that a restaurant ran less of a risk that a competitor would open nearby. Further, he used a 3% sales growth rate based on historical annual sales increases, which were between 2.5% and 3%.

He used the McDonald's opportunity report to compare the LLC's restaurants' historical data to other restaurants in the specific market and region. He said it was not "fair" to compare the LLC to 3,400 restaurants that were located over the U.S., considering the different cost structures that existed in different regions.

Just like the competing expert, he assumed $20,000 in annual reinvestment costs, but he did not factor into his calculation nearly $670,000 for additional reinvestments, calling the reinvestments "speculative." He said he was aware that the husband customarily paid 100% of the rebuilding costs but applied only $1.75 million to cover the costs of two rebuilds that were imminent.

Ultimately, he determined the LLC was worth over $16.1 million, prior to deductions—over $6 million more than the competing expert stated. The wife's expert only allowed for $4.9 million in liabilities, counting the bank debt but not the family trust debt, and concluded the LLC was worth about $11.2 million.

The wife presented additional expert testimony from a financial analyst who had worked for many years for McDonald's. This expert confirmed that, in calculating total business equity for the LLC, McDonald's chose to exclude the debt to the family trust. He explained that this decision was based on information McDonald's received about the trust and which "comforted" McDonald's and caused it to assume there was less of a risk.

Trial court's unaccountable valuation. The trial court acknowledged that both experts were "well qualified" but had "divergent views as to the factors making up the discounted cash flow valuation approach." It said it agreed with each expert on some of the factors. For example, it found the husband expert's use of the NFCA database was "more reasonable as a bench mark" than the wife expert's reliance on the opportunity report. It added that other choices the husband's expert made also were more credible.

Without further explanation, the court stated that the LLC's value was $10.6 million, less debt. It noted the parties' major disagreement over the company's debt treatment and rejected the wife's claim that the $5.8 million from the family trust was a gift to the marriage. There was "clear, convincing, and overwhelming evidence that these were [business] loans," the court found. It concluded the LLC's value "net of debt" was nearly $1.1 million.

Post-trial the wife filed a motion for reconsideration, questioning, among other things, the method the court used to classify debt. The trial judge said: "I can't remember the detail because of all of my notes as far as the calculations.... I thought I was coming to the right conclusion at the time."

The wife next appealed the judgment to the state's appellate court, contending the trial court's valuation of the LLC was error.

The appeals court agreed that the trial court had determined a predebt value of $10.6 million "without articulating its basis for its conclusion." This failure, the appeals court said, "has provided many challenges for the parties, as well as for this court, on appeal." It added that it had spent a significant amount of time to "discover the mathematical formula utilized by the trial court."

Notwithstanding its own efforts and those of appellate counsel, it was unable "to duplicate the right combination of mathematical calculations" to arrive at the exact $10.6 million predebt value.

But the appeals court went on to say that it did not believe the trial court randomly selected the $10.6 million figure as one that was between the lower predebt value of $10 million and the higher value of $16.1 million. Rather, careful consideration of the record suggested the trial court rejected the wife expert's proposition that the $5.8 million debt to the family trust represented business equity. If one were to use the wife expert's predebt value of $16.1 million and subtract $5.8 million, the result would approximate the $10.6 million predebt value, the appeals court observed. From this amount, the trial court may have deducted bank and family trust debt to arrive at a "net of debt" value of $1.1 million, the appeals court surmised. Since there was some evidence that the family trust debt was a loan, it was not error for the trial court to consider this amount debt, it noted. By extension, the trial court's valuation of the LLC was not "against the manifest weight of the evidence," the appeals court concluded and upheld the valuation.

Gallo v. Gallo

Citation: 2015 Ohio App. LEXIS 938
Date of decision: March 17, 2015
Experts: Brian Russell (husband); unknown (wife)
Judge: Klatt
State/Jurisdiction: Ohio
Court: Court of Appeals
Type of case: Marital Dissolution
SIC code: 8011 Offices and Clinics of Doctors of Medicine
NAICS code: 621111 Offices of Physicians (except Mental Health Specialists)

Court Rejects Flat Prohibition Against Double Dipping

Not even two months after the Ohio Court of Appeals issued its decision in *Bohme* on the strength of the double dipping argument, another appellate division published a different—one might say complementary—analysis of the issue and in so doing expressly repudiated the old analytical framework. *Bohme* and *Gallo* reveal an appeals court that hitches the determinations as to property division and spousal support to principles of fairness and equity.

What does 'double dip' mean? The husband was an ocular plastic surgeon who owned one practice and had ownership interests in two surgical centers. The parties stipulated the values of the businesses by using an asset-based approach for the practice and the interest in one of the centers. They valued the interest in the second surgical center, Ohio Valley Medical Center (Ohio Valley), based on the 2013 share price. Ohio Valley was a closely held corporation.

But the parties were unable to agree on the amount of income attributable to either spouse for spousal and child support purposes.

The trial court accepted the parties' stipulations for its division of property. It then determined that the husband's annual income was $700,000, including the distributions he received from Ohio Valley, and ordered him to pay $12,000 in spousal support for 66 months and to pay over $2,600 in child support.

The husband appealed, alleging the trial court's ruling conflicted with the Court of Appeals' 2008 decision in *Heller v. Heller.* Specifically, the trial court double dipped by valuing the marital interest in Ohio Valley based on future profits and then included those same profits in calculating his income for the purpose of spousal and child support.

In *Heller,* the appeals court interpreted the statutory provisions concerning marital distribution and spousal support to require it to consider "the potential 'double dip'" where the future income stream figures both into the valuation of the marital asset and into determining a spouse's ability to pay spousal support.

But the court in *Heller* went further: "Trial courts may treat a spouse's future business profits either as a marital asset subject to division, or as a stream of income for spousal support purposes, but not both." *See Heller v. Heller,* 2008 Ohio App. LEXIS 2788 (*Heller I*) (June 30, 2008) (available at *BVLaw*).

In the instant case, the Court of Appeals (the same appellate division as the one that decided *Heller*) in essence posed and answered two questions: One, did a double dip occur? And, two, does the law prohibit it, as *Heller* said it did?

As to the first issue, the Court of Appeals found *Heller* got it wrong when it defined "double dipping" as "the double counting of a marital asset, once in the property division and again in the [spousal support] award." In contrast, the appeals court in the instant case emphasized that double counting occurred only "when a court twice counts a *future income stream*—once in valuing the marital asset and once in deciding the economically superior spouse's ability to pay spousal support." For clarity's sake, it added: "It is the future income stream, not the marital asset, that is the subject of the doubling in the double dip.

The appeals court went on to say that it would be a mistake to equate the marital asset—the interest in the business—with the income the business generates. "[A] business and its income are separate entities, with the income merely serving as a tool for valuing the business."

The premise for a double dip claim, therefore, is that the asset was valued based on its future income stream, by way of a discounted cash flow analysis or a capitalization of earnings analysis, the court explained. By extension, if the asset is valued under a different approach, there is no double dip argument. Here, two of the husband's ownership interests were valued using an asset-based approach and were not at issue in the appeal, the court clarified.

In terms of the Ohio Valley interest, the appeals court found the record as to the exact valuation methodology wanting. But from some of the expert testimony it deduced that the valuation was based on the capitalization of earnings method, "which entailed dividing Ohio Valley's prior annual earnings by a 33 percent rate of return, or capitalization rate." The resulting value was multiplied by the husband's percentage of ownership to generate the "2013 share price" for his shares.

This approach, the Court of Appeals said, "opens the door to possible double dipping." It went further. Since the trial court in this case also considered the husband's income from Ohio Valley in setting spousal support, double dipping in fact occurred.

***Heller* violates statute.** As to the second issue, the Court of Appeals found several reasons to back away from *Heller.* For one, *Heller* failed to consider a crucial statutory provision, R.C. 3105.18(C)(1)(a), which expressly requires a court determining spousal support to consider all sources of income, including income derived from a marital asset divided in the property distribution. This provision, the Court of Appeals stated, "precludes us from adopting an outright prohibition of double dipping. To the extent that *Heller* did that, we must overrule *Heller.*"

Also, as the court in the instant case pointed out, in subsequent appeals (there were three in all), the court in *Heller* retreated from its earlier position by stating that the 2008 decision did not contain any "language … to suggest … a flat prohibition against double dipping applicable to every income-producing event." *See Heller v. Heller,* 2010 Ohio App. LEXIS 5136 (Dec. 14, 2010) (*Heller II*) (available at *BVLaw*).

And the Court of Appeals in the instant case said *Heller I* failed to take into account precedent from other appellate districts that allowed the consideration of pension income for spousal support purposes when the trial court already had valued and divided the pension as a marital asset.

A question of fairness and equity. Ultimately, the mandate for trial courts presiding over divorce proceedings was to craft a fair and equitable resolution, the Court of Appeals found. "Thus, in the interest of equity, trial courts should factor the impact of double dipping into their property division and spousal support decisions." True, the statute allows double dipping. But to "ameliorate the inequity inherent in double dipping," a trial court may decide to divide the income-producing asset at issue between the parties, "thus ensuring that each spouse will share in advantages and disadvantages associated with that asset," the appeals court suggested. Other times, the disparity in income between the parties may "override the unfairness in double dipping," the appeals court noted. Whether to remedy the double dip, and, if so, how, was left to the discretion of the trial court, the appeals court added.

In this case, the appeals court remanded, but only because it found the trial court had not considered the double dip in its analysis. This did not mean, however, that the trial court necessarily had to change its property division or spousal support award. The appeals court "merely direct[ed] the trial court to expand its considerations of those issues to include the effect of the double dip."

No double dip in child support. The appeals dismissed the husband's related argument that there was double dipping in regard to the calculation of his child support obligation. "Unlike a spouse, a child receives nothing in the property division," the court explained. Therefore, the trial court only "dips" once when it computes a parent's income for the purpose of setting child support, the appeals court concluded.

Estate of Giustina v. Commissioner

Citation: 2014 U.S. App. LEXIS 22961
Date of decision: Dec. 5, 2014
Experts: Robert Reilly (estate/petitioner); John Thomson (IRS/respondent)
Judge: Goodwin
State/Jurisdiction: Federal
Court: United States Court of Appeals for 9th Circuit
Type of case: Federal Taxation
SIC code: 0811 Timber Tracts
NAICS code: 11311 Timber Tract Operations

9th Circuit Calls Tax Court Out Over 'Imaginary Scenarios'

Late in 2014, the 9th Circuit issued a terse, but significant, ruling in an estate tax case involving an Oregon family holding considerable timber assets by way of a limited partnership. The appeals court faulted the Tax Court for several missteps in arriving at its valuation, having to do with the court's use of the net asset value approach and its company-specific risk premium rate.

Recap. The decedent owned a minority interest in a family-owned limited partnership (LP) that was in operation for 15 years and held large tracts of local timberland. The Internal Revenue Service assessed a deficiency of $12.66 million, which was nearly equal to the value the estate stated in its estate tax filing, and an accuracy-related penalty. The estate petitioned the U.S. Tax Court for a review. At trial, the parties' positions had come closer together because the estate's new appraiser proposed a slightly higher value and the IRS's expert a slightly lower value.

The Tax Court accepted only two methods to value the LP interest in this case: discounted cash flow (DCF) and net asset value (NAV). The former accounted for how much the partnership could be expected to earn if it continued timberland operations, and the latter valued the assets as if liquidated. The experts agreed the partnership's timber assets were worth $143 million, allowing for a 40% discount related to expected delays in selling the large tracts. However, they weighted the values from the two approaches differently and disagreed on assumptions inherent in the cash flow approach.

As for the DCF, the court not only rejected the IRS expert's analysis, but also adjusted components of the estate expert's valuation. For one, it lowered the latter's 3.5% company-specific risk premium, noting that, even though the partnership's assets lacked diversity and geographic dispersion, investors could minimize this unique risk by diversifying the portfolio of assets. Therefore, a 1.75% premium was adequate. The court also found that, pursuant to *Gross v. Commissioner*, the estate's expert improperly tax affected his annual cash flow values by 25%. And the court reduced the expert's proposed 35% discount for lack of marketability to 25% in accordance with the rate the IRS expert applied.

The court gave a 75% weighting to the DCF-derived value, which, it found, reflected the probability that the partnership would continue. But it also noted that an asset sale would reap considerably more than the current cash flow generated. The court recognized that an acquirer of the decedent's interest could only force the sale of the partnership by creating a two-thirds majority voting block with other members and that it was uncertain how many partners would favor an asset sale. But it said there was authority that allowed for some degree of speculation about the future composition of management in valuation and consequently assigned a 25% weight to the result from the NAV. It concluded the decedent's interest was worth $27.45 million. (An in-depth discussion of *Estate of Giustina v. Commissioner,* 2011 Tax Ct. Memo LEXIS 141, is available at *BVLaw* (www.bvlibary.com)).

Contradictory assumptions. In its appeal to the 9th Circuit Court of Appeals, the estate claimed there were multiple errors in the Tax Court's valuation, which stated a value that was close to $15 million higher than the estate's value appearing in Form 706.

The 9th Circuit sided with the estate on most points.

1. *NAV weight.* According to the appeals court, the Tax Court's finding that there was a 25% likelihood of liquidation of the partnership conflicted with the evidence in the record. This was a longtime partnership, and "no limited partner ever asked or ever discussed the sale of an interest," said the 9th Circuit. For liquidation to occur, one had to assume that a hypothetical buyer would: (1) "somehow" obtain admission as a limited partner from the general partners to dissolve the partnership; (2) seek to dissolve the partnership or get rid of the general partners who just approved the buyer's admission to the partnership; and (3) succeed in persuading at least two other limited partners to go along with the buyer's plan. Alternatively, and just as unlikely, the appeals court said, one had to assume that the existing limited partners who owned two-thirds of the partnership would suddenly seek dissolution.

According to the 9th Circuit, the Tax Court created "imaginary scenarios" as to the potential buyer and the buyer's willingness to wait, without receiving a return on the investment, as well as what the buyer would be able to arrange with the existing partners. For this reason alone, the 9th Circuit remanded for a revaluation based on the partnership's value as a going concern.

But there was more. The appeals court also found the Tax Court erred when it halved the estate expert's proposed company-specific risk premium. Although diversification of assets was an accepted way to reduce company-specific risk, the reviewing court said, the Tax Court did not seem to take into account how much wealth a potential buyer would need to affect diversification.

Court leaves tax affecting untouched. On several points, the 9th Circuit disagreed with the estate. As for tax affecting, it pointed out that the estate admitted that "tax-affecting is ... an unsettled matter of law." Therefore, it was not clear that the Tax Court erred in using a pretax rather than a post-tax method, the 9th Circuit stated.

As for the DLOM rate, the estate's expert proffered a 35% rate but at trial allowed that discounts typically range between 25% and 35%. Therefore, the Tax Court's 25% DLOM was not clear error.

For all of these reasons, the 9th Circuit remanded for recalculation of the valuation.

Glickenhaus & Co. v. Household International, Inc.

Citation: 2015 U.S. App. LEXIS 8424
Date of decision: May 21, 2015
Experts: Daniel Fischel (plaintiffs); unknown (defendants)
Judge: Sykes
State/Jurisdiction: Federal
Court: United States Court of Appeals for the 7th Circuit
Type of case: Securities
SIC code: 6141 Personal Credit Institutions
NAICS code: 522291 Consumer Lending

7th Circuit Proposes Solution for Loss Causation Conundrum

An unusual securities fraud case spurred a challenge from the defendants to the loss causation model the plaintiffs' high-caliber expert successfully presented to the jury. The 7th Circuit found the model insufficiently accounted for certain non-fraud-related information but declined to throw out the verdict altogether. Instead, it ordered a retrial in accordance with its burden-shifting approach.

Rare case going to trial. Few securities-fraud class actions make it to trial. This case not only went to trial, but also produced a very satisfactory judgment for the plaintiffs.

The defendants (a company and its chief executives) were in the consumer lending business. In the late 1990s, they engaged in predatory lending practices to achieve a higher stock price. When more of the company's loans became delinquent, they used improper accounting techniques to mask the reality. The truth came to light over a one-year period, starting with a lawsuit from the State of California over predatory lending at the end of 2001. Eventually, other states joined the litigation. In 2002, the defendants agreed to settle the multistate litigation for $484 million.

In 2002, the plaintiffs sued under Section 10(b) of the Securities Exchange Act and Rule 10b-5. They alleged the defendants had misrepresented the company's lending practices, delinquency rates, and earnings from credit-card agreements. The parties stipulated to class certification. The jurors determined that, of 40 potential misrepresentations, 17 statements were "actionable" because they were false or misleading, material, and caused loss. With the help of expert testimony, the jurors also determined how much the company stock was overpriced owing to the misrepresentations and arrived at a $2.46 billion judgment for the plaintiffs.

The district court denied the defendants' post-trial challenge and entered final judgment. The defendants appealed the outcome at the 7th Circuit Court of Appeals.

Two loss causation models. A critical element of a securities fraud claim is loss causation. Under the controlling U.S. Supreme Court case, the plaintiffs must show that they bought the stock at an "inflated" price, meaning at a price higher than it would have been without the false statements, and that the stock price declined once the market learned of the deception. See *Dura Pharmaceuticals Inc. v. Broudo*, 544 U.S. 336 (2005) (available at *BVLaw*). As the 7th Circuit explained: "A plaintiff's causal losses are measured by the amount the share price was inflated when he bought the stock minus the amount it was inflated when he sold it."

Calculating how much stock price inflation a false statement causes is difficult, the Court of Appeals observed at the outset of its discussion. The determination requires "sophisticated expert testimony," the court went on to say. Here, the plaintiffs were able to hire "one of the best in the field." In fact, the defendants acknowledged the expert's stellar reputation and had tried to hire him as well, but they were too late, the court noted. The defendants focused their criticism on the expert's methodology.

1. *Specific-disclosure model.* At trial, the plaintiff's expert had offered two loss causation models. The "specific disclosure model" was the simpler of the two. First, the expert identified each major disclosure event and then measured the disclosure's effect on the stock price on that specific day. To account for the fact that market or industry trends in part might have been responsible for the decline in price, the expert used a regression analysis to generate a model that predicted the movement of the company stock based on the movements in the S&P 500 and the S&P Financials Index. He calculated the effect of a disclosure event as the actual return on the day of the disclosure minus the predicted return (based on the regression model and the broader market returns that day). The amount of inflation in the stock price on any given day was the sum of the effects of all subsequent disclosures of prior false statements.

In this case, the net effect of the 14 disclosure events was a decline of $7.97 in the stock price, the expert found.

2. *Leakage model.* The second economic model was the "leakage model." It accounted for the fact that some of the information in a major disclosure often leaks out to participants in the market before it is made public. Since the specific-disclosure model focuses only on the price changes on the identified disclosure days, it fails to measure the effect of a more gradual exposure of the fraud. As a consequence, it may understate the effect of the truth on price and the amount the stock was overpriced before the truth became public.

The expert's leakage model tried to capture every difference between the stock's predicted returns and the stock's actual returns during the disclosure period. Based on this model, the total sum of the residual returns was the effect of the disclosures. The amount the stock was overpriced on any given day was the sum of all subsequent residual returns. The expert determined that the total sum of the residual returns during the class period was $23.94, which, he explained, represented a ceiling.

As the expert conceded in trial testimony, the leakage model assumed that movement in the stock price was attributable to the fraud-related disclosures. It did not account for company-specific information unrelated to the corrective disclosures. But he said that he had looked carefully for company-specific factors that were unrelated to the fraud and might explain the stock decline. He found there were disclosures that "dealt with something other [than that which] was fraud related." But their effects—some positive, some negative—cancelled each other out.

The plaintiffs also produced emails from the defendant company's executives that attributed the entire stock price decline to fraud-related disclosures. And they showed that some market analysts focused primarily on the information in the disclosures.

The jury adopted and applied the expert's leakage model for its damages determination.

Expert's testimony too general. The defendants' principal claim on appeal was that the plaintiffs failed to prove loss causation. Specifically, the leakage model that underlay the jury's verdict failed to consider firm-specific, nonfraud factors that could have had an impact on the stock price. They claimed that several law review articles that have dealt with financial fraud damages in securities class actions suggest that "to be legally sufficient, *any* loss-causation model must *itself* account for, and perfectly exclude, any firm-specific, nonfraud related factors that may have contributed to the decline in stock price" (emphasis in original). This argument was supported by an amicus brief from the Securities Industry and Finance Markets Association, an advocacy group for the financial industry.

The 7th Circuit pointed out that the plaintiff expert's regression analysis ensured that both of his models accounted for market and industry factors as well as general trends in the economy but not for the effect of firm-specific, non-fraud-related information. Nevertheless, the court was reluctant to accept the defendants' proposed standard, saying it likely would doom the leakage model as a way to quantify loss causation. On the other hand, the court noted that simply allowing an expert to make a conclusory statement that there was no firm-specific, nonfraud information that affected the stock price would make it too easy for plaintiffs to circumvent the loss causation principles the Supreme Court set forth in *Dura.*

There was a middle ground, the 7th Circuit said.

> If the plaintiffs' expert testifies that no firm-specific, nonfraud related information contributed to the decline in stock price during the relevant time period and explains in nonconclusory terms the basis for this opinion, then it's reasonable to expect the defendants to shoulder the burden of identifying some significant, firm-specific, nonfraud related information that could have affected the stock price. If they can't, then the leakage model can go to the jury; if they can, then the burden shifts back to the plaintiffs to account for that specific information or provide a loss-causation model that doesn't suffer from the same problem, like the specific-disclosure model.

The court added that one way to take care of the issue was to exclude from the model's calculation any days on which the defendants say a release of significant, firm-specific, non-fraud-related information occurred.

The court said here the prevailing loss causation model did not deal with this type of information at all and the expert's statements that any such information was inconsequential were too general to be legally sufficient. In a footnote, the 7th Circuit acknowledged that in this case the plaintiffs in fact submitted a specific-disclosure model to the jury, which the jury disregarded in favor of the leakage model. But, said the court, if, on the day of a specific disclosure there, in effect, was negative firm-specific information that was not related to the fraud, the specific-disclosure model might suffer from the same weakness as the leakage model.

The Court of Appeal's remanded for a new trial on loss causation in accordance with its instructions.

In re Groupon Securities Litigation

Citation: 2015 U.S. Dist. LEXIS 27334
Date of decision: March 5, 2015
Experts: Steven P. Feinstein (plaintiffs/investors); Dr. Paul A. Gompers (defendants/company)
Judge: Rowland
State/Jurisdiction: Federal/Illinois
Court: United States District Court
Type of case: Securities
SIC code: 7319 Advertising Services N.E.C.
NAICS code: 541890 Other Services Related to Advertising

Fraud Litigation Highlights Dispute Over 'Market Efficiency'

In the *Groupon* securities fraud lawsuit, the defendants launched a *Daubert* attack against the investors' financial expert. His testimony—particularly his event study—was unreliable, they contended, because the expert failed to use an objective scientific approach to show that Groupon traded in an efficient market during the relevant period. Market efficiency is a critical element in establishing injury in securities litigation.

Bad deal. Groupon, the deal-of-the-day company, went public in November 2011. Investors subsequently sued the company, alleging it made false statements in its initial public offering (IPO) registration statement as well as in later filings with the U.S. Securities and Exchange Commission and in oral statements by some of the individual defendants. In September 2014, the U.S. district court (N.D. Ill.) certified both a Securities Act class and an Exchange Act subclass. The latter class was the subject of this proceeding.

The Exchange Act subclass consisted of all persons who purchased Groupon stock between Feb. 9, 2012, and including March 30, 2012.

The investors relied on expert testimony to perform a market efficiency analysis under the applicable legal principles. The defendants retained an expert who contended that the rivaling expert's opinion was based on an incomplete and flawed analysis and as such inadmissible under *Daubert*.

Presumption of reliance. Under Section 10(b) of the Exchange Act and Rule 10b-5, it is a violation to make a material misstatement or omit material information in connection with the trading of a security. Reliance on the misrepresentation is one of the key elements of the case. Under the fraud-on-the-market theory, plaintiffs need not prove direct reliance on the defendant's misrepresentation to their detriment but may invoke a rebuttable presumption that they relied on the integrity and informational efficiency of the market when making trading decisions. The underlying idea—increasingly under attack by economists—is that the market price of a company's stock reflects all relevant public information about the company. By extension, falsehoods compromise the integrity of the market and the resulting loss to the investor is attributable to the fraud. In upholding the presumption of reliance, the Supreme Court last year noted: "That the price of a stock may be inaccurate does not detract from the fact that false statements affect it, and cause loss," which is all the existing law requires the plaintiff to show. See *Halliburton Co. v. Erica P. John Fund, Inc.*, 134 S.Ct. 2398 (2014).

To determine whether a stock trades in an efficient market, experts consider the *Cammer* factors (based on a New Jersey district court decision). Both experts in this case agreed that this test was the way to assess market efficiency here.

The first factor requires consideration of the average weekly trading volume during the class period. Here, the investors' expert observed that on average 2.3 million shares traded daily during the relevant period with 1.8% of outstanding shares turned over weekly. This was evidence of market efficiency, the investors' expert concluded.

Factor 2 considers the number of security analysts who follow and report on the stock during the class period. The expert found that 105 buy-side major institutions were investing in Groupon stock and 17 sell-side analysts were covering the stock. This coverage also pointed to market efficiency.

Factor 3 considers the number of market makers. The investors' expert said that, since Groupon was listed on the Nasdaq exchange, the market for Groupon shares was "presumptively efficient."

The defendants' expert did not contest these conclusions.

Factor 4 looks to whether the company is eligible for S-3 registration. The requirements are a $75 million market capitalization and having filed reports with the Securities and Exchange Commission for 12 consecutive months. The investors' expert noted that Groupon, as a new company, did not meet the 12-month minimum period requirement. However, he said it easily met the first requirement. Assuming a stock float of 302 million shares (including shares subject to an underwriter lockup provision), he calculated a market capitalization of between $5.05 billion and $6.39 billion.

The defendants' expert disagreed with the stock float figure, claiming the number of shares available for trading during the subclass period was only 40.25 million. On cross-examination, the investors' expert agreed and reduced the market capitalization figure to $800 million.

The defendants claimed that this mistake cast doubt on the investors' expert's entire market efficiency analysis. The court disagreed, finding the mistake was not critical since by all accounts this factor was not met.

Attack on event study. The defendants' major critique related to the fifth *Cammer* factor, which requires the investors to show a cause-and-effect relationship between unexpected corporate events or financial releases and movements in the stock price. Experts typically use an event study to test the relationship.

Here, the investors' expert did a regression analysis to determine whether stock movements were statistically significant in response to new information. He said he looked for "big news days" during the relevant period by identifying significant, unexpected earnings-related news. He explained that "seminal articles in the literature" supported the use of such dates. He concluded that only two dates met his objective criteria. Although that number was "on the low side," he said it was not uncommon for a class period that was only seven weeks. The first date was Feb. 8, 2012. After that day's trading, Groupon reported an earnings loss when market analysts had expected a profit announcement. The following day (the first day of the class period), the company's stock fell by 15%. The second "big news day" was March 30, 2012 (the last day of the class period). At that time, Groupon disclosed, after the close of trading, that it had overstated its fourth-quarter 2011 earnings. On the first trading day following the announcement, the company's stock fell by 19%.

There was no earnings-related news of similar importance during the class period, the expert noted. His regression analysis determined that the relationship between the date and stock movement in both cases was highly significant—both times exceeding the 95% confidence level that generally serves as a threshold for statistical significance.

Moreover, he used a one-year period to control for standard volatility—from the time of the IPO in November 2011 through November 2012. He pointed out, however, that changing the control period would not affect the results because "[t]he event date returns were so big in absolute magnitude, the drops [in stock prices] were so large, that it wouldn't make any difference whatsoever among any reasonable choice of control periods you picked."

The investors' expert concluded that the empirical data confirmed a cause-and-effect relationship existed, and he concluded that Groupon's stock traded in an efficient market during the class period.

The defendants' expert found fatal flaws in the event study, calling it unreliable and inadmissible under *Daubert*.

1. *Problematic selection of 'big news days.'* The defendants' expert contended the use of only two news days was "subjective," betraying the opposing expert's knowledge of the class period before he began his study. Further, the investors' expert should have included two other news days in his study: one representing an announcement that the company had reached record levels of mobile use and a second day regarding an announcement by U.K. regulators of potential actions against Groupon's advertising claims.

The investors' expert emphatically rejected the allegation, saying that he had preselected objective criteria—earnings surprises—before searching for dates. There was no denying that the empirical data showed a cause-and-effect relationship between unexpected earnings reports and the response of the stock price, he maintained.

The court found the investors' expert first selected the news dates based on objective criteria and only then studied their effect on price. Also, the two additional dates the defendants' expert proposed did not meet the objective criteria—unexpected earnings-related news—and, therefore, were irrelevant to the analysis.

2. *Confounding information.* The defendants' expert argued that some experts looked at the February 8 earnings report in a positive light. Their response, therefore, contradicted the investors' expert's claim that the earnings report was unexpected. Failure to consider this confounding information raised doubt about the existence of an efficient price reaction to information released.

The court agreed with the investors' expert that simply because a few analysts decided to put a positive spin on the earnings news did not mean that there was confounding information nor did it change the fact that earnings were significantly below the results the market expected.

3. *Absence of news.* The defendants' expert claimed the investors' expert should have considered whether there were stock price changes even in the absence of news. For example, although there was no news on Feb. 13, 2012, Groupon's stock that day dropped by 7.8%.

The investors' expert countered that looking at stock price movement first and then trying to find news with which to explain the movement violated all the rules of an event study and all scientific principles. Also, he said, the February 13 stock drop was irrelevant without a regression analysis. The decline could have been a result of the overall stock market or the sector in which Groupon operated.

The court sided with the investors' expert. The two news days he identified resulted in statistically significant price reactions and, "arguably, only one non-news date included a sizeable price change."

4. *Control period.* The defendants' expert argued that the one-year control period failed to represent normal Groupon stock price movement and failed to show how much of the movement is driven by the market and how much by the industry. He said that the period after an IPO was not a normal trading period, but a "quiet period when the underwriting analyst can't issue reports."

Moreover, he objected to the investors' expert's use of dummy variables in the control period after March 30, 2012. Although he conceded that using dummy variables was appropriate, he said it had to be done objectively. Here, the use of at least one dummy variable, on May 14, 2012, seemed to be "backward looking."

In terms of the control period, the investors' expert agreed that the authoritative literature suggested excluding the day after the IPO, which he said he had one. But even excluding a longer quiet period in this case would not have affected the result, he maintained.

He explained that he used dummy variables for five days during the control period to control for potentially abnormal returns related to earnings reports. He rationalized the use of the May 14 dummy variable by noting this was an atypical trading day and, what's more, the news media at that time described the day as atypical.

The court found there was no excessive use of dummy variables in this case. Further, the investors' expert used dummy variables based on an objective approach, that is, for all earnings-related trading days during the control period.

5. *Short-selling constraints.* The defendants' expert also claimed that the opposing expert failed to account for the high lending fee on shorting Groupon stocks, which left the market constrained. According to the defendants' expert, "if short selling is constrained then people with negative views of a stock can't trade, so a stock price might react too much to positive information ... [or] it may under react to negative views." Short-selling constraints interfered with market efficiency, he observed.

The investors' expert agreed with that statement but said he found that selling Groupon stock was possible, that there was an active market for selling the stock, and that there was no regulatory constraint or short-selling ban.

The court found there was no evidence to suggest that the increased cost of selling short affected the market. It pointed out that the defendants' expert admitted on cross-examination that during the class period millions of Groupon shares shorted every day, that short interest grew during the subclass period, that traders were allowed to bet against the company in the options market, and that the defendants did not identify traders who were unable to short Groupon stock.

In sum, the court found ample evidence that the investors' expert's event study met the *Daubert* requirements. The expert's testimony was "clear and credible," the court said. "He correctly analyzed 'market efficiency' from the perspective of whether unexpected information quickly affected Groupon stock price—not whether the price of Groupon stock accurately reflected *all* information," the court emphasized.

Although the defendants' expert was "clearly an expert in efficient capital markets," he failed to understand that the law did not require a *perfectly* efficient market to show fraud on the market. Debates "about the degree to which the market price ... reflects public information about the company" are "largely besides the point" in terms of determining market efficiency under legal precedent.

For all of these reasons, the court admitted the investors' expert's market efficiency analysis.

Guardian Energy, LLC v. County of Waseca

Citation: 2015 Minn. LEXIS 437
Date of decision: Aug. 12, 2015
Experts: Robert Strachota (company/relator); Clay Dodd (county/respondent)
Judge: Wright
State/Jurisdiction: Minnesota
Court: Supreme Court
Type of case: State Taxation
SIC code: 2869 Industrial Organic Chemicals, N.E.C.
NAICS code: 325199 All Other Basic Organic Chemical Manufacturing

Obsolescence Analysis Kills Tax Court's Property Valuation

The owner of a special purpose property challenged the state tax court's valuation at the Minnesota Supreme Court triggering a noteworthy discussion of how to measure external (economic) obsolescence. Although this is a difficult task even for experienced appraisers, the tax court rejected the approaches and reduction rates the parties' experts proposed and developed its own methodology. Its approach did not hold up under the high court's careful scrutiny. As a consequence, neither did its valuation of the facility.

Tax court uses 'special purpose property' designation. In 2009, Guardian Energy, a joint venture of several Midwestern ethanol facilities, bought a nearly completed ethanol producing plant for $92 million after the former owners filed for bankruptcy. Operations under Guardian Energy began in fall 2009. The facility was on 141 acres and included an industrial complex of buildings, tanks, distillation columns, wells, and septic systems, rail spur, and other land improvements.

The county's assessor provided market values for years 2009, 2010, and 2011, which Guardian Energy first challenged in tax court. At the pretrial stage, the question arose whether 27 tanks at the plant qualified as taxable real property within the meaning of the applicable statute. The tax court found they did and then held trial to determine the facility's fair market value. The company and the county presented testimony from expert appraisers.

For purposes of valuation, the tax court designated the ethanol facility a "special purpose property." Given the plant's "unique function or design," it was not likely to be sold on the market and also did not lend itself to different use in a way that was "economically feasible or practical." The parties agreed with this characterization.

Tax court opts for cost approach. Under the applicable statute, "real property" typically is assessed at its "market value"; this is "the price which could be obtained at a private sale or an auction sale," assuming there was an arm's-length transaction. To determine market value, appraisers typically rely on three approaches: the sales comparison approach, the cost approach, and the income approach.

Here, the company's appraiser used all three approaches. The county's appraiser disregarded the income approach, considered the sales-comparison approach, and ultimately relied foremost on the cost approach.

The tax court rejected the sales approach, finding there were no comparable transactions. The company's expert used sales that lacked critical data, took place within the context of bankruptcy, or were part of a stock-purchase transaction, the tax court found. For similar reasons, it rejected the county's sales analysis. It also rebuffed the company's income approach. (On this point, the state Supreme Court opinion only says that the reasons "were not at issue in this appeal.") The tax court concluded that the cost approach was the most appropriate method to value the subject plant.

Under the cost approach, it considered the value of the land, plus the replacement cost of the improvements to the land (replacement cost new (RCN)), and deductions owing to depreciation based on external obsolescence. Put differently, "the appraiser determines the current cost of constructing existing improvements on the property, subtracts depreciation to determine the current value of the improvements, and then adds the value of the land to determine the market value."

Here, the tax court's land value determination was not in dispute. It calculated $8,500 per acre for 2009 and 2010 and $9,000 per acre for 2011.

The court conducted its own RCN analysis but in so doing noted that the estimates the county's expert proposed were more convincing than those of the company's expert. Specifically, it found that, as of January 2009, the RCN for the real property was about $41.8 million. The company's estimate was $34.2 million, and the county's estimated RCN was $48.3 million.

Tax court rejects depreciation testimony. The component that caused the most controversy and prompted the company's appeal to the state Supreme Court was the tax court's depreciation analysis, specifically its economic obsolescence calculation. (Of the three forms of depreciation—physical depreciation, functional obsolescence, and external (economic) obsolescence—only the latter was at issue in the case.)

External obsolescence is "the measurement of a property's loss in value as a result of factors beyond the physical boundaries of the property and beyond the owner's control." A leading authority on the subject notes that it "often relates to the business enterprise that operates as the special-purpose property," where a change in industry conditions might result in a reduction in revenue, profit margin, or return on investment. See Robert F. Reilly, "Functional and Economic Obsolescence Procedures in Valuing Industrial Property," *J. Multistate Tax'n & Incentives,* September 2012.

Company expert. Here, both experts agreed that, during the three valuation years, the facility incurred losses as a result of "prevailing negative industry conditions." At trial, the company's expert proposed a 33.3% reduction for each of the three years based on: (1) a 40% decline in commercial market values generally; and (2) an industrywide drop in the profit margin of ethanol.

He said his calculation relied in "significant measure" on industrywide decreases in the profit margin on one gallon of ethanol as a result of overcapacity, lower demand, and the increased price of corn, the main feedstock for producing ethanol fuel. He explained that, when the plant was under construction in 2007 and 2008, forecasts pegged the nationwide profit margin of ethanol at $1 per gallon. But between 2008 and 2011, the actual margin dropped to $0.46. But at trial the company conceded that its profit margins "averaged $.666 per gallon across 2010 and 2011."

County expert. The county's expert initially proposed a decrease in reductions due to external obsolescence from 45% in 2009 to 35% in 2010 and 25% in 2011. He said he based his calculations on four transactions involving ethanol plants; all of them were distressed sales by mortgagees who had taken back idling plants. He compared the price paid per gallon of capacity to the cost of construction. In his calculation, he also considered overcapacity and deteriorating profit margins, he said. He noted that in 2010 and 2011 sales of ethanol plants "clearly show[ed] an upward trend in prices after early-to-mid 2009."

Post-trial, the county proposed a different way of measuring external obsolescence, suggesting the court use industrywide plant utilization rates. Data showed that in 2009 the utilization rate was 89% but that it increased to 94.5% in 2010 and 99.5% in 2011. As a result, the county lowered its obsolescence rates to 11%, 5.5%, and 0.5% for the three years at issue. The tax court did not address this revised analysis in its findings.

Tax court. At the outset of its obsolescence analysis, the tax court emphasized that, under the law, the company had to show the cause of the claimed obsolescence; it had to quantify the obsolescence; and it had to show that the cause of the obsolescence "*actually affects* the subject property."

The tax court found the company failed to tie the claimed industrywide trends to its facility and did not establish that the value of "*this particular plant* declined simply because the market value of other commercial properties declined." It also found that an increase in corn prices leading to a reduction in the profit margin should not factor into the calculation for external obsolescence. And it said it was inappropriate to use the price per gallon of ethanol to measure external obsolescence because the price was a function of the "machinery and equipment," which was not part of the taxable real estate.

The tax court likewise rejected the county's initial comparable transactions approach, saying it failed to consider the machinery and equipment included in the sales and differences in market conditions, location, and quality of improvements.

Instead, the tax court decided to quantify external obsolescence by looking to total ethanol production capacity in the United States. Using data from the reports of both experts, it compared demand in the U.S. with the reported ethanol production capacity in the U.S. for each of the three years. The data suggested that, in 2009, there was an 84% ethanol production capacity; in 2010, the rate was 92%, leaving 16% and 8% unused for those two years. There was no evidence of unused production capacity in 2011. The tax court decided that, because nothing indicated that the company's unused production capacity was different from that of the industry as a whole, the applicable reduction rates for obsolescence in this case were: 16%, 8%, and 0%.

Year	Company Reduction for Obsolescence	County Reduction for Obsolescence	Tax Court Reduction for Obsolescence
2009	33.3%	45.0%	16.8%
2010	33.3%	35.0%	8.0%
2011	33.3%	25.0%	0.0%

The tax court's external obsolescence calculations were of most consequence to the taxpayer. As the state Supreme Court subsequently pointed out, just by applying a 0% reduction for the year 2011, in contrast to the company's $11.1 million and the county's $5.8 million determinations, the tax court added millions of dollars in assessed tax value.

In effect, of the four valuations in play, the tax court's valuations of the facility consistently were the highest:

Year	County Assessor	Company's Expert at Trial	County's Expert at Trial	Trial Order
2009	$24,167,100	$20,320,000	$26,590,000	$36,379,100
2010	$22,157,600	$20,120,000	$29,100,000	$34,834,200
2011	$26,564,200	$19,690,000	$33,990,000	$38,593,000

Tax court has some explaining to do. The company asked the state Supreme Court for review. It contended that the tax court's order was based on two errors: (1) determining that 27 tanks were taxable real estate property; and (2) performing an improper external obsolescence analysis that invalidated the fair market value determination. The Supreme Court agreed in part.

1. *Tanks.* In terms of the tanks, the state's high court found the tax court used the proper analytical framework to reach its conclusion. First, the tax court determined whether the disputed tanks fell within the broader definition of real property, concluding "correctly" that they did. Next, the tax court considered whether the tanks met the definition of "equipment," which arguably would exclude them from taxation. It properly found that 14 tanks were involved in production and as such arguably were not taxable. However, under the third prong of the analysis, the tax court found that the remainder tanks "performed a 'structural function'" and, therefore, were subject to taxation. The state's high court agreed with all the conclusions going into the tax court's analysis and affirmed the lower court's finding.

2. *External obsolescence.* At the same time, the state Supreme Court sided with the company on the external obsolescence issue.

"The tax court's analysis of external obsolescence resulted in a percent deduction that was dramatically lower than either party's position at trial," the high court observed at the beginning of its discussion. Citing precedent, it went on to say that, even though the tax court generally does not have to accept the valuation of either side's expert, it "must indicate the basis for its calculation and adequately explain its rationale and the factual support in the record for its conclusions." This the tax court failed to do in the instant case, making its calculation of external obsolescence "clearly erroneous," the Supreme Court decided.

In terms of the tax court's methodology, the reviewing court noted that, by treating capacity as a proxy for external obsolescence, the tax court might have "intended to apply an 'inutility' approach, which is a cost-to-capacity measurement of obsolescence." It went on to say that this is a generally accepted method of calculating obsolescence "by comparing the property's capacity to its use level and adjusting the result for economies of scale." But nothing in the record explained why the tax court decided to base its entire obsolescence calculation on capacity alone when both parties' experts considered capacity as only one factor in the analysis, the reviewing court noted.

Moreover, the tax court did not explain why it "rejected entirely the decline in ethanol profit margins that both parties' appraisers found to be a primary consideration in determining external obsolescence." The state Supreme Court called the tax court's attitude "particularly confounding because the capitalization of the income loss attributable to the negative market influences is a generally respected approach to calculating external obsolescence." Also, a special purpose property has by definition only one use, making it impossible, for purposes of valuation, to separate the value of the property from its operations, the reviewing court noted, referencing the expert Robert F. Reilly.

In concluding, the state Supreme Court recognized "the complex and unique valuation challenges in calculating external obsolescence." Therefore, even though it "question[ed]" the tax court's approach, the state high court said it did not want to prescribe a particular methodology to use on remand. It also did not endorse either expert's calculation. In fact, it appeared that the company did not sufficiently tie industry-wide trends to the value of its facility, the reviewing court observed. It allowed for the possibility that the tax court use a methodology that was different from those offered by the parties. But for a different method to survive a legal challenge, the tax court had to explain the reasoning behind it, and there had to be support in the evidence as a whole for an alternative methodology.

Without a legitimate external obsolescence determination, the tax court's valuation of the ethanol plant lacked support in the record. Therefore, the state Supreme Court remanded, noting the tax court had discretion to reopen the record and conduct an additional evidentiary hearing.

In re Marriage of Hartung

Citation: 2015 Iowa App. LEXIS 688
Date of decision: Aug. 5, 2015
Judge: Mullins
State/Jurisdiction: Iowa
Court: Court of Appeals
Type of case: Marital Dissolution
SIC code: 1742 Plastering, Drywall, Acoustical, and Insulation Work
NAICS code: 238310 Drywall and Insulation Contractors

Expert's Application of Asset Approach 'Defies Common Sense'

Valuation methodology also was at the center of an Iowa divorce case in which the trial court found one method entirely inappropriate for the situation at hand and the other flawed in the way the expert applied it. Notwithstanding the trial court's fine critique of the expert opinions, its value determination prompts questions as to how it decided on the final number. An appeal of the valuation followed.

Partial interest in business. In 2000, the husband and two partners formed a sandblasting and painting contracting business. The partners had equal one-third interests. The company worked mostly for municipalities, bidding on jobs. The husband's annual income, including his salary and distributions and profits from the business, was about $300,000.

Both sides retained valuation experts who disagreed over how to value the husband's interest.

The wife's expert used an income approach and concluded the husband's interest in the company was $786,000. In contrast, the husband's expert opted for the asset approach and found the husband's one-third interest was worth about $279,400. (The appellate court decision is short on detail about the calculations.)

The trial court defined the applicable standard of value as the "price which would be agreed upon by a willing seller and a willing buyer, neither of whom is under compulsion to buy or sell and each having equal knowledge as to the matters involved."

It decided the income approach was inappropriate considering the business had a low bar of entry and relied on government agencies for customers. By law, the agencies required to choose the lowest bid. Therefore, the company could count on very little repeat business. Without a loyal customer base and a predictable annual income stream, it was hard to sell the company as a going concern, the court found. Also, the wife's expert improperly included the value of contracted work that had not been started or completed in his valuation, the court observed. According to the husband's expert, this treatment conflicted with the generally accepted accounting principles.

'Aggressive depreciation' proves problematic. But, even though the trial court found the asset approach the "more reasonable" valuation method, it concluded the value the husband's expert proposed under that approach did not represent the fair market value of the company's assets. The reason was that the expert relied on the company's depreciation schedules prepared in connection with its income tax returns. To minimize tax liability, the company opted to use a Section 179 depreciation deduction, which the Internal Revenue Code sanctions for qualifying property. As such, the taxpayer may claim a full depreciation in the year the asset was purchased and indicate zero residual value in the company depreciation schedule.

Recognizing that the law permitted the "aggressive depreciation via § 179" for tax purposes, the trial court found that using that same approach to determine the fair market value of physical assets "defies common sense." Considering in the case at hand the value of the assets was "at the crux of an asset valuation approach," the improper use of a Section 179 accelerated depreciation resulted in understating the value of the contested interest. The court observed that the parties agreed that the company's equipment had some residual value.

According to the trial court, the parties' testimony and the experts' opinions led it to conclude that the fair market value of the husband's interest was $315,000.

The appeals court affirmed without analysis, finding the trial court's value determination was "within the permissible range of the evidence."

Hewlett-Packard Co. v. Benton Cnty. Assessor

Citation: 2015 Ore. LEXIS 575
Date of decision: Aug. 6, 2015
Judge: Balmer
State/Jurisdiction: Oregon
Court: Supreme Court of Oregon
Type of case: State Taxation
SIC code: 7374 Computer Processing and Data Preparation and Processing Services
NAICS code: 518210 Data Processing, Hosting, and Related Services

Shaky Industrial Plant Valuation Survives High Court Review

Appraising an industrial plant for property tax purposes is a knotty problem and makes for interesting legal cases. In a recent decision, the Minnesota Supreme Court tackled the issue of how to determine external obsolescence. Now comes an Oregon case in which the state high court reviewed the tax court's finding on functional obsolescence. Unlike in the Minnesota case, the Oregon tax court adopted the real market valuation the taxpayer's expert offered. The Oregon Supreme Court affirmed, primarily on technical grounds, but noted an unresolved contradiction in the underlying financial feasibility analysis.

Property with core and noncore space. Hewlett-Packard (HP) owned a manufacturing and research campus in Oregon. The real property consisted of land and improvements. The improvements included 28 buildings, which the company had built between 1970 and 1990 to accommodate some

8,000 employees who worked on developing and manufacturing parts for calculators and inkjet printers. The buildings covered 2 million square feet. As the industry changed, the company's operations contracted. By 2007, HP had only 2,000 employees and used only 1.2 million square feet. HP called the space it used the "core" space. Over the next few years, it vacated the noncore space. It also started to lease out a small portion of the noncore space to outside firms.

HP disputed the county's assessment of the value of the improvements for three tax years: 2008, 2009, and 2010. HP and the department of revenue (the department) litigated the dispute in front of the tax court. The main issue was to what extent the improvements added to or detracted from the "real market value" of the property.

The tax court's valuation hinged on two interconnected determinations: (1) the "highest and best use" of the property; and (2) the "value of the loss." These terms are defined by the department of revenue and are part of a complex scheme of administrative rules governing property tax appraisals for industrial plants in Oregon.

Under the applicable statute, the "real market value" of a property is the amount "an informed and disinterested seller could reasonably expect an informed and disinterested buyer to pay for the property on the date of the assessment."

'Highest and best use' determination. The rules require appraisers to analyze what the "highest and best use" of the land is before producing a final valuation. "Highest and best use" means "the reasonably probable and legal use of vacant land or an improved property that is physically possible, appropriately supported, and financially feasible, and that results in the highest value." Put differently, the highest and best use is the most profitable use a potential owner could derive from the property given certain restrictions.

As part of their argument over the correct final valuation of the property, the parties disagreed over what use would result in the highest and best value. They offered expert testimony to bolster their positions.

HP's expert said that the highest and best use of the property was to keep using it just as HP had been using it, as a "specially designed single purpose campus style owner occupied manufacturing facility." Considering the market of potential buyers for the subject property, it was not cost-effective for a potential owner to use the noncore space, the expert claimed.

In contrast, the department's expert argued that "the space not used by a hypothetical purchaser of the property—the so-called 'noncore' space—would be absorbed by other users in the market, at very healthy lease rates and with few, if any, conversion costs to make the existing space attractive at such lease rates."

HP's expert pushed back, noting that there were significant legal obstacles to leasing out the noncore space. The property was not zoned for use as a rental property, raising questions as to whether the department's proposed conversion was legally permissible. He explained that his financial feasibility analysis showed that "the cost of conversion to marketable space exceeded the benefits of such conversion." Specifically, he concluded that a conversion would result in a $13 million net loss.

The tax court sided with HP on the highest and best use issue. It mentioned the "not insignificant" legal questions related to leasing out the excess space and factors such as demand, the location of the property relative to major transportation facilities, and the actual condition of the property.

'Value of the loss' determination. Because of their contrasting opinions on the highest and best use of the property, the experts necessarily arrived at very different real market value determinations.

The applicable statute requires appraisers to consider the income, sales comparison, and cost approaches for their final valuation. HP's expert rejected the income approach. For his sales comparison analysis, he considered prices buyers recently paid for similar single-purpose, owner-occupied research and manufacturing facilities and concluded that HP's improvements were worth about $63 million on all three valuation dates.

He next performed a replacement cost analysis. It meant determining the cost of constructing a property with "equivalent utility to the subject property." Here, he said, only the core space—1.2 million square feet—was of use to a potential owner of the plant. Constructing a new, cost-effective version of the core space would cost about $192 million.

Part of the cost analysis required calculating how much to deduct from the $192 million replacement cost due to loss in value based on physical depreciation, external obsolescence, and, most critical for this case, functional obsolescence. HP's expert deducted $89 million for physical depreciation (age and deterioration) and zero dollars for external obsolescence (economic and locational factors).

In terms of functional obsolescence, he first decided the property had a "superadequacy" of 800,000 square feet in that the 2 million-square-foot property only provided utility to a potential owner of 1.2 million square feet. Based on the governing law, he used the value of the loss method to quantify the applicable deduction. The department's rules define "the value of the loss" as the "present value of the after-tax loss in anticipated income from the continuing operation of the property." For industrial plants, according to the rules, the value of the loss often results from excess operating costs due to inefficiencies.

HP's expert compared the anticipated income from operating the property as it was, 2 million square feet, to the anticipated income from operating the 1.2 million-square-foot replacement property. He calculated $4.6 million per year in additional operating expenses due to superadequacy. After he adjusted for taxes and applied a discount rate to the additional operating expenses over the remaining economic life of the noncore space, he arrived at a $38 million value of the loss. Once he reduced the replacement cost by the amounts related to the three kinds of depreciation, he arrived at a real market value of the subject property of $65 million.

The department's expert arrived at much higher final valuations based on the highest and best use determination that a potential owner would lease some or all of the noncore space and generate rental income. The expert concluded the property's real market value was $210 million for 2008, $217 million for $2009, and $197 million for 2010.

The tax court adopted HP's final valuation for tax purposes. The real market value of HP's improvements was $65 million in 2008, $68 million in 2009, and $64 million in 2010, the court found. The final valuations were a function of the tax court's accepting HP's highest and best use analysis.

Narrow issue on appeal. The department appealed the tax court's ruling with the Oregon Supreme Court. At the outset of its analysis, the high court noted that the appeal ultimately presented a very narrow legal issue: whether the rule defining value of the loss required the tax court to calculate the value of the loss differently than it did.

It came down to this question because the department did not challenge the tax court's adoption of HP's highest and best use analysis. Nor did it challenge the values HP's expert used for the replacement cost, the physical depreciation, or the external obsolescence. Of all the steps in the cost-based analysis, the department only objected to the value HP's expert derived for the property's functional obsolescence, the high court pointed out.

Relying on the highest and best use analysis HP's expert performed, the department claimed the value of the loss should have been $13 million instead of the $38 million used by HP's expert. In considering whether converting the noncore space was a financially feasible use, HP's expert concluded that conversion was not financially feasible because an owner would lose $13 million by converting and maintaining the noncore space. On appeal, the department contended that a potential owner would rather lose $13 million by converting the noncore space than lose $38 million by leaving the noncore space vacant. Based on that assumption, the real market value under the cost approach would increase by $25 million to $90 million.

The state Supreme Court pointed to a logical disconnect in the department's argument. The department's understanding of the value of the loss was inconsistent with the valuation scheme the administrative rules prescribed. Within that scheme, the value of the loss was a component of the cost approach: It was the way with which to measure functional obsolescence, that is, the negative value stemming from inefficiencies in the subject property as compared to the replacement property. "As a result, for the purposes of determining functional obsolescence, the only difference between the subject property and the replacement property is the materials, design, and layout of the two properties," the court pointed out.

The department, on the other hand, measured functional obsolescence by comparing the value of a 2 million-square-foot property that included marketable rentable space, in addition to the 1.2 million-square-foot owner-occupied core space, with the value of a 1.2 million-square-foot property that was only used as an owner-occupied research and manufacturing facility.

As the court explained, in terms of valuing the property, that comparison was part of the preliminary highest and best use determination, whereas the value of the loss calculation was part of the final valuation of the subject property. Here, the tax court accepted HP's proposition that the highest and best use of the property was to continue as a single-purpose, owner-occupied manufacturing and research facility. Accordingly, the tax court was only concerned with valuing property as though it provided use to the potential owner of 1.2 million square feet. The department did not challenge that finding. Once this piece of the valuation analysis was in place, the next step was to quantify the cost of inefficiencies stemming from additional operating costs.

The state Supreme Court allowed that the department might have identified an error in the financial feasibility analysis underlying HP's prevailing highest and best use analysis. HP's expert suggested that it was more profitable to leave the noncore space vacant and incur $38 million in additional operating expenses than to incur a loss of $13 million stemming from the conversion of noncore space into marketable rentable property. The state Supreme Court found that proposition problematic and said it was "unclear whether the financial feasibility analysis performed by HP's expert is the correct test for the financial feasibility of improved property." It added that even the tax court, which adopted the analysis, said HP's highest and best use analysis was "perhaps not free from criticism."

At the same time, the high court pointed out that even if the highest and best use of the property were the use the department proposed—mixed-use manufacturing and rental property—it was far from certain that the final valuation would increase by $25 million, as the department claimed. Changing the highest and best use part meant changing other components of the cost approach, including the property's utility, the scope of the replacement property, the calculation of physical depreciation, and the existence of external obsolescence. "The wide-ranging effects of the department's argument on the valuation process highlight the impropriety of attempting to contain this issue entirely within the value of the loss," the high court concluded.

Here, because the department did not ask the high court to review the tax court's findings related to the highest and best use analysis, the state Supreme Court concluded it had to affirm the tax court's calculation of the value of the loss and by extension the real market value determinations that underpinned the property tax assessments.

In re Honer

Citation: 2015 Cal. App. Unpub. LEXIS 2531
Date of decision: April 9, 2015
Experts: Thomas Berg (husband); Matt Morris (wife)
Judge: Bolanos
State/Jurisdiction: California
Court: Court of Appeal
Type of case: Marital Dissolution
SIC code: 5141 Groceries, General Line
NAICS code: 445110 Supermarkets and Other Grocery (except Convenience) Stores

Court Affirms Rightness of Expert's 'Marital Value' Calculation

In a bitter California divorce, the valuation of two grocery stores was a sore point. The wife attacked the work of the husband's expert because he used what he called the "marital value." The appeals court seemed surprised by the term and discussed the validity of "marital value" in terms of valuation methodology. But a reading of the case suggests that the issue was one of standard of value. Ultimately, given the circumstances, both the trial court and appeals court endorsed the expert's approach.

Valuation dispute. During the marriage, the husband and wife bought and developed two successful grocery stores that offered specialty foods and natural and organic products. The couple owned the businesses through an S corporation in which the husband served as president and CEO and the wife as the vice president.

At the time of the divorce trial, the husband was 64 years old and working full-time at the markets. He said he planned to continue working until he was 70 and passing the business on to his daughter. He received an annual base salary $260,000. The wife suffered from a degenerative disease and stopped being involved in the grocery business. Historically, the couple used profits from the stores to invest in capital expenditures. California is a community property state.

The valuation of the businesses created bitter strife between the parties. The wife filed for divorce in fall 2009. In February 2010, the husband hired an experienced financial analyst with valuation credentials to appraise the stock of the corporation. The husband tried to persuade the wife to agree to a joint appraiser, but she refused. He also asked the wife to commit to a valuation date, but she delayed. Consequently, the appraiser prepared one valuation dated March 2010 and an updated one with a December 2010 valuation date. The trial took place a year later, in December 2011 and January 2012.

Value to the owner. The husband's expert determined the corporation was worth $2.98 million as of year-end 2010. He used both the market and income approaches because the company was a going concern with considerable cash flow. As for the market approach, he used the guideline public companies method and the industry acquisitions method and arrived at a value of $3.2 million. Under the income approach, he used the income capitalization method, which yielded a value of slightly over $3 million. He weighted the results, saying he believed the value from the income approach more accurately reflected the company's value. The operating controlling interest value of the company was nearly $3.1 million, which, after factoring in nonoperational assets and liabilities, he adjusted to $2.98 million.

He further explained that he used the "marital value" of the businesses, as opposed to the "investment value." He explained that this value did not discount for lack of control or lack of marketability. On cross-examination, he explained that, even though a marital value determination "could be different" from an investment valuation, here, the "marital value" was the same as the fair market value. In his declaration, the expert also noted that his findings complied with the Uniform Standards of Professional Appraisal Practice (USPAP).

Third-party buyer assumption. Through her attorneys, the wife eventually retained her own expert. He was a broker in Washington, D.C., whose firm focused on the food industry and who valued the company based on the assumption that the markets would be sold as a going concern to a buyer active in the grocery business. The best way to determine the value of the business would be to "expose it to the market," the analyst said. Also, he hoped to be able to sell both stores individually. This statement invited skepticism from the husband, who questioned whether it was feasible to run the markets independently. The wife's expert also observed that a third-party buyer would acquire the inventory, property, plant, equipment, and liquor licenses, leaving the remainder of the balance sheet to be liquidated.

For his valuation, the wife's expert used a June 2011 valuation date and relied on four valuation methods: comparable public company analysis, comparable transaction analysis, sales analysis, and adjusted EBITDA analysis. He arrived at a value of $5.9 million, from which he deducted $2.4 million based on the liquidation of the balance sheet, to arrive at a final value of $3.5 million.

He explained that he weighted the results, assigning the greatest weight to the value derived from the comparable transaction study. That analysis compared the value of the subject markets to the value of similar-size grocery chains that were sold to grocery operators from 2006 to 2010.

Both experts considered factors such as industry sales, the markets' historical sales, and the national, state, and local economic outlook for grocery stores.

Throughout the proceeding, the wife appeared to change her mind as to what should happen to the business, i.e., whether it should be sold or awarded to the husband. However, her other objections notwithstanding, she ultimately did not object to the trial court's awarding the company to the husband.

'Investment of sweat, toil, worry and hopes.' The trial court said it found the husband's expert more credible for a number of reasons. For one, he made an effort to speak with top management at the markets and explore the businesses' strengths and weaknesses. The wife's expert conducted no interviews. The court also disagreed with the assertion of the wife's expert that offering the business for sale would generate the most accurate indicator of value. Family businesses, the court said, "do not simply represent an investment of capital; they are also an investment of sweat, toil, worry and hopes."

Moreover, the trial court expressed concern over a possible conflict of interest, noting the wife's expert "could potentially act as broker if the markets were sold." Further, the wife's expert did not spell out the costs related to the sale of the markets nor explore the tax consequences arising out of the sale.

And the trial court noted the wife's indecision as to the business. At times, she pushed for the sale of the markets; other times, she asked to be awarded the property on which they stood, which would have made her the husband's landlady. Later, she contested the size of the equalization payment. Finally, the court pointed out that awarding the business to the husband was "essential" to ensuring he could continue to earn a living and pay spousal support to the wife.

As for the valuation date, the court pointed out that the husband paid more than $29,000 for the two appraisals, due to the wife's failure to commit to a valuation date, and that asking him to procure a third one would be "inequitable and impracticable."

The trial court expressly stated that, in crediting the valuation of the husband's expert, it valued the business "as near as practicable to the time of trial," as the applicable family code section required. Further, the court increased the value the husband's expert determined by $200,000 based on the wife's arguments and evidence. It found the corporation was worth $3.18 million. It ordered the husband to make an equalization payment of over $1.5 million and pay to the wife 20% of any distributions the corporation made to the husband. In the final analysis, the wife's award exceeded the husband's by one dollar.

Increased profit no surprise. Five months after the trial court's statement of decision, the wife asked to reopen the proceedings, arguing that, since the business valuations, the company recorded a substantial increase in earnings that represented an "undivided asset," which the court's ruling did not take into account in its division of assets. In support of her request, she presented declarations from two accounting experts. One said earnings between year-end 2010 and mid-2012 (near the time of judgment) had grown by $400,000; the other said the wife was due nearly $430,000 to cover the period of January 2011 through September 2012.

In response, the husband submitted a declaration from a CPA and business valuation expert who denied that the retained earnings had increased to the extent the wife's accounting experts suggested. He also noted that there were fewer capital expenditures during the litigation and said $250,000 was urgently needed to reinvest in the business and return the company back to industry norms. A business was "not an ATM machine," from which one could withdraw cash at whim, he testified.

The trial court denied the wife's request. It found the nature of the business had not changed since trial; the current financial results were not "substantially different from what [the wife] knew or suspected they would be at the time of trial." Also, the wife and her counsel "were well aware that [the corporation] generated profits pre-trial and, in the absence of unforeseen circumstances, would continue to do so after trial concluded," the trial court observed. Counsel made a "tactical decision of error" not to raise this issue at trial. Accordingly, there was no reason to revalue the business.

The wife appealed the trial court's valuation to the state Court of Appeals on a number of grounds:

a. *Valuation date.* The wife contended the trial court adopted the valuation of the husband's expert, which in turn was out of date and failed to consider the significant additional income to the corporation between its valuation date (December 2010) and the date of judgment (December 2012).

The Court of Appeals quickly disposed of this argument, pointing out that the trial court made it clear that it valued the business at the time of trial, not at the end of December 2010. What's more, the trial court "did not blindly accept" the valuation the husband's expert proposed. Rather, it settled on a value that was between the valuations of the two experts. They differed by about $500,000. By adding $200,000 to the value the husband's expert proposed, the court "narrowed the gap to $300,000." This approach aligned with testimony from the husband's expert that a "variance of five to 10 percent between one expert's valuation and another's would not be unusual."

b. *'Marital value.'* The wife suggested the husband's expert used a standard of value—marital value—that represented a "forbidden departure from ordinary rules of business valuation. By relying on his valuation, the trial court committed legal error. The trial court should have used the approach her expert used: determining the value the grocery stores would be worth if sold to a third-party buyer.

The appeals court tried to divine the meaning of "marital value," noting this appeared to be a term the husband's expert had coined to indicate the value to the spouse holding onto the business. (The appeal court's definition brings to mind the "intrinsic value" standard of value.) It agreed that the difference in the experts' valuations hinged on the assumption of a third-party sale.

The appeals court said it saw no legal error in the method and reasoning the husband's expert used. He was qualified as an expert and explained the facts and assumptions underlying his valuation. Even if his approach were "novel," which the court said it did not believe it was, "that would not be indicative of a misunderstanding of the concepts governing valuation of business assets in a marital dissolution action."

The court pointed out that, while the wife militated in favor of adopting the valuation her expert produced, she failed to address the reasons why the trial court rejected a sale of the business. One of them was practical: If there were a sale, the husband would lose his job; if he were awarded the business, "he will have a steady income stream from which to pay permanent spousal support, thus benefitting both parties." What's more, the wife did not actually appeal the court's decision to award the business to the husband.

If the appeals court were to reweigh the evidence, it would "overstep" the acceptable scope of review, the court concluded.

c. *Motion to reopen evidence.* The wife also attacked the trial court's refusal to allow her to introduce more evidence of an increase in the earnings of the business. Those earnings, she claimed, belonged to the community and should be divided, but they were not captured in the experts' valuations.

The appeals court found there was no error in the trial court's decision. For one, the financial information available to the wife at trial already showed an increase in retained earnings, from $1.7 million in 2000 to $4.2 million in September 2011. Likewise, the legal theory that part of the amount was a community asset subject to division was available to her attorneys at trial. Also, the husband's expert contradicted the statements the wife's accounting experts made. The wife's supposedly "new evidence" was not sufficiently material to require a reopening of the evidence.

Spousal support dispute. Finally, on appeal, the wife also challenged the trial court's determination of spousal support.

The trial court found that the husband had available $278,000 annually from which to pay spousal support. The wife asserted he had about $1 million at his personal disposal. She contended that the trial court should have considered at least part of the company's retained earnings as available for spousal support. It should have imputed to the husband any amounts not necessary for capital investment in the business, and it should have placed the burden on the husband to justify the amounts retained for reinvestment.

The appeals court firmly rejected that argument. It pointed to the statement from the husband's accounting expert that the markets were undercapitalized and in need of reinvestment. Testimony about the "realities of the grocery business supports the view that taking cash from [the company] requires restraint and careful consideration" in order not to jeopardize the future success of the markets, the appeals court said. Therefore, it also upheld the trial court's spousal award.

Immersion Corp. v. HTC Corp.

Citation: 2015 U.S. Dist. LEXIS 21555
Date of decision: Feb. 24, 2015
Experts: James Pampinella (plaintiff); unknown (defendants)
Judge: Andrews
State/Jurisdiction: Federal/Delaware
Court: United States District Court
Type of case: Intellectual Property
SIC code: 7371 Computer Programming Services
NAICS code: 54511 Custom Computer Programming Services

Court Declares Lost Profits Analysis 'Goes Too Far'

In a patent infringement case, the plaintiff's damages expert offered a novel lost profits theory that deviated from the traditional premise that there was a hypothetical world in which the infringing sales did not occur. The plaintiff conceded no case law supported its expert's analysis but noted there also was no case rejecting it. The court, ruling on the defendants' *Daubert* motion, found two reasons why the theory was not defensible.

Backstory. The plaintiff was a developer of haptic feedback technology. Haptics is the study of touch. Specifically, the plaintiff's products implemented haptic effects in mobile devices, including phones, tablets, and gaming controllers, which augmented the user's experience by conveying a sense of realism. For example, a user playing a video game might feel an explosion or gunfire eruption in his or her hands. The plaintiff also marketed a software package, TouchSense, which mobile device manufacturers could use to incorporate haptic feedback in their devices. TouchSense was not a patented product. Also, TouchSense was not the only way to integrate haptic effects in a device. The defendants were the Taiwanese manufacturer of smartphones and tablets and related North American entities.

For several years, the plaintiff and the defendants conducted negotiations over a license for the patents-in-suit. The proposed license also would have covered the plaintiff's TouchSense software. The parties discussed a rate of $0.12 per unit, but in the end they failed to reach an agreement.

Subsequently, the plaintiff sued the defendants for patent infringement and claimed reasonable royalty and lost profits damages. In the pretrial stage, the defendants attacked the testimony of the plaintiff's damages expert, arguing neither analysis met the requirements of Federal Rule of Evidence 702 and *Daubert*. The court agreed in part.

Royalty analysis looks to 'most probative' license. For his reasonable royalty analysis, the expert considered several relevant licenses the plaintiff had with third parties but ultimately decided a 2012 settlement with Motorola was "the most probative." For one, the agreement covered the same patents that were at the heart of the instant dispute. Also, the agreement covered only patents, not related software, and the infringing devices in both instances used the same operating system. Moreover, just as the parties in this litigation had no historical licensing relationship, the plaintiff and Motorola did not have one on the date of the settlement. Finally, the defendants and Motorola had similar market shares.

The expert explained that the Motorola agreement provided for an $0.11-per-unit royalty on future sales and a $500,000 lump-sum settlement payment. He explained that the Motorola license covered the plaintiff's complete patent portfolio, effectively licensing 74 patents. Part of his analysis was to calculate the value attributable to just the two patents-in-suit, he said. (The court opinion does not include further details on the steps or conclusion of the analysis.)

The defendants did not contest the expert's methodology but argued the royalty analysis was inadmissible for several reasons. One, the calculation was based on the unsupported assumption that the patents-in-suit were the most valuable patents in the portfolio. Also, the expert "cherry-picked" the license that provided the highest royalty rate even though he could have considered other relevant licenses. And, having selected the license that was most advantageous to the plaintiff, he then picked the highest payment from within that license. The defendants further claimed that the $500,000 lump-sum payment translated into "an effective royalty rate" of only $0.02 per unit for past sales. This lower rate, rather than the $0.11-per-unit rate, should have been the basis for the reasonable royalty calculation.

The plaintiff countered that the analysis was based on the plaintiff's business records, public financial disclosure data, and information from employees that were familiar with the value of its patents. The expert gave sound reasons why the Motorola license was the most meaningful to the case at hand. The defendants' own expert found it "informative." The defendants misrepresented the purpose of the $500,000 lump-sum payment, the plaintiff said. This sum was not for past sales but took care of a related issue having to do with Google's acquisition of Motorola. Therefore, there was no cherry-picking.

The court sided with the plaintiff. The defendants' objections merely indicated disagreements as to the expert's conclusions or the assumptions and considerations underlying the conclusions. The defendants did not question his methodology, which was the focal point of a *Daubert* inquiry. Further, there was no indication that the expert did any cherry-picking. He explained why he focused on the Motorola agreement, why the patents-in-suit were the most valuable patents in the portfolio, and why the lump-sum payment had no effect on the Motorola license. Ultimately, it was for the jury to decide whether the expert's analysis was credible, said the court. Therefore, the reasonable royalty testimony was admissible.

Lost profits analysis assumes sales. The plaintiff's expert presented two lost profits theories, but only one was in dispute. It assumed that, "but for" the defendants' refusal to enter into the license the parties were negotiating, the defendants would have made sales under a license for the patents as well as for TouchSense, the plaintiff's software. Therefore, he calculated lost profits by applying the contemplated rate of $0.12 per unit to the defendants' sales.

The defendants dismissed the theory as "speculative." For one, it was based on a license the parties discussed but never executed. Also, the calculation failed the *Panduit* four-factor test—specifically factor 1, that is, demand for the patented product. TouchSense, they pointed out, was not a patented product. Further, the defendants averred, lost profits legally were only possible where a patent holder was able to show it would have made the infringer's sales absent the infringement. Since the plaintiff did not make phones, it could not have made the sales.

The plaintiff responded under case law from the Federal Circuit there was recovery for lost sales of products that did not practice the patents-in-suit. As for demand under *Panduit*, the expert showed it existed. For years, the defendants had incorporated haptic technology into their devices and they had "extensive discussions" with the plaintiff concerning TouchSense. Also, the plaintiff had licenses with other mobile device manufacturers. Since the expert based his theory on the value the parties considered during their actual negotiations, it could not be speculative.

The court clarified that a patent holder could claim lost profits regardless of whether it made, used, or sold the patented device. However, the court also was clear that this did not mean the patent holder had a right to recovery based on revenue lost from just any product related to the patents-in-suit. Rather, for the patent holder to recover for lost sales of unpatented components that were sold with patented components,"[a]ll the components together must be analogous to components of a single assembly or be parts of a complete machine, or they must constitute a functional unit." See *Rite-Hite Corp. v. Kelley Co.*, 56 F.3d 1538 (Fed. Cir. 1995). Also, under the holding in *Rite-Hite*, liability does not extend to an item that does not have a functional relationship to the patented device but is sold with the latter merely as a matter of convenience or business advantage. If the patented and unpatented products can function independently, they are not a functional unit, the Federal Circuit said in *Rite-Hite*.

The court in the instant case found this described the situation here. The plaintiff's expert failed to show that the plaintiff's patented products had a functional relationship to the software package, TouchSense. There were other ways to achieve haptic effects, the court noted. It pointed out that Motorola, whose license was essential to the expert's reasonable royalty analysis, did not purchase TouchSense. The court concluded that "the fact that the patent license and the software license were being negotiated in a single contract is insufficient to base lost profits on revenue that would have been derived from the software."

But the court found there was another, equally strong, reason to reject the lost profits testimony. The expert's theory went "too far." Under existing legal principles, the analysis proceeded from the assumption that the infringer did not infringe; thus, the infringing sales did not occur. In other words, infringement was "factored out," the court said. Here, the expert created a hypothetical world in which the software sales did occur because the defendants licensed the patents. In that sense, the court observed, the expert here "factored out" infringement, too. The expert then went on to reason—incorrectly—that, but for the defendants' decision not to license the patents, they would have licensed the TouchSense software. Under this logic, whatever profits the plaintiff would have generated from the defendants' licensing the software should be recoverable.

This begged the question, the court said: Where would recovery stop under this theory? What about a situation in which the U.S. government, intent on using the software that dominated the market, might consider licensing TouchSense because the defendants did so? Would the plaintiff then be able to claim lost profits based on the royalties it would have received from the government?

The traditional lost profits theory flowed from the hypothetical situation that the infringer was excluded. The plaintiff expert's analysis started with the infringer's taking a license and then explored what else the infringer might have bought from the patent holder, the court observed. This was not a viable lost profits theory, the court concluded, and it excluded the lost profits part of the expert's testimony.

J&M Distributing, Inc. v. Hearth & Home Technologies, Inc.

Citation: 2015 U.S. Dist. LEXIS 2314
Date of decision: Jan. 9, 2015
Experts: Michael DeProspero (plaintiff); Melissa Snelson (defendant)
Judge: Nelson
State/Jurisdiction: Federal/Minnesota
Court: United States District Court
Type of case: Breach of Contract
SIC code: 3433 Heating Equipment, Except Electric and Warm Air Furnaces
NAICS code: 333414 Heating Equipment (Except Warm Air Furnaces) Mfg.

What Role for RR 59-60 Factors in Valuing Closely Held Business?

A recent *Daubert* decision addresses the use and relevance of Revenue Ruling 59-60 for purposes other than valuing estate and gift taxes and discusses how an expert's purported assumptions of liability turned into opinions on issues outside the expert's area of expertise and authority.

Two-part damages analysis. For over 25 years, the plaintiff's business was devoted exclusively to distributing the defendant's fireplace and hearth products. But, in 2011, the plaintiff suspected the defendant was trying to undercut its business by selling directly to the plaintiff's customers and generally pursuing a strategy that placed the plaintiff at a competitive disadvantage. Discussions between the parties did not resolve the conflict, and, in March 2012, the defendant gave notice of the impending termination of their redistribution relationship. The defendant also went to court seeking a declaration that it had the right to end the relationship. The plaintiff, meanwhile, sued the defendant and one of its other distributors in federal court (D. Minn.), alleging breach of contract, tortious interference with business relations, violations of the Sherman Act, and civil conspiracy.

The plaintiff and the defendant manufacturer retained experts, and both filed pretrial *Daubert* motions to exclude all or part of the opposing expert's damages opinion.

The plaintiff argued that damages must be tied to the fair market value of its business prior to any of the harmful effects stemming from the defendants' alleged misconduct. The plaintiff's expert was an experienced certified financial analyst, who stated he had valuation experience in various areas, including closely held businesses. He valued the company as of Dec. 31, 2011—the most recent full fiscal year before termination of the distributor agreement —and calculated net profits related to sales the plaintiff intended to prove it would have made but for the defendant's conduct.

The expert reviewed the plaintiff's financial statements, payroll information, a summary plan description of its 401(k) plan, and an actuarial report, as well as publicly available information about the defendant and litigation-related documents. For his calculation, he looked to Revenue Ruling 59-60, which, he said, "is viewed universally as the guiding tool for determining fair market value of closely held companies." The ruling provides eight factors it considers fundamental to any fair market valuation. The expert gave particular consideration to factor 1, which takes into account the nature of the business and its history from its inception, and factor 3, which considers the book value of the stock and the financial condition of the business. He found that among the business's unique aspects were that it distributed $300,000 to its primary shareholders and that it was reluctant to use debt in its capital structures. He said he included the distributed income, which would otherwise go to a buyer. As for debt, "this measurement assumes that an acquirer seeks to retire (pay off) all outstanding debt of the company using internal cash resources." Since the plaintiff had significantly more cash on hand than net debt, as of the valuation date, he considered this factor in his valuation, he explained.

He also considered the company's book value. He explained that shareholder equity, as reported in the company's financial statements, was over $693,000 as of the valuation date. He applied a multiplier of 2.2029 to reach a book value of $1.4 million. Belatedly he explained in a declaration (rather than in his original report) that, based on his judgment and experience in valuation, he applied a price/book value multiple discount of 25.7% to account for the company's lack of liquidity and marketability and a price/book value multiple discount of 16.3%, reducing the multiplier from 3.5 to 2.029.

He stated that the public stock of the defendant's parent company served as a point of comparison for valuation in the industry as a whole. Based on all of this information, he concluded that the plaintiff's business at the end of 2011 was worth close to $3.5 million.

He also calculated over $175,000 in net profits related to sales the plaintiff said it lost due to the defendant's actions.

The defendant presented an expert who performed her own damages analysis (not discussed) and critiqued the plaintiff expert's calculation. She said that the plaintiff's expert did not explain who provided him with the sales numbers for the calculation or why the defendant was responsible for the losses or how the sales losses were computed. He also did not show that lost sales for 2012, which according to him amounted to over $440,000, were not already part of the business valuation calculation. Further, she said that, since she had no information supporting the opposing expert's calculation or even assumptions, she was unable to respond to his computation. Until she had more information, she considered the losses "completely without merit."

The defendant's expert said she assumed liability for her own damages analysis. However, her report included numerous observations as to whether the defendant manufacturer had cause for terminating the relationship with the plaintiff. For example, she said it appeared that the manufacturer's termination was for cause. Even if the manufacturer could not terminate the relationship except for cause, she said, there were reasons that provided cause, "which would mean [the plaintiff] would have no recoverable damages." She said that there was an expectation that the plaintiff's owner would retire in the foreseeable future and believed that "any number of things could have happened in the latter half of 2012 that would have constituted cause for termination." Therefore, the plaintiff's damages "could be limited to 2012," she stated.

The defendant claimed the plaintiff's report was inadmissible on all of the *Daubert* grounds: He was unqualified, and his opinion was irrelevant and unreliable. As to qualification, he had a financial background but insufficient experience valuing small, closely held businesses, and he lacked the qualifications to calculate lost profits. As to relevancy, he based his calculation on Revenue Ruling

59-60, which was only relevant for valuations for estate and gift taxes, not damages calculations. As to reliability, he improperly considered income to the plaintiff's primary shareholders in determining the company's fair market value, even though they were not a party to the litigation. He also should not have included a "net debt calculation." And he did not provide support for his calculation of net profits lost.

Statements veer from damages calculation. None of the defendant's objections had traction with the court. The plaintiff's expert had extensive experience in finance, including valuations, the court noted. He once had worked for the U.S. Department of Treasury, in addition to working for many years in the private sector. "Such qualifications are sufficient."

The guidelines underlying Revenue Ruling 59-60 have been used in a variety of contexts, not just for estate and gift tax purposes, the court noted. Case law showed the ruling was applicable in valuing securities in income tax cases and in valuing a closely held corporation as marital property for equitable distribution purposes. A study of IRS rulings and business valuation suggested "its usage has spread as it is routinely referenced and used in the valuation of closely held businesses for various litigation purposes and its principles are applicable in the valuation of most closely held business valuations." Also, the court pointed out, the plaintiff's expert himself had used this method in the past to perform valuation analyses in regard to potential acquisitions of closely held companies. A damages calculation relying on it in this case was relevant, the court said.

In terms of the specifics of the valuation, such as consideration of income to shareholders and the debt treatment, the plaintiff's expert appeared to have used the information in applying factors from the revenue ruling, rather than to support an impermissible recovery of damages to the primary shareholders, the court found. However, the defendant would have ample opportunity to challenge the plaintiff expert's approach during cross-examination.

For its part, the plaintiff asked the court to strike portions of the defendant experts' opinion related particularly to liability, arguing many of the statements had nothing to do with the expert's expertise—the calculation of damages.

The court agreed. Although the defendant's expert said she "assumed liability" in order to analyze damages, she went beyond simple assumptions, the court noted. She debated whether the defendant manufacturer had cause to terminate the agreement with the plaintiff, when that deliberation was for the jury to perform. According to the court, "any expert testimony to this effect both invades the province of the jury and is superfluous," the court observed. Also, she lacked the qualifications to discuss substantive legal issues, such as cause for termination. These, too, were for the jury to resolve. Moreover, her statements were speculative and irrelevant, the court said. Whether the manufacturer could have ended its relationship with the plaintiff in the future had nothing to do with the termination it announced in March 2012 and the related losses the plaintiff claimed it sustained then. The expert's statements also had the potential to prejudice and confuse the jury, the court added.

For all of these reasons, the court excluded portions from the defendant expert's report.

Kardash v. Commissioner (Kardash I)

Citation: 2015 Tax Ct. Memo LEXIS 69
Date of decision: March 18, 2015
Experts: Stanley A. Murphy (petitioners); Dr. Israel Shaked (IRS/respondent)
Judge: Goeke
State/Jurisdiction: Federal
Court: U.S. Tax Court
Type of case: Federal Taxation
SIC code: 1500 Building Construction General Contractors and Operative Builders
NAICS code: 2361 Residential Building Construction

Tax Court Tacitly Approves of IRS Solvency Assessment

A recent Tax Court memo resulting from a transferee liability case includes an informative discussion of the valuation methodologies the parties' solvency experts used to determine the company's fair market value at the point when various contested transfers of payment took place. The court's analysis as to the merits of the valuations is short, but it suggests the court found the assessment of the IRS's expert more credible. Even though the IRS failed to establish liability for all of its claims, it was able to show insolvency for three out of the five relevant years.

Pinpointing insolvency. The petitioners were two minority shareholders of a Florida concrete company that flourished during the home construction boom of the early 2000s but was insolvent by the end of 2007. The company was under the control of two majority shareholders, who, from 2003 to 2007, siphoned off most of the company's cash. For 2003 and 2004, the company filed fraudulent federal income tax returns; for the subsequent three years, it filed none. Neither of the petitioners played a role in managing the finances of the company.

An eventual IRS audit found the company owed more than $120 million in taxes, penalties, and interest. Since the company could not pay, the agency agreed to an installment plan requiring monthly payments of $70,000 per month (for more than 150 years!). Under the Internal Revenue Code's Section 6901, the IRS also went after the shareholders to recover as much as possible for alleged illegal money transfers. While the IRS reached agreements with the majority shareholders as to recovery under transfer liability, the petitioners challenged the agency's claims in the United States Tax Court.

Section 6901 provides the Service with a remedy "for enforcing and collecting from the transferee of the property the transferor's existing liability." To establish the requisite liability, the IRS looks to applicable state law, in this case to the Florida Uniform Fraudulent Transfer Act (FUFTA). The IRS argued that several payment transfers to the petitioners represented actual and constructive fraud, but only the constructive fraud theory had any traction with the court. Under that theory, the IRS needed to show that the company received less than reasonably equivalent value for the transfers at issue and the company was insolvent at the time of transfer. Both sides retained solvency experts to determine the company's enterprise value and by extension the point at which it was insolvent—a key issue in the case.

Disputed transfer payments. Two sets of transfers, amounting to $5 million in total, were under consideration. One set included 2003 and 2004 bonus "advances" to the petitioners. Specifically, after the company suspended its performance-based bonus program under which the petitioners received hundreds of thousands of dollars in addition to their salary, the majority owners gave the petitioners so-called "bonus advances" to enable the petitioners to keep up their standard of living. The majority owners told the petitioners they did not have to report the payments in their tax returns. When the IRS subsequently discovered the advances, it characterized them as dividends. The petitioners settled the disputes and paid tax on the advances.

The second set of transfers included dividends the company gave to all the shareholders based on the percentage of stock ownership, which the petitioners reported on their individual returns. The dividends were for 2005, 2006, and 2007.

Asset-based valuation. The IRS's expert decided the best method to determine solvency was the "asset accumulation approach." Under this method, he valued the company at the price at which a willing buyer would pay for the company's tangible assets and land. As the expert saw it, any potential buyer would insist on reviewing the company's tax returns and audited financial statements prior to buying it. Since the company could produce neither, no buyer would be willing to pay more than the value of the company's tangible assets and land. The expert also said he did not believe the company had intangible assets of value.

The expert relied on a 2006 appraisal of the company's assets, which indicated that the assets' fair market value (FMV) at that time was 102% of the undepreciated book value of the company's property, plant, and equipment. He simply applied this multiplier to the book value of the company's assets on the relevant dates and concluded that the company was insolvent at all times during the five years at issue.

He also performed a backup analysis using the market approach to value the company's assets. He said it was appropriate to use the revenue-to-sale-price ratio because "that is what most buyers use." He found 13 sales of companies similar to the subject company. He explained that he adjusted the sales price for each company to account for the subject's financial mismanagement and also applied a 25% key man discount (the court's opinion includes no details on the reasoning behind it). For each company, he then divided the five-year average of revenues by the sales price. He determined that the median revenue-to-sale-price ratio was 0.9. Finally, he applied this ratio to the company's average revenue for the five-year periods ending on each valuation date. He concluded that the value of the company's income tax liabilities exceeded the FMV of the company's assets by the end of January 2006 and that the company remained insolvent through the end of March 2007.

Three-pronged valuation approach. The petitioners' expert used three methods, weighting them evenly at 33.3%, to compute a weighted market value of invested capital. From that value, he subtracted debt and liability to arrive at an equity valuation.

The first approach was performing a discounted cash flow (DCF) analysis. The petitioners' expert based the cash flow projections on three sources. For Year 1, he used management's forecast; for Years 2 through 4, he used industry growth statistics capturing expectations as to the growth of the residential construction market in the U.S., inflation expectations, and the historical relationship between growth in Florida residential construction and U.S. residential construction. For Year 5, he used industry statistics capturing expectations of inflation in the U.S. and projections of Florida's population growth.

He explained that a willing buyer and willing seller would have relied on the available management forecasts and used estimated revenue growth or a long-term growth rate forecast when there were no management forecasts. He did not account for fraud in his estimates. He found that EBIT in 2002 was just over $7 million and nearly $59.8 million at the end of 2006. He calculated the rate of return on equity capital using the modified capital asset pricing model (MCAPM) and used the Gordon growth model to determine the terminal value of the company. He capitalized the projected cash flows beginning in the terminal period into perpetuity. First, he normalized depreciation, capital expenditures, and working capital requirements to match long-term expectations of revenue. Then, he normalized available cash flows (The court's opinion does not give further specifics.)

The IRS's expert rejected this approach because the company did not have reliable historical cash flow information on which to base cash flow projections. According to the expert, no prospective buyer would value the company using a DCF analysis.

The petitioners' expert also performed a guideline public company analysis based on six publicly traded companies that operated in a similar line of business. The multiples he used included enterprise value divided by revenue and enterprise value divided by EBITDA.

Finally, he conducted a guideline company transactions analysis, comparing the subject company to similar businesses that had been acquired in private transactions, including mergers and acquisitions. He said he searched for similar transactions based on business descriptions. The multiples again included enterprise value divided by revenue and enterprise value divided by EBITDA. (The court's opinion is short on detail as to the comparative analyses.)

The petitioners' expert concluded that the company was not insolvent at year-end 2006 or any date before but was insolvent at year-end 2007. This conclusion led the petitioners to argue that the company did not become insolvent until after they had received the last of the contested transfer payments.

Both experts largely agreed on the value of the company's debts.

Mixed solvency ruling. In terms of establishing fraud by first showing lack of reasonably equivalent value, the IRS argued the 2003 and 2004 bonus advances to the petitioners were loans that were never repaid. Consequently, the company did not receive reasonably equivalent value for the transfers during those two years.

The Tax Court disagreed, finding these advances were compensation that the petitioners received instead of the suspended bonuses. The company never expected repayment. Since the petitioners gave reasonably equivalent value for the transfers during 2003 and 2004, insolvency for those years was not an issue. The transfers were not constructively fraudulent. Moreover, the court found that, even with the 2003 and 2004 advance payments, the company's assets then exceeded the FMV of its debts. Therefore, it was not then insolvent.

In terms of the IRS's fraud claim pertaining to transfers in 2005, 2006, and 2007, the court found the company "likely did not receive reasonably equivalent value" for payments to the petitioners. Under the state's fraudulent transfer act, "a distribution of dividends that is not compensation or salary for services rendered is not a transfer in exchange for reasonably equivalent value." Therefore, there was constructive fraud assuming the company was insolvent at the time of the various transfers that occurred during those years, the court said.

Without providing a detailed discussion of the expert testimony, the court in effect found the company was insolvent on all of the transfer dates starting in 2005, that is, once the company made dividends to the four shareholders. These large payments and the accumulation of tax liability stripped the company of its assets and rendered it insolvent, the court said. Consequently, the petitioners were liable as transferees for 2005, 2006, and 2007, the Tax Court held.

Kardash v. Comm'r (Kardash II)

Citation: 2015 Tax Ct. Memo LEXIS 198
Date of decision: Oct. 6, 2015
Judge: Goeke
State/Jurisdiction: Federal
Court: United States Tax Court
Type of case: Federal Taxation
SIC code: 1522
NAICS code: 236118

Tax Court Explains Valuation Method Behind Solvency Ruling

The Tax Court amended its prior ruling on transferee liability by determining that the taxpayer company was solvent a year longer than the court originally had found. In so doing, the court acknowledged errors that had crept into its earlier assessment and it used the opportunity to explain its valuation in greater detail than it had done in its original decision. Ultimately, however, the revised solvency determination did not change the outcome of the case.

Prior ruling. The petitioners were two minority shareholders of a Florida concrete company that was insolvent by the end of 2007. The company was under the control of two majority shareholders who, from 2003 to 2007, siphoned off most of the company's cash. Subsequently, an Internal Revenue Service audit found the company owed more than $120 million in taxes, penalties, and interest. Since it could not pay, the IRS instituted an installment plan requiring monthly payments of $70,000 per month (for more than 150 years!). Under the Internal Revenue Code's Section 6901, the IRS also went after the shareholders to recover as much as possible for alleged illegal money transfers. While the IRS reached agreements with the majority shareholders as to the recovery under transfer liability, the petitioners challenged the agency's claims in the United States Tax Court.

At issue were several payment transfers to the petitioners, which the IRS claimed represented if not active than constructive fraud. Under the latter theory, the IRS had to show that the company received less than reasonably equivalent value for the transfers at issue and the company was insolvent at the time of transfer. The contested transfers included dividends the company gave to all the shareholders based on the percentage of stock ownership in 2005, 2006, and 2007.

At trial, the IRS's expert explained the best method for determining solvency in this case was the "asset accumulation approach." Based on this method, he valued the company at the price a willing buyer would pay for the company's tangible assets and land. He said he did not believe the company had intangible assets of value. He concluded that the company was insolvent at all times during the five years at issue.

He also performed a backup analysis using the market approach to value the company's assets. It was appropriate to use the revenue-to-sale price ratio because "that is what most buyers use," he said. Using this method, he concluded that the value of the company's income tax liabilities exceeded the FMV of the company's assets by the end of January 2006 and that the company remained insolvent through the end of March 2007.

The petitioners' expert used three methods—a discounted cash flow analysis, a guideline public company analysis, and a guideline company transactions analysis—which he weighted evenly to compute a weighted market value of invested capital. From that value, he subtracted debt and liability to arrive at an equity valuation.

The petitioners' expert concluded that the company was not insolvent at year-end 2006 or any date before but was insolvent at year-end 2007. Accordingly, the petitioners claimed that the company did not become insolvent until after they had received the last of the contested transfer payments.

In its original ruling, the Tax Court found there was constructive fraud. It ruled the company was insolvent in 2005, 2006, and 2007, once it made dividends to the shareholders. The court added that the company "likely did not receive reasonably equivalent value" for payments to the petitioners. Consequently, the petitioners were liable as transferees for 2005, 2006, and 2007, the Tax Court held.

The court's ruling did not include a detailed valuation discussion, but the ruling suggested the court's solvency determination was informed by the IRS expert's asset accumulation valuation. (An extended discussion of *Kardash v. Comm'r*, 2015 Tax Ct. Memo LEXIS 69, begins on page 147.)

Reconsideration. In their subsequent motion for reconsideration, the petitioners claimed the court's finding that the company was insolvent in 2005 was error. And, they said, assuming the company was solvent in 2005, the petitioners were not liable for the 2005 transfers.

The court, revisiting the solvency issue, said "for the sake of clarity, we deem it necessary to discuss our valuation in greater detail than we did previously." It clarified that, although the IRS's expert had recommended the use of the asset accumulation value, the court instead decided to rely "largely" on the expert's market multiple valuation. The latter approach valued the company as a going concern and factored in intangible assets, which the court said it believed the company in fact had.

The court admitted that it previously had used the wrong estimates as to the company's tax liabilities and had stated the IRS expert's business enterprise value incorrectly. All told, adopting the IRS expert's market multiple calculation, the court ruled that the company had a negative equity value of over $12.3 million on the January 2006 transfer date and remained insolvent through March 2007. But the company was not insolvent in 2005.

At the same time, the court noted that the company's solvency in 2005 did not change the fact that the 2005 payments to the petitioners were constructively fraudulent. The reason was that they were part of a series of transfers that "in total" left the company insolvent, the Tax Court explained. The transfers, beginning with the 2005 payments, were not for reasonably equivalent value and rendered the company insolvent. Accordingly, the Tax Court declined to change its prior liability ruling.

K.T. v. M.T.

Citation: 2015 Tex. App., LEXIS 8558
Date of decision: Aug. 13, 2015
Experts: Bryan Rice (husband/appellee); James Francis (wife/appellant)
Judge: Livingston
State/Jurisdiction: Texas
Court: Court of Appeals
Type of case: Marital Dissolution
SIC code: 6282 Investment Advice
NAICS code: 523930 Investment Advice

Court Declines to Attribute Commercial Goodwill to Solo Practice

A recent Texas divorce case featuring the solo practice of a financial advisor raised questions about valuation methodology and goodwill. One expert's use of the excess earnings method prompted criticism from the rivaling expert that this approach was particularly ill suited for valuing a business that had almost no tangible assets. Relatedly, the experts disagreed over the allocation of goodwill, which made up most of the value of the business.

Valuation pivots on individualized service. The husband was a licensed financial advisor who sold financial products to clients. The business was incorporated, but he was a registered representative of a broker dealer, from whom he received commissions and whom he paid a monthly fee for back-office support and insurance.

At trial, the husband's expert described the husband as a quasi-employee or independent contractor of the broker dealer. What mattered most, however, was that sales depended on the husband's cultivating his own clients, the expert emphasized. Trust in the husband's advice was one reason why it would be difficult to transfer the clients to another professional. Also, the husband sold products based on his evaluating a client's needs.

The expert said he used an income approach, which must consider "any net profits, discretionary cash flows, cash distributions, or other measures of economic benefits from the company's portfolio of assets." He explained that income in this context did not necessarily mean income in the accounting sense but referred "to future benefits accruing to the owner."

But he also said that under the applicable fair market value standard of value he ultimately "went straight to the net assets of the business" as of the valuation date because "nobody would pay a penny more than the net assets of the business." He explained that, without the husband's signing a noncompete agreement, a potential buyer of the business would "not be able to rationalize paying more for it." He went on to say that, given the husband's average cash compensation in recent years was approximately $240,000, taking into account pretax distributions and salary, there was no reason for the husband to sign a noncompete for less than $500,000 to $720,000. The noncompete amount represented the husband's personal goodwill, the expert claimed. It was one-and-a-half to three years of the husband's total emolument from the practice.

The expert decided a 25% discount for lack of marketability was appropriate considering the business's main asset was the ability to serve customers, which, in turn, hinged on the relationship between the working owner and the customers. He noted that the assets of the business were "extremely limited." The value of the business lay in customer relationships.

Using a 25% discount rate, he concluded the business was worth $443,200. In contrast, the adjusted net book value of its assets was $27,000. He contended that the difference between the two figures represented goodwill and that 100% of the goodwill was "allocable to the personal goodwill of [Husband]."

He explained that, under Texas law, it was important to determine how much of the goodwill in a business was transferable. In a professional practice, goodwill was "highly dependent upon the individual practitioner," he explained. Without a covenant not to compete, it was "virtually impossible" to transfer a professional's goodwill, he said. When valuing a solo practice, he said he did not assess "any divisible goodwill" because the relationship between the practitioner and the client was "so strong and so paramount in driving the business."

He defined "goodwill" as "the ability of a business to retain patronage after a change in ownership." If a potential buyer acquired a business and was able to keep customers, the buyer was acquiring commercial goodwill. But, "if you are not sure you get to keep the customers after buying the business, you will not pay for that goodwill, so it is personal." Assuming there was no noncompete agreement from the husband, the value of the business was $27,000—the adjusted net book value of its assets.

Valuation based on excess earnings approach. The wife's expert said that he was looking for the fair market value of the business by considering not only how the business had performed recently, but also "what it looks like the business is going to continue to be doing."

He said he used the excess earnings method, which, he claimed, for years has been accepted by the IRS and the courts for valuing small, professional practices. This approach "considers both the tangible assets of the business, as well as the earnings capacity of the business, using a type of capitalized cash flow method," he explained.

Specifically, he added the business's tangible assets—mostly office furniture and equipment—to a weighted average net income of business, including the husband's salary. As for goodwill, the expert said he started with the return on the tangible assets from the total earnings and then capitalized the outcome at 28.24%. The result was the value of intangible assets, including the business goodwill and the personal goodwill, he stated.

He clarified that personal goodwill required determining what the risk was to a potential buyer of losing customers "because they don't know who you are.... Maybe you're not as personable as [Husband]." He said he perceived a "huge risk" without the husband's running the business and pegged the risk at 25% of the calculated value. This amount represented personal goodwill in this case. The remainder was business goodwill, the expert claimed. After discounting the capitalized net income by 25% and adding back in the cost of the fixed assets, the wife's expert concluded the business was worth nearly $413,700.

The wife's expert criticized the opposing expert for concluding that, if the business were sold, there would be a risk that the husband might compete with it. He also claimed the opposing expert's application of a 25% discount for lack of marketability equaled a deduction for personal goodwill. He contended that, under the methodology the husband's expert used, the latter deducted personal goodwill twice.

Finally, the wife's expert noted that he also used "some rule of thumb methods" from a pricing guide as a check on the value he had generated by way of the excess earnings method.

The husband's expert objected to the opposing expert's use of the excess earnings methodology. He explained that this method segregated tangible from intangible value by calculating a perceived rate of return on the intangible value. He said that the IRS, which created the method almost a hundred years ago to value distilleries during Prohibition, currently disfavored it, as did the valuation profession. Barring a better approach, this method was really only appropriate for businesses with tangible assets. Here, however, the business had few tangible assets and they were not instrumental in generating income. Rather, it was the husband's "clients, his expertise, and his knowledge" that generated income, the husband's expert explained.

The wife's expert conceded that the IRS had been critical about the excess earnings approach. But he maintained that he testified "quite often before the IRS" and found the agency accepted the method "all the time."

In cross-examination, the wife's husband also argued that "the book of business of those clients' money and the servicing of those clients constitutes 'business goodwill,' not commercial." At the same time, he conceded that if the husband were to die the next day, the clients would be assigned to a new broker-dealer and the husband's estate would not receive trailing commissions. He also admitted that a third-party buyer of the business could not simply find out the names of the husband's clients or obtain their business without their first leaving the business. Regardless, the wife's expert said he stood behind his valuation because "someone else could come in and … do a good job."

The trial court adopted the $27,000 value the husband's expert placed on the business. The wife appealed, arguing there was insufficient evidence to support the valuation.

Goodwill jurisprudence in Texas. At the start of its analysis, the Court of Appeals noted the distinction under state law between the goodwill attributable to the individual professional and the commercial goodwill of a business. It went on to say:

> To determine whether goodwill that is subject to division upon divorce attaches to a professional practice, goodwill first must be determined to exist independently of the personal ability of the professional spouse, and then if such goodwill is found to exist, the court must determine whether that goodwill has a commercial value in which the community estate is entitled to share.

(citing *Hill v. Hill*, 2014 Tex. App. LEXIS 292) (available at *BVLaw*).

The court noted that the case in front of it involved a "classic battle of the experts." It was the province of the trial court whom to believe. Here, the wife did not dispute the qualifications of the husband's expert, the court stated. Rather, she claimed the opposing expert's valuation was "merely conclusory."

The Court of Appeals saw it differently. The husband's expert discussed the method he used for his valuation and critiqued the method the wife's expert used, the court noted. The husband's expert explained "more than once" how he arrived at the conclusion that the goodwill attached to the business was personal. To reach this conclusion, he applied Texas law concerning personal goodwill to the facts of the case, the appeals court noted.

In contrast, the wife's expert claimed that 25% of the calculated value was personal goodwill and the remainder was commercial goodwill. However, the appeals court said, he never explained how whatever goodwill existed could be attributed to the business "separate and apart" from the professional's personal skills, ability, and reputation.

Accordingly, the Court of Appeals affirmed the trial court's business valuation.

Lane v. Lampkin

Citation: 2014 Miss. App. LEXIS 497
Date of decision: Sept. 16, 2014
Judge: Carlton
State/Jurisdiction: Mississippi
Court: Court of Appeals
Type of case: Damages
SIC code: 5200 Building Materials, Hardware, Garden Supply, and Mobile Home Dealers
NAICS code: 444190 Other Building Material Dealers

What Rationale for Net Book Value in Damages Analysis?

How do you assess damages in a situation in which one of two equal shareholders died and the surviving partner feels compelled to open a new company that does the same work as the original company? A divided appeals court recently dealt with the issues of proper method of recovery and whether the trial court erred when it dismissed disagreement between the experts as just "getting bogged down in an argument over the terminology used to describe the valuation of [the company]."

Two companies, same function. Two men jointly owned land and decided to set up a business on it that bought and sold rocks. Each man owned a 50% interest in the company. One partner also owned a construction company that was one of the rock supplier's major clients. The rock business operated on a line of credit that both partners personally guaranteed and that was the primary source of funds for buying inventory. Ten years after the company's formation, in 2006, one partner died; his stock in the company and the land transferred to the estate. Meanwhile, the line of credit necessary to keep the business going was about to expire. When the surviving partner was unable to obtain a timely loan guarantee from the estate's executors, he set up a new company on the same property performing the same services as the subject company and selling to the same customers. He completed the subject company's contracts and paid its debts. He tried to keep profits attributable to the subject company separate from profits belonging to the new company.

He then asked the court for a judgment declaring that: (1) he had the right to invest in and operate his own rock-supplying business; (2) he had not breached a fiduciary duty to the subject; and (3) he had the authority to sell the subject's existing inventory, collect its accounts receivable, and use incoming money to pay the company's debts. The estate countersued, accusing the surviving partner of breach of fiduciary duty and usurpation of a business opportunity. It sought lost profits damages.

The trial court determined that the balance sheets showed the company was solvent, but it lacked "a substantial amount of equity with which to continue on with the business." Without credit, it was not likely to stay in business for very long. The court also found the surviving partner had a duty to cooperate with the estate. He failed to give the estate adequate time and the financial information it needed to make a considered decision on the loan guarantee issue. Therefore, his argument that the estate's failure to renew the credit line relieved him of his fiduciary duty to the subject company lacked merit.

A matter of semantics? A separate trial took place for damages. Both sides presented experts, who disagreed as to the proper valuation method, prompting the trial court to say: "Whether you call it asset based or net book value or lost profits, this Court is merely concerned with how and whether to value this business." The court's opinion does not describe the expert testimony in great detail, but it says that the court ultimately fashioned a remedy by taking parts of both experts' calculations and by reviewing the financial records of the two companies.

The court found that the company "was never all that profitable." It added that, if the court "were to carry its business assessment forward to the year 2012 based on the financial records of both companies, the Court would merely be placing a net loss in the hands of the corporation." For equity's sake, it said, it would look to the subject's past performance to calculate lost profits after 2007. It first adopted the book value calculation the surviving partner's expert offered to capture the value of the business as of the end of 2007. Specifically, the expert took the year-end net book values for 2006 and 2007 and backed out all expenses, all erroneously placed expenses personal to the surviving partner, and all accounts receivable from the partners. He then added in the value of the corporation's remaining assets—a front-end loader and a heating and cooling unit—and arrived at a total net book value of over $125,500.

In terms of lost profits, the court adopted the $21,000 average net income figure the estate's expert determined for the period 2000 to 2007. It decided to award lost profits for five years, 2008 through 2012, considering the acrimony between the parties and the likelihood that the business would not have continued for very long. Adding the total net income to the net book value yielded $230,100 in total damages owed to the subject company, the court decided. Because the estate was one of two shareholders of the company, it had a right to half of the total damages.

The court dismissed the estate's claim to one-half of the lease payments owed to the subject company since 2007. It credited the surviving partner's testimony that there had been no such payments in the past five years. Also, said the court, both partners were equally responsible for any lease payments and equally entitled to one-half of the proceeds. Therefore, the issue "creates a wash."

The court also rejected testimony from the estate's expert that the surviving partner had failed to account for nearly 650,000 tons of rock the subject company had bought and that this "diversion" caused lost profits to the subject company. There is no indication in the court's opinion that the expert quantified the loss "due to the circumvention of the accounting system." The surviving partner's expert admitted that the purchase of the rock did not appear in the subject's books. The court found the surviving partner and his expert adequately accounted for the whereabouts of the rock. This was a closely held corporation, it said, where on occasion rock was delivered to different places and billed to the surviving partner. This mode of doing business did not give rise to lost profits, the court said.

Lost income vs. lost profits. The estate appealed the trial court's damages calculation to the state Court of Appeals for several reasons. The essence of its argument was that the trial court erred by relying on the opposing expert's calculation. The latter performed a business valuation calculation when he should have used a lost profits analysis, the estate claimed. At the least, the expert's mistake should have prompted the trial court to defer to the estate expert's damages determination. At the most, the trial court should have excluded the erroneous opinion under the state's Rule 702.

The surviving partner contended that the trial court's calculation properly relied on parts of both experts' analyses and that it "fell within accepted methodologies to arrive at a reasonable calculation."

The appeals court sidestepped the issue of whether the trial court erroneously built its damages on the opposing expert's net book. Instead, it found that the trial court properly determined future lost profits for five years by looking to "historical lost net profits" and adopting the figure the estate's expert proposed. The methods the trial court used did not constitute an abuse of discretion, the appellate court said.

The estate also claimed the trial court's damages calculation "greatly underestimated" the lost profits by failing to consider unreported rock. That argument also had no traction. There was conflicting expert testimony on the issue, the appeals court said. The trial court had discretion to find in favor of the surviving partner's expert.

Conflict of interest claim. In an argument related to admissibility, the estate claimed there was another reason to exclude the opposing expert under the state's Rule of Evidence 702. On cross-examination, the expert admitted that his firm did tax work for the surviving partner and his businesses. This relationship represented a conflict of interest and compromised his objectivity in the case at issue, the estate maintained. It rendered his valuation opinion unreliable.

Once again, the appeals court disagreed. Rule 702 required that the expert be qualified and the testimony be relevant and reliable. Here, the expert had decades of experience as a business valuator. He was certified in financial forensics and had served as an expert in all types of accounting-related areas, including business valuations and lost profits calculations. There was no doubt that he was qualified. At the same time, at trial, the estate had an opportunity during voir dire and cross-examination to question the expert about his ability to provide an objective and independent opinion in the case. He said he could. The trial court was in the best position to assess the credibility of the expert witnesses, and it accepted the expert, the appeals court noted.

'Illogical' calculation? Four judges on the Court of Appeals disagreed with the majority's decision. They found that the trial court committed reversible error when it reduced the experts' arguments over the damages calculations to a matter of "just splitting hairs." In fact, the court's minority said, "[The experts] were testifying about detailed and important accounting terminology."

The law required the use of a lost profits analysis where there was a claim of breach of fiduciary duty as well as where there was a claim of usurpation of a corporate opportunity, the dissent pointed out. There was no authority supporting the trial court's use of a business valuation analysis in this case. In fact, it was "illogical" to include a "net book value" calculation in a damages calculation, as the trial court did. In a dissolution case, a shareholder has a right to the distribution of the proceeds of the corporation's remaining assets, the minority explained. "'Net book value' is simply an accounting term that is not directly related to the actual value of the corporation's assets," it went on to say. "There is simply no case to support this conclusion," the dissent said, rejecting the trial court's damages analysis.

LongPath Capital, LLC v. Ramtron International Corp.

Citation: 2015 Del. Ch. LEXIS 177
Date of decision: June 30, 2015
Experts: David Clarke (petitioner); Gregg Jarrell (respondent)
Judge: Parsons
State/Jurisdiction: Delaware
Court: Delaware Court of Chancery
Type of case: Dissenting shareholder
SIC code: 3674 Semiconductors and Related Devices
NAICS code: 334413 Semiconductor and Related Device Manufacturing

Adjusted Merger Price Superior to Other Valuation Methods

The Delaware Court of Chancery has been a hive of activity during summer 2015. In two months, the court issued a number of key valuation decisions—all long and deep. The following statutory appraisal ruling falls in line with a suite of other decisions in which the court held the merger price was a more accurate indicator of value than the values achieved with other techniques, including the often-favored discounted cash flow (DCF) model. In this case, irreparably compromised cash flow projections rendered the DCF meaningless.

Hostile deal. The petitioner was an investment vehicle that pursued an appraisal arbitrage strategy. The respondent was a fabless semiconductor company that produced F-RAM. "Fabless" means the company outsourced the manufacture of the silicon wafers used in its products. RAM stands for random access memory. The company's F-RAM was a relatively unique product; it had fast read and write speeds, could be written to a high number of times, and used low power. Also, it retained memory if power were lost.

The company was the target of a hostile bid by a third party, Cypress Semiconductor Corp. (Cypress), which was not a party to the litigation. In March 2011, when the subject was experiencing serious cash management problems, Cypress made a nonpublic written offer for $3.01 per share, which the company rejected as inadequate. The offer was a 37% premium over the then closing price of the company's stock.

In mid-June 2012, Cypress issued a bear hug letter offering to buy the company for $2.48 per share. Again, the company rebuffed the bid. About a week later, Cypress commenced a hostile tender offer at $2.68 per share. This offer, too, represented a 37% premium over the company's stock price, which by then had fallen. The company's board again found the offer inadequate and announced it was exploring strategic alternatives.

Meanwhile, in July 2012, the company acknowledged that its second-quarter 2012 earnings were below expectations and there was a good possibility that the company would come in below the full-year 2012 estimate by at least $10 million. That same month, Merriman Capital, the only analyst covering the company, stated that, if Cypress were to pull its offer, the company's shares might return to the $2.00 range or even lower.

While Cypress pursued its hostile bid, the company engaged a financial advisor to find other potential buyers and explore other strategic options. The advisor contacted over 20 possible suitors, including Cypress. Six parties were sufficiently interested to sign nondisclosure agreements, but, ultimately, none made a firm bid, except for Cypress. Two serious contenders expressed concern over the company's cost structure.

Cypress, on the other hand, increased the offer to $2.88 per share and extended the term of the tender offer. In fall 2012, Cypress and the company were negotiating in earnest, settling on $3.10 per share as the final transaction price. The parties signed the merger agreement in September 2012, and stockholders approved it in November 2012.

The merger price was 25% higher than Cypress's starting bid. It represented a 71% premium over the company's unaffected stock price of $1.81.

A month after the merger announcement, the petitioner bought shares in the company. Three weeks after the transaction closed, it filed suit, claiming the market undervalued the shares and asking the Delaware Court of Chancery for a fair value determination.

Company's operational problems. Because the company did not manufacturer its products, its life and success depended on its relationship with its foundry. At the time of the merger, the company had a contract with Texas Instruments (TI). Before that, it had a different primary foundry. Transitioning from the first foundry to TI was a difficult process that took seven years, causing problems in day-to-day business, related to the company's sales and revenue recognition models.

The company sold mostly to distributors that sold to end-users. And it used a point-of-purchase model that recognized revenue when the product shipped rather than when the product sold to the end-user. At trial, witnesses explained that this approach made it difficult to forecast future sales because distributors served as buffers and could mask actual demand. Specifically, the difficult transition to a new foundry forced the company to place its customers—mostly distributors—on allocation. Concerned about supply shortages, the distributors reacted by overordering. By 2011, the company faced a "massive inventory bubble," overrecognition of revenue, and a cash crunch since the company had to pay for the extra inventory it ordered. During 2011 and 2012, the company either missed or had to renegotiate its loan contracts with its primary lender. Also, in July 2011, the company undertook a secondary public offering of about 20% of its outstanding shares. This transaction occurred at $2 per share. The company used the proceeds to pay off its excess inventory. However, by spring 2012, the company faced another cash crisis, which continued until the signing of the merger agreement.

Another "pitfall" of the point-of-purchase system was that it allowed for channel stuffing. The record showed that company management, concerned over making the revenue forecast in the first quarter of 2012, stuffed excess inventory into its distribution channels. As a result, the second-quarter numbers suffered.

Management projections. Prior to 2012, the company had created five-quarter forecasts but never multiyear forecasts. Witnesses explained that the semiconductor industry made forecasting difficult because of the stiff competition among players, technological change, and "macroeconomic factors." But, in June 2012, just days after Cypress announced its public bid, the company's new CEO ordered an equally new management team (most of the executives had been in their jobs for less than two years) to create long-term projections. He specified he wanted a "product by product build up, with assumptions, for it to hold water in the event of a subsequent dispute." He also wanted the projections done by using a point-of-sales approach, as opposed to the company's customary point-of-purchase method. At trial, the company's CFO explained the projections had a dual purpose: "marketing the company to a white knight and creating inputs for a DCF analysis." The head of sales, at the time, noted that even the car industry was more predictable than the semiconductor industry and proposed to "simply plug in 30% CAGR" for "out years."

Polar opposite views of the company. In trial, the parties presented two polar opposite views of the company—which found expressions in the "widely disparate" value conclusions the parties' appraisers reached. According to the petitioner, the company was "on the verge of taking off like a rocket." It had strong intellectual property protections for core products and a successful new management team; also management projections reflected the company's excellent business prospects, the petitioner contended. According to the company, however, it then faced a bleak future and might have folded if the Cypress deal had not ended well.

The petitioner's expert claimed the company's stock price was $4.96 per share. This price, the court pointed out, was more than 274% of the company's unaffected stock price. The expert used a combination of the DCF analysis and a comparable transaction analysis to arrive at this value conclusion. He weighted the former at 80% and the latter at 20%.

The company's expert arrived at a fair value of $2.76 per share. He rejected a DCF analysis, finding the management projections were overly optimistic and said there were no comparable transactions. Instead, he used the transaction price and backed out synergies. Despite his misgivings about the management projections, he performed a DCF as a check, which produced a $3.08-per-share value.

Both experts agreed that there were no comparable companies.

DCF lacks sound foundation. "Much has been said of litigation-driven valuations, none of it favorable," the court said in reaction to the parties' positions. It emphasized that the petitioner rejected the merger price but bought its shares *after* the merger's announcement, "thereby effectively purchasing an appraisal lawsuit." Such arbitrage can be lucrative when the market in fact undervalued the company, the court said. But, in this case, the petitioner invested so little that, even if it prevailed in this action, it would probably not break even because of the litigation expenses. As for the company, the court stressed that it "submitted an eyebrow-raising DCF that, based on projections its expert *presumed* were overly optimistic, still returns a 'fair' value two cents *below* the Merger price."

The court agreed with the company's expert that the DCF model was inappropriate in this case. "The foundational inputs of a DCF are the company's cash flows," the court said. Here, there were numerous reasons to question the accuracy of the cash flow projections underlying the petitioner's DCF study. Most obvious, they were prepared by a new management team, not in the ordinary course of business, and using a methodology the company had never used before. What's more, the record showed that, even using traditional methods, management's ability to forecast its own business more than two quarters was "of middling quality," the court pointed out. At trial, the company's CEO described the quality of the projections he saw when he assumed his position, in early 2011, as "probably mediocre." When asked whether he succeeded in making improvements, he said, "No." Part of the difficulty stemmed from a lack of understanding the market, he suggested.

The court also noted that the projections at issue were based on unrealistic assumptions regarding the company's ability to transition to another foundry that was to serve as a second foundry. The company had reached a management agreement with that foundry in late July 2012; the projections assumed the transition would take place in early 2013 even though the first transition took *seven* years and went so badly that it caused the company to place distributors on allocation, the court said with emphasis. Moreover, establishing a foundry requires substantial financial resources, which the company did not have in July 2012, the court pointed out. To assume the company could expect to start commercial production at the second foundry in 60 days and start experiencing cost savings within six months, as the projections did, was not reasonable.

Moreover, the management projections relied on inaccurate 2011 and 2012 revenue figures. Because of customer allocation issues and channel stuffing, they did not reflect actual demand for the company's products. Also, the projections did not align with the company's historical performance; they stated revenue growth and gross margins that required dramatic improvements to the business when there were no changes. The court said that the final nail in the coffin for the management projections was that they were not prepared in the ordinary course of business. There was testimony that the company used other sets of projections for managing the company's finances, including providing estimates of revenue and cash flow numbers to the company's bank. The contested projections were in anticipation of litigation as well as to shop the company to potential white knights, the court concluded.

'Dearth of data points.' The court also rejected the comparable transactions analysis the petitioner's expert had done and by which he arrived at an implied value of $3.99 per share. He used two transactions involving companies that produced memory products and that also did not have their own foundry. He determined multiples based on three metrics: (1) equity value/last 12 months' revenue (EV/LTM); (2) equity value/next 12 months' forecasted revenue (EV/NTM); and (3) EV/NTM + 1. Averaging the multiples, he generated an implied value for the subject company.

The company's expert noted that one of the companies featured in the transactions might not be comparable because the proxy statement for the transaction did not show the subject company on the list of comparable companies. But he also observed that the multiples for that company indicated the merger price in the transaction at issue was fair value.

A "dearth of data points" raises doubt about the reliability of the comparable transactions approach, the court noted. In the past, the court had rejected analyses that used as few as five and two transactions. Here, there were only two data points and the multiples differed considerably, the court said. The EV/LTM multiple produced a synergy-adjusted per-share value range of $3.99, with per-share values of $2.74 to $6.13. The EV/NTM multiple indicated equity values of $2.72 to $4.55, a range of $1.83. The EV/NTM + 1 multiple generated a closer range of $3.27 to $4.53.

These concerns and the fact that the petitioner's expert himself accorded little weight to the value stemming from the approach militated against using it to determine the company's fair value, the court concluded.

Transaction produces reliable value. Under case law, when a sound transaction process likely results in an accurate valuation of the acquired company, the court may give the merger price 100% weight, the court stated. It determined that this was the situation here, even though only one company, Cypress, actually made a bid and even though the merger was a hostile deal. For one, the company repeatedly resisted the bidder's offer causing Cypress to raise its price *five separate times*, the court said with emphasis. Ultimately, management succeeded in extracting a substantial premium—25% higher than Cypress's starting offer—from the bidder.

Also, during the three months in which Cypress pursued its hostile bid, the company tried hard to sell itself "to anyone but Cypress," the court said. But even though the company's financial advisor contacted about two dozen potential buyers, six of whom signed nondisclosure agreements, other than Cypress, no one bid. The lack of interest had to do with the company's operative reality, not with flaws in the merger process, the court concluded. Therefore, the merger price was a reliable indicator of value.

Synergy adjustment. The final step in the fair value analysis was excluding any merger-specific value, the court noted. Here, the company's expert, who had advocated for the merger price as the indicator of value, deducted $0.34 per share to account for synergies. In contrast, the petitioner's expert claimed the synergistic value was only $0.03 per share. He noted that negative revenue synergies and transaction costs had to be added back to the value the opposing expert determined for synergies. And the petitioner contended the deduction was applicable to the value Cypress attributed to the subject company, somewhere between $3.90 and $5.44, rather than the merger price.

The court disagreed with the latter proposition, noting it ran counter to the applicable statute, which required the court to determine fair value *exclusive of* any element of value attributable to the merger. The court also rejected the figure—over 10% of the transaction price—the company's expert suggested to account for synergies. It was based on a marketwide analysis of premiums paid by financial as opposed to strategic buyers. That analysis, the court said, "does not tell me anything about *this specific* transaction," which was the focus in a statutory appraisal action. Here, there was evidence that the acquiring company expected negative synergies of between 10% and 15% of revenue. Accordingly, the court used the petitioner expert's $0.03 synergy figure to arrive at a fair market price of $3.07 per share.

Lunn v. Lunn

Citation: 2015 Tenn. App. LEXIS 515
Date of decision: June 29, 2015
Experts: Robert Vance (wife/appellee); Brent A. McDade (husband/appellant)
Judge: Frierson II
State/Jurisdiction: Tennessee
Court: Court of Appeals
Type of case: Marital Dissolutiion
SIC code: 8021 Offices and Clinics of Dentists
NAICS code: 621210 Offices of Dentists

Tennessee Appeals Court Straddles Goodwill Issue in Divorce

Tennessee divorce courts seem divided on how to treat the goodwill of a business, specifically on the question of whether to adopt a distinction between enterprise and personal goodwill. The current rule seems to be that, if the business is a solo practice, goodwill is never divisible, but, if there are more partners involved and/or a business has pre-established contracts, courts may pay attention to the distinction. A recent case probes the issue further and in so doing provides a valuable summary of the state's goodwill jurisprudence.

Including enterprise goodwill. The husband was a dentist who started his own practice during the marriage. The business was a sole proprietorship. Its valuation became a point of contention at trial, with both parties presenting expert testimony in support of their claims.

The husband's expert stated that he understood Tennessee law to require that the value of the business be based solely on its net tangible assets. There should be no consideration of personal goodwill, he said. Accordingly, he valued the practice at $52,000.

In contrast, the wife's expert explained his valuation excluded the value of personal goodwill (about $210,000) but included enterprise goodwill, which amounted to nearly $278,000. Adding to enterprise goodwill the value of the business's hard assets and subtracting total liabilities, he determined the practice was worth nearly $430,400. He asserted that, since the husband had worked in another place at one point, "any dentist could step into [the husband's] practice." Consequently, it was appropriate to also consider the personal goodwill related to the subject practice.

The expert's personal goodwill argument carried no weight with the trial court. Citing precedent, it said: "There is a disturbing inequity in compelling a professional practitioner to pay a spouse a share of intangible assets of a judicially determined value that could not be realized by a sale or another method of liquidating value. *Smith v. Smith*, 709 S.W.2d 588 (Tenn. Ct. App. 1985) (citing *Holbrook v. Holbrook*, 103 Wis. 2d 327 (Wis. Ct. App. 1981).

At the same time, the trial court adopted the $430,000 valuation the wife's expert proposed, which excluded personal goodwill but included hard assets and enterprise goodwill. Although the valuation was "somewhat optimistic," it was acceptable because it aligned with the value ($450,000) the husband himself had assigned to the practice in a 2005 loan application, the court decided.

It found the $52,000 figure the husband's expert proposed "grossly" undervalued the company. Moreover, the court stated that "a valuation of the business that does not account for the enterprise goodwill that results from building a successful operation for eight years, especially when the business has been posting its best profits in the most recent years, seems unreasonable."

Excluding enterprise goodwill. Appealing the judgment at the state Court of Appeals, the husband contended the trial court was wrong to adopt a valuation that included enterprise goodwill.

The appeals court agreed. It allowed that some courts in the state recognized the distinction between enterprise and professional goodwill. But it continued to say: "[T]his Court has been reluctant to allow enterprise goodwill to be divided as a marital asset upon divorce when the business involved is a sole proprietorship as here." (referencing *Hartline v. Hartline*, 2014 Tenn. App. LEXIS 7). Since the husband's business was a solo practice, the trial court's adopting a valuation that expressly included enterprise goodwill was error, the Court of Appeals held.

In a final remark on this issue, the appeals court dismissed the trial court's effort to justify the final value by reference to other evidence, specifically the husband's "own admission" on a financial statement that the practice was worth $450,000. Looking more closely at the document, one could see he also had listed a debt against dental equipment of $240,000, the appeals court observed. Therefore, the total value as it appeared on the statement was only $210,000 and did not comport with the $430,400 figure the wife's expert proposed based on the inclusion of enterprise goodwill.

For all of these reasons, the Court of Appeals remanded, ordering the trial court to produce a valuation "without consideration of professional or enterprise goodwill."

Editor's note: All of the cited cases are available at BVLaw.

In re Mauer

Citation: 2015 Iowa App. LEXIS 172
Date of decision: Feb. 25, 2015
Experts: Dennis Redmond (wife); Eric Engstrom (husband)
Judge: Doyle
State/Jurisdiction: Iowa
Court: Court of Appeals
Type of case: Marital Dissolution
SIC code: 8042 Offices and Clinics of Optometrists
NAICS code: 621320 Offices of Optometrists

Asset Approach Avoids Double Counting of Future Earnings

Double counting remains a preoccupation for divorce courts across all jurisdictions. Recently, the Iowa Court of Appeals affirmed the trial court's decision to circumvent the problem by endorsing one expert's use of the asset approach to value the owner spouse's eye clinics. Using an income approach runs the risk of counting the owner spouse's future earning capacity twice, the trial and appeals courts said.

Income vs. asset approach. The husband was an ophthalmologist and the sole owner of three closely held professional corporations. At trial, the parties focused their valuation disputes on the two profitable businesses and agreed that the third entity had a value of zero and debts amounting to $390,000.

For the valuations, the wife's expert "primarily" used an income approach that considered goodwill. The analysis was based on the history of profit and prospect for profit for each business. He concluded that the first business was worth nearly $4.2 million and the second clinic approximately $1.2 million.

The husband's expert relied primarily on an asset approach and valued the businesses twice. Under the earlier, March 2013, valuation date, the first business was worth slightly over $1.2 million and the second was worth $300,000. Using information based on a later, August 2013, date, the expert arrived at a lower value for both businesses: $970,000 for the first business and $190,000 for the second practice. He said the decrease in value had to do with the changing healthcare laws. Also, the second business had experienced considerable turnover in optometrists. Statements from the husband suggested that he was trying to hire replacements but might have to close the second clinic.

The wife also introduced financial statements the husband had given to a lender before and around the time of separation. In the documents, the husband claimed a net worth of between $10 million and $14 million.

Expert fails to adjust downward. The trial court dismissed the financial statements as "not probative of the actual value of a business." These types of statements, the court said, were "commonly used in cases like this to gain an undeserved advantage over a business loan applicant by exploiting the loan applicant's exaggerations of his or her net worth to convince the lender that he or she is credit worthy."

The court also said it would consider goodwill in setting spousal support due to the wife. It said it favored the valuations of the husband's expert because he used primarily an asset approach. "Because [the husband's] earning capacity will be accounted for in setting spousal support, it would be improper to count it twice by using the income approach to value the corporations."

Specifically, as to valuing the second entity, the trial court noted that the wife's expert failed to make a downward adjustment to account for the business's 60% collection rate. Moreover, when valuing the business by the income approach, the expert failed to consider serious staffing problems and the attendant decline in income. The valuation proposed by the husband's expert was "more realistic," the court said. The court noted that, even though the resulting value might seem conservative, it was appropriate considering evidence that the business in the year of trial was not the same as in the years immediately preceding the present year. The odds that the husband would close that business or that the business would return to prior profitability were about even.

In conclusion, the court valued the first clinic at $1.02 million and the second at $190,000.

In terms of spousal support, the record showed the husband had a net income before taxes of over $750,000, $1.2 million, and $1.4 million in the three years preceding trial. In terms of the more successful first business, the husband's expert determined a salary of $900,000, which exceeded the husband's current wage of $500,000 and the three-year average of $324,000.

The trial court ordered the husband to pay $9,100 per month in alimony, which would taper off to $7,000 per month and finally to $5,000 per month until "the death of either party." The wife had requested $25,000 per month, decreasing to $15,000 and finally to $10,000. She said her starting amount was based on an actual monthly budget and a list of expenditures she had created.

Appeals court modifies spousal support. The wife appealed the trial court's decree at the state Court of Appeals, attacking both the business valuations and the spousal support order.

In terms of the business valuations, she claimed the trial court's failure to adopt her expert's methodology and conclusions led to an inequitable distribution of property. She also contended that the trial court failed to consider goodwill attributable to the businesses in valuing the entities.

At the outset of its analysis, the appeals court noted that valuing professional practices was difficult "because their income flows almost exclusively from the efforts of the professional who owns the business." Under legal precedent, goodwill attributable to the professional practice was a marital asset and subject to division. See *In re Marriage of Hogeland*, 448 N.W.2d 678 (Iowa Ct. App. 1989) (available at *BVLaw*). However, the appeals court went on to say, "Goodwill bears on the professional's future earning capacity (for the purposes of determining alimony), but should not be additionally listed as an asset in the valuation of a professional practice."

Here, the trial court explicitly stated it would consider the enterprise goodwill in determining spousal support, the appeals court observed. Moreover, to avoid counting the husband's earnings capacity twice, the trial court expressly said it preferred the valuations from the husband's expert as these were based on the asset approach, as opposed to the income approach. For these reasons and the fact that the trial court's valuations were within the permissible range of evidence, the appeals court upheld the business valuations.

But the Court of Appeals disapproved of the trial court's spousal support order. Considering the long marriage and the wife's limited earnings capacity, she was entitled to traditional, or permanent, spousal support providing her with "support comparable to what [she] would receive if the marriage continued." Although she "overstated" many of the expenses and included items in her budget for which she was not and would not be responsible in the future, the district court awarded an amount that failed to be equitable, the appeals court said. To award her $25,000, as per her request, was fair. It was best to broach step decreases related to the husband's retirement in a future modification action.

McCarter v. McCarter

Citation: 2014 Tenn. App. LEXIS 778
Date of decision: Dec. 1, 2014
Experts: Renee Harwell (wife/appellant); Jason Fleming (husband/appellee)
Judge: Frierson II
State/Jurisdiction: Tennessee
Court: Court of Appeals
Type of case: Marital Dissolution
SIC code: 6531 Real Estate Agents and Managers
NAICS code: 531210 Offices of Real Estate Agents and Brokers

Goodwill Determination Turns on Classification of Auction Business

A Tennessee divorce ruling deserves close reading for what it says and what it implies about professional and enterprise goodwill. The crux of the matter is whether a business owner who is not a professional in the usual sense, i.e., a lawyer, doctor, or CPA, can have professional goodwill that is nontransferable and not subject to division.

Goodwill value changes. The husband was a licensed auctioneer and real estate agent, who was the sole shareholder of a thriving auction business that he built during the marriage. The valuation of the company became a flashpoint during the parties' messy divorce proceedings.

At trial, the husband presented expert testimony from a CPA and experienced business valuator. The expert provided two reports, each based on the company's financial records for the past five years, from 2007 through 2011. He explained that he had completed an initial valuation based on the company's draft 2011 federal tax return and a revised report based on the 2011 final tax return.

Although both reports were admissible evidence, the appraiser said the revised report more accurately represented his opinion as to the business's value.

He said in both instances the valuation was based on two methods. One was an asset approach that he described as "adjusted book value—going concern method"; he also used an income approach, the "capitalization of cash flow method," which he said "effectively determin[ed] the present value of the Company's ongoing benefit stream growing perpetually at a fixed rate and discounted at the required rate of return."

In both reports, he determined that under the income approach the fair market value was $210,000. In the first report, the adjusted net book value was $176,000, but in the final report it had dropped to $125,000. He explained the change had to do with the different numbers that appeared in the company's 2011 draft and finalized federal tax returns for accumulated depreciation and cost of fixed assets. When he first prepared his valuation, the company's CPA had not yet made the requisite adjustments to the tax returns.

The expert also explained that the goodwill attributable to the husband was the difference between the enterprise value—$210,000—and the adjusted net book value—$178,000 initially and $125,000 in the final report. Accordingly, the goodwill value increased from $34,000 to $85,000.

Further, he reviewed a profit-and-loss statement for the first quarter of 2012, which ended approximately three weeks before trial. It suggested a $71,000 loss during that period, prompting the appraiser to lower the adjusted net book value from $125,000 to $104,000 as of March 31, 2012. At trial, the husband explained that this loss was in keeping with the seasonal nature of land auction sales.

The wife offered rebuttal expert testimony from a CPA who also had a background in business valuation. However, this valuator did not perform an independent valuation of the company but instead reviewed both versions of the opposing expert's report. The expert said her main concern was the significant change in goodwill: how could it reasonably have increased from $34,000 to $85,000, she asked. She did not contest the $210,000 figure resulting from the husband expert's capitalization of cash flow analysis and also did not argue with his approach to determining the adjusted net book value.

The wife's expert said the drop in enterprise value from $176,000 to $104,000 was completely the result of the first-quarter-2012 loss and did not credit the adjustment the husband's expert made based on the finalized federal tax return. If the first-quarter loss was seasonal, then the enterprise value would not change and the goodwill would be $34,000, she suggested.

Finally, she proposed that some of the husband's professional goodwill was attributable to the business rather than the husband personally.

The husband's expert explained that the husband's goodwill was not marketable; therefore, there was no enterprise goodwill. If the husband were to ask him to sell the business, "I would simply say, 'I'm sorry, I can't do that because his business isn't transferable in that sense.'" According to the husband's expert, the husband was "providing a professional service. It's not like manufacturing....

That's the reason we opine that all of the goodwill in excess of the adjusted net book value was personal goodwill."

The trial court adopted the valuation of the husband's expert, finding the business was worth $125,000 and rejecting the adjustment for seasonal loss. The expert used valuation methods that were acceptable under state law, the court said. It expressly stated that it "did not feel comfortable with the testimony of the wife's expert witness."

Flexibility on goodwill? The wife appealed the trial court's findings on multiple grounds to the state Court of Appeals. In terms of the business, she argued that the trial court failed to give due consideration to her expert's testimony and inflated the value of the husband's goodwill.

The appeals court disagreed. The trial court heard both experts, but only the husband's appraiser conducted a valuation of the business. The trial court explicitly stated that he used "competent" methods. The wife's expert did not object to either methodology. At the same time, she seemed not to understand how to calculate the goodwill. "It appears from her testimony that [the wife's expert] interpreted the goodwill estimate as a fixed amount rather than a remainder derived from subtracting the adjusted net book value from the total market value," the appeals court said. It also noted that the trial court expressed its lack of comfort with the testimony the wife's expert gave. According to the appeals court, as the fact finder, the trial court was in the best position to assess the credibility of the witnesses.

As for the goodwill in particular, the appeals court noted that under state law professional goodwill was not a marital asset. Without specifically saying so, both courts appear to have adopted the position the husband's expert took when he described the goodwill at play as "professional" and called the husband, an auctioneer, "a professional." Once characterized in this way, the goodwill was nontransferable and, therefore, not subject to division in a divorce proceeding. The appeals court did allow that under a recent decision some goodwill might be attributable to the business, "where the practitioner has one or more partners or pre-established contracts that could be assumed by another practitioner." See *Hartline v. Hartline*, 2014 Tenn. App. LEXIS 7 (Jan. 13, 2014) (available at *BVLaw*). However, in this instance, the husband was the only licensed auctioneer in the company and its sole shareholder, the Court of Appeals said.

For all these reasons, it affirmed the trial court's valuation.

Editor's note: This opinion leaves a lot unsaid, but a number of points deserve amplification. It is noteworthy that the husband's appraiser called an auctioneer a professional, a status that makes the husband's goodwill nontransferable. This attempt (successful) aligns with other divorce cases in which parties sought to expand the scope of what qualifies as "professional service" beyond the traditional professions such as law, medicine, and accounting. See Brave v. Brave, *2014 Ark. LEXIS 232 (April 17, 2014) (available at* BVLaw*) (chef and restaurant owner arguing unsuccessfully all goodwill in business is professional and nontransferable). Here, both courts accepted the characterization without explaining what makes the auctioneer a professional. Was it the license? Also, the appeals court suggests that where a business has only one partner it cannot have enterprise goodwill—a proposition with which appraisers might argue.*

Merlin Partners LP v. AutoInfo, Inc.

Citation: 2015 Del. Ch. LEXIS 128
Date of decision: April 30, 2015
Experts: Donald Puglisi (petitioners); Mark Zmijewski (company/respondent)
Judge: Noble
State/Jurisdiction: Delaware
Court: Delaware Court of Chancery
Type of case: Dissenting Shareholder
SIC code: 4731 Arrangement of Transportation of Freight and Cargo
NAICS code: 488510 Freight Transportation Arrangement

Chancery Adopts Merger Price Sans Cost Savings Reduction

In a Delaware statutory appraisal action, the Chancery once again determined that the merger price trumped values resulting from other valuation analyses. But before "placing full weight on the Merger price," Vice Chancellor Noble performed a DCF analysis as a check and in so doing provided a useful discussion related to the size premium. In line with the court's 2014 decision in *Huff Fund*, the judge also rejected a downward adjustment based on purported merger-related cash savings

Backstory. The respondent was a public transportation services company. It owned no assets, and it operated under a somewhat unusual business model, relying 100% on independent sales agents in the U.S. and Canada. The agents maintained all client relationships. In contrast, most other transportation logistics companies followed a store model in which brokers were direct employees of the company. Concerned that the market undervalued the company, in summer 2011, the subject company's board hired an investment bank with extensive experience in the transportation industry to explore strategic options.

The bank observed that the company "consistently traded at valuation multiples well below its peer group due to the Company's relatively small scale and corresponding lack of interest from the investment community." The bank also said that, if the company were able to increase its market capitalization from $20 million to about $400 million or $500 million, it would attract more attention from Wall Street and obtain capital at lower cost. The bank's preliminary valuation showed a range of $0.59 to $1.76 per share, yielding an average of $0.98 per share. The company traded at $0.60 per share at the time.

After some inconclusive efforts to shop the company, the board formally retained the bank to run a sales process. For purposes of the sale, the bank asked management to prepare bottoms-up five-year financial projections, directing that the forecast be optimistic. A representative working on the deal stated: "You certainly don't want to be conservative and leave potential shareholder value on the table." Because management had never done long-term projections, managers questioned their ability to achieve an accurate forecast of future performance. One person described the efforts at projecting as "a bit of a chuckle and a bit of a joke." Ultimately, management developed a forecast by projecting agent revenue, considering each agent's historical revenue and taking "the most optimistic view of agents' performance in the marketplace." Managers assumed that larger agents would grow at a lower percentage than smaller agents but acknowledged there "was no science" behind the assumptions.

Serious accounting deficiencies. The first 10 bidders offered prices ranging from $0.90 to $1.38 per share. Ultimately, a bid at $1.26 per share from a private equity investment (PEI) firm emerged as the highest and most serious offer. As part of due diligence, the PEI firm hired its own financial advisor to test the company's stated historical earnings and ability to meet projections. The advisor found the company's financial records were "unusually bad for a publicly traded company." It noted that the company used QuickBooks accounting software, which, while popular with small businesses, was rarely the tool of choice for public companies. It also was puzzling that the subject, a Florida-based public entity, used a one-office accounting firm based in Connecticut. The PEI firm's advisor said the subject's practices violated generally accepted accounting principles. An investigation also showed that the company's 2012 adjusted EBITDA was nearly a quarter less than management had estimated. In the face of these weaknesses, the bidder lowered the offering price to $0.96 per share. Negotiations between the company's special committee and the PEI firm ensued, hampered by additional discoveries of accounting deficiencies.

Ultimately the parties reached a deal at $1.05 per share. The bank advising the company declared the deal fair in its fairness opinion, and shareholders approved the merger in April 2013. There was no topping bid between the deal's announcement and its closing.

Two former common stockholders challenged the transaction and petitioned the Delaware Court of Chancery under the state's appraisal statute, 8 Del. C. § 262, to determine the fair value of their stock. "Fair value" means "the value to a stockholder of the firm as a going concern, as opposed to the firm's value in the context of an acquisition or other transaction."

Both sides engaged "well-qualified" experts to press their positions.

All valuation methodologies in play. The petitioners' expert valued the company at $2.60 per share. This value was the result of three calculations, which he weighted equally.

In essence, he performed a discounted cash flow (DCF) analysis, using management projections to forecast the company's future performance. Next, he conducted two comparable companies analyses: For the first treatment, he used a 2012 EBITDA figure he derived from the company's 2012 10-K; for the second treatment, he used an estimated 2013 EBITDA that he derived from modifying management projections.

In contrast, the company's expert found both the DCF analysis and the comparable companies analyses inappropriate under the circumstances. He noted that a key component, management projections, here was unreliable and generated an unreliable indicator of value. At the same time, he performed a DCF analysis "for illustrative purposes" for his rebuttal. For this analysis, he said he used five-year "base case" projections the acquirer had prepared during due diligence. The company's expert noted, however, that those projections also did not yield a reliable indication of fair value. And he explained that the DCF outcome did not affect his value conclusion.

Further, the company's expert contended that in this case a comparable companies analysis lacked the data necessary to perform it accurately.

He analyzed the merger price and the market evidence to determine the strength of the sales process and decided the merger price was the best indicator of fair value. But he decided to adjust the price downward to the tune of $1.4 million per year (before tax) to factor out cost savings related to the merger. He explained that one group of cost savings included public-company costs the company would eliminate once it stopped trading as a public company; the other group included savings related to executive compensation. He said that, according to academic literature, "target firms capture virtually all of the value created by corporate combinations through the price paid by the acquirer." Backing out the anticipated cost savings, the company's expert arrived at a fair value of $0.97 per share.

The court took issue with all expert valuations but overall found the company's expert most credible.

'Indisputably optimistic' projections. Given the problematic management projections, the Chancery swiftly dismissed the significance of the petitioners' expert's DCF analysis. This was an instance where management had never prepared projections in the ordinary course of business and, when it did, it did so to "maximize the effort to market the company." The projections were "indisputably optimistic," the court said, such that the petitioners' own expert noted he would have "implied a discount factor to back out the optimism if the record had provided a basis for calculating one." All of these factors triggered skepticism about the reliability of the projections. Also, the record showed that management had no trust in its own ability to forecast, which made the projections all the more unreliable.

Failure to consider size in comp selection. According to the Chancery, there were at least two reasons not to trust the petitioner expert's comparable companies analyses. For one, the companies the petitioners' expert used as points of comparison were all significantly larger than the subject company. All but two of the comparables had a market capitalization of more than 10 times that of the subject.

In testimony, the petitioners' expert contended there was no meaningful relationship between size and a company's multiples. He said he did not remember "ever discriminating inclusion in comparable companies based on company size … [because] size itself should not have an impact on the ultimate valuation."

The court found this statement unconvincing. It noted that there was empirical support in the valuation literature and in the court's decisions for discriminating among comparables based on size. Also, the company's expert in his publications suggested that it was inappropriate to choose comparables "without regard to relative market capitalization without otherwise controlling for risk and other differences." Further, the investment bank overseeing the sales process had extensive experience in the transportation sector and noted that the market usually perceived smaller firms to be riskier and valued them at lower multiples. The market afforded premium multiples to larger companies, considering them more stable, a representative of the bank said.

The court noted that, before the investment bank issued its fairness opinion, it prepared its own comparable companies analysis. It opted to use a lower multiple range based on the differences between the subject company and comparable companies. The differences focused on size, business model, and the quality of management.

Another of the court's concerns was the failure of the petitioners' expert to account for the risk that attached to the subject's 100% agent-based business model. The market perceived this model to be inferior to the company store model. According to testimony from a representative of the investment bank, "agent-based models ... are generally less desirable. They're perceived as riskier. The company does not have control over the customer relationship. The agent does."

The court observed that, at trial, the petitioners' expert was unable to identify which of the comparables used which type of business model but "suspected" most of them were agent-based businesses. In contrast, based on its knowledge of the industry, the investment bank advising the company used a below-median multiple for its comparable analysis, the court pointed out.

Because size and business model influenced the multiples at which companies traded in the transportation brokerage industry, the court declined to give any weight to the values resulting from the petitioner expert's comparable analyses. That the values were unreliable seemed borne out by the bids the company received during the sales process, all of them implying market multiples well below those produced by the petitioners' expert, the court said. Moreover, the company sold at a price less than half of the expert's comparable companies valuations.

Sales process substantiates merger price. The company's expert advocated in favor of the merger price, subject to cost savings adjustments. His proposition prompted at least three objections from the petitioners.

Speaking categorically, they contended the merger price was not a valid business valuation method. Moreover, a court could not rely on the price if there was no business valuation analysis to corroborate the merger price. Finally, even if the merger price were a legitimate indicator of value, it was not in this case because of the deficient sales process.

The Chancery gave little consideration to the first two contentions. It pointed out that in other statutory appraisal cases the court had exclusively relied on the merger price where that price proved to be the best indicator of value. Also, there was no requirement to substantiate the merger price through a particular valuation methodology. And, in this instance, the sales process validated the price. The process was comprehensive; it included arm's-length negotiations, a lack of compulsion, and the parties' having had adequate information. The merger price reflected a 22% premium to the company's average stock price during the six months that preceded the last trading day before the public announcement of the merger. It was noteworthy that, in the two years before the merger, the company's stock price never even reached $1.00 and that the merger price surpassed the highest price the stock had commanded during the previous five years, the court observed.

Also, the company retained an experienced investment bank to direct the process. "Part of the reason for hiring the bank would have been to educate the market and assure the Company that it was not leaving value on the table," the court noted. Even if the market had little information on the company before the sales process began, it gained ample information as the sale proceeded, the court added.

DCF as check on merger price. Before committing to the merger price, however, the Chancery performed its own DCF analysis. It said it used the financial projections the acquirer's financial advisor prepared during the due diligence process. Not only did the company argue that they were a more accurate forecast of the company's future performance than the projections its management had created, but also the petitioners' expert agreed that they were reasonably reliable.

The court noted a disagreement between the two experts as to the weighted average cost of capital (WACC) input. The company's expert used a WACC of 17.57%, whereas the petitioners' expert used 11.30%. The debate boiled down to the percentage of the equity size premium that was added to the company's cost of equity. Both experts used the capital asset pricing of equity (CAPM), and both added a size premium. Whereas the petitioners' expert used 3.81%, the company's expert used 11.65%.

Both relied on 2013 data from Ibbotson Associates, but while the petitioners' expert opted for the microcap category including the 9th and 10th percentiles—companies whose market capitalizations ranged from $1.13 million to $514.2 million—the company's expert used the 10z subdecile—featuring companies with market capitalizations from $1.13 million to $96.2 million. At the time of the merger, the subject's market capitalization was about $30 million.

The petitioners' expert said he would have used a size premium close to the 10z category or even the 10z category itself, but he thought it necessary "to strip out a marketability factor." The court found this type of adjustment to the size premium was plainly in conflict with the court's ruling in *Gearreald v. Just Care, Inc.*, 2012 Del. Ch. LEXIS 91 (April 30, 2012) (available at *BVLaw*). It dismissed the petitioners' argument that an illiquidity discount, as proposed in *Gearreald*, was distinct from the marketability discount applicable here. That distinction may apply in a separate context, the court said, but here the company's "cost of capital directly affects transactions between the Company and providers of capital, and is thus part of its value as a going concern."

The court selected the 10z size premium and a WACC of 17.5% and arrived at a DCF-based fair value of about $0.93 per share on the merger date. Ultimately, it decided against ascribing any weight to the DCF-derived value and adopted the merger price.

Insufficient basis for cost savings claim. In so doing, the court rejected the company expert's downward adjustment to the merger price; the adjustment was based on the principle that the appraisal award must not include merger-specific value. The expert's calculation relied on adjustments the acquirer's financial advisor had made when it prepared its base case projections during the due diligence process. The court said it was unclear how the financial advisor had arrived at its numbers. The Chancery declined to allow for a "near automatic reduction in price," finding that doing so would unduly reverse the burden on the party militating for the adjustments. Here, the company had failed to show that a downward adjustment to the merger price was warranted, the Chancery concluded. Consequently, the fair value of the company's shares was the $1.05-per-share merger price.

Moore v. Getahun

Citation: 2015 ONCA 55
Date of decision: Jan. 29, 2015
Judge: Sharpe
State/Jurisdiction: Ontario-Canada
Court: Court of Appeal
Type of case: Evidence

Canadian Ruling on Use of Expert Draft Reports Crumbles on Appeal

When a Canadian trial court last year decided to impose strict rules of interaction between attorneys and experts and compel production of expert draft reports, valuation and legal professionals in Canada balked and organized to intervene in an appeal. Their efforts met with success when an appeals court recently struck down the prior ruling.

Since financial and legal professionals in Canada and the United States maintain a lively exchange, the case also generated considerable attention (and concern) in the U.S. Even though the Canadian decisions carry no weight in U.S. courts, valuators practicing in U.S. jurisdictions will find the discussion of evidentiary issues instructive.

Activist trial court. In a medical malpractice case, the Ontario Superior Court of Justice grappled with a number of evidentiary issues related to the admissibility of expert evidence under Rule 53.03 of the Ontario Rules of Civil Procedure. One issue that became a flashpoint concerned the use of expert witness reports.

The defendants (a doctor and the hospital in which he worked) retained an expert who filed a first report in 2009 and a second report in September 2013. During discovery, the plaintiff found notes indicating a 90-minute telephone call had taken place between defense counsel and the expert. During cross-examination, the expert indicated that he had sent a draft of one of his reports to defense counsel. A phone conversation followed in which the attorney made "suggestions … of what to put in" the report. The expert made "the corrections over the phone." The expert then produced his final report.

The plaintiff did not pursue this issue, but the trial court found this interaction disturbing. It asked the expert to arrange his file in chronological order and furnish the court with his draft reports. The court—not opposing counsel—subsequently questioned the expert about the drafts and his discussions with counsel. When it became clear that there was another file (not in evidence), the court directed defense counsel to provide all instruction letters and records of any conference calls and asked the expert to return the next day for further questioning. The court embarked on a detailed review of the draft reports and found the interaction between counsel and the export led to significant changes in the testimony. Given "the conflict between the evidence at trial and the contents of the expert testimony," the court ultimately discredited the expert's testimony.

The trial court explained that amendments to the civil procedure rules occurring in 2010 specifically sought to counteract the "hired gun approach" to ensure the expert witness's independence and integrity.

According to the trial court:

> The expert's primary duty is to assist the court. In light of this change in the role of the expert witness, I conclude that counsel's prior practice of reviewing draft reports should stop. Discussions or meetings between counsel and an expert to review and shape a draft expert report are no longer acceptable.

The trial court went on to say that "if after submitting the final expert report, counsel believes that there is need for clarification or amplification, any input whatsoever from counsel should be in writing and should be disclosed to opposing counsel."

The decision generated strong opposition from the legal as well as the expert witness communities. The Canadian Institute of Chartered Business Valuators and the Advocates' Society were among the six organizations that intervened in the appeal to the Ontario Court of Appeal. They essentially argued that the trial court's ruling had no basis in precedent and the prohibition on communication between attorneys and experts interfered with the "normal, reasonable and prudent litigation practices" and increased litigation costs.

Collaboration is 'essential.' The appeals court sided with the interveners. It first addressed the trial court's declaration that the 2010 amendments to rule 53.03 triggered a "change in the role of expert witnesses." Not so, said the appeals court. There was nothing in the record underpinning the amendments that indicated new duties applicable to expert witnesses or that justified "altering the long-standing practice of counsel reviewing draft reports." Rather, the 2010 amendments reflected the basic common-law principle that an expert witness had to provide "fair, objective and non-partisan" testimony. The Court of Appeal acknowledged that some judges have voiced concern about the impartiality of expert testimony but found that "banning undocumented discussions between counsel and expert witnesses or mandating disclosure of all written communications is unsupported by and contrary to existing authority." The most effective way to expose "partisan expert evidence" is the use of cross-examination, the appeals court said.

The Court of Appeal went further. "Consultation and collaboration between counsel and expert witnesses is essential" to ensure that the expert witness understands his or her duties. A review of the expert's draft report allows the attorney to make sure the expert understands critical legal concepts, such as who has the burden of proof and "scientific certainty," and that the report conforms to the applicable rules of civil procedure. Also, the attorney has a chance to ensure the report addresses only matters within the expert's area of expertise and the expert does not "usurp the court's function as the ultimate arbiter of the issues." The trial court's approach would lead to increased delay and cost in a system that already struggles with delivering justice in a timely and efficient manner, the appeals court observed.

In an effort to avoid disclosure of communication between the testifying expert and the attorney, counsel would resort to "shadow experts" for advice and would opt to destroy draft reports that could be improved through editing, the reviewing court added. If anything, precluding collaboration between the two would provide an incentive for attorneys to use a "hired gun" because someone who makes it his or her career to testify in court will require less guidance and preparation from the attorney.

Litigation privilege protects draft reports. The appeals court also reviewed the disclosure requirements applicable to expert draft reports under the existing rules. Consultation between counsel and the experts typically is protected by the litigation privilege, which shields communication with a third party from disclosure "where the dominant purpose ... is to prepare for litigation." (This rule seems akin to the work product doctrine applicable under U.S. law.)

The law protects draft reports of experts the attorney does not intend to call. The litigation privilege also protects "draft reports, notes and records of any consultations between experts and counsel, even where the party intends to call the expert as a witness." According to the appeals court, imposing a rule that provides for the automatic disclosure of preparatory drafts and discussions, as the trial court did, would discourage "the participants from reducing preliminary or tentative views to writing, a necessary step in the development of a sound and thorough opinion." Also, allowing the trial court to engage in an "open-ended inquiry into the differences between a final report and an early draft," as the trial court in this case did, would lead to interference in the orderly preparation of a party's case and might needlessly prolong the proceedings, the Court of Appeal explained.

The existing rules require disclosure of the opinion of an expert witness before trial as well as disclosure of the expert's report and other "foundational" information, including the facts underlying the opinion of the testifying expert. The appeals court noted that the litigation privilege also "yields" when "the ends of justice" make disclosure necessary—for example, if the opposing side can show reasonable grounds to suspect that counsel interfered with an expert's duties of independence and objectivity.

"Absent a factual foundation to support a reasonable suspicion that counsel improperly influenced the expert, a party should not be allowed to demand production of draft reports or notes of interactions between counsel and an expert witness," the Court of Appeal said. In this case, the 90-minute telephone conversation between the testifying expert and the attorney "plainly does not meet the threshold" for supporting an allegation of improper influence. The trial court erred as a matter of law when it required routine documentation of changes in reports and disclosure.

The Court of Appeal also found that discrepancies between an expert's report and life testimony are the proper subject of cross-examination. If an expert's report was not entered into evidence and the expert was not cross-examined about alleged contradictions between his or her testimony and the report, the report carries no evidentiary value. "This is not a mere technicality but rather a matter of trial fairness," the appeals court said. An expert has a right to explain or clarify what may appear to be inconsistencies. According to the appeals court, in this case, opposing counsel did not cross-examine the expert on inconsistencies and the draft reports were not exhibits. Therefore, the trial judge erred "to the extent that she relied on perceived contradictions" between the expert's testimony and reports.

Notwithstanding the trial court's evidentiary errors, the Court of Appeal found they did not lead to a miscarriage of justice. The trial court carefully considered the evidence and gave "convincing reasons" why it preferred one expert's testimony over another's. Since the trial court "would necessarily have reached the same result," there was no basis for granting the appellant's request for a new trial, the Court of Appeal concluded.

Moore v. Moore

Citation: 2015 S.C. LEXIS 343
Date of decision: Oct. 7, 2015
Experts: Raymond E. McKay (Expert 1, wife), Jay E. Fishman (Expert 2, wife); B. Perry Woodside III (husband)
Judge: Kittredge
State/Jurisdiction: South Carolina
Court: Supreme Court
Type of case: Marital Dissolution
SIC code: 5719 Miscellaneous Home Furnishings Stores
NAICS code: 442299 All Other Home Furnishing Stores

S.C. Supreme Court Makes New Law on Business Goodwill

A South Carolina divorce case recently presented the state's high court with an issue of first impression concerning the treatment of enterprise goodwill. The case, which featured illustrious valuation experts, also triggered an informative discussion of issues related to discount for lack of marketability and valuation date.

Who steered company to success? The flashpoint in the parties' divorce proceedings was a retail store called Candelabra that sold high-end light fixtures and home furnishings and accessories. The wife, who had extensive education and training in sales and marketing, founded the business in 2001 just prior to the marriage. She served as president and was responsible for managing all of the business's operations, including the selecting and display of products. She also built long-term relationships with vendors and manufacturer representatives. The shop won an industry award for best lighting store in 2007 and was nominated again in 2012 for the same award. An employee said without the wife "it wouldn't be Candelabra. [The wife] is Candelabra."

The husband did not become involved in the business until 2005. In 2007, while the couple experienced serious problems in their relationship, the husband urged the wife to sell the business. A buyer offered to pay $1.7 million, which, at the time, seemed "surreal" to the parties; they did not think it was worth that much. In fact, the offer fell through in fall 2008. In the first years of the recession, the business suffered net operating losses. The husband was a driving force in the decision to shift focus to online marketing and to build a strong Web presence. The change in strategy proved successful, with the shop's website generating as much as 80% of the company's sales at the time of the divorce.

Since most of the company's value was in intangible assets—goodwill—who deserved most credit for the new business strategy became another sticking point during litigation. The husband claimed he "had to drag Wife kicking and screaming into the technological age." The wife acknowledged the husband's contribution to developing an Internet strategy and to finding the right people to implement the website update. But, she emphasized, she was the one who worked with outside people on making the website unique and accessible. And her ongoing monitoring and updating have made the website and the company a lasting success.

As sales began to increase, the couple's marital problems became more acute. In May 2011, the wife fired the husband. In June 2011, the parties filed for divorce. Based on a court order, the husband stopped being involved in the business.

Three aspects to valuation. During litigation, three valuation-related issues emerged: goodwill, discount for lack of marketability (DLOM), and valuation date.

Both parties hired highly qualified appraisers to support their claims as to the business's fair market value (FMV) and the goodwill allocation. The parties' experts agreed that the business's fixed assets were worth about $354,000 at the time litigation began.

The wife presented testimony from two experts.

Expert 1 was an attorney and CPA who testified that the unadjusted FMV of the business was $1.2 million. For his valuation, he interviewed the wife as well as employees of the business and he examined its history of operations and finance. He said he used a variety of valuation methods, including the net asset approach, the excess earnings method, the capitalized earnings methods, the discounted cash flow approach, and the market approach

He said that $846,000 represented goodwill. In his view, "at least" 20% to 25% of the goodwill was attributable to the wife (personal goodwill) and not subject to marital distribution. It was appropriate to assign at least this much to personal goodwill considering the wife had sole responsibility over day-to-day operations and she was the only one who selected products, monitored the website, and kept it fresh. Also, the wife had built important relationships with vendors and manufacturers. Without her expertise, the company would not be able to offer the unique mix of products that made it so successful with clients.

He applied a 20% discount for lack of marketability to capture the illiquidity of a closely held business. He acknowledged that there was an argument in the valuation community that "since the sale of the company is not anticipated as a consequence of most divorce litigation, no [marketability discount] should apply," but he concluded that under the FMV standard of value a DLOM was justified. Expert 1 concluded that the company's adjusted FMV was $960,000.

Expert 2 was a nationally recognized business valuator. For his determination, he reviewed the company's financial documents; conducted extensive interviews with company employees, vendors, and suppliers; and closely examined the company's website as well as the website of competitors. He concluded that the two factors that drove the business's success were its Internet presence, specifically its website, and its special product mix. The company was easily accessible on the Internet, and its website was user-friendly; the products, as selected by the wife, were stylish.

Website layout and product selection were critical if a company selling nonexclusive product on the Internet hoped to stand out, he explained, because "the competition is fierce [and] the barriers to entry here are rather low." There was no guarantee that sales and profit followed just because a company used search engine optimization (SEO) strategies, he noted. The wife's creative approach to the website's layout and her eye for presenting products were instrumental in converting Internet users from visitors to clients, he said.

He dismissed the opposing side's argument that anyone could take the wife's position and achieve the same good results. "That's a field of dreams. [Businesses] have to figure out a way. What differentiates me from the competition and [here] I think it's product selection, customer service, all those things."

On the subject of DLOM, he said that, because there were no "exceptional circumstances" in this case, it was inappropriate to discount for lack of marketability, particularly since no one contemplated a sale of the business.

The husband's expert also was an accomplished business valuator. That expert said he relied on conversations with the husband to understand how the business operated. He did not visit the store or interview the wife or other store employees. He determined the company was worth $2.96 million as of June 30, 2012. The valuation date he used was almost a year after litigation began. Under state law, the date of filing for divorce is the presumptive valuation date.

The husband's expert did not determine personal goodwill, but on cross-examination admitted there was "some" personal goodwill in the business. How much was "difficult to know," but it might be from "5% to 10%."

Since the company could be sold "fairly readily," there was no argument for a DLOM, he concluded.

The court record included emails from the husband to the expert that showed the husband tried to pressure the expert into producing a high valuation. "You are the only offense I have. Let's keep the wheels turning and get me the value [I am] deserving for a company with this type of opportunity," one of the messages said. At trial, the husband admitted to arguing with the expert over a "multiplier" but losing: "I fought him on it and he didn't give in."

In her subsequent appeal, the wife asked the court to dismiss the entire expert opinion based on this evidence, but the court declined, noting that a highly respected expert, such as the husband's appraiser, would not succumb to that kind of pressure.

Trial court adopts high valuation. The trial court credited the opinion of the husband's expert in its entirety. The company was worth $2.96 million as of June 30, 2012, it found. Based on the expert's reply during cross-examination, the court decided to assign 10% of the company's goodwill to the wife as personal goodwill. The remaining 90% of the company's value, excluding the value of its fixed assets, was enterprise goodwill and includable in the marital estate, the trial court found.

In terms of the valuation date, the trial court said it was appropriate to use the later date because there was an appreciation in the marital asset while the divorce case was pending—after the litigation had begun and before a final judgment. This appreciation was passive in nature and includable in the marital estate. That is, the growth of the business was primarily the result of the "market force of the Internet," as opposed to the wife's management of the company, her work on the website, or her product selection, the trial court said.

'Cautiously' following majority. Both sides appealed the trial court's decision with the state Supreme Court.

The wife claimed it was wrong for the trial court to include *any* goodwill in the value of the business. The husband contended the court erred in assigning *any* part of the company's value to the wife's personal goodwill.

According to the state high court, the parties' appeals raised a novel issue as concerns enterprise goodwill. Although South Carolina had a "categorical rule" against the inclusion of personal goodwill in the marital estate, the high court for the first time was asked to consider "whether enterprise goodwill can be a marital asset subject to division."

At the start of its analysis, the court noted that goodwill posed a particular challenge for family law courts around the country. In aiming to reach a fair and equitable outcome, trial courts "often and purposely" ignore "real world valuation principles," the court said. Among other things, trial courts wrestle with the construct of a hypothetical buyer and seller when "in reality there rarely is a true sale, for one spouse typically retains the business interest which is the subject of the goodwill valuation and apportionment dispute."

To answer the question at hand, the high court discussed in detail the differences between enterprise and personal goodwill, referencing *BVR's Guide to Personal v. Enterprise Goodwill* 19 (Adam Manson and David Wood, eds., 2011). It also reviewed the approaches other states have taken to resolving the issue.

Ultimately, the high court decided it would "follow the emerging majority approach and hold enterprise goodwill is marital property subject to equitable division." Personal goodwill, "which follows the owner and is entirely dependent on the owner's personal or professional services and skills, is not marital property," the court stated. And, it said, "enterprise goodwill, which inheres in the business itself and is transferrable in the market, should be distinguished from personal or professional goodwill."

The court said it answered the question in front of it "cautiously, knowing that today's decision does not and could not possibly answer the myriad questions that will arise."

High court applies new law to facts. The state high court had words of praise for all three experts involved in the case. Ultimately, it chose to credit the opinions of the wife's experts, except when it came to the issue of DLOM.

The reviewing court found there was "undisputed" evidence that some of the goodwill in the business was personal to the wife. The record as to the wife's role in product selection and website design supported the conclusions of the wife's experts. The evidence also showed that the husband "vastly overstate[d] his contributions to the implementation and management of the website development." According to the court, the husband was "a purveyor of ideas" who "left the details of putting his ideas into action to others with a solid work ethic, such as Wife."

The court also saw signs of enterprise goodwill. For example, the website's domain name was specific to the business, not to the wife. And, although the website once was a "minor feature of Candelabra's overall marketing strategy," it had become the business's central feature, being responsible for 80% of all sales.

The court quickly dismissed two claims the husband made as to the wife's personal goodwill. One argument was that only professionals, such as lawyers, doctors, and accountants, were able to develop personal goodwill. The court cited, with approval, opinions from different jurisdictions that found personal goodwill being developed in all kinds of businesses. The other argument was that, since 80% of the sales resulted from the website, only 20% of the company's value was in play when considering goodwill that was personal to the wife. There was substantial evidence that personal goodwill of the wife was linked to the website, the court said.

It held that the trial court erred in merely assigning 10% of the overall goodwill to the wife personally. The correct number was 20%, based on the opinion of the wife's experts.

The state Supreme Court also found the trial court was wrong to use June 2012, instead of June 2011, as the valuation date. Any efforts the husband made to keep the company afloat (around the time of the recession) occurred before the filing for divorce. Only post-filing activities affect the analysis of the active-passive distinction, the high court pointed out. Here, the wife's efforts after the filing date contributed to the increase in the business's value. Also, the court said, "it is not faithful to the record" to credit "market forces" with the successful website sales—which is what the trial court did. The evidence showed that growth was to a large extent the result of the wife's "active and continuing managerial efforts" for the website.

The reviewing court did "adopt a central feature" of the analysis the husband's expert presented—a zero DLOM. Although it declined to make a bright-line rule as to whether DLOM was ever appropriate in divorce-related business valuations, it found that in this case there was no justification for it. "Because Wife will retain ownership of Candelabra, we see no legitimate reason to indulge in the fiction of a marketability discount." This approach, the court noted, was in accord with existing jurisprudence regarding the valuation of closely held businesses and was even supported by the testimony of the wife's Expert 2.

It concluded the value of the business was $1.2 million. Deducting the value of the tangible assets resulted in an overall goodwill value of about $843,300. Only 80% of the goodwill was enterprise goodwill subject to marital distribution. The Supreme Court affirmed the award of the business to the wife and ordered her to pay the husband approximately $338,500.

Nordock, Inc. v. Systems, Inc.

Citation: 2015 U.S. App. LEXIS 17117
Date of decision: Sept. 29, 2015
Experts: Dr. Stan V. Smith (plaintiff); Richard F. Bero (defendant)
Judge: O'Malley
State/Jurisdiction: Federal
Court: U.S. Court of Appeals for the Federal Circuit
Type of case: Intellectual Property
SIC code: 3569 General Industrial Machinery and Equipment
NAICS code: 333999 Material Handling Equipment Manufacturing

Trial Court Misinterprets Damages Rules for Design Patent Violation

In a design patent infringement case, the Federal Circuit recently clarified the interplay between compensatory damages, such as lost profits or reasonable royalty, and special damages under Section 289. It found the defendant's expert used an improper method to calculate design patent infringement damages and the trial court failed to ensure the jury met its obligations under the applicable statute to determine the infringer's profits.

Improper methodology. The plaintiff and the defendant both designed, manufactured, and sold loading dock levelers. These are bridge-like contraptions that connect the loading dock with the truckload beds. The plaintiff sued the defendant over selling various kinds of dock levelers that illegally incorporated its protected lip lug and hinge plate design.

A jury trial on the issues of validity, infringement, and damages followed. The court denied the defendant's repeated motions before and during the trial to find the patent invalid. The jury subsequently found that certain of the defendant's dock levelers violated the plaintiff's design patent.

Both sides presented expert testimony on damages. The plaintiff's expert said that the defendant sold 1,514 infringing levelers resulting in over $912,000 in net pretax profits.

In contrast, the defendant's expert stated in his report that the defendant's operating profit per accused unit was $433. At trial, he indicated that the defendant sold 1,457 of the infringing devices. He also said that the plaintiff had not shown that it had suffered lost profits; therefore, lost profits were not applicable damages. He maintained that in this case "royalty was the proper form of damages, that $15 per allegedly infringing dock leveler was the appropriate amount of royalty, and that, based on the 6,000 accused units, total damages were about $91,650."

At the same time, he proposed an alternative calculation based on what he called the "cost savings methodology." This approach amounted to a form of apportionment. Specifically, he said that the cost savings the defendant made as a result of using the portion of the dock leveler that contained the protected design were "something less than $15 per unit. It's the same number as the royalty damages. It's actually less than that." He said he understood the plaintiff's position "that it should get the entire dock leveler, and to the extent that's the case the number would be, you know, higher obviously."

Instructing the jury on the applicable measure of damages, the district (trial) court said:

> For design patents, [the plaintiff] can prove either actual damages, known as compensatory damages, or it may prove [the defendant's] profits as its measure of potential recovery with respect to the sale of each unit of an infringing product. As compensatory damages, [the plaintiff] may prove either its own lost profits, or a reasonable royalty for the design patent. [The plaintiff] is not entitled to recover both compensatory damages and [the defendant's] profits on the same sale.

But the district court also advised the jury that, if it found there was an infringement of the plaintiff's design, it had to award the plaintiff the defendant's total profit stemming from the sale of the article to which the design was applied, not just the portion of the profit stemming from the design aspects of the patent.

The jury, relying on the testimony of the defendant's expert, found that 1,457 of the defendant's dock levelers infringed the protected design, and it awarded the plaintiff a reasonable royalty in the amount of $46,825. It also found that the defendant made zero ($0) profit from the infringement.

In a post-trial motion, the plaintiff asked the court to amend the judgment or to order a new trial on damages. Under the applicable statute, 35 U.S.C. § 289 (Section 289), the plaintiff had a right to recover the defendant's total profits from the sale of the infringing dock levelers. Here, the jury's verdict assigned zero profit to the defendant when the defendant's own expert determined that the defendant made a net operating profit of at least $433 per unit for the dock levelers, the plaintiff pointed out.

The court dismissed the plaintiff's arguments, saying the jury received detailed instructions as to the damages it could award. Here, it chose to award compensatory damages in the form of a reasonable royalty. The verdict aligned with the jury instructions and "a reasonable basis exists in the testimony and evidence presented at trial to support the jury verdict."

The plaintiff appealed the judgment with the United States Court of Appeals for the Federal Circuit. It challenged the jury's finding that the defendant made zero profit from the infringement as well as the district court's finding that the jury had no obligation to determine Section 289 damages in light of the jury's award of a reasonable royalty.

Misunderstanding the law. The Federal Circuit agreed with the plaintiff. It noted that a general misunderstanding pervaded the damages calculation in this case.

At the start of its analysis, the Federal Circuit explained that 35 U.S.C. § 284 (Section 284) sets forth the general rule in patent infringement cases. The provision says that damages must be "adequate to compensate for the infringement, but in no event less than a reasonable royalty for the use made of the invention by the infringer." Compensatory damages include the patent holder's lost profits or a reasonable royalty resulting from an arm's-length negotiation.

But, in the case of design patent infringement, Section 289 provides an additional remedy. A design patent holder may claim either $250 or the infringer's "total profit" from the sale of "any article of manufacture to which such design or colorable imitation has been applied," whichever is greater. At the same time, a design patent holder may not recover both compensatory damages and infringer profits.

Here, the jury's verdict was problematic for several reasons. For one, the methodology the defendant's expert used and on which the district court relied when it sanctioned the jury's verdict was fatally flawed. The expert applied the so-called cost savings method, rather than the legally appropriate gross profits method, the court observed. In calculating damages, he improperly limited the profits the defendant made from the infringement to the portion of the dock levelers that included the patented design. But, the Federal Circuit said, Section 289 does not allow for apportionment. Rather, it requires basing the award on the total profits from the "article of manufacture"—in this case, the entire dock levelers.

Further, it was clear from the patent that the protected design applied to the entire dock leveler; moreover, there was no evidence that the defendant ever sold the portion containing the protected design separately from the dock leveler. What's more, the defense expert's method also contradicted the district court's instructions to the jury, which defined the defendant's "total profit" as "the entire profit on the sale of the article to which the patented design is applied."

The plaintiff had a right to the determination of the defendant's profits based on the gross revenue method, the Federal Circuit stated.

Also, the court continued, there was no credible evidence to support the jury's finding that the defendant's profit from the sale of the infringing dock levelers was zero dollars.

Leaving aside the testimony of the plaintiff's expert, who calculated net pretax profits to the defendant of over $912,000, the defendant's expert found the defendant sold 1,457 accused dock levelers and made a profit of $433 on each unit. His testimony indicated a profit to the defendant of over $639,800. Also, even if the jury relied on the expert's improper cost savings method to determine damages, it should have found that the defendant made some profit on the infringing products.

The jury's finding that the defendant's profit was $0 was "against the manifest weight of the evidence," warranting a new trial, the Federal Circuit concluded.

Finally, the Federal Circuit agreed with the plaintiff that, even though the jury instructions accurately stated the law, the trial court misinterpreted them "to read out" Section 289. Rejecting the plaintiff's request for a new trial, the trial court said that the jury decided to credit the opinion of the defendant's expert and award a reasonable royalty rather than credit the testimony of the plaintiff's expert on lost profits. According to the trial court, the jury's decision to award one form of compensatory damages was all that was required of the jury.

The Federal Circuit disagreed. It said the trial court improperly "blended its discussion of [the plaintiff's] compensatory damages with the evidence of [the defendant's] profits. In so doing, the trial court overlooked the jury's obligation under Section 289 to determine the amount of the defendant's total profits. It was not enough for the jury simply to decide between awarding compensatory damages under Section 284 and infringer profits under Section 289. "Only where § 289 damages are not sought, or are less than would be recoverable under § 284, is an award of § 284 damages appropriate."

For all of these reasons, the Federal Circuit remanded, ordering the trial court "to revisit and re-structure its jury instructions on damages" to ensure the jury understands its obligation pursuant to Section 289 to determine the defendant's profits.

Editor's note: The Section 289 issue recently came up in the Apple v. Samsung *case with Samsung arguing on appeal for apportionment not only in cases involving utility patents, but also in those involving design patents. A number of law professors submitted a "friend of the court" brief supporting Samsung's position on this issue. They contended that allowing entire profits for design patent infringement "makes no sense in the modern world." The court was not receptive to the argument. It noted that the proper address for policy arguments was Congress, which, in drafting the statute, expressly removed the need for apportionment. See* Apple, Inc. v. Samsung Electronics Co., *2015 U.S. App. LEXIS 8096 (May 18, 2015) (available at* BVLaw).

Owen v. Cannon

Citation: 2015 Del. Ch. LEXIS 165
Date of decision: June 17, 2015
Experts: Yvette R. Austin-Smith (plaintiff/petitioner); E. Allen Jacobs (company/respondent)
Judge: Bouchard (Chancellor)
State/Jurisdiction: Delaware
Court: Delaware Court of Chancery
Type of case: Dissenting shareholder
SIC code: 8999 Services NEC
NAICS code: 541990 All Other Professional, Scientific, and Technical Services

Chancery Validates Tax Affecting in Fair Value Case

A joint fiduciary duty and statutory appraisal suit provided an opportunity for the Delaware Court of Chancery's new chief, Chancellor Bouchard, to rule on the issue of tax affecting. In discussing the choices that informed his discounted cash flow analysis, the chancellor explained in detail how he used the controlling *Kessler* model to calculate a 22.71% hypothetical corporate tax rate.

Success and disunity. Around 2000, three partners built a successful company that provided software-related services to the then-nascent retail energy industry. The company was organized as a subchapter S corporation. Pursuant to a stockholder agreement, the plaintiff/petitioner owned a 35.20% interest and his partners, the individual defendants (one of whom was the plaintiff's brother), owned 61.80%. Another executive, who was not a party to the litigation, owned the remaining 3%. The plaintiff served as president, and he and the two defendants were directors of the company. The plaintiff's exact ownership interest became a point of contention later on.

The company made pro rata distributions of most but not all of its income to stockholders. The three executives received salaries that were below market rate. They also received monthly "draws," that is, interest-free loans against their distributions, and they received distributions that covered their tax liabilities.

In the five years before the contested transaction, the company experienced consistent growth, notwithstanding competition. For example, revenue climbed from $14.9 million in 2008 to $32.2 million in 2012; during the same period, EBIT increased from $5.6 million to $17.3 million.

But by the late 2000s, an irresolvable disagreement over the direction of the company prompted the defendants to terminate the plaintiff as president and start working toward a buyout. One of the defendants took over as interim president. There was a problem, however: The ouster started to become costly for the company because, even though the plaintiff stopped working in 2009, he continued to receive his base salary, benefits, and stockholder distributions. In the five years preceding the 2013 merger, he received over $14 million in distributions, with the majority of them made after his ouster.

Valuations in contemplation of buyout. In 2012, the defendants hired a major accounting firm to assist the company in obtaining financing for the buyback of the plaintiff's shares. The accountants prepared a series of valuations based on projections by the defendant who was serving as president and in charge of day-to-day operations of the company. In his new role in the company, the defendant president developed a solid understanding of the company's future prospects, holding weekly and other meetings with the company's senior management. By the middle of the year, he had heard some company employees expressing concern "about possible attrition" in their customer base and had asked the accounting firm to revise its valuation.

In the fall 2012, the firm prepared a discounted cash flow (DCF) analysis for purposes of mediation that assumed a discount rate of 15.1%, a tax rate of 40%, and a perpetuity growth rate of 2.5%; it excluded the cash on the company's balance sheet. The firm arrived at an enterprise value of the company of approximately $118.5 million. Assuming the plaintiff owned 33.3% on a fully diluted basis, the firm valued the plaintiff's interest at about $39.5 million on a going-concern basis, excluding his pro rata share of any cash on hand.

Further assuming a 20% discount for lack of marketability (DLOM) and a 20% discount for lack of control (DLOC), the firm found the enterprise value of the plaintiff's interest was approximately $25.3 million, not counting his share of the company's cash.

Around that time, the company offered to buy out the plaintiff for $18 million, based on a 2011 valuation, rather than the contemporaneous DCF-based valuation. The plaintiff rejected the offer, arguing the company was "exploding in growth."

By December 2012, the company was aware that its largest customer would switch to one of its major competitors. There also was an increasing risk that customers, to cut costs, would do some of the work the company was doing for them in-house. Regardless, the defendant president saw the loss of the company's big customer as a "one-time event," rather than a "defect in the business model." In a sales and marketing presentation at the beginning of 2013, he talked about a "[v]ery full sales pipeline" and about his expectation of a significant amount of deals to come.

2013 projections. In March 2013, the defendant president revised the annual budget to reflect the recent loss, more competition, and some other changes in the business. The company provided the updated projections to the accounting firm. When compared with the 2012 projections, the 2013 forecasts revealed an expectation of lower revenue growth and operating margin. The 2013 projections also appeared to include "normalized" salary expenses for the two defendants and the fourth shareholder.

Based on the 2013 projections, the accounting firm prepared another DCF valuation that assumed a discount rate of 16%, a tax rate of 40%, and a perpetuity growth rate of 2.5%; it excluded $13.6 million in cash on the company's balance sheet. Under this valuation, the plaintiff's interest in the company was $22.3 million, excluding cash. On client instructions, the accounting firm sent the 2013 projections to a bank to obtain financing for the buyout.

The company also provided the 2013 projections to the plaintiff and in a cover letter proposed to buy out his interest for $26.3 million, including $4 million for his share of cash on hand. The plaintiff declined to respond.

In early May 2013, the defendants scheduled a special board meeting to vote on a proposed merger resulting in the plaintiff's buyout for $26.3 million. At that time, the accounting firm stated that there had been "no material changes to the business operations or forecast assumptions since completion of the analysis back in March."

When the plaintiff asked to push the meeting back one day to give him time to review the relevant documents, the defendants refused. At the meeting, the two defendants approved the merger and transferred their stock to an acquisition company in exchange for acquisition corporation stock. Shortly afterwards, they filed a certificate of merger. According to the plaintiff, the merger was "boom, done, Blitzkrieg style."

The plaintiff subsequently filed a complaint with the Delaware Court of Chancery, alleging the individual defendants and acquisition corporation had breached their fiduciary duty and asking the court for a fair value determination of his shares under Delaware's appraisal statute, Section 262.

'Delta' between valuation. For purposes of the statutory appraisal claim, both sides presented expert testimony. Both experts, and the court, relied on a DCF analysis to value the plaintiff's interest. But, instead of adopting either expert's analysis completely, the court performed its own valuation. It noted that disagreements over several key components created a "delta" between the experts' final values.

The plaintiff's expert based her valuation on the 2013 projections. Because she thought it appropriate to tax affect the company's tax rate to reflect the company's S corp status, she used a tax rate of 21.5%. Her weighted average cost of capital (WACC) was 13.28%, but the plaintiff subsequently accepted the opposing expert's rate of 14.13%. The plaintiff's expert assumed a terminal growth rate of 5.0%. She said she based her calculation on an ownership interest of 33.3% and acknowledged that the plaintiff's share of $17.4 million cash on hand might require adjustment for tax liabilities. She determined that the plaintiff's stock in the company was worth $51.7 million. After a post-trial adjustment of the plaintiff's percentage ownership and changes to the cash on hand figure, the plaintiff claimed his interest was worth $52.65 million.

In contrast, the company's expert rejected the 2013 projections but instead created a 10-year set based on per-unit calculations of revenues and costs. This meant that his projections for the five years covered in the 2013 projections were significantly lower. He also argued it was inappropriate to tax affect the company's earnings and used a 44.8% tax rate. At the same time, he proposed that the court use a 31.4% tax rate should it approve of tax affecting. The expert's WACC was 14.3%, and he calculated a 3% terminal growth rate. He concluded that, at the time of the transaction, the company was worth $65 million. Considering an ownership interest of 33.08%, the plaintiff's fair value of his stock was worth about $21.5 million.

Most of the value gap could be ascribed to the differing cash flow projections and the disagreements over tax affecting, the court said.

Litigation-driven projections. The plaintiff argued that, at the time of the transaction, the 2013 projections reflected management's best estimate of the company's future. They were based on assumptions the defendant president had made and revised as he was preparing to cash out the plaintiff.

In an about-face, the company cited a number of reasons why its own 2013 projections were inappropriate for a DCF valuation. It said they "were not the product of a robust process that included a broad management team, were not developed within [the company's] ordinary course of business, did not involve a thorough review of [the company's] or industry drivers, and were accepted by Defendants in the hope that a high merger price would avoid litigation." Accordingly, the company militated in favor of basing a DCF analysis on its expert's post-transaction 10-year projections.

The court found the company's arguments unconvincing. As a general rule, it explained, Delaware courts place great weight on contemporaneous management projections because "management ordinarily has the best first-hand knowledge of a company's operations" as well as "the strongest incentives to predict the company's financial future accurately and reliably." Here, the court said, the defendant president had undertaken a "deliberate, iterative process over a period of three years to create, update and revise multi-year projections." The process culminated in the 2013 projections, which the accounting firm prepared at his direction and in consultation with him. The record showed that the growth assumptions underlying the projections came from the company, not the accounting firm. Also, even though the defendant president may have been the only one creating the projections, he did so based on steady exchanges of information with the company's management. In testimony, he admitted that he was "very familiar" with the company's business lines and that its revenues 'have generally been predictive." The defendant president was well informed about the company and "brought this knowledge to bear on the 2013 Projections," the court said.

The court pointed out that there was evidence that he worked with the accounting firm to make significant downward revisions to his earlier projections at a time when he knew he wanted to force the plaintiff out of the company—if necessary based on a valuation using the 2013 projections. The revisions led to material decreases in the company's future performance, which were justifiable given the loss of a major customer and other pressures, the court noted. When the plaintiff failed to respond to the buyout offer based on these projections, the merger went through at essentially the same price. According to the court, the motive for the buyout was to "stop the hemorrhage," that is, paying millions of dollars in distribution to the plaintiff who had not worked for the company for years. The defendant president admitted as much at trial, the court said.

Also, the company authorized the accounting firm to submit the projections to a bank for purposes of obtaining a $25 million credit card facility that would finance the buyout. Considering it is a federal felony "to knowingly" obtain funds from a financial institution based on fraud or misrepresentation, the Chancery typically accords "great weight" to projections given to a financing source, said the court.

The post-merger 10-year projections the company's expert prepared were not management's best estimate of future performance at the time of the merger, the court concluded. They were created in the context of litigation and were too pessimistic, projecting noticeably lower revenue in a line of business that between 2009 and 2012 had grown from $12.34 million to $18.76 million. In contrast, the expert projected that going forward revenue would drop to $12.74 million in 2020 and slowly increase to $13.67 million in 2023. All told, the court said, there was no sound reason to replace the 2013 projections with the post hoc forecasts.

Tax-affecting dispute. What corporate tax rate to apply in calculating the company's projected cash flows was another point of contention between the experts. The plaintiff's expert argued a valuation of the plaintiff's interest had to capture the denial—due to the merger—of the future benefits of the company's S corp status.

The court agreed with this proposition. "A critical component of what was 'taken' ... in the Merger was the tax advantage of being a stockholder in a Subchaper S corporation," it said. Accordingly, adequate compensation for the plaintiff's loss required tax affecting the company's earnings as part of a DCF valuation.

In terms of how much of the earnings should be subject to tax affecting, the court rejected the company expert's contention that the plaintiff should only receive the value of being an S corp stockholder for the actual distributed earnings (76.7%), not for earnings the company retained and reinvested in the company (23.3%). It stated that "the operative metric under the *Kessler*-based valuation method is not the actual distribution made by a Subchapter S corporation, but the amount of funds that are available for distribution to stockholders." To conclude otherwise would deprive the petitioner of "his proportionate interest" in the company as a "going concern," the court said.

As for reinvesting in the business, the court pointed out that historically the company had not actually reinvested significant amounts of its undistributed earnings. Instead, it had kept the earnings as cash on its balance sheet. Nor was there any evidence that it intended to reinvest its cash as of the merger. Nor did it need to reinvest earnings to grow. Both experts, the court said, testified that the relevant projections included all of the capital expenditures necessary to enable the company to generate the projected future cash flows.

Using the *Kessler* model, the court determined the hypothetical corporate tax rate was 22.71%, assuming zero entity-level tax and a 47.25% rate applicable to the plaintiff's distribution from corporate earnings. The latter is the result of 35.5% actual federal income tax, 3.8% net income investment tax, and 7.95% state tax.

Additional disputed inputs. The experts also differed on what an appropriate terminal growth rate should be for the company. The plaintiff's expert calculated a 5% rate, which, she explained, represented a 0.5% premium to the midpoint of three estimates of nominal U.S. GDP growth prepared in March 2013, the month of the merger, for 2017 and beyond. The company's expert computed a 3% rate, which represented a 1% premium to the Federal Reserve's projection of inflation as of the merger.

Two principles should guide the calculation of the terminal growth rate, the court said at the beginning of its analysis. First, the rate "should not be greater than the nominal growth rate for the United States economy" because, if it were, the company's cash flow at some point would surpass the gross national product. Consequently, the 5% rate was too high for the subject company, which had developed into a company confronting increasing competition and flatter growth. Second, the rate of inflation represented a floor for calculating a terminal growth rate in circumstances where a company recorded solid profits and there was no noticeable risk of insolvency. This was the case here, the court said, adopting the 3% rate the company's expert proposed.

Moreover, the parties argued over the amount due to the plaintiff as a result of the company's $17.4 million "excess" cash at the time of the merger. They agreed that it was appropriate to deduct $2.3 million for certain tax liabilities. However, the company's expert proposed deducting an additional $916,000 as working capital, which represented 3% of the company's 2012 revenue. He called it an "extremely conservative estimate" and said not having cash on hand was not "a prudent thing to do." The plaintiff's expert said the company did not need extra working capital since it generated millions of dollars in capital every month.

The court agreed with the company's expert. Moreover, for its DCF analysis, the court decided to deduct an additional $1.2 million from the "excess" cash to account for outstanding liabilities related to the company's nonpayment of Texas use and sales tax.

Determining that the plaintiff had a 33.85% ownership in the company, the court valued his shares at $42.16 million.

Fiduciary duty claim. Lastly, the court found the merger was self-interested and unfair to the plaintiff. The defendants breached their fiduciary duty when they approved it. They timed the merger to exploit the loss of a major customer, which translated into a downward revision of the 2012 projections to the 2013 projections. The latter became the foundation for the company's $22.3 million valuation.

Also, in terms of process, the court noted that it was "inequitable" to reject the plaintiff's reasonable request to postpone the merger-related board meeting by a day. Moreover, under the court's DCF-based fair value determination, the price the defendants offered to the plaintiff was not within a range of fair value.

In conclusion, the court found that damages in this instance represented the fair value of the plaintiff's shares, that is, $42.16 million.

Perez v. Bruister

Citation: 2014 U.S. Dist. LEXIS 148314
Date of decision: Oct. 16, 2014
Experts: Dana Messina (DOL/plaintiffs); Z. Christopher Mercer (plaintiffs); Gregory Range (trustees/defendants); Matthew Donnelly (appraiser)
Judge: Jordan III
State/Jurisdiction: Federal/Mississippi
Court: United States District Court
Type of case: ESOP
SIC code: 4899 Communication Services N.E.C.
NAICS code: 517410 Satellite Telecommunications

Averaging Multiple Appraisals Yields Most Reliable FMV

An appraiser of dubious background proved to be a linchpin in a complex ESOP case that centered on allegations from the Department of Labor and individual plaintiffs against the plan's trustees for buying stock above its fair market value. In an undertaking full of obvious conflicts of interests, the transgressions on the part of the appraiser are noteworthy. Although he represented himself as the plan's independent appraiser, he blatantly aligned himself with the stock seller, shaping his valuations in accordance with the latter's instructions. The court's opinion includes a trove of damaging correspondence and serves as a cautionary tale that no misdeed goes undiscovered.

'ESOP possibility.' The company was a home service provider (HSP) for Direct TV, installing and servicing satellite television equipment. Direct TV was the company's sole client, which meant it had all the leverage. This included the right to terminate its contract with the company unilaterally and without cause and being under no obligation to promise the company exclusivity over service areas. Starting in 2000, when the company's founder and owner explored ways to divest himself of the company, the Direct TV contract proved a major obstacle to finding a buyer. With the help of a friend, the owner then developed an alternative exit strategy—what the court called the "ESOP possibility."

In a series of transactions that took place between 2002 and 2005, he sold 100% of the company's shares to its employees by way of an employee stock ownership plan (ESOP) and using a family limited liability company (LLC) that held the company stock. Three of the transactions gave rise to the case in front of the court. In each, the plan bought company stock through an employee stock ownership trust (ESOT) for which the owner-seller and two persons with a close working relationship to him served as trustees. The transactions involved a combination of cash payments and transaction loans.

A December 2004 transaction included cash and a transaction loan from the LLC to the ESOT for the purchase of pledged stock. The company, not the LLC, held pledged stock subject to the loan in a suspense account. Contributions the company made into the ESOT were used to make payments on the principal and interest. At the end of the year, the company would release a proportional amount of pledged stock from suspension. The loan was refinanced the following year to reflect a "mirror" loan whereby the company was substituted for the LLC as creditor incurring an obligation to repay the LLC as the company received payments from the ESOT. A second transaction that took place in September 2005 involved all cash. And a third transaction occurring in December 2005 was another mirror loan with no cash. The total amount of principal and interest the ESOT paid from employer contributions was about $9.6 million; the total price for the three transactions was about $19.2 million.

The trustees based the share price on valuations an appraiser had performed. In 2010, the U.S. Department of Labor (DOL) sued the trustees in federal court, alleging violations of ERISA under sections 404(a)(1) and 406 for breach of fiduciary duty, failure to monitor, and engaging in prohibited transactions. The district court (S.D. Miss.) consolidated the case for trial with a separate case two plan participants had brought based on similar allegations. The key issue was whether the trustees paid too much for the stock because the appraiser's valuation did not reflect the fair market value (FMV) of the stock.

The company stopped operating in 2008 after negotiating a deal with Direct TV under which the latter assumed the company's debt and acquired its assets in a foreclosure sale.

At the start of its decision, the court pointed out that "this is not a normal case," considering the "enormous" record and many factual and legal disputes. But the crux of the case was whether the appraiser and the trustees were truly independent and looking out for the interests of the ESOP and whether it was reasonable for the trustees to rely on the appraiser's valuations. The court's answer to these questions was "no."

Appraiser requires help with valuations. The court found the appraiser was compromised in several ways. Although he purported to work for the ESOT, he had a history of working for the owner-seller of the stock and his allegiance was to the seller and the seller's legal advisor. The seller hired the appraiser around 2000 to do a feasibility study for him. At the time, the appraiser lobbied to be retained as the future "independent" ESOP appraiser by offering to cut his fee. He also was eager to please the seller's lawyer, promising to "get you one good ESOP project every month, for the next 20-30 years." No one in the company investigated the appraiser's background, and, therefore, no one knew that he lacked a college degree and that he had a prior felony conviction for fraud and operated under an assumed name.

The appraiser claimed to have performed over a thousand valuations, many involving ESOP transactions. Yet, because there were gaps in his understanding of valuation concepts, he relied "heavily" on California-based Business Equity Appraisal Reports Inc. (BEAR) to assist with the calculations. Typically, he sent data and instructions to BEAR, which BEAR plugged into a computer program to generate an analysis or report. Contemporaneous emails and deposition testimony from a BEAR valuator who was the appraiser's main contact revealed her concerns about the appraiser and his valuations.

While working on valuations on behalf of the ESOT, the appraiser communicated directly with the owner-seller and the seller's counsel rather than with the two lay trustees or ESOT counsel. He sent draft valuations to the seller and his lawyer, modified valuations to align them with the lawyer's instructions, and forwarded only the final valuation to the ESOT trustees and counsel.

The December 2005 transaction, the court found, best illustrated the undue influence the seller and his lawyer had over the appraiser. This event represented the last chance for the owner to sell stock because afterward the employees would own all of the company stock. The appraiser initially provided data to BEAR specifying a 17% capitalization rate. BEAR's representative sent an email noting the calculated result was significantly less than one from five months ago, but she did not specify a value. In response, the appraiser said the company had incurred considerably more debt in the meantime. He went on to say that, since there was a proposal to buy the company's assets for $50 million, "the owner needs to get his fair share or the ESOP will get it all." He then considered the company's profitability during the preceding three years and directed BEAR to give more weight to the most profitable year and to decrease the cap rate to 16.1%—all in an effort to increase the ultimate value. He also contacted the seller's lawyer to relay the bad news, all the while assuring the latter he would "tweak" the valuation" to approximate the $50 million number.

He did, the court said. After the first valuation came in at $30 million, he kept changing the variables, including reducing the weight he had given to the 2005 numbers from three to one and dropping the cap rate to 16%. Based on instructions from the seller's attorney, he told the BEAR representative to include an explanation in the valuation that 2005 was an aberrant year given the effect of Hurricane Katrina and a few other unusual events. When ESOT counsel was included in the correspondence and noted he had not seen the draft valuation that the appraiser had been discussing with the seller and the latter's lawyer, the appraiser declined to provide the draft; instead, he promised to send ESOT counsel a finalized valuation at the same time he sent it to the seller.

"There is no legitimate reason why this appraisal was higher than the previous appraisals," the court said. Trial expert testimony and the record showed that the company's value dropped in the months prior to the December 2005 transaction. What's more, the appraiser in his earlier message to BEAR explained why that was the case. But he subsequently increased the value, "showing that [the appraiser] followed through with his stated intent to help [the owner] in his final opportunity to sell stock." This history showed the appraiser's divided loyalties and put in doubt each of the transactions. "In sum, these were not arm's-length transactions," the court concluded.

Trustees lack valuation knowledge. According to the court, the structure of the transactions was rife with conflicts of interest, starting with the composition of the board of trustees. It included the owner-seller and two lay trustees, one of whom worked directly for the owner, as did her husband. She later testified that she always considered the owner's and the company's interests, even when acting on behalf of the ESOP. The other trustee was a CPA who considered the owner-seller a friend and noted he was a major client of her firm. She later said she was concerned about the owner's interests, but those concerns were secondary to the concerns for the ESOT.

What's more, the court observed, both lay trustees, although "decent people" and "certainly likable," lacked the understanding of business valuation necessary to challenge the appraiser's calculations. The employee trustee said so in writing and from the get-go voiced doubts about her ability to serve as trustee. The CPA trustee had an MBA and stronger qualifications, but she also did not understand the appraiser's valuation methods to the degree that she could challenge his decisions and conclusions. Frequently, both trustees turned to the owner and his lawyer, asking for guidance on ESOP-related questions, including issues such as "accounting adjustments made for 'valuation purposes.'"

But, said the court, the trustees' lack of knowledge of the valuation process did not justify their total reliance on the appraiser. Although both persons understood accounting principles and the way the company operated, they failed to "spot a few glaring mistakes." One involved a $6 million error the appraiser made in the December 2004 valuation when he added instead of subtracted $3 million. The trustees' failure to catch this mistake may have resulted in considerable overpayment, the court observed. It also noted that the appraiser subsequently brought the mistake to the trustees' attention and purportedly fixed it in a new report but, nevertheless, achieved the same FMV he obtained using different data earlier. "The Court has considerable suspicion that this post-closing fix could occur without manipulating the numbers."

Also, the appraiser's calculations for 2003 and 2004 included a "projection risk," which he said reflected "our estimate of the risk that the projections may not be realized." For 2003, he used an 8% risk, but for 2004 he lowered the risk to 3%. In testimony, the CPA trustee could not articulate a reason for the drop. For 2005, which was by all accounts a particularly difficult year for the company, the appraiser decreased the risk to 2.5%. "If anything, [the company's] projection risk should have increased with the obstacles it faced in 2004 and 2005," the court noted.

Protection for the plan participants could have come from ESOT counsel had he or she been independent, the court said. But this was not the case. When the first ESOT attorney, who was paid by the company, "proved too thorough and expensive," the owner's attorney replaced him with one of his former law partners. "Thus, the seller—acting through an agent—terminated the buyer's independent counsel," the court stated. The second ESOT counsel played a limited role and failed to ask relevant questions. Once he learned there was a draft report he had not seen, ESOT counsel failed to push back regarding the appraiser's refusal to provide the report and failed to ask why the seller's attorney had instructed the plan's independent appraiser to adjust EBITDA in a draft report that he had not shared with the ESOT trustees or counsel.

According to the court, "the bigger picture is that the purchase price was always [the appraiser's] number." There was little communication involving the trustees and the ESOT counsel before the transactions took place. The latter rarely saw valuations before the eve of closing. Unlike the seller's attorney, the trustees never negotiated with the appraiser over valuation reports. For all these reasons, the court determined that there was no reasonable justification for the trustees' reliance on the appraiser.

Appraiser works with spotty data. The trustees also failed to provide the appraiser with accurate and complete financial data, the court concluded. They provided financial data that they said complied with GAAP, when they knew the data did not. Even their trial valuation expert acknowledged that the internal financial results "have known accounting inaccuracies and divergences from generally accepted accounting principles in the U.S." Also, the appraiser based his valuation on an overly optimistic view of the company's relationship with Direct TV, which he formed from conversations with the company's owner and which no one seemed to correct. For his part, the appraiser never reviewed the contracts the company had with Direct TV. As a result, he concluded that it would be difficult for a competitor to take the company's market. No one seemed to have informed him about crucial risk factors in the parties' relationship, including Direct TV's unilateral decision to keep reducing the rates it would pay to HSPs, its requirement that HSPs lease or purchase company vehicles in 2005, and the company's growing cash flow problems.

The trustees' argument that the rate changes were less significant because the company was able to generate revenue from other sources had no traction with the court. It found that the standard professional installation fees made up the majority of the company's revenues and the dropping margins sent shock waves through the HSP community. Also, the court said, "a legitimate appraiser would want to know that the company's sole client had begun slashing rates" because rate reductions "necessarily impact [the company's] company-specific risk and projected EBITDA margins."

Similarly, the vehicle policy was "a game changer that the trustees should have explained to [the appraiser]," the court pointed out. It meant increased expenses as far as gas, leases, maintenance, and insurance were concerned. The owner admitted that the added cost from gas alone was between $25,000 a day and $40,000 a day, depending on the price of gas. Direct TV's policy change left HSPs squeezed, the court observed, but the appraiser was "generally oblivious to these dramatic shifts." Therefore, he did not account for them in developing his projections. Rather, he assumed that the expenses would be reflected in the financial statements after they had been incurred, the court added.

The decreasing margins contributed significantly to the company's cash flow problems in 2004 and 2005. For a while, the company's owner loaned millions of dollars to the company to make payroll and cover other expenses, which the company paid back promptly. But after Hurricane Katrina hit in 2005, its ability to repay the owner was wanting. What the effect of the storm on the business was remained unclear, the court said, but the trustees should have explored the debt repayment issue with the appraiser.

While the trustees openly discussed questions as to the company's viability among themselves at the time of the third transaction in December 2005, they painted a rosy picture to the appraiser, watching as the seller's lawyer "coaxed [the appraiser] to the highest-ever valuation," said the court.

For all these reasons, the court found the trustees had breached their fiduciary duty and paid an inflated stock price.

Court grapples with remedy. The court said determining an appropriate remedy was more difficult than determining liability in this case. The three parties advocated for different measures of damages. The DOL urged the court to rescind the transactions, noting the difficulty of determining the stock's FMV at the time the transactions occurred, and it asked for an $8.77 million surcharge payment from the fiduciaries. The individual plaintiffs wanted an award representing the difference between the full contract price for each transaction and the actual fair market value on the date the transaction closed. The trustees objected, claiming they should only be liable for the difference between what was actually paid and what should have been paid. Considering there was debt related to the transaction loans that was never repaid, the amounts paid for the December 2004 and 2005 transactions were less than the FMV the plaintiffs' own experts determined; consequently, the plan suffered no loss from these events, they claimed.

The court dismissed the trustees' argument, as well as the DOL's. The correct measure of damages was the amount the plan participants overpaid, it said. Although difficult, calculating that amount was not impossible. For its FMV determination, the court considered the testimony of the three noted valuation experts the parties presented at trial. Different experts used different methods or applied the methods they used differently, but they all used multiple methods to produce several FMV estimates on the transaction dates, the court pointed out. To arrive at a final conclusion, they averaged or weighted the results. "This method tempered the outliers that some methods produced," the court observed with approval. Accordingly, it decided to take a number of valuations resulting from different methods and assumptions and average them. "In this way, the Court's sample pool is larger than those averaged or weighted by the individual experts," it explained.

This approach was reasonable because no expert was more credible than the others and no one methodology was clearly correct or incorrect, the court added. It noted conceptual and technical differences. For example, the trustees' expert saw the company as a growth company during the relevant 2004 and 2005 years, based on interviews with the trustees. But, said the court, these interviews took place years after the transactions and after a lawsuit was underway. The information the expert received did not accord with contemporaneous records and overestimated the company's projected EBITDA margins and long-term prospects. The government's expert and the plaintiffs' expert were on the other end of the spectrum, assuming a no-growth company. This perception may have been influenced by the company's ultimate demise and seemed to lead to undervaluation, the court said. The trustees' expert used the guideline public company method but made large adjustments, which prompted criticism from the plaintiffs' expert that the need to do so showed the method was inappropriate. Unlike the other two experts, the government's expert declined to rely on the company's financial statements but instead re-created the numbers based on industry norms. This approach prompted critique from the trustees' experts. According to the court, this showed that there were different ways to address the same ultimate issue and their validity depended on the validity of the expert's judgment.

The valuations the court did not include in its calculation were those from the appraiser, "because they are not credible." Based on the above approach, the court generated a per-share price for the three transactions and compared it with the per-share price the appraiser determined. The court noted that its own FMV numbers were consistently below the appraiser's final results. The court's calculations also showed that "the margin by which the numbers were inflated grows with each transaction." This picture aligned with the record, the court said. It concluded that the total amount of overpayment was over $4.5 million, for which the trustees were jointly and separately liable. The owner-seller-trustee was also liable for nearly $2 million in prejudgment interest.

The court seemed to foresee an appeal, noting that, just as the individual appraisals lend themselves to critique considering the many subjective decisions the appraisers made to arrive at them, the court's findings may be "vulnerable." But, it added, in the end, "the undersigned is comfortable with this approach and the results."

Rabe v. Rabe

Citation: 2015 Ky. App. Unpub. LEXIS 379
Date of decision: May 29, 2015
Experts: Robert Sicking Jr. (wife); Gary Jennings (husband)
Judge: Vanmeter
State/Jurisdiction: Kentucky
Court: Court of Appeals
Type of case: Marital dissolution
SIC code: 4212 Local Trucking without Storage
NAICS code: 484110 General Freight Trucking Local

Court Infers Nature of Goodwill From Nature of Business

A recent opinion in a divorce case from the Kentucky Court of Appeals, although unpublished, merits attention because it shows the court ruling on the nature of goodwill in a business valuation based merely on the type of business at stake. The opinion also serves as a reminder to appraisers that failure to address questions regarding the nature of the goodwill head-on may put the client at a disadvantage in trial and on appeal.

Recap. This case has a business valuation history. The husband was the sole owner and operator of a transportation company that he brought into the marriage. The business provided him with an income of between $350,000 and $400,000. In the original proceeding, the issue for the trial court was the company's increase in value during the marriage. That amount was divisible marital property.

Both parties presented expert testimony, with the husband's expert concluding the increase in value was about $149,000, whereas the wife's expert claimed it was nearly $462,000. The husband's expert explained that, based on information he had received from the husband, the company was "fragile." Some 60% to 80% of the company's business stemmed from one customer that could terminate its relationship with the company on 30 days' notice. For this reason, the expert used a low earnings multiplier of one.

The trial court found this testimony "more accurate" than the testimony from the wife's expert, but it decided to modify the amount to arrive at an increase in value of nearly $205,000.

In the first appeal, the wife successfully argued that the trial court erred by crediting the testimony of the husband's expert. The expert blindly relied on information from the husband that proved to be inaccurate as concerned the company's business relationship with its alleged sole client. Rather than being the subject company's largest customer, the latter had an agency relationship with the subject company. Under the parties' franchise agreement, the company generated all of its business independently and had many customers.

The appeals court remanded, ordering the trial court to reconsider its determination. If the trial court decided to rely again on the opinion of the husband's expert, it had to provide specific findings of fact that justified its reliance. (A digest and the court's opinion for *Rabe v. Rabe*, 2008 WL 4998483, are available at *BVLaw*.)

Tables turned. On remand, with a different judge presiding, the trial court decided to rely on the wife's expert for its valuation of the business.

Once the trial court had entered its supplemental judgment, the husband filed a motion asking the court to reconsider its calculation of the wife's interest in the company and also to determine the nature of goodwill included in the business valuation. The trial court declined to do so.

New appeal addresses goodwill. The husband next appealed the valuation a second time. He claimed it was error for the trial court suddenly to rely on the wife's expert when it simply could have made new findings of fact that supported its earlier reliance on the valuation from the husband's expert. The husband blamed the court's change in position on the fact that two different judges oversaw the case. He also contended the valuation the wife's expert offered included goodwill value but failed to distinguish between enterprise and personal goodwill.

As to the first objection, the appeals court said that, even though it sympathized with the husband's frustration about multiple judges presiding over the case, the trial court's crediting the valuation of the wife's expert on remand was not an abuse of discretion.

As for the goodwill issue, the court noted that under state case law only enterprise—not personal—goodwill was subject to division. See *Gaskill v. Robbins*, 282 S.W.3d 306 (Ky. 2009) (available at *BVLaw*). The appeals court said that, in the case in front of it, it seemed that the trial court, by including the goodwill in the value of the business, attributed the goodwill to the business and as such considered it divisible. The trial court had discretion to do so, the Court of Appeals said.

The appeals court explained that, in *Gaskill*, the business at issue was a professional practice. Personal goodwill, it said, was "most commonly found in similar professional practices that receive business as a result of the professional's reputation. The business would not have the same value absent the professional because the professional's reputation cannot be transferred to a buyer."

In contrast, the business in this case was not a professional practice, the appeals court observed. Consequently, "it seems likely that the business's name and reputation earn it business rather than [the husband's] name and reputation." Further, neither party offered testimony that any of the goodwill was personal rather than enterprise goodwill. "Hence, the goodwill of [the company] is enterprise goodwill, something which would be transferable in a sale of the business," the appeals court concluded. Consequently, it found the trial court did not err in including goodwill in the value of the business and upheld the valuation.

Reedy-Huffman v. Huffman

Citation: 2015 Alas. LEXIS 56
Date of decision: May 20, 2015
Judge: per curiam
State/Jurisdiction: Alaska
Court: Supreme Court of Alaska
Type of case: Marital dissolution
SIC code: 8049 Offices and Clinics of Health Practitioners N.E.C.
NAICS code: 621399 Offices of All Other Miscellaneous Health Practitioners

Court Validates Zero Goodwill for Naturopathic Practice

A short but informative Alaska divorce ruling involving a professional practice provides a helpful summary of the state's position on goodwill. The court's opinion also sounds a cautionary note about the importance of presenting valuation testimony—whatever form it may take.

Evidentiary void as to value of practice? The husband was a licensed naturopathic physician who owned two practices on the Kenai Peninsula in Alaska that operated under the same name. Alaska is an equitable distribution state but allows for community property agreements between spouses.

After filing for divorce, the wife obtained an order from the trial court directing the husband to pay $10,000 to allow her to cover interim attorney fees and hire a business valuator. The wife noted that the husband had "possession and control of all of the business documents." Even though the husband paid, the wife did not retain a valuation expert.

Neither did the husband. But, at trial, he testified that his business had zero market value, reasoning that the only similar business on the peninsula was for sale for over a year but did not sell. Ultimately that business was taken off the market, he explained. The wife did not present any contrary evidence or, for that matter, any alternate valuation. Instead, she claimed there was an "evidentiary void" as to the business value and maintained that the practice should be valued at $500,000 "to account for its goodwill as an ongoing established business." She did not point to any support for that claim.

But she provided evidence of the business's various assets and their individual values, which the trial court adopted for purposes of dividing the marital estate. At the same time, based on the husband's testimony, the trial court found the business had zero goodwill value.

The wife appealed the trial court's business valuation to the state's high court. She admitted that she had not offered valuation evidence, but she repeated her argument that there was an "evidentiary void" at trial as to the value of the business. The trial court should have directed the party with the best access to data—that is, the husband—to fill the void, the wife contended.

The husband countered that there was no evidentiary void since he had testified as to the market value of the business.

The state Supreme Court noted that the burden of supplying sufficient evidence for the record lay with the parties, not the court. If a party fails to do so, he or she may not later attack the adequacy of the evidence on appeal, the court added. In this instance, the trial court provided the wife with the resources to gather valuation evidence, which she failed to do. Accordingly, the trial court did not abuse its discretion when it declined to order the husband to present additional evidence about the value of the practice.

Three-part goodwill determination. The appellate court also affirmed the trial court's goodwill conclusion. At the outset of its analysis, the reviewing court noted that, under the applicable case law, valuing goodwill required three determinations:

1. The trial court must determine whether goodwill exists;
2. If the trial court finds there is goodwill, it has to determine whether the goodwill is marketable since only marketable goodwill is includable in the marital estate; and
3. Finally, if there is marketable goodwill, the trial court must calculate the value of the goodwill by using "principled methods of valuation."

The state's high court observed that, in this case, the trial court had adopted the husband's testimony as to goodwill and had halted the analysis after making the first determination—there was no marketable goodwill. The trial court's approach accorded with precedent, the appellate court found, citing *Richmond v. Richmond*, 779 P.2d 1211 (Alaska 1989) (available at *BVLaw*). The state Supreme Court added that, even though *Richmond* involved expert testimony as to the goodwill of the husband's law practice, "valuation evidence from the parties alone is sufficient to determine marital property value."

Here, since neither party furnished evidence that the husband's business had marketable goodwill, the state Supreme Court affirmed the trial court's judgment.

Ross v. Rothstein

Citation: 2015 U.S. Dist. LEXIS 30180
Date of decision: March 12, 2015
Judge: Crabtree
State/Jurisdiction: Federal/Kansas
Court: United States District Court
Type of case: Contract
SIC code: 1382 Oil and Gas Field Exploration Services
NAICS code: 213112 Support Activities for Oil and Gas Operations

FRE 702 Ruling Puts Expert in 'Uncommon Position'

May a court exclude an expert's opinion (conclusions) but still admit his or her "nonopinion" testimony under Federal Rule of Evidence 702? The plaintiff claimed that the entire expert testimony was inadmissible. To credit one aspect while rejecting the expert's ultimate conclusions, as a magistrate judge had done, was error. The reviewing court saw it differently.

The plaintiff and the defendant litigated a dispute over the plaintiff's failure to repay a loan to the defendant. A judge found the plaintiff liable of several breaches of contract and said the defendant was entitled to obtain a certain number of common stock of the plaintiff's company, which served as collateral for the loan. The defendant subsequently sold the shares, realizing over $220,000 from the sale. The stock traded on the Over-the-Counter QB Tier Market (OTCQB); it was not publicly traded or sold on any other stock market. The plaintiff then sued the defendant for wrongfully disposing of the collateral. He argued that OTCQB was not a "recognized" market under state law and the sale was not commercially reasonable. By selling the stock in the way the defendant did, the defendant failed to preserve the value of the stock.

The defendant offered expert testimony on over-the-counter securities trading. The expert submitted an affidavit that included four opinions and eight factual statements. Among other things, the expert concluded that OTCQB qualified as a "recognized market" under the state's uniform commercial code.

Court finds part of testimony helpful. The plaintiff filed a pretrial motion to exclude the testimony under Rule 702. The magistrate judge concluded the witness was qualified as an expert but precluded him from testifying about the four opinions because they were impermissible legal conclusions. At the same time, the judge ruled the expert had other "knowledge, skill, experience, training or education" that helped the court understand the evidence and decide the legal issues. Specifically, the magistrate judge could consider the expert's factual statements as to "the operation, function, and trading of stocks on over-the-counter securities markets generally, as well as the OTCQB in particular and how it functions, operates, and how stocks trade on the OTCQB." For the purpose of formulating a recommendation, the magistrate judge also considered the expert's statements as to "the details of [defendant's] actual trades" of the shares at issue. Ultimately, the judge recommended summary judgment in favor of the defendant. The facts showed that the defendant had sold the shares in a commercially reasonable manner, she concluded.

The plaintiff attacked the magistrate judge's recommendation in the federal district court (D. Kan.). The crux of his argument was that the magistrate judge erred when she admitted the factual testimony of the defendant's expert while excluding his opinions. You cannot permit the witness "to testify about any 'facts' that support his properly excluded opinions," the plaintiff contended.

More to expert testimony than opinion. At the start of its discussion, the district court noted that the magistrate judge's ruling "left [the witness] in a relatively uncommon position for an expert."

According to the court, the issue came down to: "May an expert in this position still testify about the 'non-opinion' aspects of the expert's 'knowledge' or 'experience?'" It said the plaintiff failed to cite any legal authority to support his position. In contrast, "the available authority on the issue" strongly suggested the magistrate judge's ruling was correct. For one, Rule 702(a) provides that a witness who qualifies as an expert "may testify in the form of an opinion *or otherwise* if: (a) the expert's ... other specialized knowledge will help the trier of fact." (emphasis added) Further, the advisory committee notes to Rule 702 "amplify this principle," the court found. The notes state: "Most of the literature assumes that experts testify only in the form of opinions. The assumption is logically unfounded."

Case law, too, rejected the notion that "opinions are essential to an expert's currency," the court added. It pointed to cases where experts provided background information but no opinions. In the instant case, the magistrate judge's exclusion ruling did not nullify the expert's qualifications to provide helpful background information on over-the-counter markets, including OTCQB. Consequently, it was not error for the magistrate to exclude the expert's conclusions while admitting the facts underpinning the conclusions.

Rowe v. DPI Specialty Foods

Citation: 2015 U.S. Dist. LEXIS 110605
Date of decision: Aug. 19, 2015
Experts: Jeremy Sharpe (plaintiff); Derk G. Rasmussen (defendants)
Judge: Nuffer
State/Jurisdiction: Federal/Utah
Court: United States District Court
Type of case: Damages
SIC code: 5141 Groceries, General Line
NAICS code: 445110 Supermarkets and Other Grocery (except Convenience) Stores

Damages Opinion Reveals 'Serious Misconception' of Role of Expert

What's the proper role of a damages expert? This question was at the heart of a *Daubert* challenge in which the court found the rebuttal expert ascribed to himself an outsize role that made him fact finder, proponent of evidence, and advocate of theories. He seriously misread the authorities he cited on what it means to be a damages expert and did not apply reliable principles and methods to achieve his conclusions, the court concluded.

Loss of employment. The plaintiff worked for a food broker that worked with the defendant company, DPI Specialty Foods, to market deli food items to retailers. He claimed that DPI Specialty Foods, through one of its employees who was working with the plaintiff on a retail account, made defamatory statements about him that ultimately cost him his job at the food broker. First, he was removed from the client account; then, several months later, the food broker terminated him. The plaintiff asserted two claims against the defendants: defamation and tortious interference with economic relations.

He sought damages for loss of earnings and benefits; loss of reputation; loss of economic relations; emotional distress, pain, and suffering; and value of reparative work.

Whether and to what extent the defendants' alleged defamatory statements caused the plaintiff's eventual termination was a key issue in the case.

Assumption of liability. The plaintiff retained an expert to calculate damages, and the defendants offered a rebuttal expert. In his opinion, the plaintiff's expert cited allegations in the plaintiff's complaint and said that his report was "based on an assumption of liability. I have done no work to determine liability and do not expect to do any such work."

The defendants' expert was an experienced CPA who held numerous business valuation credentials and stated that he had served as an expert witness in 127 separate engagements. The crux of his rebuttal testimony seemed to be that the opposing expert's calculations were based on flawed assumptions. But he went further.

Notably, his report included a section, "Financial experts and economic causation," that not only identified the opposing expert's assumptions, but also included an extended discussion of how to perform a proper economic damages analysis. According to the expert's report, "when evaluating a damage claim, one must ensure that each claimed economic impact can be traced back to the incident. This is where the concept of causation or causal link is integrated into the analysis of economic damages." Citing three editions of the *Litigation Services Handbook: The Role of the Financial Expert*, the rebuttal expert proposed: (1) that there were "two different contexts of causation, legal and economic"; (2) that the issue of causation "continues to be expanded"; and (3) that "an expert has a duty to understand and prove that a causal link exists between the incident and each of the damages elements." Moreover, "an expert is specifically precluded from relying upon an assumption that economic causation exists," the rebuttal expert claimed.

He also contended "the consideration of all facts available in a case is critical to any economic loss analysis." When he was asked during his deposition whether there was any limit to the facts that were subject to the damages expert's review, the rebuttal expert replied: "[Y]ou have to assess all of the facts that are available and determine whether or not they support or don't support your assumption of causation." When asked whether the issue of causation provided him with "license to weigh and compare facts and reliability of witnesses," he replied: "From an economic point of view, yes." For this reason, he said, "Expert witnesses are allowed to sit in the courtroom and listen to all of the testimony, because all of that has a bearing on causation, for example."

As for the case at issue, he said that "based on the economics and my review of the economics," the plaintiff's "professional goodwill evaporated because of people being removed out of the situation, and because he's got new people in there that maybe his personality doesn't match up well with." He said he was prepared to offer this testimony to the jury because "[t]hat's the economics that I see."

He further maintained that it was necessary for a damages expert to assess the opinions of other experts, including medical and vocational experts, to determine whether the evidence supported "any assumptions they make or the data points upon which they form their analysis."

Usurping function of other trial participants. The plaintiff attacked the testimony under *Daubert* and Federal Rule of Evidence 702, arguing the expert's opinions "invade the proper province of the jury to weigh the facts and evaluate witness credibility." The expert's report was "loaded with factual assertions" but lacked economic analysis, and the factual assertions were not mere assumptions but opinions that the expert intended to share with the jury. Also, he lacked the qualifications to render vocational and industry opinions outside his expertise, the plaintiff claimed.

The court dispensed with any detailed analysis of the legal principles at issue but focused its discussion on statements the expert made in his report and deposition testimony. It agreed with almost all of the plaintiff's objections. "Most of what [the rebuttal expert] does is in the province of the witnesses in offering evidence, of the jury in determining facts, and of counsel in arguing theories."

There was only one "proper portion" of the testimony, and it concerned the rebuttal expert's identifying the assumptions the plaintiff's expert made and noting factors the plaintiff's expert failed to consider in his damages analysis. However, the rest of the rebuttal testimony was not helpful to the jury.

The court found the expert "twist[ed]" reference material into a concept the texts did not support: a "dichotomy between economic and legal causation that he attempts to exploit." The court said there was no evidence that this difference of causation existed and that it was an expert's role to opine on either. The rebuttal expert's "misreading" of the cited authorities was "very troubling," the court said, but it found the expert's assumptions about the role of an expert in the courtroom "significantly more troubling." According to the court:

> An expert witness has no duty to prove causal links between incident and damages. An expert opines on facts which the expert assumes will be proven, and an expert can explain the bases for an opinion. But an expert is not to opine on the weight of the facts or take a principal role in sifting, weighing and reciting them for the jury.

By insisting that a damages expert had "to assess all of the facts that are available," the rebuttal expert wrongly believed there was no limit to the scope of his review, the court went on to say. It added that by "invoking economics," the rebuttal expert allowed himself to opine on issues outside the scope of his engagement and expertise, such as the factual cause of the plaintiff's termination.

The court observed that the expert's 20-page report reflected the expert's theory of his role. Seven pages were direct recitations of deposition testimony the expert weighed and critiqued. About three pages were a summary or characterization of facts as the expert saw them based on the record. He spent about four pages to state, "incorrectly," his role as an expert witness, the court noted.

Finally, the court found that in assigning to himself a responsibility to evaluate other expert testimony, he abandoned his role as an economic damages expert. He had no authority to second-guess the assumptions and conclusions underlying the opinions of experts on issues outside his area of expertise.

Noting the expert's "serious misconception of his role," the court only admitted the rebuttal expert's critique related to the assumptions that informed the plaintiff expert's calculations.

Russell v. Allianze Life Insurance Co. of North America

Citation: 2015 U.S. Dist. LEXIS 1946
Date of decision: Jan. 8, 2015
Experts: Robert Vance (plaintiff); N/A (defendant)
Judge: Brown
State/Jurisdiction: Federal/Mississippi
Court: United States District Court
Type of case: Contract
SIC code: 6411 Insurance Agents, Brokers and Service
NAICS code: 524210 Insurance Agencies and Brokerages

Expert's Failure to Adhere to Objective Standard Spoils Analysis

A recent *Daubert* case in which an insurance agent sued the insurance company for breach of contract and sought lost profits serves as a reminder to valuators of the high cost to credibility resulting from the expert's abandoning due diligence and standard practice in an effort to accommodate the client's narrative.

Comparative analysis. In 2000, the plaintiff signed an agreement with an insurance carrier to act as its agent/broker for long-term care insurance and health products. In 2009, the plaintiff complained to the insurer that it was not performing well. In 2011, the insurer informed the plaintiff that effective immediately it had terminated the relationship for cause. It subsequently filed complaints with insurance commissioners in two states and informed the plaintiff's clients of the termination. After repeated questions from the plaintiff as to the cause, it claimed he had tried to commit fraud against the insurer. At the time of termination, the plaintiff was 70 years old.

The plaintiff, in turn, sued for breach of contract, breach of the covenant of good faith and fair dealing, breach of fiduciary duty, and "intentional interference with business relations." He contended that, because of the improper termination, he lost contracts and was unable to "gain a similar agency status" with another company.

To show damages, the plaintiff offered expert testimony from a CPA who specialized in business valuation and forensic accounting. The defendant filed a *Daubert* challenge to preclude the opinion.

The expert performed a forensic accounting study of lost profits for a period of 10 years after termination. The analysis had four steps: (1) analyzing the plaintiff's "historical gross revenues from commissions, the related business expenses and resulting net profits" from 2005 to 2012; (2) determining that the plaintiff had a work-life expectancy of 10 years; (3) using data from the Insured Retirement Institute regarding sales of annuities on a national level as a yardstick to project the plaintiff's future annual gross commissions income; and (4) valuing the plaintiff's "book of business" at 1.5 times the projected gross commission income for the year 2020.

As for specifics, he explained that he used the plaintiff's 2010 gross income of approximately $116,500 as the base year—rather than the actual year of termination, 2011, which showed revenue of only about $70,000. He said he increased the base by 0.4% for 2011, 0.4% during 2012, and 0.9% for the remaining work life through 2020. The projections ended in 2021with the sale of the book of business. He said he deducted business expenses of 61.5% from the projected gross commissions for the years 2011 to 2020, as well as the actual mitigating earnings for 2011 and 2012, and he used 2012 as a basis for years 2013 through 2020 for a total of nearly $102,000. The loss of future profits was approximately $554,000. To discount to present value, he used a 2.64% rate, based on the 10-year Treasury bond safe rate. He noted that the projected income figures were "effectively" risk-adjusted, "since this book of business has grossed much more in the past, and the level projected requires only 2-3 annuity sales or renewals per month." The present value of future lost profits was over $486,000, the expert concluded.

Expert ignores facts of case. The defendant called the damages calculation speculative and inadmissible under *Daubert* because it assumed there was a saleable book of business and also because it "grossly" overestimated the plaintiff's work-life expectancy. The expert's approach did not comply with the requisite scientific methodology, the defendant claimed. The court examined both aspects in turn.

Book of business. Of the total lost profits, the plaintiff's expert allocated $151,700 to the sale of the book of business. He explained that he arrived at that value by comparing the plaintiff's business to the annual revenues and sale prices of insurance agencies that were similar in size to that of the plaintiff. He admitted that, even though he used a 1.5 multiplier, the multiplier could be anywhere in the range of one to three times the projected gross commission income for 2020.

He also said he based his calculation on the assumption that the plaintiff lost his entire customer list as a result of the termination. However, in testimony, the plaintiff admitted that after his termination he was able to sell insurance products to clients on the list through other carriers.

The defendant contended the expert's comparative approach was inappropriate since the plaintiff's annuity book of business was "grossly dissimilar" from books of business of other insurance products that formed the basis of the comparison. Further, the defendant pointed out that, even though the expert claimed the value of a book of business flowed from an agent's reputation and customer list, the expert admitted he did perform an analysis of whether and how the plaintiff's termination affected his customer list.

The court agreed that the expert's opinion was "fundamentally unsupported" and not helpful to the jury. He based his calculation on the plaintiff's assertion that the latter lost his complete book of business owing to the termination and on declining business revenue. But, had he actually reviewed the client list, he would have known the plaintiff continued to sell insurance to some of the people on the list, the court observed.

Moreover, the expert based his loss analysis on a comparison to other insurers, but, when pressed to provide further information, he was unable to. He said he "inadvertently lost" documentation of the specific insurance agencies he used to determine the value of the plaintiff's book of business. In the end, there was no evidence with which the plaintiff could counter the defendant's claim that the insurance agencies were not sufficiently similar.

Work-life expectancy. The expert's lost profits calculation assumed that the plaintiff would continue to live and work for another 10 years, based on the plaintiff's statements that he was in good health, loved working as an insurance agent, and thought of the work as "retirement work."

The expert testified that he normally used objective data for his calculation, such as the Skoog-Cieka work-life expectancy study. Skoog-Cieka, he said, was based on Bureau of Labor statistics and other government data and featured tables that address work-life expectancy based on gender, age, education, and work experience. He said that in this instance he was unable to use the tables because the plaintiff was older than the maximum age listed in any of the tables.

In deposition, the expert also noted that other work-life expectancy tables were available besides Skoog-Cieka, derived from studies of self-employed persons. He did not remember the names of the studies, but "recalled" they showed self-employed people "typically work five to ten years longer than the work-life expectancy tables." He said that, even though he had used these studies in other cases, in this instance, he solely relied on the plaintiff's statements.

The defendant claimed that the expert's failure to adhere to an objective standard made the analysis inadmissible.

Once again the court sided with the defendant. It observed that all of the tables in the Skoog-Cieka study listed a maximum age of 75. The mean work-life expectancy for a 70-year-old male with a high school diploma was 3.74 years and the median was 2.5 years. The expert's estimate, therefore, was three times higher than the estimate suggested by the Skoog-Cieka study.

Although the expert's failure to use the Skoog-Cieka study did not in itself render his calculation unreliable, his failure to use *any* objective standard did, the court said with emphasis. It pointed out that he did not even use the self-employed work-life expectancy studies that he said he had used in other cases but chose to base his analysis solely on the plaintiff's "self-serving testimony." There was no basis from which to conclude that the expert's estimate was based on a reliable methodology, the court concluded. Accordingly, the expert's testimony was inadmissible under *Daubert.*

Schickner v. Schickner

Citation: 2015 Ariz. App. LEXIS 48
Date of decision: April 16, 2015
Experts: John Pinto, Stephen Koons (husband); Calvin Swartley (wife)
Judge: Brown
State/Jurisdiction: Arizona
Court: Court of Appeals
Type of case: Marital Dissolution
SIC code: 8042 Offices and Clinics of Optometrists
NAICS code: 621320 Offices of Optometrists

No Automatic Bar to Minority Discount in Divorce Cases

In the context of divorce, may a court apply a minority discount when valuing a minority interest in a business to determine the nonowner spouse's fair share? This was the primary issue the Arizona appeals court recently addressed in ruling on the wife's claim that the trial court undervalued two jointly owned business interests.

Interest in two professional practices. The husband was an ophthalmologist who, during the marriage, acquired a 50% community interest in an eye clinic and a 20% interest in a surgery center in which he performed eye operations. Arizona is one of nine community property states.

At trial, the valuations of the two interests for purposes of equitable distribution of the property became the flash point. Both parties retained seasoned business appraisers to support their positions.

In all, for each of the two business interests, four valuations were in play.

1. *Fifty percent interest in eye clinic.* The husband's first appraiser applied discounts for lack of control and for lack of marketability and valued the 50% interest in the eye clinic at $475,000.

The husband's second appraiser valued the interest by: (a) applying minority interest and lack of marketability discounts to arrive at a value of $620,000; and (b) applying no such discounts to achieve a value of $830,000.

In contrast, the wife's expert valued the entire business at over $3.2 million and from the total value concluded the community's 50% interest was worth $1.6 million.

2. *Twenty percent interest in surgery center.* Again, the husband's first appraiser applied both minority share and lack of marketability discounts to conclude the community's 20% interest in the surgery center was worth $580,000.

The wife's second appraiser determined the interest was worth $490,000 when discounted for lack of control and lack of marketability and was worth $540,000 without discounts.

In contrast, the wife's expert determined the surgery center as a whole was worth just under $5.3 million, which he concluded translated into $1.05 million for the community's interest. (The court's opinion does not include a detailed discussion of the appraisers' valuation methodologies.)

At trial, the husband attacked the valuations of the wife's expert, claiming the expert used too high a capitalization rate and for both businesses failed to account for lack of marketability and lack of control. The wife challenged the valuations from the husband's experts, arguing his appraisers addressed the issue from the standpoint of the husband's selling to a third party when there was no intent to do so. She also maintained that both discounts were only relevant factors if an outside buyer was buying into the practice but not where the present owner was "buying out" the co-owner, as was the case here. Further, the wife claimed the valuations were based on the use of "inflated rents" and excessive salaries to family members.

Valuator as 'Zen master.' The trial court said the husband's first appraiser used a "Zen master" approach to valuation (no further explanation available) that it found "disconcerting." It then went on to say that since this expert's calculations aligned with those of the husband's second appraiser, the first appraiser was credible.

At the same time, the trial court disapproved of certain "foundations" informing the calculations of the wife's expert. For one, the court objected to the use of the 11% capitalization rate. A rate this high typically applies to a large publicly traded company, not to small businesses like the ones at issue, the court said. Further it pointed out that the expert did not value the specific interest of the community in each of the entities but instead determined the total value of the respective entity. Once he had ascertained that value, he divided it based on the share the community owned. But, said the trial court, a "minority interest has less value than the total interest of a company on a per-share basis." Since the community did not own a controlling interest in either entity, this distinction was meaningful, the court said.

The trial court concluded that: (1) the fair market value of the 50% interest in the eye clinic was worth $602,000; and (2) the 20% interest in the surgery center was worth $536,000. Accordingly, it ordered the husband to pay the wife $569,000 for her half of the community's interests in both businesses.

Facts don't support discount. The wife appealed the trial court's decision to the state's Court of Appeals, contending that the lower court improperly applied a minority share discount that resulted in undervaluation. Use of this discount in a divorce setting violated Arizona law, she claimed.

The appeals court found the wife relied on the wrong case to support her position. Specifically, she cited a dissenting shareholder case that centered on the applicable statutory provisions requiring a "fair value buy-out." But a marital dissolution proceeding is subject to an equitable division principle, thus a different standard, the appeals court pointed out.

It went on to say that no Arizona case prohibited the use of a minority interest discount in a marital dissolution case. It went on to say: "Consistent with the majority of other jurisdictions that have addressed the issue, we decline to adopt such a bright-line rule here."

Rather, the appeals court said whether or not to apply a minority discount in the divorce context was a case-by-case determination requiring the trial court to "consider factors such as the minority shareholder's degree of control, lack of marketability, and the likelihood of a sale of the minority interest in the foreseeable future."

When applying these considerations to the facts of the case, the appeals court found the trial court's valuation as to the eye clinic did not hold up. For one, the husband held the same interest in the business—50%—as the only other member of this limited liability company. The husband also had considerable power over financial decisions, including determining how much of his compensation he wanted to take in the form of salary and how much by way of distributions. Other than an inability to change the terms of rent, the record showed few limitations on the husband's joint control of the business, the appeals court observed. What's more, he did not indicate that he had any plans to sell his interest in the business. None of the justifications for a minority discount applied here, the appeals court concluded.

The appeals court also pointed out that the trial court's valuation ($602,000) was not only substantially below the value the wife's expert calculated ($1.6 million), but also below the fair value determination the husband's second appraiser produced ($820,000). The trial court's value even fell below that appraiser's discounted value ($620,000). Therefore, the Court of Appeals remanded, ordering the trial court to revalue the interest in the eye clinic.

At the same time, the appeals court detected a rationale for applying a minority share discount to the valuation of the surgery clinic. The husband only owned 20% of the business, and there was no evidence in the record that his control "is not substantially limited by the holder of the 80% interest." Consequently, the trial court did not abuse its discretion when it decided the fair market value of the community's interest in the surgery center was $536,000, the appeals court said.

Distributions-related dispute. A second point of contention had to do with the husband's compensation. In 2009 and 2010, the husband received "exactly the same" amount of compensation, $500,000, from the eye clinic. However, his CPA testified that, in 2010, the husband decided to change the form of payment from all salary to one-half salary and one-half distributions, ostensibly to avoid paying Medicare. In June 2010, the husband filed for divorce. The husband had an employment agreement with the eye clinic specifying a base salary for his medical services of $250,000.

The record did not show what the reasonable amount of compensation was for the husband's "toil and labor" at the surgery center. Both businesses had operating agreements that specified that distributions of cash or other property to members were to be in proportion to their percentage interests.

After the husband had filed for divorce, the wife asked the trial court for a declaration that she was entitled to all the distributions from the two businesses issued prior to the court's entering a final decree. The trial court declined to do so. It determined that the distributions represented salary or earned income and, therefore, were the husband's separate property.

On appeal, the wife contended the trial court's finding on this point was erroneous.

Under the applicable legal principles, "the community is generally 'entitled to the profits and gains attributable to community assets,'" the appeals court explained. Further, "although property acquired by either spouse after service of a petition for dissolution of marriage is the separate property of the acquiring spouse, the service of a petition for dissolution does not alter the status of preexisting community property." Here, the appeals court noted, the parties agreed that the husband's $250,000 base salary was his separate property once he filed for divorce. At the same time, for him to be able to claim all of it as separate property meant proving in court that the remaining $250,000, which he received annually in the form of distributions over a three-year-period, was compensation for his toil and labor.

The appeals court concluded that the trial court had failed to "adequately consider Wife's community interest in the two businesses." Nor had it imposed the requisite burden of proof as to the distributions on the husband. Accordingly, the appeals court remanded, ordering the trial court to determine the reasonable amount of compensation as to each business and to credit any excess to the community "as profits derived from existing community assets and subject to equitable division."

SEC v. Wyly (I), (II)

Citation: 2014 U.S. Dist. LEXIS 135671
Date of decision: Sept. 25, 2014
Experts: Dr. Chyhe Becker (SEC); Prof. Daniel Fischel (defendants)
Judge: Sheindlin
State/Jurisdiction: Federal/New York
Court: United States District Court
Type of case: Securities

Citation: 2014 U.S. Dist. LEXIS 175940
Date of decision: Dec. 19, 2014
Experts: Dr. Chyhe Becker (SEC); Prof. Daniel Fischel (defendants)
Judge: Sheindlin
State/Jurisdiction: Federal/New York
Court: United States District Court
Type of case: Securities

Court Sanctions SEC's Novel, Alternative Disgorgement Measure

In a "highly unusual" securities case centering on the use of numerous offshore trusts to enable a complex tax deferral scheme, the SEC was able to prove the defendants' liability for numerous violations. In the remedy phase, the court initially approved the agency's tax-based disgorgement measure under which the defendants would be liable for over $187 million. Anticipating an appeal and wanting to further a resolution of the case, the court recently approved the SEC's alternative, and novel, way of calculating the value of ill-gotten gains.

Background. The SEC's civil enforcement action in federal district court (S.D. N.Y.) alleged the defendants, Sam and Charles Wyly, engaged in an elaborate tax deferral scheme that went on for 13 years. They established a number of offshore trusts and subsidiary companies in the Isle of Man (IOM) that they used to trade shares in four public companies (issuers) on whose boards they were, without properly disclosing their beneficial ownership of the stock. By transferring valuable options and warrants to the trusts, exercising the options and trading in secret, and reinvesting the proceeds in other ventures, the Wylys were able to accumulate tremendous tax-free wealth.

The trial was divided into liabilities and remedies phases. In May 2014, the jury found the Wylys liable for nine securities violations, including securities fraud under section 10(b) of the Securities Exchange Act and failure to make various disclosures. In August 2014, the court held a bench trial on the remedies issue. At that time, the SEC sought disgorgement based on unpaid taxes. Under this measure, the agency: (1) calculated the total profits on the sale of the issuer securities by the IOM trusts; and (2) approximated the amount of taxes that would have been paid on those profits had the Wylys accurately disclosed beneficial ownership of the securities.

The defendants argued that the Tax Code prohibited disgorgement measured by unpaid taxes. Also, since they were currently under an IRS audit that covered some of the same years of security fraud, there was a potential for duplicative recovery or conflicting orders.

The court disagreed, noting that "[m]easuring unjust enrichment by approximating avoided taxes does not transform an order of disgorgement into an assessment of tax liability." Further, the risk of duplication or conflict was avoidable by crediting amounts disgorged in the SEC case toward any subsequent tax liability the IRS may determine. Accordingly, it ordered Sam Wyly to disgorge approximately $123.8 million and Charles Wyly to disgorge approximately $63.4 million.

Profit-based alternative model. At the same time, the court allowed the SEC to propose an alternative measure of disgorgement based on an expert report that approximated the unlawful gains by "calculat[ing] the difference between the Wylys' gains from their offshore transactions in the Issuers' securities, and the gains that an ordinary buy-and-hold equity investor would have earned in those securities."

The defendants presented expert testimony that critiqued the SEC expert's methodology and proposed two different approaches to measuring the gains, if any.

At the outset of its discussion of the expert testimony, the court noted that this alternative measure was only appropriate if an appeals court were to strike down its prior order. According to the court, disgorgement based on unpaid taxes was the best measure of the Wylys' improper gains.

The law required the SEC to provide a "reasonable approximation" of the amount subject to disgorgement. Under the alternative model, the SEC's expert assumed the fraud period began in April 1993, when the defendants first transferred securities to the offshore trusts, and ended in February 2005, when one of the issuers acknowledged it was under government investigation. The expert compared the defendants' gains during this period to the gains that an ordinary buy-and-hold investor would have earned in those same securities.

Her calculation hinged on four key dates: (1) the date the options were transferred offshore; (2) the date they were exercised; (3) the date the stock was sold; and (4) the end of the fraud period. She considered the transfer date as the beginning of the holding period, treating it as if the Wylys were "purchasing" the options for the value of the option on that date. She posited that there was an additional "purchase" on the date of exercise for the strike price. She treated the securities that were still being held at the end of the fraud period as if they were being sold by the defendants—thus including the value of securities the defendants then held but never sold. But she excluded any unrealized gains the defendants earned from the securities before transfer to the offshore system.

She first calculated the total gains earned from the issuer securities transactions in the offshore trusts during the fraud period. Next, she calculated the Wylys' rates of return and average holding periods using the "dollar-weighted rate of return," which takes into consideration the timing and the amounts of the investments. Using the rates of return, she then calculated the Wylys' average holding periods for each of the four issuers. She explained that the average holding periods allowed a comparison of the Wylys' total gains to what they would have earned if they had invested the same amount, for the same length of time, but earned instead the average buy-and-hold equity investor return for each issuer. She found the Wylys' average holding period for the offshore securities ranged from 1.6 years to 4.7 years. She then calculated the rate of return for a buy-and-hold investor in each of the four securities during the 13-year fraud period. Finally, she determined the hypothetical gains that the Wylys would have generated if they earned the same rates of return buy-and-hold investors earned. This calculation, she explained, represented what an investor would have earned if it had invested the same amount as the Wylys over the same average holding period but earned the annualized rate of return for that specific security. She then subtracted the buy-and-hold investor's gains from the Wylys' total gains to determine the ill-gotten gains. She concluded that the numerous securities law violations allowed Sam Wyly to make over $115.5 million and Charles Wyly to make nearly $77.2 million in gains in excess of the gains a buy-and-hold investor could earn.

Five deadly flaws? The Wylys' expert attacked the SEC's expert's analysis on five grounds, which the court considered in turn.

1. *Using a method not generally accepted.* The Wylys' expert said the competing expert had failed to point to any authority supporting her methodology, making her approach unreliable. According to him, there was an extensive body of economic literature for analyzing "whether the profitability of trades by insiders results from an informational advantage as compared with uninformed trades." It required that the analysis focus solely on the insiders' sales of securities and whether the stock showed abnormal returns in the period after the sale.

The SEC's expert defended her approach, saying it was informed by studies that showed that disclosure requirements cause insiders to trade in a fundamentally different way to keep some information from the investing public. Her approach, she said, tried to measure the benefit to the Wylys from a lack of disclosure. She pointed out that, "because of this invisibility, the Wylys appeared more like a buy-and-hold investor than what they really are." Comparing their actual trading to a buy-and-hold benchmark was a way to measure the difference between what the

Wylys actually earned and what they would have earned if they had been buy-and-hold investors, which she said was "the image they projected to the investing public."

The court found her testimony that the established method for measuring the value of secrecy was not appropriate for this case persuasive. This case had unique facts—the lengthy fraud period, the large volume of offshore and undisclosed transactions, and the fact that the Wylys were not "garden variety" insiders—that made the standard method of measuring ill-gotten gains, i.e., performing an event study for each trade, unhelpful. The SEC's expert used a method that could reasonably approximate the profits "causally connected to the Wylys' violations," the court stated.

2. Irrelevant dates make holding period meaningless. The Wylys' expert objected to the opposing expert's calculation of the holding period. She improperly treated transfers and exercise of the options as purchases based on insider information. The Wylys owned the options before and after the transfers and would have received the same gain on the securities resulting from the exercise of the options and the subsequent sale of the stock regardless of when the options were transferred offshore. Relatedly, he alleged that the SEC's expert improperly compared the rate of return on options with the rate of return on stock.

The SEC's expert maintained that the transfer date mattered because it was when the secrecy began. On the day of the transfers, the Wylys had the ability to "do anything they want with these options without disclosure." Also, charts the SEC prepared for each of the issuers for which the expert calculated a profit revealed that the Wylys transferred the options when the stock price was relatively low. This timing suggested that they used their informational advantage when selecting a transfer date for the options.

The court agreed that using the transfer date as the start of the holding period made sense, since that date marked the beginning of when the Wylys made the options "invisible" to the investing public. To calculate the gains to the Wylys that were in excess of those of a buy-and-hold investor, the SEC's expert had to choose a start date for the holding period, the court noted. The transfer date marked the filing of a misleading disclosure, "misleading" in that the Wylys disclaimed beneficial ownership of the options after the transfer.

The court also found the exercise date was relevant because on this date there was either false information or no disclosure. Also, using this date as the start of the holding period for the amount of the exercise price was a way to track the period during which the Wylys tied up additional capital "over and above the value of the option at the date of transfer" in the offshore system and to establish a weighted average holding period.

Moreover, the court observed, using both dates enabled the SEC's expert to compare the rate of return in the underlying stock. Specifically, the expert used the value of the option and the exercise price to "effectively turn the Wylys' options into stock." According to the court, on the transfer date, the expert treated the Wylys as having "purchased" the underlying stock for the value of the option. On the exercise date, she treated the exercise price as an additional "purchase." Raising the Wylys' basis to that of an investor who bought stock allowed for a comparison of the Wylys' rate of return with that of a buy-and-hold investor in stock, the court concluded.

3. Improper inclusion of unrealized gains. The Wylys' expert said the SEC's expert should not have included the gains related to securities that the IOM trusts retained until the end of the fraud period or until the issuers were acquired. The Wylys did what a buy-and-hold investor would have done, holding on to the securities, and never used an informational advantage to "cash out." According to the Wylys' expert, 38% of the gains in the SEC's expert's calculation of ill-gotten gains related to securities the defendants did not sell.

The court sided with the Wylys on this point. To include unrealized gains from securities that were never sold did not result in a reasonable approximation of the Wylys' ill-gotten gains, it said. Although there were real benefits to the Wylys related to these securities, such as the ability to use them as collateral for a loan and to hide the Wylys' beneficial ownership from the investing public, it was not appropriate to use them to measure gains in excess of those of a buy-and-hold investor.

4. Failure to consider unrelated reasons for trading. Another reason why the SEC's expert's method was defective was because it failed to consider that not every trade reflected the use of an informational advantage, the Wylys' expert claimed. Many trades took place for unrelated reasons.

The court dismissed this argument. Since all offshore trades occurred without accurate disclosures, it said, it was appropriate to consider the total of trades made during the fraud period. It agreed with the SEC's expert that a trade that was made because the Wylys needed money—to repay a loan, for example—did not mean the transaction was not motivated by an informational advantage. Also, the court said, by comparing the total amount the Wylys earned to the total amount a buy-and-hold investor would have earned during the same holding period, the SEC expert was able to account for any individual trades that did not result in a gain to the Wylys or even resulted in a loss.

The court also mentioned some of the intangible benefits that the Wylys derived from their securities law violations. These included "reputational benefits"—being able to project an image of owners "standing by their company" and "not trading opportunistically in companies that they controlled." They also included a liquidity advantage.

Claim of zero ill-gotten gains. The Wylys' expert used two methods that, he said, showed the defendants received, in the aggregate, no improper gains. Under the first method, he determined whether there were abnormal returns after the Wylys sold securities from the offshore system. Looking at any abnormal performance over the entire fraud period, he found that the Wylys had $47 million in net losses—a $51.4 million net loss for Sam Wyly and a $4.4 million net gain for Charles Wyly.

The court discredited this approach, saying it only spoke to the issue of whether the defendants used an informational advantage but did not capture the value of other benefits they received as a result of their violations. Also, the expert did not use the method in a standard way. Instead of using a window of six months to two years to determine whether trades were informed, he used the entire fraud period, up to 13 years. If the stock price increased beyond the sale price at any point during the remainder of the period, he did not consider it a benefit to the Wylys. But, said the court, had he followed standard practice, he would have captured a sale whose stock price drastically dropped for a significant time after the sale and subsequently increased long afterward.

Under the second method, the expert compared what the Wylys would have earned if they had held the securities until the end of the fraud period with what they hypothetically could have earned if they had invested sales proceeds in the S&P 500 or in one-year Treasury bills. He concluded the Wylys would have been better off if they held the securities and never made any sales.

The court also rejected this treatment. It failed to account for the many benefits the Wylys did receive from making sales—using their profits to make other investments, starting new businesses, and buying personal possessions. Being able to monetize their offshore assets and use the money for other purposes was a benefit, even assuming they would have made more money if they had held the securities and never sold them, the court pointed out. In sum, both methods failed to rebut the SEC's calculation, the court said.

The court concluded that, even if the SEC expert's method was not without blemish, it provided a reasonable way to approximate the Wylys' ill-gotten gains. The approach used dates related to disclosure violations and linked the gains to specific amounts "invested" on the dates that capital was tied up in the offshore system. Also, it properly accounted for the differences in the rate of return between an investment in options and one in stock. Therefore, the court adopted the calculation but ordered the SEC to recalculate the disgorgement amount by taking out 38% of gain related to securities never sold.

Settele v. Settele

Citation: 2015 Ohio App. LEXIS 3629
Date of decision: Sept. 15, 2015
Experts: Richard Ferguson (husband); Brian A. Russell (wife)
Judge: Sadler
State/Jurisdiction: Ohio
Court: Court of Appeals
Type of case: Marital Dissolution
SIC code: 8021 Offices and Clinics of Dentists
NAICS code: 621210 Offices of Dentists

Court Nixes Double Dip Claim Based on Accounts Receivable Treatment

Raising a double dip argument seems par for the course in Ohio divorce cases notwithstanding recent decisions from the Court of Appeals that have limited the applicability of the theory to the context of an income-based business valuation and have gone as far as to say that double dipping is permissible. Recently, the owner-spouse tried to fit the case into a double dip framework by analogizing the opposing expert's use of accounts receivable in the asset-based valuation to using a future stream of income. There was no prior law directly on point.

Adjustments to balance sheets. The parties narrowed their dispute to the valuation of the husband's dental business. The husband initially set the practice up as a sole proprietorship but during the divorce proceedings reorganized it as a single-member limited liability corporation (LLC).

The wife's expert used an adjusted net asset approach to value the practice. He said the income approach marked the value as less than the business assets, which generally represented the floor of a business. The market approach resulted in a range of results that was too wide to be reliable.

He explained that the asset approach considered the value of "certain assets, bank accounts, accounts receivable, equipment" at a certain point in time. He used the company's balance sheets, he said, and made three major adjustments.

First, he added over $53,000 in expense payments made at year-end 2013 to the business value because those payments did not "absolutely" have to be paid then. Also, under generally accepted accounting principles, they would represent prepaid expenses that were an actual asset to the company at that date.

Second, he added over $206,000 in accounts receivable to the value. In so doing, he followed the standard method of aging accounts to capture risk related to collectability.

Third, he changed the book value of the practice's furniture and equipment, first adding back in part of the value of furniture bought at the end of 2013, which was depreciated entirely, and then subtracting nearly $17,000 in leasehold improvements. He acknowledged that he did not perform his own appraisal of the equipment but said an appraisal likely would not produce a different value than what appeared on the company's balance sheets.

Based on the three adjustments, he concluded the assets of the business totaled nearly $358,400. After subtracting liabilities and using a 7% discount for lack of marketability, he arrived at a net asset value of approximately $313,000.

The expert's accounts receivable treatment prompted questions on cross-examination. He explained that in terms of taxes "[w]hen those receivables are collected in the subsequent period or in the following year, they would be recognized as taxable income as the collection of those receivables in that subsequent year." He clarified that "there's going to be approximately 200-some thousand dollars of accounts receivable in existence and those are going to, as a rolling advantage, continue being collected and recognized as cash-basis income."

The wife's expert also was asked about the applicability of the 2008 *Heller* case ruling, which ostensibly prohibited double dipping. See *Heller v. Heller*, 2008-Ohio-3296 (available at *BVLaw*). He responded:

> The double-dipping issue has no bearing on an instance where the company is valued based on an asset approach. That issue is relevant when the company is based on a capitalization of earnings approach with the argument, or the potential double counting, being that you counted a net earnings stream and capitalized it to determine the business value, and then you may also be using that same

> earning stream for determining income level for support purposes. Therein lies the potential for a double counting.

The husband's expert used an income approach, specifically the capitalization of earnings method. To determine the appropriate future earnings base, he used figures in the Schedule C tax forms for 2011 and 2012 and the company's financial statement for 2013. He adjusted for officer compensation and arrived at a "going forward income" for the business of $74,000. Using a capitalization rate of 19%, he concluded the business was worth $390,000.

He stated that he had "[n]o problem" with the opposing expert's approach or calculations. He noted that he thought the business typically prepaid expenses each year, but he acknowledged that there was no record that it had done so prior to December 2013. He also explained that, even though appraisers should visit the business they are valuing, it sometimes proved hard to do so because the opposing side might not cooperate.

Spousal support calculations. The wife's expert also performed an analysis of the parties' incomes and earnings for the court's determination of spousal support. He explained that he calculated the husband's gross income by averaging earnings from the business from 2011 through 2013 and subtracting child and spousal support paid. The 2011 and 2012 figures were based on the net profit in the federal Schedule C tax forms; the 2013 figure reflected the net profit appearing on the company's profit and loss sheet. The pretax spousal support amount per month was nearly $6,300, he calculated. On cross-examination, he said he did not discuss the 2013 earnings with the husband or the company's CPA. (The court's opinion does not include any spousal support opinion from the husband's expert.)

Asset approach prevails in trial court. The trial court adopted the business valuation the wife's expert proposed, saying it was the "most conservative and directly relevant—and therefore the most equitable"—determination. Using the three-year average earnings the wife's expert had determined, the court found the husband's earning capacity was nearly $255,000. Accordingly, it ordered the husband to pay monthly spousal support of nearly $6,300 for an indefinite period, reserving the right to change the amount and spousal support period.

No future income stream in play. The husband attacked the trial court's findings essentially on two grounds: double dipping and relying on a valuation whose methodology was fatally flawed. The Court of Appeals considered the arguments in turn.

Double dip. The gist of the husband's double dip claim was that, notwithstanding the asset-based valuation, the testimony of the wife's experts showed that the accounts receivable in play was analogous to "future business profits" or a "future stream of income," as contemplated in *Heller* and subsequent decisions from the Ohio Court of Appeals. Under these circumstances, an asset-based approach does not preclude the occurrence of a double dip.

Citing to a 1990 Wisconsin case that prohibited any account receivable from being classified as a marital asset and as income includable in the spousal support calculation, the husband claimed the wife's expert did just that in his business valuation and determination of income subject to the spousal support award. The trial court should have adjusted the income for 2014 to counteract the double dip attributed to the accounts receivable.

The Ohio Court of Appeals dismissed the argument for several reasons. First, the record suggested that the portion of the accounts receivable the expert considered in the business valuation was eliminated when he averaged the husband's earnings to determine income available for spousal support.

Further, Ohio's statutory provision on spousal support expressly requires the trial court to consider income of the parties *from all sources.* (court's emphasis) "Thus, in a divorce where a spouse owns a business, merely considering the same assets in both a business valuation and in an income evaluation is not in error and is likely unavoidable." According to the Court of Appeals, the risk of double counting arises only when a court twice dips into a *future income stream*, which is avoidable if the business valuation is based on an asset approach, as it was in this case (citing *Gallo v. Gallo*, 2015-Ohio-982) (available at *BVLaw*).

Also, not only was the Wisconsin case not controlling authority, but it was also not persuasive, the Court of Appeals in the instant case found. The Wisconsin decision left it unclear whether the Wisconsin court considered only the accounts receivable on hand, future accounts receivable, or both.

Moreover, the accounts receivable the wife's expert in the instant case added into his business valuation did not represent "future income streams" for the purpose of a double dip analysis. The cash and accounts receivable were *present* assets of the company, the Court of Appeals emphasized.

The court explained that Ohio law did not provide a ready definition of "future income streams," but cases such as *Gallo* and *Bohme* suggested the phrase meant the "projected, ongoing value of an asset." *Gallo* specifically mentioned "pensions, business and professional goodwill, and dividend-yielding stock" as the kind of asset that produces future income streams, the court observed. *Bohme* mentioned pensions and annuities as future income streams to which the double-counting framework might be applicable. See *Bohme v. Bohme*, 2015-Ohio-339 (available at *BVLaw*).

Further, in a post-*Gallo* decision, the trial court treated the accounts receivable that was included in the prevailing asset-based valuation as present, not future, income, the Court of Appeals noted. See *Sieber v. Sieber*, 2015-Ohio-2315 (available at *BVLaw*).

Accordingly, "under *Gallo* and considering the facts of this case, even if the record could establish that the same cash and accounts receivable were actually considered twice, no double dip occurred," the Court of Appeals concluded. The trial court did not err when it calculated the husband's income for spousal support and adopted the asset-based valuation of the wife's expert.

Flawed methodology. The husband claimed it was wrong for the trial court not to consider the tax increase resulting from the expert's adding back expenses when adjusting the company's balance sheet. The applicable statute required the trial court to consider the tax consequences of the awards to each spouse.

The Court of Appeals said the applicable statutory provision did not require the trial court to perform an independent examination of the tax consequences of the adjustments an expert made in valuing the business. Nor was there evidence in the record of what the tax benefits were of prepaying expenses.

Another argument as to why the valuation was defective was that the wife's expert did not obtain appraisals of the business assets and did not visit the site or talk to the husband or his business accountant.

This argument also had no traction with the court. The husband did not cite to any case supporting his claim that it was a "fundamental concept" that asset valuations require the fair market value of the assets. Moreover, the husband's expert affirmed the accuracy of the opposing expert's calculations and methodology and noted the difficulties in divorce cases of obtaining access to a business. Also, at trial, the husband did not contest the equipment values the wife's expert used.

The trial court did not abuse its discretion when it relied on the adjusted net asset valuation the wife's expert offered, the Court of Appeals concluded. It affirmed the judgment.

Shaffer v. Visaggio's, Inc.

Citation: 2015 Pa. Super. Unpub. LEXIS 2403
Date of decision: July 29, 2015
Experts: William Boles (company/appellant); James Smelzer (shareholder/appellee)
Judge: Allen
State/Jurisdiction: Pennsylvania
Court: Superior Court of Pennsylvania (Court of Appeals)
Type of case: Dissenting Shareholder
SIC code: 7011 Hotel and Motels
NAICS code: 721110 Hotels (except Casino Hotels) and Motels

Appraiser Lacks Necessary Valuation Expertise, Dissent Says

A Pennsylvania dissenting shareholder case raised questions about who is qualified to resolve valuation issues as well as what constitutes competent financial evidence. Valuators may find the dissent's analysis more compelling than the majority's opinion because it displays a greater appreciation of the professional discipline.

Backstory. In 1980, three partners formed a company that held real estate including land, a restaurant, hotel, garage, and banquet facilities. The restaurant had various pieces of equipment related to the business. In 1981, the dissenting shareholder left the business but held on to his 25% ownership interest. In 2008, the company was poised for a merger, which prompted the dissenting shareholder to demand the fair value of his interest. The company offered him $35,000, but he claimed his stock was worth $500,000. When the company rejected his proposal, he filed suit in state court

Under the statute governing valuation proceedings in a dissenting shareholder action, the trial court appointed an appraiser "to receive evidence and recommend a decision on the issue of fair value." The appraiser was an attorney.

Experts' three-method approach. An evidentiary hearing took place in front of the appraiser at which both sides presented real estate and business valuation experts. The business valuators' proposed values were the result of three methodologies.

1. *Company's expert.* The company's valuation expert was the only expert who performed independent valuations.

- Income approach: Using a capitalized earnings approach, the expert arrived at a "[t]otal indicated value before contingent liability" of over $101,700. It was based on the weighted average of annual net income for the three years preceding the merger and a capitalization rate of 21.80%.
- Market approach: Using the invested capital to sales method, the expert calculated weighted average of annual sales for the three years preceding the merger and applied an industry multiple of "0.34" to arrive at an "[i]ndicated value of operating assets plus goodwill" of about $487,700.
- Net asset approach: The expert used the excess earnings approach to value the company's goodwill. He then added shareholder equity based on financial statements, the net value of the real estate (approximately $333,200), and goodwill to determine a "[t]otal indicated value before contingent liability" of about $191,500.

He said that the financial statements that management provided showed contingent liabilities related to deferred salaries for the majority owners and unfunded pension obligations of about $1.8 million. Since the liabilities dwarfed all three values, he assigned zero ($0) value to the company's stock.

He conceded that if pressed he would caution the owners or employees of the company that it was not likely that they would ever receive the amounts claimed for deferred wages or unfunded pensions given the company's operative reality. He doubted that the company would have borrowed money to pay the accrued but unpaid salaries, and he denied that the company was able to pay the deferred compensation at the time of the merger.

2. *Dissenting shareholder's expert.* The minority shareholder's expert did not perform his own valuation. Instead, finding the opposing expert's approach "reasonable," he used the numbers the company's expert generated as a baseline and made several adjustments.

- He relied on his client's real estate valuation;
- He increased the shareholder equity value from (-$148,300) to (-$119,400);
- He added the value of certain marketable securities as nonoperating assets (approximately $111,750); and

- He made no deductions related to claimed unpaid wages and/or pension obligations.

He pointed out that the claimed wage liabilities were "approximately 147 percent higher on the accrued wage schedule than what is reasonable for an operating business of this nature." The alleged accrual period was considerable, starting in 1981 and going to about 2010, he said. If the company had been paying the claimed compensation amount since 1981, it would have been close to $2 million in deficit, he said. Under industry standards, the claimed wages were excessive and there was no expectation that they would be paid. He said the excessive numbers led him to conclude that the liability was created such that it would reach a number that would make the minority shareholder's interest worthless.

He determined that the invested capital to sales method was "the most appropriate approach." Using the opposing expert's $487,700 value resulting from that method and applying his modifications, the dissenting shareholder's expert found the company's stock was worth nearly $799,500. This yielded a value of nearly $199,900 for the minority shareholder's interest.

Appointed appraiser's determination. Following the hearing, the appraiser inspected the property and operations and asked to see the company's insurance policies. Subsequently, he determined that the real estate was worth $1.8 million, noting the hotel rooms and liquor license should be factors in the valuation but not to the extent the minority shareholder's expert proposed. Based on insurance information and his inspection, the appraiser concluded the equipment, which he said was "used, readily available, not unique and in some cases, very dated," was worth $325,000.

Both sides objected to the appraiser's report, claiming there were factual and legal errors. Nevertheless, the trial court adopted it. After noting there was a $1.6 million debt on the real estate and subtracting that amount from the $1.8 million, the trial court concluded the company was worth $525,000, yielding a $131,250 value for the dissenting shareholder's 25% interest. In so doing, the trial court paid no attention to the business valuators' conclusions.

The company appealed the trial court's decision at the Superior Court of Pennsylvania, an intermediate appellate court, claiming two errors: One, there was no evidence to support the business equipment value, and two, the trial court's valuation failed to consider the $1.8 million unpaid wage and pension liabilities.

Flexibility under the law. Under the state law applicable in a dissenting shareholder suit, determining the "fair value" of the stock requires establishing the going concern as opposed to the liquidation value. The Pennsylvania Supreme Court recognized three principal valuation methods with which to determine fair value: asset, market, and income approaches. Using what is known as the "Delaware Block" method, a trial court essentially assigns weight to each of the three values generated by the three methods to arrive at the fair value of the company.

But, under a subsequent ruling from the state appellate court, trial courts are not limited to these methods but may take a "more liberal approach [which] must include proof of value by any technique or methods which are generally considered acceptable in the financial community and otherwise admissible in court." See *Glosser Bros. Inc.*, 555 A.2d 129 (Pa. Super. 1989) (citing *Weinberger v. UOP, Inc.*, 457 A.2d 701 (Del. 1983)).

The majority of the state appellate court drew on this flexibility in the law when reviewing the trial court's findings on the value of the business equipment and its decision on wage and pension liabilities.

1. *Business equipment valuation.* The company in essence contended that neither business expert specifically valued the equipment and the appraiser's valuation of business equipment based on his site visit and the insurance policies was not a proper valuation method. Therefore, there was no competent evidence to support the trial court's valuation.

The majority of the appellate court disagreed, finding that the testimony of the real estate experts and the business valuation experts touched on the value of the equipment. For example, both sides' real estate experts visited the company and the condition of the property, including the business equipment, came up during the proceedings. The majority noted that, even though both sides confined their real estate appraisal to real estate only, "it does not follow based on the [applicable] jurisprudence" that the appraiser was confined to the real estate expert reports to evaluate the business, the court said.

Moreover, the majority said, the business equipment was an asset that appeared on the company's balance sheets, and it came up when the parties' business valuators discussed the treatment of certain marketable securities in the amount of $111,750. The company's expert excluded this amount from his valuation because at the time of the merger the securities had been liquidated "and had been rolled into the operations of the company either for equipment or to continue operations during the economic downtown" in 2008. The dissenting shareholder's expert rejected this approach, treating the securities instead as nonoperating assets.

The court's majority said the company's business valuators also referenced the equipment in generally describing the asset approach and the market approach. For example, the dissenting shareholder's expert noted that the opposing expert "refer[red] to *Pratt's Stats* which is an analysis of sales transactions and concluded … 34 percent of gross sales is an indicator of what a restaurant's operation's value would be, which would include the operating assets, which is property—which is equipment plus any goodwill and conclude[d] the value was $487,714."

And, the majority said, the equipment was listed in the company's insurance policies that the appraiser requested. The appraiser's impressions from his site visit and his review of the insurance policies for the equipment likewise represented competent and relevant information. Finding the appraiser's report was based on substantial and competent information, the appellate court affirmed the trial court's adopting the appraiser's recommended valuation of the business equipment.

2. *Wage and pension liabilities.* The appellate court also found the testimony from the business valuation experts on the subject of unpaid wages and unfunded pension obligations was competent and substantial evidence in support of the appraiser's exclusion of the $1.8 million liability claim.

Therefore, the court's majority affirmed the trial court's fair value determination.

Dissent discredits equipment valuation. The dissent said it agreed with the majority's "thoughtful" analysis of the wage and pension liability issue. At the same time, it found the trial court's adopting the appraiser's business equipment valuation was error.

It noted that, even though there was no statutory requirement that the appointed appraiser be a business valuator and no appellate court had spoken to this issue, a trial court "could presumably appoint an expert in business valuation." The dissent suggested that it might be preferable to do so. It pointed out that the trial court in adopting the appraiser's report in fact cited to an admonition from the state Supreme Court that valuation issues in a dissenting shareholder litigation were "rather economic than legal in character" and could "better be derived by consulting the business man, the banker, and the industrial engineer, than the jurist legal scholar, or lawyer."

Here, the dissent said, the appointed appraiser was an attorney and the record "contains no indication that he has any expertise or qualifications as a business valuation expert." It added that the appraiser functioned more as a special master, receiving evidence in the form of conflicting expert testimony and making a recommendation to the trial court based on that evidence. In this role, the appraiser failed, the dissent concluded.

Although the appraiser received expert valuations based on the Delaware Block method, he ignored them. Instead, he used the value the company's casualty insurance placed on the equipment and then made a downward adjustment based on his own observation of the equipment. This approach, the dissent said, "bore no relation to, and did not rely in any respect upon, the work performed by the two business valuation experts." The appraiser's valuation did not represent a going-concern value for the equipment but an estimate of its liquidation value, which itself was improper, the dissent added.

Further, the majority's citation to testimony from the company's valuation expert that the value of the furniture, fixtures, and equipment and inventory was about $191,500 was misplaced. A review of the record showed that this number included other items, including real estate and goodwill, and, therefore, did not represent the value of the business equipment.

Similarly, the majority's pointing to testimony from the dissenting shareholder's opinion to find the equipment was worth about $487,700 was misguided. This figure represented a capitalization of the company's annual sales, not the value of the business equipment.

In sum, there was no competent or substantial evidence in the record to support the $325,000 valuation and it "does not even reflect a going concern valuation as is required by law in this context." Since the appraiser had no expertise in valuing business equipment, "his report constitutes, at best, his speculation regarding the liquidation value of the business equipment." The trial court's adopting the appraiser's valuation was reversible error, the dissent concluded.

Sieber v. Sieber

Citation: 2015 Ohio App. LEXIS 2256
Date of decision: June 15, 2015
Experts: Alan C. Duvall (wife/appellee); Joseph Rippe (husband/appellant)
Judge: Hendrickson
State/Jurisdiction: Ohio
Court: Court of Appeals
Type of case: Marital Dissolution
SIC code: 5065 Electronic Parts and Equipment, NEC
NAICS code: 423690, Other Electronic Parts & Equipment Merchant Whlsrs

Husband's Roles in Company Negate Need for DLOC

In early 2015, the Ohio Court of Appeals ruled on two cases in which the owner spouse of a business claimed the spousal award involved double dipping. Both times, the court questioned the validity of the double dip framework and retreated from its earlier analysis in the seminal 2008 *Heller* case. Nevertheless, the parties are not giving up on the double dip theory, as a recent Ohio divorce case shows. The new case also includes an informative discussion about valuation methodology and the discount for lack of control.

Background. Since 1986, the husband worked for two closely held S corporations that shared common ownership and had an interdependent business relationship. Company A manufactured drive-thru systems and sold them exclusively to Company B, which, in turn, sold the products to the banking, food, and pharmacy industries. The husband was the principal salesperson, president, and CEO of both corporations. He also owned a minority interest in both businesses: 1.73% in Company A and 1.37% in Company B.

Besides his annual salary, he received bonuses, including a W-2 bonus based on profitability, director's fees, and Schedule K-1s from both companies. In 2011, the year when the spouses separated, the companies lost their biggest customer, Walgreens. It meant that Company B would continue to service Walgreens's existing accounts, but Walgreens would no longer buy new systems. At trial, in fall 2013, the husband claimed that losing the account caused revenues to drop by about $10 million. He said that in 2012 Company B was still struggling to earn a profit and that he did not expect to receive the large W-2 bonuses he had received in the past.

Other evidence showed Company B had been in business for about 55 years, almost 30 years by the time the husband joined it. It did business in 21 states and, after the loss of Walgreens, was able to obtain other accounts.

Valuing the husband's ownership interest in both companies became a sticking point. At trial, both parties offered expert testimony to promote their positions. The experts agreed on the valuation date, and both used fair market value as the standard of value—i.e., the price on which a willing buyer and a willing seller with a reasonable knowledge of the relevant facts would agree to trade the stock.

The company resisted the parties' efforts to access its records. It obtained a protective order that prohibited any copying or scanning of documents and required both experts to sit at its headquarters and copy information from balance sheets and other company documents.

Expert paints a bleak picture. Given the companies' interconnectedness, the husband's expert decided to value them as one entity using the capitalized earnings approach. His inquiry focused on what a buyer could expect as a return on his or her investment, he explained. For this purpose, he considered the corporate structure of the companies, the loss of Walgreens, the loss of sales, and the husband's minority interest. He said that the decline in revenue made him believe the companies might be out of business by 2015 or 2016. By his calculation, the husband's interest in both companies was worth under $11,400. The expert contended that it was appropriate to apply a 24.3% discount for lack of control (DLOC) and a 15% discount for lack of marketability (DLOM) because of the husband's minority interest and his limited control over decisions within the company.

The expert said he rejected an asset-based approach for valuing the stock because any attempt to liquidate the businesses would be futile considering the husband owned less than 2% in each company. Also, an asset-based approach would result in "pennies on the dollar" at auction or liquidation.

Expert's sudden change of method and value. The wife's expert submitted his initial valuation by the deadline for expert reports, but at the final hearing he proposed a different valuation that stated lower values for Company B. The reason for this change at the last minute was that he only learned about certain key facts—the companies' interdependency and the losses to Company A—after handing in his "preliminary valuation," he explained. The trial court acknowledged the difficulty both experts had in obtaining company information and decided to admit the revised valuation despite the husband's objection.

In his initial report, the wife's expert used an asset approach to value Company A given the liquidity of the company's assets. He adjusted fixed assets for depreciation, cash, accounts receivables, and inventory and offset the company's few liabilities, including payroll expenses and accounts payable. He concluded the husband's 1.73% interest in the company was worth $63,000, including a 10% DLOM.

For Company B, the wife's expert originally used a capitalized earnings approach, which yielded a $78,000 value for the husband's 1.37% interest. He explained that, only when reviewing the husband's deposition transcript, he learned that Company A sold exclusively to Company B and that Company B had lost Walgreens. This new piece of information prompted him to change the capitalization rate, which resulted in a $24,000 drop in the value. Combining the $54,000 Company B value with the $63,000 Company A value resulted in a combined value of $117,000. The expert considered this value an upper limit. As for the lower limit, he said that valuing both companies under a net asset approach resulted in the same value for Company A, but a decrease in value to $20,000 for Company B, including a 10% DLOM. Consequently, the change in methodology produced a lower limit of $83,000.

The wife's expert disagreed with the opposing expert's 24.3% DLOC. It was inappropriate, he said, because the husband was a top-ranking executive in both companies. "[W]e are not talking about a 2% investor in California who's outside the company and doesn't know what's going on ... we're talking about an insider who is running the company, who's in control of that company from a day-to-day standpoint." The expert also pointed out that the companies had not compelled the husband to sign noncompete agreements.

After finding the revised valuation from the wife's expert was admissible, the trial court adopted the lower value—$83,000—as the fair market value of the husband's interest in the two companies. The way the husband's expert described the companies' future was too bleak, the court decided. Although the loss of new business from Walgreens was significant, it was important to remember that Company B had been in business for a long time, had customers in many parts of the country, and had brought in new accounts since the Walgreens decision. Company B was a "mature company with an established, albeit narrow niche." Similarly, the court found the facts did not support the lack of control argument the husband's expert made. By his own testimony, the husband was not only a "figurehead but the primary salesperson and key driving force behind the company's success," the court said. The majority shareholder had to take into account the husband's influence and control, and it did as the lack of a noncompete showed, the court concluded.

Spousal support includes share of bonuses. In addition to ordering the husband to pay the wife 50% of the value of the stock, the court awarded the wife temporary spousal support. The husband was to pay 40% of his "gross bonuses" for 11 years. The term "gross bonuses" included, but was not limited to, W-2 bonus pay, 1099 bonus pay, 1099 director's fees, and any K-1 shareholder distributions, the court clarified.

A case for the asset approach. In challenging the trial court's decree at the state Court of Appeals, the husband assigned error both to the lower court's business valuation and spousal support award.

The husband attacked the trial court's valuation ruling on three grounds.

1. *Late admission.* The trial court erred when it allowed the wife's expert to revise his valuation on the day of trial. The husband claimed that this late admission denied him the opportunity to prepare for cross-examination.

The appeals court noted the trial court's considerable discretion when it came to deciding whether evidence was admissible or excludable. Unless the appellant was able to prove abuse of discretion, the reviewing court would uphold the evidentiary ruling. Here, the trial court's decision was reasonably based on the "arduous process" experts had to go through to obtain important company information. Moreover, the husband suffered no harm from the late admission, the appeals court observed. At trial, he was able to cross-examine the wife's expert on the change in methodology and numbers. More importantly, the husband benefitted from the revised valuation since the value of his interest in the companies dropped from $141,000 to as low as $83,000. This represented a decrease in value of nearly $60,000, the Court of Appeals pointed out. Admitting the revised valuation was not an abuse of discretion.

2. *Adopting wrong valuation.* According to the husband, in crediting the valuation of the wife's expert, the trial court failed to consider the husband's inability to force liquidation as a minority shareholder. For that reason, the husband's expert expressly rejected the asset approach. The husband also suggested that, in adopting the opposing valuation, the trial court did not fully appreciate the negative effect the loss of Walgreens had on the companies' prospects.

The Court of Appeals disagreed. It noted that the trial court had discretion to "believe all, part, or none of any witnesses' testimony." Here, the trial court explained why it rejected the bleak view the husband's expert offered of the companies' future. Also, there was credible evidence to support the asset-based approach the wife's expert used given the companies' significant liquid assets, including Company A's cash accounts receivables and "inventory that becomes cash in three to four months." The trial court was "in the best position to weigh the [experts'] credibility," the appeals court said.

3. *Failure to apply DLOC.* The husband contended the trial court adopted the wrong valuation because the latter did not include a lack of control discount.

This argument, too, lacked the power of persuasion. The experts disagreed over the appropriateness of a DLOC. The trial court agreed with the way in which the wife's expert interpreted the husband's position within the company, noting specifically that a DLOC was not necessary considering the husband's key roles in the companies. Accordingly, the trial court decided "it cannot be ignored that the majority shareholder(s) must consider the significant influence and control Husband exerts in the business."

In sum, the evidence supported the trial court's decision to adopt the $83,000 value for the husband's interest, the Court of Appeals said.

Inapplicable double dip theory. The husband's other main target was the spousal support award. He asserted that ordering him to pay the wife a percentage of his K-1 distributions amounted to double dipping because that income was already included in the value of the business shares, of which the wife received half. The husband cited *Heller v. Heller*, 2008-Ohio-3296 (available at *BVLaw*) as support.

In its 2008 *Heller* decision, the Ohio Court of Appeals said: "[W]here a court uses a business owner's 'excess earnings' to value the interest in the business and also fixes support on that spousal's total income (inclusive of the 'excess earnings' used to value the business), a 'double-dip' occurs."

The facts in the instant case were different from the facts in *Heller*, the Court of Appeals said. It explained that in *Heller* the husband's expert valued the husband's interest in a company using an income approach—capitalization of earnings—to determine the "present worth of the future benefits of ownership." The trial court then divided the value of the stock evenly as a marital asset. It also ordered the husband to pay the wife 20% of future dividends from the company as spousal support. On review, the *Heller* Court of Appeals said the trial court committed error because it treated the husband's shares of the company's expected future profits as both an asset and an income for spousal support.

Here, the appeals court said, the prevailing valuation valued both Company A and Company B under the asset approach. As such, the business valuation did not include the potential future K-1 income stream. Given the use of the asset approach, there was no double counting of the husband's income in the present case, the appeals court decided, citing to recent precedent. *See Bohme v. Bohme*, 2015-Ohio-339, and *Gallo v. Gallo*, 2015-Ohio-982 (both available at *BVLaw*).

For all of these reasons, the Court of Appeals upheld both the trial court's valuation and spousal support determinations.

Tilstra v. Boumatic LLC

Citation: 2015 U.S. App. LEXIS 11183
Date of Decision: June 30, 2015
Experts: Rinaldo Sciannella (plaintiffs); unknown (defendant)
Judge: Posner
State/Jurisdiction: Federal
Court: United States Court of Appeals for the 7th Circuit
Type of case: Contract
SIC code: 3523 Farm and Garden Machinery and Equipment
NAICS code: 333111 Farm Machinery and Equipment Manufacturing

'Blunderbuss of Objections' Aims to Kill Loss of Goodwill Calculation

In litigating a contract dispute that turned on the covenant of good faith and fair dealing, the defendant launched a variegated attack on the plaintiff expert's damages calculation. Its allegations included the expert's failure to verify the client's financial information, his reliance on improper assumption, and his failure to consider all the dimensions of the applicable contract provision. Ultimately, the defendant's offensive persuaded neither the trial court nor the 7th Circuit Court of Appeals.

Capitalization of earnings approach. For 20 years, the plaintiff's company was a dealer for the defendant's dairy farm equipment. The plaintiff was from Southwestern Ontario, Canada; the defendant was a manufacturer from Wisconsin. The dealership agreement entitled the dealer to terminate the contract without notice and allowed the manufacturer to change the territory it assigned to its dealers. But, under the contract, the manufacturer was only allowed to change or end the agreement for good cause and upon giving the dealer at least 90 days' advance, written notice. The agreement precluded damages for the loss of goodwill.

The plaintiff's territory included "arguably the richest dairy country in Canada" and was making a profit of about $400,000 per year.

In his suit, the plaintiff claimed that the defendant forced him to sell his dealership to a neighboring equipment dealer at below market price by threatening to stop supplying him with equipment or eliminate his territory altogether. The defendant's conduct was a violation of the rule of contract to perform in good faith, the plaintiff alleged.

Further, the plaintiff contended the value of goodwill in the dealership was $1.5 million, but, owing to the defendant's conduct, he felt compelled to sell it for half that amount.

To calculate damages, the plaintiff retained a certified management accountant who had numerous professional certifications. The expert used the capitalized earnings method to estimate the fair market value of the plaintiff's company. For his valuation, he said he considered the economic and industry outlook for the company and the dairy farm equipment market, as well as the company's financial health.

The manufacturer's overarching defense was that it did not improperly terminate the agreement. But it also claimed that under the agreement the plaintiff had no right to goodwill damages. And, even though the contract did not permit the defendant to shrink the dealer's territory to zero, it did allow the manufacturer to change the sales territory. A change in sales territory could have resulted in a decrease in the plaintiff's profits.

The defendant initially attacked the damages calculation in a *Daubert* motion, noting in particular that the expert failed to perform a market study of the present and future market conditions. He should have based his calculations on a restricted market, not an unrestricted market, the defendant said. Moreover, the expert did not rely on comparable sales and made incorrect assumptions about the viability of the plaintiff's dealership.

The district court dismissed the objections. The defendant offered a "laundry list of factors" that the expert should have considered, said the court, but all of those factors affected the weight to be given the expert's valuation, not the testimony's admissibility. Moreover, the court found the factors did not suggest that the expert used an improper or unreliable methodology for his calculation. The testimony was admissible, and cross-examination was the way by which to test its reliability.

The jury decided the defendant constructively terminated the dealership agreement, and it awarded the plaintiff over $470,000 in damages.

The trial court denied the defendant's post-trial motions for judgment as a matter of law or a new trial. Subsequently, the defendant appealed the judgment to the 7th Circuit.

No faulty assumptions. According to the Court of Appeals, the defendant "fire[d] a blunderbuss of objections" at the expert's damages calculation, but none of the defendant's arguments were convincing.

For example, the defendant claimed the expert failed to verify the company's financial statements on which he based his calculation.

The appeals court first noted that the financials were prepared by outside accountants in the ordinary course of business, not in the context of litigation. Under Federal Rule of Evidence 703, an expert need not verify all the facts or data on which he or she relies. In other words, the expert may rely on otherwise inadmissible hearsay—here, the accountant's statements in the financials—if reliance on such information is an accepted practice in the expert's field. This was the case here, the court explained.

The defendant reiterated its argument that the agreement specifically did not entitle the dealer to any termination compensation or compensation for goodwill.

The Court of Appeals pointed out that this statement appeared in the same paragraph, "Termination of Dealership Agreement," as the for-good-cause requirement and the 90-day-written-notice requirement that applied to the defendant. Since the jury found the defendant had failed to comply with both of these requirements, the defendant could not rely on the goodwill exclusion.

The defendant contended the expert's calculation was speculative because it was based on the mistaken assumption that, if there had been no termination of the agreement, going forward the plaintiff's dealership would have retained the same value it had in recent years.

The court disagreed. It said the expert used a standard business valuation method, the capitalized earnings approach, to determine the discounted future earnings of the dealership.

The defendant further claimed the expert failed to consider that the plaintiff could have obtained a dealership from another manufacturer of dairy farm equipment or remained independent.

The 7th Circuit also dismissed this proposition as unrealistic. It noted first that securing a dealership was difficult; moreover, without a new dealership, the plaintiff's company would have been forced to manufacture its own equipment—an option that assumed it was able to do so. A dealership was essential to remaining competitive, the court observed.

The court briefly mentioned the defendant had other complaints about the plaintiff's expert but declined to be more specific other than to say these arguments went toward the weight of the testimony, not its admissibility. The court pointed out that the defendant had had a chance to challenge the testimony during the trial and had done so. The defendant's challenge was somewhat successful, said the court, since the jury only awarded about half of the damages the expert had proposed. For all these reasons, the 7th Circuit upheld the judgment.

Tri Cnty. Wholesale Distribs. v. Labatt USA Operating Co. LLC

Citation: 2015 U.S. Dist. LEXIS 81914
Date of decision: June 24, 2015
Experts: Lamont Seckman (plaintiffs); Dr. Samuel Kursh (defendants)
Judge: Marbley
State/Jurisdiction: Federal/Ohio
Court: United States District Court
Type of case: Damages
SIC code: 5182 Beer and Ale
NAICS code: 424820 Wine and Distilled Alcoholic Beverage Wholesalers

'Hybrid' Approach to Quantify Loss of Beer Franchise Contracts

What is the best way to determine loss of business value resulting from the termination of franchise contracts? This question recently took center stage in a suit by two beer distributors against a major beer supplier and related corporate entities. The court's decision includes an informative discussion of the factors affecting beer distributorships and brand valuation.

Litigating 'diminished value.' The two plaintiff companies had distribution franchises for a number of well-known brands of beer. In spring 2013, the defendant supplier notified each plaintiff of the termination of its distributorship under Ohio's "successor manufacturer" statute. The law provides that a manufacturer that complies with certain requirements may terminate or not renew a franchise without the distributor's consent. Typically, the manufacturer buys back the distributor's inventory of the terminated brand(s) and then must compensate the distributor for the diminished value of the business "that is directly related to the sale of the product or brand terminated or not renewed by the successor manufacturer." Under the statute, the value of such a business includes, but is not limited to, the "appraised market value of those assets ... principally devoted to the sale of the terminated or nonrenewed product or brand and the goodwill associated with [it]."

The plaintiffs initially contested the lawfulness of the terminations, but the defendants prevailed on summary judgment. Subsequently, the court held trial on damages. To prove the diminution in value, both sides presented opinions from veteran experts. In addition, the plaintiffs offered testimony from top executives on the nature of beer distributorships generally and their businesses in particular.

Plaintiffs' valuation evidence. The plaintiffs proposed two ways to determine diminished value.

1. *DCF analysis.* The plaintiff's expert had been active in the beer industry for over two decades, both as an employee and a principal in a consulting firm working primarily with beer and other beverage distributors across the country. To quantify the loss to the plaintiffs stemming from the loss of the supplier's brands, he performed a discounted cash flow (DCF) analysis that he applied to the plaintiffs' businesses in their entirety with the brands and without the brands.

- *Discount rate.* To calculate the discount rate the DCF analysis requires, he used a capital structure of 65% debt and 35% equity, even though both businesses had 100% equity and zero debt.

He said he knew from his experience working in the industry and observing transactions that this structure was typical of a buyer of a beer distributorship. Assuming first the plaintiffs' businesses had the brands, he arrived at an 8.95% discount rate for Plaintiff 1 and a 9.2% rate for Plaintiff 2. Without the brands, the applicable discount rate was 10.15%, he found.

- *Cost savings.* As for how much each plaintiff could save as a result of losing the brands, the expert found that for Plaintiff 1 the warehouse and delivery costs were largely fixed but there was some decrease in labor-related costs. Plaintiff 1 would save about $21,000 in operating costs for the relevant year. In contrast, Plaintiff 2 would see a drop in operating expenses of nearly $187,000, a considerable portion of which related to avoiding certain warehousing and delivery costs.

He concluded that for Plaintiff 1 the drop in value was $646,000. For Plaintiff 2, it was close to $6.1 million, based on the company's fair market value of nearly $2.3 million with the brands, but almost minus $3.8 million without them.

2. *Comparable transactions.* Another methodology the plaintiffs asked the court to consider when calculating diminished value, at least as a check on any DCF valuation, was a gross profit multiple approach. For this purpose, the president of Plaintiff 1, who was also a CPA and who had worked at the company for over 35 years, testified that he regularly used this approach to assess the value of a brand of beer. Brand multiples, he said, were a function of the potential for growth of the brand and the relationship between a brand that is to be acquired and the brands that are already in the business's portfolio. He explained that Plaintiff 1 had bought the subject brands in 2009 at a multiple of 6x gross profits and the then-executed agreement provided for a buyback at the same multiple.

Moreover, he said, if the company lost the subject brands, it would try to obtain new, smaller brands and grow them to replace the lost brands. This process would take five to 10 years.

Plaintiff 2 offered testimony from its vice president and director. The executive said that in 2013 the subject brands accounted for 49% of the total number of case equivalents (CE) of beer sold by the company, but 42% of the gross profit for beer sold by the company. Considering the operating losses that were sure to follow the loss of the subject brands, the company had considered liquidation. In the end, it decided to rebuild by buying and growing new brands. This process would take three to five years during which the company expected to use $4 million in cash and securities to cover its operating losses. He explained that, after receiving the termination notice, while litigating the case, the company had entered into a services agreement with another company to provide warehousing and delivery services on a per-case fee. For 2013, the year the franchise was terminated, the rate was $1.39 per case.

In terms of beer brand transactions, he said he also negotiated brand values based on multiples of gross profits. Transactions might occur within a range of multiples of 1x and 6x gross profits, he said. For the subject brands, a multiple of 6x to 7x gross profits would be appropriate, given the brands' sales volume and profitability. He noted that the company's independent appraisers, Stout Risius Ross, had used a gross profits multiple approach to appraise the business. Although the appraiser could not identify comparable brand transactions, it concluded that in the beer industry brands usually transfer at 2x to 5x gross profits multiples. To value the beer distribution rights of Plaintiff 2, the appraiser had used a multiple of 2.25x the annual gross profits on all beer sales.

Both executives explained that multiples for brand transactions were increasing. The rise in prices was in part a function of consolidation among suppliers and distributors. At the same time, in some instances, manufacturers were able to pressure distributors into accepting low multiples as consideration for retaining other lines of business or for avoiding litigation. The witnesses also observed that high-profile brands, such as the subject brands, enabled a synergistic relationship between brands that was difficult to quantify. The well-known brand provides distributors with a chance to interact with customers and cross-sell the other brands.

Defendants' valuation evidence. The defendants' expert held a doctorate in business administration with a concentration in applied economics and taught "commercial damages" at several universities. He had done appraisals for the beverage industry since the early 1990s. In this instance, he only conducted a DCF analysis for the value of the lost brands. He said that, while he intended to value the businesses in their entirety, the available evidence failed to show a noticeable impact on the plaintiffs' other assets from the termination of the franchises.

Discount rate. In terms of the discount rate, he used two different capital structures. One was based on the companies' actual structure: 100% equity and zero debt. In the alternative, he used what he called a "long term industry capital structure" of 6.8% debt and 93.2% equity. There was no publicly available report of discount rates that were used industrywide, he noted. He said that, even though he disapproved of the opposing expert's use of a buyer's capital structure, he recognized that experts might reasonably disagree over the choice of a capital structure.

He observed that there were no centralized databases of brand transactions. To determine weighted cost of capital (WACC), he assumed that brands would be valued at a multiple of 2.5x gross profits across the county but noted that "in the popular press" transactions occurred at multiples between 2x gross profits and 5x gross profits. He acknowledged that many sales occur at 3x gross profits or higher.

Assuming 100% equity, the discount rate was 25.16%, he concluded. Based on the "long term industry capital structure," it was 23.71%.

He rejected a comparable transaction analysis in this case, finding the very few transactions the plaintiffs cited were not similar enough to produce a statistically reliable result. In general, he considered using multiples to value brands a "short cut approach to calculating discounted cash flow."

But he conceded that if the results of a DCF analysis did not align with market-based numbers, the DCF outcome was "probably incorrect." It was common among valuation analysts to use more than one approach to test and reconcile values, he said.

Cost savings. Based on the warehousing and delivery agreement Plaintiff 2 had made with a third party, the defendants' expert considered 100% of those costs as avoided costs. In addition, he deducted savings in sales commissions, state taxes, and merchandising costs.

For Plaintiff 1, in contrast, he assumed the business provided the lost brands and other products to the same customers and, therefore, did not avoid costs in delivery costs. He did determine avoided warehouse labor costs, sales expenses, merchandising costs, and taxes.

Post-termination profits. Moreover, he maintained that, since Plaintiff 2 had not yet transferred the lost brands, it derived a post-termination benefit that was deductible from the damages award. Allowing Plaintiff 2 to retain profits generated after the termination date, while also compensating it for the loss of the brands by way of a DCF-based valuation, would result in a windfall to the plaintiff, he claimed.

In conclusion, he found that damages for Plaintiff 1 were nearly $134,000 and for Plaintiff 2 were nearly $723,500.

Two critical damages components. At the outset of its analysis, the court noted that the applicable statute failed to define "diminished value" and failed to prescribe a method for determining the loss in value. But, said the court, it was clear that a damages calculation required determining the value of the businesses before and after termination of the brands. Moreover, the concept of "diminished value" included at least two discrete components: (1) the fair market value of the assets primarily devoted to the sale of the terminated brand; and (2) the goodwill associated with the brand. But, because diminished value was not limited to those components, in theory, at least, the distributors were able to prove other losses.

Here, said the court, neither distributor possessed assets dedicated to the sale of the brands and neither party defined "goodwill." Both sides seemed to assume that the value of the brands was the same as their goodwill but failed to provide support for this proposition, the court observed. However, case law suggested that the value of the terminated franchises was a part of the fair market value of the distributorships in their entirety and was distinct from the brands' goodwill.

The court said it would use a "hybrid" approach to determine the diminished value in this case. This required determining the fair market value of the franchise contracts using a DCF analysis and adding any loss in the fair market value of other tangible or intangible components of the distributorships "directly resulting from loss of the Brands."

One question was whose DCF analysis was more credible. Both experts presented fairly similar models that differed in two regards, the court observed. For one, the experts disagreed over the appropriate capital structure to calculate WACC, and they disagreed over the cost savings input. According to the court, the defendant expert's opinion overall was more persuasive. Valuing the businesses in their entirety, as the plaintiffs' expert had done, "adds unnecessary complexity to what is a much more straightforward determination." The court also faulted the plaintiffs' expert for not explaining his calculations and charts during trial, making it impossible for the court to assess the witness's credibility and having the unfortunate consequence of devaluing the testimony.

Also, the court said, other courts have accepted many of the assumptions underlying the analysis of the defendants' expert. According to the court, the defendant expert's credentials (Ph.D. in business administration and his teaching "commercial damages" at a law school) were "particularly applicable to the task at hand."

Finally, the defendants' expert used the proper valuation date—the date of the termination notice—the court pointed out. In contrast, the opposing expert used a number of end-of-year dates that were inappropriate in this case.

While the court declined to perform its own DCF analysis, it found it was necessary to modify the defendant expert's DCF-based valuation in three regards.

1. *Capital structure.* The court noted that, when assessing the fair market value of the subject brands, it had to determine a value that approximated the price a hypothetical buyer and a hypothetical seller agreed upon on the open market. Here, the defendants argued on the one hand that the diminished value to the plaintiffs' businesses was limited to the brands' fair market value while at the same time claiming that the discount rate in the DCF analysis should be based on the actual capital structure of the businesses. This approach to the capital structure was one of the reasons for the "chasm" in the experts' value determinations.

According to the court, the discount rate should be based on the average industry capital structure. Because neither expert offered "foundational data or evidence" that showed how he arrived at his capital structure, the court decided to average the experts' capital structures and arrived at a 35.9% debt rate and a 64.1% equity rate.

2. *Cost savings.* In terms of avoided costs, the controversy focused on Plaintiff 2's avoidance of warehouse and delivery costs.

For Plaintiff 1, the court said it found both experts persuasive and decided to average their estimated savings—$35,270 versus $21,000—to arrive at a total cost savings of about $28,150.

For Plaintiff 2, the court pointed out that the defendant expert's reliance on the plaintiff's warehousing and delivery agreement was inappropriate since that contract came into being after the termination date. The defendants claimed, and the court agreed, that the appropriate valuation date was the date of termination. Therefore, what mattered were the conditions of the company at that date, the court said. Since the defendants' expert did not determine the costs related to warehousing and delivery separately but simply subtracted the full amount of those costs, the court had to adopt the figure the plaintiffs' expert calculated for that item. However, the court used the defendant expert's estimate for avoided state taxes, and it averaged the remaining cost savings to arrive at a total avoided costs of nearly $198,000.

3. *Post-termination benefits.* The court rejected any deduction for profits stemming from the sale of the subject brands after termination of the franchise contracts. It agreed with the plaintiffs that the applicable statute did not authorize such a deduction and there was no precedent for it. It credited the plaintiffs' statement that this type of deduction would represent a windfall to the defendants,

which would keep all the profits earned during the litigation. Both parties gained from the status quo, the court said. If the plaintiffs were made to disgorge their profits, so should the defendants.

As for the defendants' double counting argument, the court pointed out that the DCF was only one of several ways to value an intangible asset. The court went on to say that, if it had decided to value the brands based on a market approach, the defendants would not be able to argue for the deduction of future profits. And it said: "Although the DCF method is based conceptually on projected future cash flows, it is not, in actuality, merely a representation of future cash flows, but is, instead, an estimate of the total value of the intangible asset."

Finally, the court noted the inconsistency, even "hypocrisy," in the defendants' position. On the one hand, they urged that the court value the brands as of the date of termination and not take into account any post-termination events. On the other hand, they asked the court to look to post-termination events. And, while the defendants used the termination date to calculate diminished value, they would deduct all profits made from the date of termination until January 2015.

Qualified no to use of gross multiples. The court agreed with the defendants that there were no transactions that were sufficiently comparable to the transaction at issue. At the same time, it recognized the practice in the industry to use multiples for brand valuations. It pointed out that an independent valuator for Plaintiff 2 had determined an average gross multiple of 2x to 5x gross profits and had used an average multiple of 2.25x annual gross profits for all of Plaintiff 2's brands. The defendants' expert also had assumed a multiple of 2.5x gross profits for fashioning his industrywide WACC.

All of the "collective" testimony confirmed that the DCF-based values the defendants' expert produced were "discordant" with market conditions, the court observed. Specifically, the expert's DCF-based value was equal to only 1.91x to 2.1x gross profits for Plaintiff 1 and 1.21x gross profits for Plaintiff 2. There was no evidence that beer brands sold for such low multiples, the court said.

But it found that, by adjusting components of the defendant expert's DCF analyses, it achieved an outcome that was 3.25x gross profits for Plaintiff 1 and 3.47x gross profits for Plaintiff 2. These figures fell within the industry average, the court noted. The expert's modified DCF analyses, therefore, reflected the value of the lost brands more accurately.

In conclusion, the court awarded Plaintiff 1 $302,700 and Plaintiff 2 approximately $2.76 million as compensation for the loss of the subject brands of beer.

TWC I, L.L.C. v. Damos

Citation: 2015 Iowa App. LEXIS 438
Date of decision: May 20, 2015
Experts: Eric Engstrom (plaintiffs); Ronald Nielsen (defendant)
Judge: Vogel
State/Jurisdiction: Iowa
Court: Court of Appeals
Type of case: Dissenting Shareholder
SIC code: 1542, General Contractors-Nonresidential Buildings, Other than Industrial Buildings and Warehouses
NAICS code: 236220, Commercial and Institutional Building Construction

Discovery Evidence Casts Doubt on Valuator's Independence

A state statutory appraisal case illustrates how discovery may reveal compromising communication involving the expert, the client, and the latter's counsel. In discrediting one expert's testimony, the trial court noted written communication that indicated that the expert's valuation "backtracked" to the values the client and counsel had proposed.

Buyer's interest 'unique.' The plaintiffs were employee-owned construction companies that confronted a dire financial situation in the wake of the recession. They had to lay off half of their employees but at the time were unable to pay them the value of their shares. Because of decreased working capital, the companies also had difficulty retaining their bonding companies and stopped making distributions. They experienced a significant operating loss in 2011.

An investment banking firm specializing in the industry found the companies were "generally unsaleable" but said it knew of a potential buyer that had a "unique" interest in the subject. As part of due diligence, the prospective buyer's attorney estimated that the liquidation value of the companies' accounts receivables was about $18.2 million. In contrast, the companies' general counsel stated the likely recovery would be about $35.8 million and the worst-case scenario would be a recovery of about $16.4 million. The companies hired an independent appraiser that considered the proposed sale fair to the shareholders. After the companies' independent board members unanimously approved the sale, the full board recommended it to the shareholders. The sales price in December 2012 was $75.01 per share.

During his 10-year term at the companies, the defendant served as CFO, CEO, and chairman. At the time of the sale, he had left but had retained a minority interest. He was one of two shareholders objecting to the transaction. He argued that the $75.01-per-share price did not represent the fair value of his shares, which he put at approximately $216 per share. The companies asked the trial court for an appraisal.

Both parties offered expert testimony from CPAs who also were credentialed business valuators and who agreed that in this instance the net asset value approach was the preferred methodology to value the companies. The considerable gap in their value determinations came down to their differing treatment of the companies' accounts receivables and "backlog." Backlog referred to "future work that the [companies] had contracted to do but which had not yet been completed."

The defendant's appraiser valued the accounts receivables higher than the companies did in their financial statements, explaining that there were three major claims whose anticipated collection was higher than the companies assumed. He estimated the accounts receivables were worth over $42 million.

For the backlog, he reduced the gross margin only by direct costs but did not factor in indirect overhead costs. The backlog was worth about $16.5 million, he found. His calculation yielded a per-share price of approximately $199. This figure was lower than the defendant stated earlier and apparently was based on updated company information the defendant obtained in discovery. Consequently, the defendant lowered his demand to $199 per share.

The companies' expert did not perform a completely new appraisal for purposes of the litigation but, in critiquing the defendant's expert, relied on information and findings he had obtained while working for the subject before and after the sale. He said he relied on the valuations the buyer's and seller's counsel had done for the accounts receivables before completion of the sale. Making adjustments of their valuations, he estimated the accounts receivables were worth a little over $18 million.

The companies' expert admitted that he prepared the backlog valuation after the transaction, in the course of creating an "opening balance sheet" for the new company. He included indirect overhead costs and discounted for the risk of making a profit to the buyer of a company that has a significant backlog. He concluded that the backlog was worth only $1.5 million, yielding a per-share price of $70.81.

Record contradicts expert report. The trial court discredited the defendant's expert's valuation. It noted "clear errors" in the expert's report, which the companies' expert had corrected. More importantly, it questioned the independence of the appraiser based on letters from the appraiser to the defendant and his counsel and the defendant's responses to discovery questions from the opposing side. This discovery evidence suggested that the appraiser used the client's valuation as a "starting and stopping point," the court said.

Moreover, the expert failed to account for the obligations the company incurred to the workers it had laid off but whose shares it could not buy at that time. The court pointed out that "such reporting is clearly required under all applicable standards for business value reporting." Also, the record belied the defendant's expert's statement that he independently investigated facts by communicating with the companies' current management and its counsel. Rather, he simply relied on information the defendant had provided to him, having obtained the information from the companies in the process of discovery. Finally, the expert failed to discuss and explain the significant assumptions underlying the increased values he calculated for the accounts receivables and backlog values.

Ultimately, the trial court adopted the company expert's valuation that pegged the share price at $70.81. The court further ruled that since the plaintiff had paid the defendant $75.01 per share—the sales price—he was not entitled to further payment and, under the law, the plaintiff had no claim for overpayment.

Both sides appealed to the state Court of Appeals. The defendant challenged the trial court's fair value determination, while the plaintiff objected to the denial of attorney fees.

Purchase price is relevant. The defendant assigned numerous errors to the trial court, which the appeals court considered in turn.

According to the defendant, it was a mistake for the trial court to rely "almost exclusively" on the transaction price.

The state Court of Appeals observed that state law provides that the facts of the case control the methodology for determining fair value. The "record of the corporation, its prospects for the future, the selling price of stocks of like character, the value of [a company's] assets, book values, market conditions, [and] the reputation of the corporation" are all some of the factors that may guide the court's analysis.

The appeals court found no error. Here, the trial court did not exclusively rely on the purchase price but instead considered expert testimony in light of the companies' financial condition and the circumstances surrounding the sale.

The defendant also maintained the trial court "misunderstood purchase price accounting" and improperly relied on the company expert's testimony even though the latter failed to perform a "full," fresh appraisal. Moreover, instead of basing whatever valuation the opposing expert did perform on presale values, he "worked backwards" from the opening balance sheet he created for the new company postsale.

The appeals court dismissed this claim as well, noting the failure to provide an entirely new appraisal "out of whole cloth" was inconsequential in this case, where both experts agreed on the proper valuation method and the only sticking points were the values assigned to the various assets. The company expert's accounts receivable determination was based on presale information and reports, including the valuations by counsel for the buyer and seller. And, even though the companies' expert determined the value of the backlog during his work for the new company, his value conclusion was substantiated presale evidence—based on the opinions from the investment bank brokering the deal and the seller's financial advisor, which approved of the deal in its fairness opinion.

The defendant also claimed use of the purchase price was improper because the sale was not an arm's-length transaction considering the circumstances surrounding the deal.

The appeals court found this argument unconvincing. It pointed out that the defendant tried to have it both ways. On the one hand, he claimed that the companies were not "a sinking ship" but were "weathering the storm" of the recession; therefore, the purchase price since did not accurately reflect the companies' fair value. On the other hand, he said that the companies did not have enough reserves to pay their debt and felt compelled to sell at whatever price.

The sale was arm's length, the appeals court found, and there was substantial evidence to bolster the trial court's conclusion that the purchase price was relevant to the valuation.

The defendant's final argument was that his expert provided the only reliable opinion as to the presale value of the shares.

It was the trial court as the fact finder that had to assess and weigh the expert opinions, the appeals court observed. Here, the trial court gave detailed reasons why the company expert's report was more credible. Therefore, the appeals court affirmed the trial court's valuation and judgment.

Utah Resources International, Inc. v. Mark Technologies Corp.

Citation: 2014 Utah LEXIS 216
Date of decision: Dec. 23, 2014
Experts: Jeff Wright (company, fairness opinion), Francis Burns (company, trial); Roger Smith (court-appointed)
Judge: Durrant
State/Jurisdiction: Utah
Court: Supreme Court
Type of case: Dissenting Shareholder
SIC code: 6531 Real Estate Agents and Managers

Use of Asset-Level Deductions Hinges on Business Strategy

A recent decision from the Utah Supreme Court adds a new dimension to the debate on the use of discounts, particularly the marketability discount, in fair value proceedings. In reviewing the district court's valuation, the state's high court clarified why the lower court's reliance on prior law prohibiting the use of all discounts and tax deductions was misguided under the circumstances of the case.

Winding-down strategy. The impetus for the contested fair value proceeding was a 2004 share consolidation transaction. When the petitioner, a Utah company that was involved in various business activities, including land development, ran into financial problems in early 2000, it decided to wind down by selling its land holdings. From that point on, its major activity was holding and selling undeveloped real estate. As a company representative later put it, under this business strategy, "everything [was] for sale." Company management expected that it would take about 10 years to sell all of the company's property. The company also owned oil and gas mineral leases and collected royalty on them.

In subsequent years, most of the shareholders sold their shares to the company's president for anywhere from $1,000 to $4,000 per share. By 2004, the company president, via another company he owned, held about 87% of the subject's outstanding shares. In an effort to generate added liquidity for the remaining shareholders, the subject's board of directors decided to conduct a two-part share-consolidation transaction. First, the company would conduct a 500-to-1 reverse stock split, and then it would buy out any fractional shareholders. The result would be a buyout of all shareholders except for the president and his other company.

The subject's board hired a financial advisor to value the company. In his fairness opinion, the appraiser proposed several values, including a market value of $2,750 per share, an investment value of $4,908 per share, and a net asset value of $5,644 per share. The board approved the transaction, and it became effective in June 2004. Based on the fairness opinion, the subject repurchased fractional shares for $5,250 per share held before the reverse stock split.

Two "activist" investors (so described in the opinion), who in the past had filed numerous suits against the company, dissented. They contended that the transaction was the contrivance of the company's president to finally secure an "unpaid-for majority position" in the company and "squeeze out" minority shareholders. Their shares were worth nearly $32,000 per share, they maintained.

Because the parties could not reach an agreement, the company petitioned the state district court for a fair value determination. Its business strategy became a determinant in the valuation. "There is accordingly no dispute that the vast majority of [the company's] value as of the valuation date, and its only realistic means of generating earnings, came from its assets," the company stated.

There were four types of assets: (1) approximately 345 acres of undeveloped real estate; (2) a minority interest (49.58%) in a closely held real estate company; (3) oil and gas royalty rights; and (4) miscellaneous assets, including cash and receivables.

Initial appraisal based on asset approach. The trial court appointed an appraiser who prepared an initial appraisal. The court disagreed with numerous deductions (discussed below) related to the first three assets and instructed him to amend the valuation. It also allowed the company to offer its expert opinion.

Initially, the appraiser used an asset-value approach to value the dissenters' shares. Accordingly, he valued each asset separately. For the company's real estate holdings, he used an appraisal another company—Fortis—had done based on the market approach. However, he then reduced the gross value by 5.5% to account for anticipated broker commissions and closing costs. Moreover, he adjusted for trapped-in capital gains taxes—reducing the adjusted value of the real estate by 37.3% of the difference between the adjusted value and the real estate's book value (net appreciation of the real estate).

The appraiser valued the oil and gas interests using an income capitalization approach. "This approach quantifies the present value of the future economic benefits that Management expects to accrue to the Company. These benefits, or future cash flows, are discounted to the present at a rate of return that is commensurate with the Company's inherent risk and expected growth," he explained. Consequently, he accounted for costs necessary to generate income, including adjusting for income taxes.

To value the company's minority interest in the third-party real estate company, he again relied on a Fortis appraisal to compute the value of the real estate company. He then calculated the asset value of the subject's interest in the real estate company, applying a 15% discount to account for transaction costs related to selling the interest.

Both parties attacked the valuation. The company objected that it was "incomplete, insofar as it did not offer an investment value or market value" of the company. The dissenters objected to the appraiser's use of discounts for lack of control and lack of marketability and his deductions for projected liabilities. These deductions, they said, conflicted with state law, which did not allow for a minority discount or marketability discount in dissenting shareholder actions. Moreover, the tax and transaction costs deductions for future land sales were "speculative."

The district court dismissed the company's claims but sustained the dissenters' objections. It ordered the appraiser to perform a new appraisal without any marketability discounts or adjustments for built-in capital gains taxes.

Appraiser disavows amended appraisal. The appraiser defended his initial appraisal but agreed to amend it, noting that appraisers are "not attorneys and not qualified to interpret Utah law." The new appraisal produced significant increases in value:

- The difference for the real estate asset was $5.8 million;
- The difference for the oil and gas interests was $1.4 million; and
- The difference for the minority stake was $150,000.

The initial appraisal stated a total value for the four assets of nearly $17.8 million—translating into a $7,600-per-share price. In contrast, the amended appraisal resulted in a total value of nearly $25.2 million and a $10,700-per-share price.

The appraiser subsequently distanced himself from the amended valuation. He protested that it was "not consistent with how [he] normally value[d] businesses." He explained that he had never valued an asset without accounting for the costs of selling it and factoring in related taxes. He said that the amended valuation for the gas interests, which he valued under an income approach, produced a "mathematically and factually erroneous" result. But the calculation followed the district court's instructions. He contended that his initial appraisal accurately valued the assets and believed no reasonable buyer would have paid more than $25 million for the company on the valuation date.

Company expert blends market value and NAV. The company retained a financial expert to perform yet another valuation. He agreed with the court-appointed appraiser that the amended appraisal was not a reliable indicator of the company's fair value. He by and large agreed with the asset value the court-appointed appraiser used in his initial appraisal. And he concluded it was appropriate to consider tax liabilities and other transaction costs in calculating net asset value.

Because the company pursued a business strategy of selling its real estate assets, a hypothetical buyer would similarly discount the company's value.

The company's expert offered a market value and a net asset value for the company's shares. The company's market value, he concluded, was around $11.1 million. He considered prior transactions, including the most recent sale of company stock for $2,750 per share. Although this was "an established market price between parties negotiating at arm's length," it required adjustments "to remove the impact of discounts for lack of control and lack of marketability." Data on transactions of real estate limited partnership interests suggested the $2,750-per-share price represented a 42% discount, he determined. He concluded the adjusted fair market value was $4,700 per share. He also explained that he had searched Bloomberg to find guideline public companies similar to the subject, but to no avail.

He said he was unable to provide a traditional income value for the company's shares "because [the company's] historical earnings did not reflect the earnings it could expect in the future from selling its large portfolio of real estate." Instead, he computed a net asset value, which he said combined "the income and asset methods—with appraised property on the balance sheet capturing future revenues and liabilities capturing future operating expenses and taxes." The company's net asset value was $15.7 million, he concluded. He weighted the adjusted net asset value at 60% and the market value at 40% and arrived at a $5,900-per-share price.

The district court adopted the $10,700-per-share value resulting from the amended valuation. This price was more than twice the price the company proposed to pay for the shares.

In essence, the district court said that the state's dissenters' rights statute and controlling case law from the state and other jurisdictions prohibited deductions for lack of marketability or capital gains taxes. As for discounts, it pointed out that the state Supreme Court had held "that discounts at the shareholder level are inherently unfair to the minority shareholder who did not pick the timing of the transaction and is not in the position of a willing seller." *Hogle v. Zinetics Medical, Inc.*, 2002 UT 121 (2002) (available at *BVLaw*). In the same case, the *Hogle* court explained that "fair value of dissenters' shares is the dissenters' proportionate share of the value of 100% of the [corporation's] equity." The district court in the instant case noted that *Hogle* "did not carve out any exceptions for asset-level discounts."

'Unwarranted extension' of prior ruling. The company asked the state Supreme Court for review. It argued the district court misapplied state law and relied on noncontrolling law from other jurisdictions when it disallowed the deductions for lack of control, lack of marketability, transaction costs, and trapped-in capital gains taxes. A key point was that the lower court erroneously relied on the *Hogle* case because *Hogle* concerned a shareholder-level discount whereas the present case dealt with asset–level discounts.

The dissenters responded that discounting, whether on the shareholder level and asset level, had the same effect in that it "allow[s] an end-run around the prohibition against minority and marketability discounts." They cited a law review article suggesting that the difference between the two is "tenuous at best."

The state Supreme Court sided with the company. A shareholder-level discount "involve[s] varying 'fair value' based on the characteristics of the shares in the hands of particular shareholders," it explained. On the other hand, an asset-level discount "reduces the value of a specific asset because of that asset's particular characteristics." *Hogle*, the court went on to say, dealt with shareholder-level discounts, not with asset-level discounts. The district court's ruling represented an "unwarranted extension" of *Hogle*. The rationale that applied in *Hogle*, but not here, was that it would be unfair to dissenting shareholders who "are unwilling sellers with no bargaining power" to penalize them for their shares' lack of marketability or lack of control, the Supreme Court noted.

"But these concerns are not at issue where a company discounts the value of an asset that it intends to sell for reasonable transaction costs," the high court went on to say.

Here, the company's "undisputed" business strategy was to hold and sell its real estate. This business plan was in place some four years before the share-consolidation transaction became effective. Under these circumstances, it was appropriate to consider reasonable transaction costs, including broker commissions and closing costs, arising from the sale. All the appraisers agreed on this point, the reviewing court said. Moreover, the court-appointed appraiser noted that the transaction costs would have affected equally the majority and minority shareholders. The district court erred when it equated these transaction costs with the shareholder-level marketability discounts at issue in *Hogle*, the state Supreme Court held.

It dismissed the dissenters' argument that shareholder-level and asset-level discounts amounted to the same thing by pointing out that the law review article they cited as support discussed corporate-level discounts not asset-level discounts. "Nowhere does the article suggest that it is improper to distinguish asset-level discounts from shareholder-level discounts," said the high court.

It also disagreed with the district court's finding that the transaction costs were "speculative." This reasoning was based on inapplicable case law from other jurisdictions. In those cases, the subject company had no intent to sell its assets before the "triggering event," the high court explained, whereas in the instant case the company was pursuing a strategy of selling real estate long before the valuation date.

The district court's rejection of the use of a marketability discount when valuing the company's minority interest in the third-party real estate company was similarly misguided, the high court said. While the lower court correctly recognized that courts must not use a marketability discount with respect to a dissenter's interest, it was wrong to apply this principle, articulated in *Hogle*, to discounts on assets held by the company in general. The appraisers in this case did not discount the dissenters' interests based on the dissenters' minority position. Rather, they discounted one of the company's assets. The company's lack of control over the real estate company affected all shareholders, on a pro rata basis.

'Ordinary course of business' rule. One of the company's largest liabilities was trapped-in capital gains tax. On appeal, it argued that disallowing the 37.3% adjustment in the initial valuation of the real estate produced a seriously inflated value. The district court disapproved of it because the sale of the real estate was not "imminent." Also, it said, it was "improper" to deduct capital gains tax liability in a fair value determination "where the dissenters have already or will pay capital gains taxes on the appreciation of their shares."

The state Supreme Court agreed with the company's argument that whether to allow for trapped-in capital gains deductions should not depend on the triggering event or whether a sale was "imminent." It declared: "Deductions for trapped-in capital gains are appropriate where the taxes are reasonably foreseeable in the ordinary course of business."

It added that not to consider capital gains taxes in this fair value proceeding would give the dissenters a windfall. Even if the triggering event had not occurred, the court said, the company under its business strategy would still have sold the real estate and incurred capital gains tax liability, "which would have necessarily affected the value of the Dissenters' shares." Moreover, considering trapped-in capital gains taxes when appraising an asset for sale was a "generally accepted, proper financial technique," the court pointed out. All the appraisers in the case deducted for taxes, which proved the point.

Erroneous income valuation. The Supreme Court also found it was error for the district court to disallow a deduction for income taxes in the valuation of the oil and gas royalty interests. Taxes figured into the income-based analysis the court-appointed appraiser performed for his initial valuation in two ways, the high court explained. First, he deducted associated expenses and income taxes related to the estimated future revenues to compute future net cash flows. Had he not done so, the future cash flows would have been significantly inflated, the high court said.

Also, under the income approach, he had to apply a discount rate to the future cash flows. One way to compute the discount rate was to use the capital asset pricing model (CAPM), and one component of CAPM is the WACC. "The cost-of-debt component requires an appraiser to determine the after-tax rate of return on debt capital, which necessarily requires consideration of the applicable tax rate," the reviewing court explained. Considering tax rates in an income approach valuation is not only appropriate, but also "necessary," the state Supreme Court said. Not to consider taxes leads to an incorrect calculation. Based on the district court's instructions, the court-appointed appraiser was obligated to perform an erroneous income valuation, the reviewing court observed. He either should have applied a posttax discount rate to the posttax revenue stream (as he did in his initial valuation) or used a pretax discount rate for the pretax revenue stream.

For all of these reasons, the state Supreme Court vacated the district court's ruling and remanded for new fair value proceedings consistent with the high court's opinion.

Warsaw Orthopedic, Inc. v. NuVasive, Inc.

Citation: 2015 U.S. App. LEXIS 3133
Date of decision: March 2, 2015
Experts: John Kevin Neels (plaintiff); Ryan M. Sullivan (defendant)
Judge: Dyk
State/Jurisdiction: Federal
Court: United States Court of Appeals for the Federal Circuit
Type of case: Intellectual Property
SIC code: 3841 Surgical and Medical Instruments and Apparatus
NAICS code: 339112 Surgical and Medical Instrument Manufacturing

Federal Circuit Sweeps Aside Lost Profits Theories and Award

At trial, the plaintiff, a nonpracticing patent holder, successfully navigated around the legal principle that a patentee could not claim the lost profits of a related company. But on appeal its attempts to justify its substantial lost profits award as a combination of lost convoyed sales, lost royalty payments, and lost true-up payments encountered stiff resistance from the Federal Circuit.

Nonpracticing patent holder. The plaintiff sued the defendant for infringing two of its patents: one that allowed oversized spiral implants by way of lateral insertion and one that related to instruments and methods enabling minimally invasive tissue retraction during surgery.

The plaintiff did not use the patented technologies or sell the patented products. Rather, it licensed the patents to two related companies (Deggendorf and Medtronic Puerto Rice) for a royalty. The licensees in turn manufactured and sold the patented products to a third party (MSD). In addition, the plaintiff produced "fixations" (rods and screws for holding the implant and vertebrae in place), which it sold to MSD. The fixations were not patented. MSD then packaged the fixations and the patented products in medical kits and sold the kits to hospitals and surgeons.

At trial, the plaintiff requested both lost profits and a reasonable royalty. The jury found the defendant liable and awarded damages totaling almost $102 million. The jury's verdict form said the award was for "lost profit damages (with royalty remainder)" and suggested royalty rates for each patent. The trial court set an ongoing royalty rate of 13.75% of sales of the infringing implants and of 8.25% of sales of the infringing retractors. But the court rejected the plaintiff's post-trial request for supplemental damages as well as the defendant's objections to the lost profits award. (For its part, the defendant sued MSD for infringement of one of its patents and prevailed.)

Both parties appealed the award at the Federal Circuit. The appeals court affirmed the liability rulings but not the damages.

No basis for convoyed sales claim. Under the applicable case law, a patent holder may not claim as its own damages the lost profits of a related company. By its own admission, the plaintiff was not entitled to the lost profits of the three related companies.

But at trial the plaintiff successfully argued it was owed lost profits for the fixations under a theory of convoyed sales. Specifically, its damages expert proposed that, because of the defendant's infringement, the plaintiff made fewer sales of the fixations to MSD since MSD lost sales of the patented medical kits. According to the expert, the plaintiff lost sales in the amount of $27.8 million, of which $24.5 million was lost profits.

On appeal, the defendant argued that to recover lost sales under a theory of convoyed sales a product that is not protected must be sufficiently related to the patented product. Here, there was no functional relationship between the claimed convoyed sales and the patented products. The plaintiffs' nonpatented parts "can be and are frequently used independently of the patented implants and retractors," the defendant stated. The plaintiff countered that its unpatented components were an integral part of the medical kits that "contain everything necessary for a fusion procedure."

The Federal Circuit found there was no basis for lost profits for convoyed sales. It noted that at trial the plaintiff merely offered marketing language that promoted the kits' "comprehensive set of instruments and implants." But a business strategy to sell both components together or the convenience that comes from selling or buying the patented and related products together does not establish the functional relationship the law requires, the Federal Circuit observed. Put differently, the plaintiff did not offer testimony that its fixations "would not work as well in other surgeries not involving the patented technologies." The trial court erred in allowing lost profits for lost sales for the fixations, the Federal Circuit said.

No basis for 'true-up payments.' Next the defendant claimed the lost profits improperly included lost royalty payments to the plaintiff from the two licensees, Deggendorf and Medtronic Puerto Rico. At trial, the plaintiff successfully argued that because of the defendant's wrongful conduct the licensees made fewer sales and by extension made fewer royalty payments to the plaintiff.

Arguing to the Federal Circuit, the defendant said that the plaintiff simply fashioned another theory to get around the prohibition against claiming the lost profits of a related company. To the extent there was harm in his case, it was harm to the two licensees, not on the plaintiff.

The Federal Court agreed and struck down this portion of the damages calculation. It explained that under controlling case law a plaintiff had to sell something in order to be able to claim lost profits as a result of the infringing sales. In this case, there was no showing of lost sales to the plaintiff.

Finally, the defendant objected to including "true up" payments in the award. At trial, the plaintiff's accounting expert explained that the plaintiff has a transfer pricing agreement with MSD (and other related companies) that ensured the parties compensated each other for the fair market value of the exchanged property. If the initial transfer did not reflect the market value of a product or service, a post-hoc transfer rectified the situation. Here, the true-up payments should be recoverable because they included in part royalty payments from MSD to the plaintiff related to sales of patented products to surgeons and hospitals.

The Federal Circuit noted that the money MSD sent back to the plaintiff was substantial: It amounted to 95% of the profit MSD made from the sale of patented technologies. This component accounted for the majority of the total lost profits the plaintiff claimed. But the Federal Circuit also noted that the plaintiff had failed to detail what true-up payments correlated with what transaction and what patent. In effect, the applicable transfer pricing policies suggested that the true-ups occurred on a company-by-company basis, not a technology-by-technology or product-by-product basis, the court observed. Considering the missing crucial detail, the plaintiff was not able to recover as lost profits the true-up payments.

The Federal Circuit added that, even though none of the plaintiff's theories supported an award for lost profits, the plaintiff might qualify for a reasonable royalty to compensate it for the value of the patented technology. But since the jury's verdict sheet was too unclear to use it for the computation of a reasonable royalty, the Federal Circuit remanded for a new trial in which to determine a royalty.

Finding that the ongoing royalties the trial court had calculated improperly included a lost profits component, the Federal Circuit also ordered the trial court on remand to redetermine the appropriate ongoing royalty rate.

Washington v. Kellwood Co.

Citation: 2015 U.S. Dist. LEXIS 63457
Date of decision: April 21, 2015
Experts: Scott A. Barnes (plaintiffs); Gary R. Trugman (defendant)
Judge: Dolinger
State/Jurisdiction: Federal/New York
Court: United States District Court
Type of case: Damages
SIC code: 5136 Men's and Boy's Clothing and Furnishings
NAICS code: 423910 Sporting and Recreational Goods and Supplies Merchant Wholesalers

Daubert Allows for Generous View on Yardstick Analysis

A recent *Daubert* case centering on the alleged breach of a license agreement put the spotlight on the use of the yardstick method for calculating lost profits. The defendant sought to preclude the opposing expert testimony by claiming a yardstick analysis had to use a "nearly identical" business as a comparator. Since the benchmark business was the market leader and the plaintiff company was in its infancy, the value conclusions from the expert's yardstick analysis were unreliable. The court took a more generous view of the test for reliability as to that method. But the court's liberality reached its limit when it came to the expert's alternate "market forecast analysis."

Breaking into sports apparel market. The plaintiff and his company owned the "Sunday Player" brand and wanted to use it in designing and selling compression sportswear apparel and accessories. Sometime in 2002, they teamed up with the defendant, a large manufacturer, marketer, and seller of private labels and brands. The defendant introduced the plaintiff to some retailers and later allegedly told the plaintiff "that the initial orders with Target and Foot Locker would easily exceed $10 million."

More auspiciously, the defendant allegedly told the plaintiff that MTV was interested in partnering with Sunday Players. An MTV promotion would result in hundreds of millions in product sales.

At the end of 2003, the plaintiff and the defendant developed a license agreement. In broad strokes, it granted the defendant an exclusive license to use the Sunday Player mark "with the production, manufacture, advertising, merchandising, promotion, importation, distribution and sale" of different types of apparel and accessories. The initial term was for three years; however, the defendant had the option to renew the agreement for another three years. The defendant was to pay the plaintiff a 5% royalty on net sales and spend 3% of net sales on marketing.

The plaintiff claimed his main motivation for entering into the license agreement with the defendant was the belief in an "imminent MTV promotional agreement." Although the defendant and MTV got as far as a draft agreement and MTV, according to an MTV employee involved in the negotiations, was prepared to finalize the deal, the defendant called it off. In spring 2005, the defendant ended its arrangements with the plaintiff.

According to the defendant, it was unable to make a single sale even though it pitched the brand to some 18 large retailers and spent about $220,000 in marketing. Its expert calculated that total sales during the license agreement period amounted to $147,000; they apparently were made by the plaintiff.

The plaintiff sued in federal district court (S.D. N.Y.). In essence, it claimed the defendant "fail[ed] to use its best, or even reasonable, efforts to generate profits under the agreement." Also, the defendant breached the license agreement and defrauded the plaintiffs by misrepresentations and omissions. The plaintiff asked for damages in excess of $50 million.

Both parties relied on expert testimony to support their positions, and both sides challenged the opposing testimony under *Daubert*.

Plaintiff's expert uses two valuation methods. The plaintiff retained a CPA and certified financial forensics expert with extensive experience in business valuation. The expert stated that he had assessed the value of intellectual property and infringement-related damages in various fields, "from oil field equipment to computer software to golf equipment." Moreover, he "had literally hundreds of assignments that involved me having to make and/or evaluate sales and revenue projections, using market share data, financial projections and other business records."

He submitted an initial report and later a supplemental report that accompanied the plaintiff's opposition to the defendant's expert testimony. The defendant tried to exclude the supplemental report, describing it as "an eleventh hour effort to rescue a deficient expert report." But the court found the report was "within the scope of the initial expert report" and admitted it into evidence.

For his damages calculation, the expert used two approaches: a yardstick analysis and what he called a "market forecast analysis." He then used the values from both analyses to calculate net sales, royalties, and lost value of the Sunday Players brand, for the license agreement's initial three-year term as well as for the three-year renewal term. He also said he examined a number of underlying documents, including SEC financial disclosure statements for the defendant, for MTV, and for the company that served as point of comparison for his yardstick analysis. Further, he reviewed profit-and-loss statements for the defendant and the comparator, as well as relevant depositions, case documents, and numerous accounting and valuation secondary sources.

The defendant first attacked the plaintiff expert's qualifications, arguing he lacked the expertise to testify to the defendant's marketing efforts. The plaintiff countered that *Daubert* does not require experts to have industry-specific knowledge, and the court agreed. To the extent the defendant claimed the expert was not qualified to testify to the valuation of a business in the apparel industry, it "overplays its hand," the court said.

But the court added that whether the expert was qualified to discuss the defendant's marketing efforts was "a much closer question" and one that was pertinent to the expert's yardstick analysis that tied the plaintiff's theoretical success to the performance of the benchmark company. According to the court, the expert's yardstick analysis not so much discussed "reasonable marketing and promoting" efforts as provided facts to support the expert's comparison between the plaintiff and the benchmark company. Therefore, the expert was qualified to testify on that level, but his valuation expertise did not qualify him to assess what marketing and promotional efforts would be reasonable and whether the defendant met the standards.

As for the yardstick method, the plaintiff's expert defined it as an attempt to quantify "lost profits by using a benchmark, comparable circumstance, index or similar guideline entity that reasonably resembles the economic opportunity or economic performance that the plaintiff would have reasonably experienced but for the alleged actions or inactions of the defendant." He decided that, for the purpose of gauging the various losses to the plaintiff, the most appropriate benchmark company was Under Armour, the market leader in the compression sportswear industry.

According to the expert, in 2003, Under Armour executed a promotion agreement with ESPN. This development illustrated the growth potential in the market and brought to mind the joint venture efforts between the plaintiff and the defendant and the never-executed promotion agreement with MTV. Other reasons for using Under Armour as an example of what could have been for the Sunday Players brand was Under Armour's then focus on selling compression sportswear and the fact that it, like Sunday Players, was then in "its early startup period." Also, MTV, like ESPN, had a significant geographical reach and cultural influence. The expert also indicated that the negotiations between the defendant and MTV suggested the defendant and MTV believed the Sunday Players brand could have broken into this market with success. The plaintiff anticipated that the way in which Under Armour was marketed might parallel the marketing strategy for Sunday Players had the defendant realized the promotional agreement with MTV.

The expert then reduced the comparative figure he derived from Under Armour's sales history by 50%. He suggested this reduction was to account for the increased competition in the compression apparel market during the relevant period, as well as Under Armour's 2005 IPO and competition from other industry players, such as giants Nike and Reebok. At this deposition, the expert characterized this discount as an "assumption." He admitted that if there had been actual projections from the defendant and MTV, "we may not have used that methodology."

'No' to rigid yardstick test. The defendant attacked the yardstick analysis on two grounds. First, it claimed that Under Armour was an inappropriate comparator. A review of the characteristics that guided the expert's comparison made it clear that "Under Armour and Sunday Players are so dissimilar as to render [the expert's] selection of Under Armour laughable."

The court disagreed. Under *Daubert*, "[e]xpert testimony should not be rejected simply because the conclusions reached by the witness seem subjectively improbable," the court said. Even if in this case the expert's claim that Sunday Players could have had a success similar to that of Under Armour seemed an improbable conclusion, the expert provided reasons for arriving at that conclusion and a methodology to support it, the court said.

The court also clarified that there was no bright-line test for yardstick analyses. "Reliability," it noted, was a "flexible" concept and no one set of factors, "not those listed in *Daubert* for purposes of scientific inquiries and not those applied by particular courts to accounting methodologies," applied to all experts in every case.

In so holding, the court rebuffed the defendant's proposition that the standard for a reliable yardstick analysis was set in *Celebrity Cruises Inc. v. Essef Corp.*, 478 F.Supp. 2d 440 (2007) (available at *BVLaw*). Moreover, to the extent that case spelled out what a reliable yardstick analysis was, the expert satisfied the test because the company that served as the yardstick was "similar to [plaintiff] in material respects," the court said.

In sum, any objections the defendant had to the expert's ultimate conclusion went to the weight of the evidence and was for the factfinder to assess.

The defendant's second line of attack on the yardstick analysis was to say that the expert applied the analysis in an unreliable way. He made two wholly arbitrary decisions. One concerned the period his analysis of Under Armour's growth focused on, January 2002 to March 2004. The defendant contended that this framing allowed the expert to rely on the sales record of a six-year old company (Under Armour) as a yardstick for a new undertaking such as Sunday Players.

This argument had no traction with the court, which found that the expert based his comparison on the assumption that a well-established entity such as the defendant would have taken direct control of the Sunday Players brand and would have teamed up with the cultural powerhouse MTV to sell the brand "in circumstances that would not have neatly fit the definition of a 'start-up.'"

The defendant claimed the other serious flaw in the application of the method lay in the expert's decision to reduce Under Armour's actual sales by 50% for his calculations. The court agreed that this "assumption" on the expert's part suggested the expert attempted "to temper possible attacks on the soundness of the comparison between Under Armour and Sunday Players by rounding out the edges of that comparison." The expert admitted that he engaged in some "estimating and, perhaps, even speculation," which could render the analysis vulnerable, the court observed. But the expert's use of the yardstick method was not "so unrealistic and contradictory as to suggest bad faith." Therefore, testimony as to the yardstick analysis was admissible under *Daubert*.

Regarding the market forecast analysis, the plaintiff's expert explained he used it to "quantif[y] estimated lost profits by developing financial models and forecasts of the financial performance of the plaintiff using various hypothetical assumptions and empirical data to model the financial event at issue." He called this approach the "market forecast analysis" and explained that it "generally requires preparing financial projections and forecasts based on plaintiff's expected performance and/or prior historical performance."

The biggest hurdle for the analysis was that there was no documentary evidence available to the expert that the defendant had prepared financial projections to quantify its arrangement with Sunday Players. The only tangible evidence as to the expectation underlying the arrangement was deposition testimony from the MTV employee who took part in the negotiations over the potential promotional deal. She suggested that, in discussing Under Armour's success, the defendant mentioned it hoped to "carve out 10 or 15 percent" of the market share.

The court noted that the employee's statements could be read as an indication that the defendant and MTV "engaged in some sort of financial projections for the Sunday Players undertaking." But, said the court with emphasis, "what these statements *do not* contain is a description of what form those projections may have taken and what conclusions they may have drawn."

Even if the court allowed that the expert's yardstick analysis was an appropriate way to circumvent the lack of projections, it said there was no basis on which to find the market forecast analysis reliable. Therefore, it precluded any testimony as to damages based on this approach.

As a final objection to the testimony, the defendant contended that any lost profits and lost value damages related to the three-year renewal term were inappropriate.

The court agreed. It pointed out that the licensing agreement specified that the option to renew was the defendant's alone. For his calculations, the plaintiff's expert said he assumed that there would be a renewal of the agreement because he was asked to do so by the plaintiff, but he was unable to offer a justification for the assumption.

'Thin' arguments against rebuttal testimony. The defendant's expert was an experienced CPA and seasoned business valuator. In 2010, a state court called him arguably "THE most qualified and respected business evaluator in the profession."

The defendant's expert did not perform an independent damages analysis but offered "archetypal rebuttal testimony." He detected a series of defects in the opposing expert's calculations. As such, he contended the plaintiff's expert failed to do sufficient independent analysis in his reports, was unqualified to assess reasonable marketing practices, and used the yardstick and market forecast methods in a way that resulted in an unsound analysis. The defendant's expert also pointed out the serious historical underperformance of Sunday Players merchandise and provided examples of other companies that failed to secure control of a significant market share of the compression sports apparel industry. The plaintiff expert's methodology was not "accepted by experts in the field," the defendant's expert asserted.

Moreover, in the introductory letter to his rebuttal report, he accused the plaintiff's expert of "violating professional standards. The expert "ignores" standards and guidelines of the American Institute of Certified Public Accountants and "violates" proper accounting standards and rules, the defendant's expert stated. Finally, he accused the plaintiff's expert of violating "our ethical standards."

In attacking the qualifications of the rebuttal expert, the plaintiff seemed to claim that the rebuttal expert lacked the expertise to evaluate whether there was a violation of professional codes of conduct.

Considering the defendant expert's acumen in "a general field closely related to the subject matter in question," the court found there was no basis for this claim.

The plaintiff also contended the rebuttal testimony was unreliable because it was not "accepted by experts in the field." This conclusion seemed based on an exchange in which the defendant's expert, when asked about the methodology he applied in rendering his report, said he had no idea what methodology other experts use to produce a rebuttal report, had never seen his method described anywhere, and confirmed that the method he used had not been peer reviewed.

The court said the plaintiff's objection "borders on the absurd." The plaintiff would require rebuttal expert testimony to be grounded in knowledge of how to give rebuttal expert testimony, the court said, adding that "[n]othing in Rule 702 requires the witness to be an expert in being an expert."

The plaintiffs' claim that the rebuttal testimony was not relevant either under *Daubert* or Federal Rule of Evidence 403 was "similarly thin," the court found. The testimony was admissible because it would assist the trier of fact in determining whether the plaintiffs' expert followed proper methodology and whether he properly reached his conclusions, the court concluded.

In sum, in response to the *Daubert* motions, the court merely excluded the market forecast analysis testimony the plaintiffs' expert proposed.

Wright v. Irish (Hudson Valley Clean Energy, Inc.)

Citation: 2014 N.Y. Sup. Ct. Index No. 2111/2014
Date of decision: Nov. 7, 2014
Experts: Greg Scheig (petitioner); Wayne Day (respondent)
Judge: Forman
State/Jurisdiction: New York
Court: New York Supreme Court (Trial Court)
Type of case: Judicial Dissolution
SIC code: 3674 Semiconductors and Related Devices
NAICS code: 334413 Semiconductor and Related Device Mfg

Expert's Solid DCF and Industry Research Sway Court

Two recent fair value proceedings in New York—*Zelouf* and *AriZona Beverages*—have given valuators much to chew on, particularly when it comes to the courts' positions on the discount for lack of marketability. Now, a third New York buyout case has added another dimension to the DLOM discussion, illustrating how one expert managed to score a decisive victory against the opposing expert.

Business plan. In the early 2000s, two brothers-in-law formed a solar energy company that installed panels on houses and commercial properties throughout the Hudson River Valley in Upstate New York. The petitioner owned 10 shares of the company and the respondent 11 shares. The partners' business savvy and state and federal government policies to promote the use of the panels led the business to an early success. By 2010, the situation had changed. There were more competitors, including companies that offered customers the choice to lease rather than buy the panels. The subject company did not have a leasing program. There also was uncertainty over the duration of the tax incentives the governments had made available. As a consequence, despite the growth in the solar energy market, the company's share of the market dropped precipitously, from 80% in 2003 to 11% by 2010.

Friction between the owners ensued, particularly over the direction of the business. In April 2014, the respondent and his wife—the petitioner's sister and a newly minted director—persuaded the board to adopt a strategic growth plan that called for an expansion into new markets. The petitioner objected and subsequently filed for dissolution of the company under New York Business Corporation Law Section 1104-a. The respondent and his wife (co-respondent) opted to buy out the petitioner following a fair value proceeding pursuant to BCL Section 1118.

Both sides presented expert testimony about the fair value of the petitioner's interest in the company.

Limiting DLOM to goodwill. The petitioner's expert used both the income and market approach for his calculation of value. The income approach relied on the discounted cash flow (DCF) method. He used the five-year projections the management board had approved but applied a company-specific risk premium to account for "forecast risk." At the end of the forecast period, he reduced the growth rates during the remainder of the 10-year discrete forecast to only inflationary growth in the terminal value. He studied the company's balance sheets and financial statements, reviewed its corporate structure, and assessed the recently adopted business growth plan. He also researched the industry and found both owners to be capable managers who had built a company whose revenue had grown "exponentially" during the past decade. Moreover, he learned that New York state had extended the tax credits through 2016 and had initiated another program to incentivize consumers to install the panels. Greentech Media, a leading source of news and analysis of green technology, forecast 60% annual growth in the industry over the next three years. Also, the company's 2013 revenue exceeded that of the previous year by 35%.

The expert explained that investors evaluating the growth potential of a company frequently relied on the DCF, as did the Internal Revenue Service. This method considered all the relevant components of a business: capital, cash, and debt levels. Based on the DCF, he determined the company's equity was worth $9.3 million. For his final calculation, he assigned this value 75% of the weight.

Under the market approach, he used a group of guideline public companies operating in the same industry and facing similar risks as the subject company. The set consisted of 12 solar and green-energy type businesses. Because many of them were larger and more geographically diverse than the subject company, he used the lower quartile of values in calculating multiples for EV/EBITDA and EV/sales. On cross-examination, he acknowledged there was an unnecessary EBITDA adjustment in his analysis due to a misunderstanding on the client's part but was able to recalculate the equity value on the stand, reducing it from $7.9 million to $6.9 million. He assigned this value 25% of the weight.

He concluded that the fair value of the company was nearly $10.3 million. He used a 21.4% DLOM, which he only applied to the company's goodwill, not its entire equity value, and concluded that the petitioner's share was worth over $3.8 million.

Ignoring *BIZCOMPS* user guide. The respondent's expert also used the income and market approaches, but his methodology in both instances was different. Under the income approach, he used the capitalization of weighted earnings method, which assumes that a company has long-term stable cash flow. On cross-examination, he conceded that, even though the company was profitable for years, its cash flows and earnings were not stable during the preceding four years. He admitted his calculation did not include a growth rate and he had not considered management projections. He was unaware of the growth strategy that had fueled the owners' dispute and that the board of directors had adopted. And he did not know that the board had voted to reinvest dividends in the company to stimulate growth. He also admitted that the DCF was his preferred approach.

His market-based analysis relied on actual closed transactions of companies that operated in the same sector as the subject company. He also used the *BIZCOMPS* database but seemed not to have followed the methodology the *BIZCOMPS* user guide prescribed. He focused on HVAC and electrical contractors as base companies for comparable sales without filtering for profitability or closely held companies. He proposed a 25% DLOM applicable to the entire equity value of the corporation. The court's opinion states that he weighted the results of the two approaches, but it does not provide the weight he accorded the value stemming from each method. He concluded that the petitioner's share was worth approximately $1.1 million.

Valuation with 'severe deficiencies.' The court discredited the respondent expert's valuation for its many errors in the income- and market-based analyses. For example, the expert did not know critical facts, such as the existence of a strategic growth plan. In performing his income-based analysis, he "severely underestimated even his clients' own projections," the court said. He used a weighted average of historical net income as opposed to the next year's expected income, which includes growth.

His market-based calculation revealed even more "severe deficiencies." Regarding *BIZCOMPS*, he chose "comparables" that were as much as 10 times smaller than the subject company—the selected companies had averaged sales of only approximately $1 million, whereas the subject company had 10 times that many. Regarding the IBA market data, he selected companies as comparables that were even smaller. After he was shown a copy of the *BIZCOMPS* user guide during cross-examination, he admitted to mistakes. For example, he did not add all short- and long-term assets to the *BIZCOMPS* value, less the value of all fixtures and equipment. He failed to subtract liabilities. He did not know that the sales multiple derived from *BIZCOMPS* already accounted for a private company being on the market for over seven months, plus a 10% business broker commission.

Accordingly, the court adopted the opinion of the petitioner's expert almost in its entirety. Its one point of disagreement was the DLOM. The issue in this case was not whether to apply a DLOM, since both parties applied it. Rather, the foremost question was whether the DLOM was applicable to the company's entire equity value or just to its goodwill value, as the petitioner advocated.

Without discussing an earlier split among New York appellate divisions on the issue of DLOM scope, the court simply found that "the law does not limit this discount to the goodwill of a corporation in all instances," citing *Matter of Murphy (U.S. Dredging Corp.)*, 74 A.D.3d 815 (2d Dept 2010). There was no reason in this case to limit DLOM to the goodwill of the company, the court said without providing further explanation. At the same time, it adopted the petitioner expert's 21.4% rate. Applying that rate to the expert's proposed $10.3 million value, the court found the discounted fair value of the company was about $8 million and the petitioner's share was worth about $3.8 million.

Editor's note: In a 2010 discussion of Murphy, *Peter Mahler, a New York attorney and frequent commenter on fair value proceedings, notes the earlier rift among New York appellate courts on the DLOM issue. The court in* Murphy *quietly rejected the precedent coming out of its own department (Second Department), which had limited DLOM to goodwill, in favor of the First Department's approach to applying DLOM to the entire enterprise value. At the same time, the court in Murphy did not create a bright-line rule. Instead, it proposed that the issue of whether to apply DLOM only to a company's goodwill or its entire enterprise value was a case-by-case decision. As Mahler sees it, "so ends with a whimper what had been the most controversial, open issue in stock valuation proceedings under the fair value standard used in oppressed minority shareholder and dissenting shareholder buyout proceedings."*

Zelouf International Corp. v. Zelouf

Citation: 2014 N.Y. Misc. LEXIS 5595
Date of decision: Dec. 22, 2014
Judge: Kornreich
State/Jurisdiction: New York
Court: Supreme Court of New York (Trial Court)
Type of case: Judicial Dissolution
SIC code: 5099 Wholesale Durable Goods
NAICS code: 4239 Miscellaneous Durable Goods Merchant Wholesalers

Zelouf Court Reasserts Its Objection to DLOM

Late last year, a New York court transfixed the valuation community when it ruled in a statutory fair value proceeding that the facts of the case militated against the application of a discount for lack of marketability (DLOM). As one might expect, the court's ruling is not the end of the case. The parties swiftly filed post-trial motions seeking to modify or vacate aspects of the decision. For its part, the court used the motions as an opportunity to explain in further detail why a DLOM was inappropriate.

Recap. After the founder of a very successful textile business died, a family feud erupted over its management. The controlling members of the business were the founder's grandson, Danny, and his uncle, Rony. The minority member was Nahal, the wife of the founder's other son, Emil, who had been left comatose in a separate incident shortly after he complained about the controlling members' conduct. Eventually, Nahal won the right to Emil's shares and sued, alleging corporate waste and self-dealing by the controlling shareholder. But, on the eve of trial, the court allowed the majority shareholders to proceed with a freeze-out merger based on certain contingencies. After Nahal rejected the company's offer of $1.5 million for the "fair value" of her 25% stake, the appraisal proceeding went forward. Both sides used as a baseline for the valuation an appraisal a neutral valuator had prepared earlier within the context of unsuccessful mediation talks. At trial, the parties' own experts limited themselves to critiquing the third-party appraiser's report.

A major point of contention was whether to use a DLOM and, if so, what the rate should be. The neutral appraiser found a DLOM was inapplicable in the case, but the company's expert contended New York law required it in fair value proceedings. The court rejected that claim. The idea underlying a DLOM is that the recovery of a frozen-out, minority shareholder should amount to less so as to account for the difficulty of selling a closely held company in a niche business as compared to a publicly traded company, the court explained. However, this rationale did not apply here because it was unlikely that the company would or could ever be sold. According to the court, a liquidity risk in this instance was "more theoretical than real." Applying a DLOM would "artificially depress Nahal's recovery due to a hypothetical sale that will never occur," the court found. The result would be imposing "the very sort of minority penalty that New York law prohibits." Based on this reasoning, the court declined to apply a DLOM to the valuation. (Find an extended discussion of *Zelouf International Corp. v. Zelouf*, 2014 N.Y. Misc. LEXIS 4341 (Oct. 6, 2014) at *BVLaw*.)

Court relies on context and fairness. Post-trial, the parties filed reargument applications with the same court in an effort to change the outcome of several aspects of the court's ruling. The most noteworthy challenge was to the court's decision not to apply a DLOM.

The controlling shareholders' particularly objected to the court's no-likelihood-of-sale rationale. New York appellate courts have regularly applied DLOMs even where there is little likelihood of sale, they claimed. "This is because New York law is unambiguous in requiring the appraising court to assume a hypothetical sale; the willingness of the owners to sell is irrelevant." They also suggested that to decline to apply a DLOM to the minority holder's interest amounted to overcompensating Nahal, especially in light of normalizing adjustments the neutral appraiser made to his calculation and which increased the value of the company.

The court stood firmly behind its decision not to apply a DLOM. First, it said, with emphasis, "no New York appellate court has ever held that a DLOM *must* be applied to a fair value appraisal of a closely held company." It reiterated that to apply a DLOM in this case would be the economic equivalent of imposing a minority discount, which New York law prohibits:

> Indeed, it is the tension between the application of a DLOM, which is done in most cases but is not *legally required*, and the practical effect of a DLOM here serving as a minority discount, repugnant to New York courts and *never allowed*, that drives the court's ruling.

The court also referenced another recent New York fair value decision, *AriZona Beverages*, to show that considerations as to the likelihood of illiquidity are a factor in a court's DLOM analysis. Specifically, in *AriZona*, the court said its use of a DLOM was warranted because there was actual evidence of the company's illiquidity, including expressions of interest from two buyers in the company that never ripened into a sale and an owners' agreement with sales restrictions. Therefore, the facts in *AriZona* were not like the facts in *Zelouf*. (Readers may find a discussion of *Ferolito v. AriZona Beverages USA LLC*, 2014 N.Y. Misc. LEXIS 4709 (Oct. 14, 2014) in the December issue of *Business Valuation Update* and at *BVLaw*.)

The court here emphasized it was *not* saying that a DLOM was always legally inappropriate in valuing closely held companies. "Such a holding would be incompatible with binding New York precedent." In essence, the decision of whether to apply a DLOM depended on what was fair under the unique facts of a case, the court said. While corporate valuation principles ought to guide the court's analysis, "this court's role is not to blithely apply formalistic and buzzwordy principles so the resulting valuation is cloaked with an air of financial professionalism." According to the court, in this case, the valuation the neutral appraiser offered, and the court adopted, was based on sound valuation principles. "Nonetheless, the gravamen of the court's valuation is *fairness*," a notion that requires "contextualizing the applicable valuation principles to the actual company being valued."

In a footnote, the court also stated that, if it were to apply a DLOM, it would not be at a rate of 25% or higher, as the company wanted. Rather, the rate would be 10%, a rate that aligned with the DLOM rate in yet another recent New York fair value decision, *Cortes v. 3A N. Park Ave Rest Corp.*, 2014 N.Y. Misc. LEXIS 4693 (Oct. 28, 2014) (Slip Op) (reviewed on page 72 and available at *BVLaw*).

The question of whether there was a rationale for DLOM in fair value proceedings has become "an area of heated debate in the legal and valuation communities," the court observed. It surveyed decisions from courts in other jurisdictions that have refused to apply a DLOM for various reasons. In sum, it said, "more compelling appellate resolution of these issues would surely be welcomed by all."

www.ingramcontent.com/pod-product-compliance
Lightning Source LLC
LaVergne TN
LVHW062156300926
849161LV00010B/2680
9781621500612